802.11 (Wi-Fi)

Networking Handbook

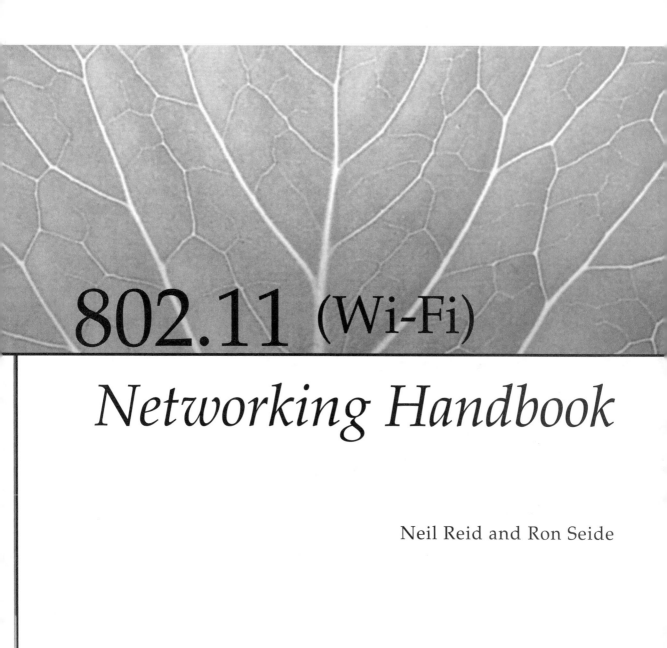

802.11 (Wi-Fi)

Networking Handbook

Neil Reid and Ron Seide

McGraw-Hill/Osborne

New York   Chicago   San Francisco
Lisbon   London   Madrid   Mexico City   Milan
New Delhi   San Juan   Seoul   Singapore   Sydney   Toronto

McGraw-Hill/Osborne
2600 Tenth Street
Berkeley, California 94710
U.S.A.

To arrange bulk purchase discounts for sales promotions, premiums, or fund-raisers, please contact **McGraw-Hill/**Osborne at the above address. For information on translations or book distributors outside the U.S.A., please see the International Contact Information page immediately following the index of this book.

802.11 (Wi-Fi) Networking Handbook

567890 CUS CUS 01987654

ISBN 0-07-222623-4

Publisher	**Copy Editor**
Brandon A. Nordin	Bill McManus
Vice President & Associate Publisher	**Proofreaders**
Scott Rogers	Susan Carlson Greene,
Editorial Director	Lisa Wolters-Broder
Tracy Dunkelberger	**Indexer**
Acquisitions Editors	Valerie Robbins
Tracy Dunkelberger,	**Computer Designers**
Lisa McClain	Tabitha M. Cagan, Lucie Ericksen
Project Editor	**Illustrators**
Lisa Wolters-Broder	Michael Mueller, Lyssa Wald
Acquisitions Coordinator	**Series Design**
Martin Przybyla	Lyssa Wald, Peter F. Hancik
Technical Editor	**Cover Series Design**
Bruce Alexander	Jeff Weeks

This book was composed with Corel VENTURA™ Publisher.

With thanks and love to my wonderful wife Mary, along with our son Martin and daughter Kelly. Ever the source of my greatest joy, it's you three who make it all worthwhile. This is my last book—no, really...
Neil Reid

To my sons, Hunter, Chandler, Spencer, and Cooper.
With enough effort and perseverance, you can accomplish anything.
Ron Seide

ABOUT THE AUTHORS

Neil Reid is a business development manager for 802.11 and fixed wireless systems at Cisco Systems, Inc. He has worldwide field responsibilities for 802.11 and fixed wireless product requirements, tactics, and strategies for systems engineers engaged in network solutions for Cisco.

Ron Seide has more than a decade of experience in data communications. He's served in marketing and management capacities at various technology companies and is currently a product line manager at Cisco Systems. There, he plays a part in shaping the near- and long-term direction for Cisco's industry-leading line of Wi-Fi equipment. Ron interacts regularly with high-profile customers, industry analysts, and the trade media both to communicate product and industry trends and to understand first hand the needs of the marketplace. He has an undergraduate degree in economics and a master's degree in business administration, is an avid amateur winemaker, and is a former Jeopardy! champion. Ron, his wife Vicky, and their four children reside in their native northeastern Ohio.

CONTENTS

Part III   WLAN Equipment and Component Selection

Part IV   Integrating WLAN into Your Network Infrastructure

ACKNOWLEDGMENTS

The premise that no man is an island is perhaps never truer than when attempting a significant work like writing a book. There have been many people in my life who have been exceedingly generous with their time, talents, and patience in their support of this and many other endeavors of mine.

My first note of thanks is to my co-author and colleague, Ron Seide, who is enormously capable as a leading 802.11 industry professional, always upbeat, quick with a good joke, and an outright pleasure to work with. Your expertise and views have taken this book to a higher level than if I had gone the project alone. I must publicly state that you have the best writing style of any technology book author I can think of and it is a style I would very much like to emulate. If I have a momentary lapse of judgment and decide to do a third book, it's my hope you'll be a willing accomplice.

A special note of thanks to Bruce Alexander, who is the primary technical editor of this work and the author of Chapter 8, "Selecting the Right Wireless LAN Equipment Components." Ever in high demand from people all over the planet, you continually amaze me with your generosity of time and talent. You are the best.

Thanks to Mike Tibodeau for your contributions and Peter Argumentiz from TXU for the use of his site survey questions.

Thanks also to my manager, Vince Pandolfi, for allowing me to do this book. It's a privilege to work for you, Mike Rau, Jim Smith, and Joe Wojtal. Each of you consistently provides the right mix of support and hands-free management. Thanks for your trust and generosity.

Many thanks to my colleagues at Cisco who keep up the pressure to always perform at a peak and ever-improving level. There are too many of you to list, but you know who you are. An enormously competitive environment, both internally and externally, it's an incredible company because of the people who work there. I still pinch myself about the privilege of being part of that team.

Neil Reid

I think the image of the lonely writer scribbling away in solitude must be a lot more applicable to fiction than to technical nonfiction. While there might be just two names on the front cover, this book really was a team effort. An acknowledgement here, a complementary copy of the book, and maybe a free bottle of wine doesn't go nearly far enough to express the gratitude I have for the many smart and generous people who helped to make this book a reality. Still, I hope that they accept this sincere and humble thanks for all their indispensable contributions. In a word, thanks.

I'll state the obvious: without Neil Reid, none of this would have happened. He's a wealth of information, a great motivator, a cagey negotiator, a real asset to Cisco Systems, and, oh yes, one heck of a writer. I am so glad this worked out, and that you agreed to take a chance on an unknown entity—it's been a great experience for me. I couldn't have asked for a better writing partner. Thanks, Neil, for everything.

Bruce Alexander would have been the George Martin of this project except that neither Neil nor I bear any resemblance to any of the Beatles. His involvement was beyond that of a technical editor; Bruce brought to the project his typical passion and insistence on excellence. Thanks, Bruce, for agreeing to do this, for your usual excellent follow-up, and for the last-minute diving catch.

Whether it's recommending delis in Montreal, trading obscure art-rock references, or detailing the early days of wireless LANs, Harvey Ikeman is a pretty extraordinary guy. His generosity with his time and collected materials made writing Chapter 1 a pleasure—I hope the readers find it half as engaging as my conversations with Harvey.

It's rare to find in a single person a comprehensive understanding of international radio regulations, certifications, and laws. It's even more rare to have this sort of knowledge base and a great attitude as well. Jim Nicholson is *the* go-to guy for wireless regulations, a genuinely good guy, and the foundation of Chapter 7.

Pej Roshan is so money and doesn't even know it. Pej does a great job of taking some *very serious* security concepts and making them understandable to those without an NSA clearance. Security expertise without all the troublesome paranoia is a nice combination and was indispensable for Chapter 11. Best wishes for *your* book.

"Hi, you don't really know me, but would you mind giving me a crash course in QoS and saving my skin? Oh, and proof the chapter, too?" Many people would ignore such a request, but Bob Meier is a much better guy than that. A driving force behind 802.11e, Bob made the QoS chapter infinitely better than it would have been.

All the way from Germany, Michael Kaemper provided the book with an international point of view with some well timed and insightful edits to the public access chapter.

Given its reputation, I was expecting the folks at McGraw-Hill/Osborne to be consummate professionals. What I wasn't expecting was that they would be so cool. Tracy Dunkelberger and Lisa McClain herd cats with polished expertise and uncommon good humor. Lisa Wolters-Broder ("the girl of a hundred lists") and Martin Przybyla are nothing but wonderful. Readers would thank Bill McManus for the amazingly thorough copy edits—he made this a much better book.

I've saved my biggest thanks for last. Vicky Seide, my wife, my partner, and the mother of my four sons, provided the foundation and the support I needed to play my part in this project. Thanks for the coffee, for shooing the kids out of the office, and for the diversions. Thanks most of all, Vicky, for being my wife.

Ron Seide

FOREWORD

When I installed one of the original NCR WaveLAN network cards almost ten years ago, I knew the wireless LAN market would be big. But I'd be fibbing a bit if I said I knew it would be *this* big. In less than a decade, an exotic technology that was both bulky and expensive has been transformed into one of the hottest networking technologies available, used by millions of people every day for work and play.

Despite the technology's success, we've only scratched the surface of possibilities. To reach full market potential, technical obstacles must be overcome. Higher performance. Better security. Quality of Service. The list goes on. Just as important, there is a compelling need for technical information on WLAN system design, implementation, and management. Too much of the information currently available is either too technical or too business-oriented.

In the meantime, many organizations have struggled with WLAN integration issues, stubbing their toes on pilot projects that cause as many problems as they solve. Not only is the world of analog microwave radio alien to most data networking experts, it is complex enough that I have often deflected questions about how it all works, referring to it as the magic of physics.

But magic is not really what wireless networking is all about. Instead, modern wireless LANs merge the complexities of two technologies that first appeared in the 1960s: digital microwave radio and packet-switched data communications. Each one is complex. Together, they are much more so.

Neil Reid and Ron Seide fill an important void by presenting an authoritative and readable treatise on today's most popular WLAN technology: IEEE 802.11, also known as Wi-Fi. They cover all key points, from technical protocol details to security and regulatory issues. The information they provide is technically comprehensive and accurate (thanks in part to the contributions of technical editor Bruce Alexander, a respected industry veteran), but it is also presented in a down-to-earth manner, with attention focused on real-world applications. Whether you're a beginner or an expert with WLANs, you'll likely come away from this book with some new insights.

Dave Molta
Director, Syracuse University Center for Emerging Network Technologies (CENT)
Senior Technology Editor, Network Computing Magazine

PREFACE

One of the hottest Internet technologies today is the wireless local area network (WLAN). The preeminence of this technology can be measured in part by the fact that it is one of, if not the only, technology that has remained "recession proof" during the last two years. Another suitable metric would be that of the billions of dollars in annual sales that this technology generates on a worldwide basis. The predominant standard for this technology was, and continues to be, assembled by the IEEE with an array of workgroups under the general heading of 802.11. These workgroups cover a multitude of challenging issues, such as carrier frequency, modulations, security, quality of service, interoperability, and many others.

Technical literacy on this subject, the practical application thereof, and a contextual understanding of the wide array of issues are every bit as important today as is understanding Ethernet. Whereas the bulk of discussions between network administrators, technology vendors, and CxOs used to center on how a radio performed, the discussions are much more centered now on security and mobility in general. The scope of this technology is now way beyond that of radio technology fundamentals. The authors of this work along with the technical editor are part of the team at the very forefront of this technology, given their respective positions at Cisco Systems, which designs and ships more 802.11 technology for enterprise networks than any other company. This book is essentially a detailed response to the most commonly asked questions from network managers and end users around the world.

It is our hope that, through this book, you'll not only gain an understanding of this wonderful and important technology, but also be part of a technology revolution that has no equal in human history in terms of adoption rate—the Internet.

Best Regards,
Neil Reid and Ron Seide

PART I

Moving from Wired to Wireless Networks

1

CHAPTER 1

A Brief History of Wireless LANs

Although the technology is referred to as wireless local area networking (wireless LAN), at its core, it's radio. And so, while the history of Wi-Fi or 802.11 only goes back to the mid-1980s, the history of the technology began over 100 years earlier. In this chapter, we provide a brief history of the technology that forms the foundation of wireless LANs. We do this both because the development and deployment of radio and data communications are among the most fascinating technology stories of the twentieth century and because having at least a passing acquaintance with what came before today's wireless LANs helps you to understand the evolution to today's standards and, more importantly, where they're likely to go.

RADIO, THE FOUNDATION OF THE WIRELESS LAN

As radio technology is the foundation of the wireless LAN, the early work in electromagnetics is in turn the foundation of radio. The Scottish theoretician James Clerk Maxwell first put forth the notion of electromagnetic waves in 1864, postulating that they arose as an electronic current changed direction. A device designed to produce electromagnetic waves by changing the direction of an electrical current, a process known as oscillation, is in essence a transmitter. The German Heinrich Hertz built upon this, developing equipment in the 1880s that actually sent and then received electromagnetic waves over the air. This equipment was capable of increasing the number of waves produced in a given period of time, their frequency, and their rate of change or oscillation. His name, of course, became a common unit of measure for frequency, where 1 hertz (Hz) means one complete oscillation or cycle per second. In radio, the more common kilohertz (KHz) means thousands of these waves per second, megahertz (MHz) means millions of waves per second, and so on through gigahertz (GHz). In this way, the increasingly shorter electromagnetic waves may be quantified and placed in increasing order of frequency or descending order of wavelength—it's the same idea since the more frequent the cycle, the shorter the wave will be. This linear quantification is today known as the radio frequency or electromagnetic spectrum.

It was Guglielmo Marconi who took this pioneering work to the next step and then on to practical application. While his name is forever linked with what we today colloquially refer to as radio, the transmission of sound, his first application was actually an early form of data communications. In the decade following the work of Hertz, Marconi synthesized his developments with those of Samuel Morse. Marconi reasoned that if it were possible to transmit binary signals (dots or dashes) across a wire, it should be possible to send these same signals across an electromagnetic wave and use them as a means of communication.

In 1895, when he was just 21 years old, Marconi sent and received his first radio transmissions across the attic of his parent's villa in the Italian countryside. The following year, he was achieving transmissions of over a mile. With improvements to his transmitters and antennas, distances increased quickly and dramatically, moving radio from the realm of science into that of technology. Marconi realized the commercial potential for his radio telegraphy equipment, obtaining his first patent in 1896 and forming a company, the Wireless Telegraph and Signal Company Limited, in England the following year. By 1898, Marconi's wireless telegraphy equipment was being used for ship-to-shore communications as well as terrestrial applications in lieu of wired systems—an early example of wireless supplanting more traditional wired infrastructure. The next year, a wireless link between England and France was established, and in 1901, a message was sent from England to Newfoundland across the Atlantic ocean.

Thomas Edison was the driving force behind the first commercially deployed wireless systems in the United States, which became the foundation of General Electric, one of the largest and most successful companies in the world. Edison's work was based on that of Marconi and one of Edison's own former employees, Nicola Tesla, a recently arrived immigrant from Europe. Interestingly, after many years of controversy, in 1998 Tesla was given formal recognition by the U.S. Patent Office as an inventor of radio, a distinction formerly held solely by Marconi.

The world of wireless technology has come a very long way from the days of Tesla, Marconi, and others. From the crude but brilliant devices built in their labs, differing types of wireless technologies have proliferated on every continent and are deemed mission-critical business tools for efficiency as well as important items for personal safety and convenience.

It is interesting to compare the early days of radio with those of the personal computer industry. In our time, the development of the PC is held up as the standard for rapid development from theory and concept to practical application. The early PC industry was driven by energetic and brilliant young people like Bill Gates and Steve Jobs. The development of radio is no less astounding. From theory to application in a decade, from proof of concept to commercialization (in the form of a multinational company!) in two years. All driven by a man in his early twenties. Marconi and others like David Sarnoff, Alexander Popov, Lee DeForest, and Reginald Fessenden made additional advancements and refinements, ushering in the "golden age" of radio in the 1920s with commercial broadcasting and the societal change it fostered. In 1923, the United States government first began the process of dividing up the radio frequency spectrum into allocations for specific uses and users. Eleven years later, the Federal Communications Commission (FCC) was chartered. Today, Marconi Corporation, while being a worldwide communications technology provider, is one that, ironically, plays little role in radio and wireless LANs.

A FOUNDING MOTHER OF WIRELESS LANS

Innovation often comes from unlikely sources, and few are more unlikely than a glamorous actress and a noted composer sitting together at a piano at a 1940s Hollywood cocktail party. Hedy Lamarr was a well known movie star and widely held to be one of the most beautiful women in the business. What was unknown to the general public and even her adoring fans was that she possessed a sharp intellect and, as a native of Austria, a hatred for the growing Nazi régime in Germany.

George Antheil was a noted composer, one of his compositions in which airplane propellers were used as drumsticks having been performed at Carnegie Hall. The story goes that when Hedy was married to an arms dealer in her native country, she picked up fragments of ideas for radio innovation in Europe. George, of course, was well versed in music theory, in particular the patterns of the 88-key piano keyboard. At that party, these two areas of knowledge came together to aid in the Allied war effort.

A system of spreading narrowband radio communications across a broad band of the frequency spectrum was devised by Lamarr and Antheil as a means of guiding torpedoes to their targets in a manner that was less susceptible to frequency jamming techniques or eavesdropping. This was accomplished by having the frequency that the controller and the torpedo used to communicate move or "hop" from one channel to the next with a predetermined and coordinated pattern. Their resulting patent, awarded August 11, 1942, was the first spread spectrum system. Not surprisingly, the number of hops in these patterns was 88, matching the number of keys on the piano keyboard. Player piano rolls were envisioned as a means of controlling these hopping patterns.

To jam a signal that is spread across a wide portion of the frequency spectrum, all of the spectrum that the signal is spread across would have to be jammed. By having the signal hop from one frequency to another, in a pattern predetermined by and known only to the sender and receiver, the pattern would have to be "hacked"— the code would have to be broken—by the intercepting party. While this general concept invented in front of a piano at a party may today seem intuitive, it was unique and unobvious enough to warrant a patent.

Spread spectrum radio communications was well before its time and was never actually used during the Second World War. It was, however, considered to be important enough by the U.S. military to have been classified and kept secret until the 1960s. Given the secrecy shrouding the patent and the development stemming from it, it's impossible to estimate the degree to which the patent was employed in future developments. What is known is that by the 1960s, when data processing technology advanced to the point that a computer (not a piano roll) could control hopping patterns, spread spectrum frequency hopping indeed did become the foundation for secure, robust, and nonjammable military communications. The value of this approach for commercial purposes is clear: private radio users often require secure communications in the same way that the military does. Although it's relatively uncommon for private communications to be intentionally jammed, unintentional jamming, and resulting performance loss or complete breakdown of the system, is inevitable if many users are sending radio communications in the same frequency band.

In 1981, the U.S. government declassified Lamarr and Antheil's now-expired patent for a "Secret Communications System." The timing of this release into the public domain wasn't a coincidence: in 1985, the FCC first allocated portions of the radio frequency spectrum for use without license by "industrial, scientific, and medical" (ISM) parties. The operation in these ISM bands was, and today still is, covered under FCC Part 15 rules, which stipulate the types of radio communications permitted. One of the schemes allowed for use in the ISM bands is spread spectrum technology. Prior to this, spread spectrum had been used on only a limited commercial basis for communications with multiple satellites. With spread spectrum, a greater number of users, with no specific knowledge of or coordination among each other, can operate in the band without unintentionally jamming each other's communications. While spread spectrum transmission was ideal for the military for one set of reasons, it was additionally ideal for unlicensed private use for other reasons—a most useful and extensible technology!

WIRELESS DATA ACQUISITION SYSTEMS: THE PRECURSORS OF THE WIRELESS LAN

The first systems that bear any real resemblance to today's wireless LANs began to appear in 1985. A thread that runs through the history of this technology is that if an application is so ideal for wireless connectivity, users will accept a suboptimal solution. Retail is just this sort of application. Indeed, in retail and associated warehousing and distribution center environments, there is an obvious need for a retail associate or inventory manager to roam freely throughout the facility with a data acquisition terminal like a bar code scanner. This "wirelessness" can of course be accomplished by batching the collected data and then uploading it at the end of a session, but this doesn't provide for the real-time, up-to-the-minute information that is so critical to making just-in-time (JIT) inventory systems work. A far better solution is for the data collection device to be in continual, real-time contact with the inventory system. Communication via radio waves is the natural way to do this as dragging a cord through store aisles is impractical to the point of comical.

It's something of a stretch to refer to these wireless systems as being local area networks. Rather, these first wireless data acquisition systems were simply a collection of devices that were modified in some very clever ways that were not envisioned by their original designers. Unlike a LAN, these systems were actually point-to-multipoint polling systems where user devices don't contend for or simultaneously share the transmission medium but rather use it in turn. The design for these early data acquisition systems was actually based on a far-flung wide area system, ALOHANET, a wireless system that connected the Hawaiian Islands. Operating at 9600 bits per second (bps), ALOHANET was the first system for sending data packets over radio and represents not only a precursor to wireless LANs but also the foundation for the predominant *wired* local area technology—Ethernet.

Telxon Corporation of Akron, Ohio, then a leading manufacturer of batch-processing data acquisition terminals, developed one of the first wireless systems by bolting a 1200bps modem to a batch-processing terminal via the asynchronous serial interface that typically was used for uploading data at the end of a session. In *addition* to the cable that ran from this terminal to the handheld scanning gun, a cable was run to what is essentially an off-the-shelf walkie-talkie onto which a cable connector had been soldered. This three-piece system—radio, terminal, and scanner—was inelegant to say the least; the user with a system of three heavy pieces would often literally drag the radio across the floor as they moved down an aisle (suboptimal, but not nearly as bad as dragging a cable through the entire facility!). On the receiving side, an off-the-shelf walkie-talkie was similarly modified and attached to a modem to demodulate the data coming in over the air from the remote units. This device then interfaced into a modified batch-processing collection terminal. The fact that this system sold at all indicates just how well wireless fits in a retail environment. In addition to the user, the inelegance of this system impacted those who managed these systems. This system was based on serial interfaces with no real networking protocols involved, putting it beyond the reach of most information technology departments. Even though the traffic on the system was unidirectional, was time sliced such that two terminals never transmitted simultaneously, and was typically just bar code scans, the low bit rate of the modem coupled with the radio described below limited the number of users per base station to ten.

But it was on the radio side where most of the inconvenience was concentrated. The rugged, commercial-grade walkie-talkies used were not the toys found under Christmas trees but rather licensed devices used commonly on construction sites, by security firms, and by municipal workers. Although the FCC had declassified the spread spectrum patents in 1981, and, at the request of the FCC, the Institute of Electrical and Electronics Engineers (IEEE) began to study the commercial applicability of spread spectrum communications, the radios pressed into service in wireless data acquisition systems were narrowband devices and not based on spread spectrum technology. Indeed, it wasn't until 1985 that regulations were in place to allow for the regulated use of spread spectrum technology by the public.

Operating in the ultrahigh frequency (UHF) portion of the frequency spectrum in the 450- to 470MHz range, these narrowband crystal-controlled radios were set at the factory to a particular 25KHz-wide narrowband channel that could only be retuned to a different channel by changing the crystal at the factory. To operate on any of these 25KHz-wide channels, a geographic operation license from the FCC is required. The implications here are numerous. First, it is of course desirable for a geographically distributed organization like a retailer to have interchangeable devices. It is, however, unlikely that a single channel is available for licensing in all geographies where that retailer operates. The upshot is that licensed radios that are incapable of being tuned to a different channel are specific to their location, which adds administrative, support, and inventory burdens. Worse still, if all 25KHz-wide channels are already licensed in a particular location (a likely scenario in heavily populated areas), wireless operation is simply not possible. Finally, in retail, it's common for periodic physical inventories to be done by contracted firms that move from location to location, performing full inventory over a single night with a large team. Here, the requirement for a geographic license is either a major inconvenience or a motivator for noncompliance. Additionally, the ten-user limit, which is also driven by the narrow license band, makes for a less efficient operation.

By 1988, incremental improvements to these early data acquisition systems were being made. By integrating the radio into the data acquisition terminal, the user's system went from being a three-piece unit back to the same two pieces found in batch-processing units. By migrating from the first 1200bps modems to what were then state-of-the-art 9600bps modems, the user count per base station increased from 10 to 30 users. It's interesting to note that this increase in system performance, and corresponding increase in user count, was achieved not by increasing the available bandwidth (it was still limited to the narrow 25KHz-wide band) but rather by using a higher-order modulation system found in the 9600bps modem. This same means of improving performance through better data modulation algorithms (not increases in bandwidth) is today driving performance increases in contemporary wireless LANs.

These improvements contributed to wireless data acquisition systems breaking out of their first retail markets. Most any business traveler has some familiarity with the next market to adopt these real-time wireless systems. Airport-based car rental agencies, Avis in particular, were the next set of customers to embrace these systems. Here again, the need to rapidly acquire data about the returning cars and process the transaction in real time was so great that these companies were willing to take the risks and bear the inconvenience that are inherent in being an early adopter of a technology. In addition to the multipart user system, the licensed radio negatively impacted the use of the system for car rental companies in much the same way as it did retailers. In outdoor airport environments, this effect was even more pronounced, as signals from nearby licensees had greater potential for interference when outdoors. Additionally, airports are in general "noisier" environments for radio frequencies, creating a general interference impact on these narrowband systems set to static channels. Clearly, improvements to these early systems needed to take place to address their limitations.

THE FIRST WIRELESS LANS

With the 1985 changes to FCC Part 15 regulations that allowed for the use of spread spectrum radio in commercial applications, the door was opened to commercialize the technology. A little more than a year after the FCC regulation change, a company, Telesystems SLW, was formed in Toronto to exploit this development.

It's interesting to note that while the system designed by Telesystems was indeed spread spectrum, it used a variation on this theme that is different than the frequency-hopping system put forth in the original spread spectrum patent. Rather than having a narrowband signal hop from one frequency to the next over a given wide band, Telesystems employed a system referred to as *direct sequence*, whereby a narrowband signal is spread over the given wide band by multiplying the width of the signal across a greater set of frequencies. The result of this system is similar to that of frequency hopping; that is, the narrowband signal that is spread out over a wider band is less susceptible to interference because only some portion of the multiplied signal needs to reach its intended receiver for the transmission to be successful. Additionally, and much like with frequency hopping, the direct sequence signal at that time provided some level of security insofar as the decreased power per unit of bandwidth made the signal less discernible from the surrounding noise when using contemporary eavesdropping equipment.

In 1988, the first commercial systems based on Direct Sequence Spread Spectrum (DSSS) technology were released to the market. In addition to incorporating DSSS, these systems operated not in a licensed band, but rather in the unlicensed band newly established by the FCC between 902- and 928MHz. Because this band was located close to the licensed band allocated for analog cellular telephone use in North America, it provided manufacturers with the advantage of being able to build their unlicensed devices with repurposed components originally intended for use in cell phones. With license-free operation, the administrative burden and lack of commonality across geographies that was so troublesome to early adopters of wireless data acquisition systems was addressed. With DSSS, cohabitation with other unlicensed users in the same band was possible, allowing users to sort out interference problems by themselves. In general, license-free operation using DSSS was an ideal solution for retailers, car rental agencies, and similar vertical market applications. Naturally, these first unlicensed DSSS systems were targeted at a completely different application.

The first products from Telesystems were designed as cable replacements, either to connect multiple desktop computers to a central base station in much the same way as an Ethernet network would, or to connect the networks in separate buildings together in much the same way as a bridge. Running Novell NetWare, the predominant network operating system at the time and providing a data rate of about 200,000bps (200Kbps), these very first wireless LANs for office environments carried a retail price of $1,500 per node. Although the product found critical favor, it was ultimately well ahead of its time and provided an insufficient price-to-performance ratio to gain the sort of mainstream acceptance needed to sustain a company. Indeed, today the proliferation of wireless LANs into typical office environments is only just beginning.

Rather, it was the vertical market applications then being served by the licensed narrowband radios where spread spectrum technology first gained a commercial foothold. Recognizing the scalability and geographic consistency advantages of unlicensed spread spectrum operation, Telxon began to offer the Telesystems unlicensed radios in its data acquisition terminals as an alternative to the licensed narrowband radios that were then provided in large part by Motorola. Ironically, to gain a foothold in the marketplace, the Telesystems radios were designed to match the physical specifications of the Motorola radio such that they could be swapped into the same data acquisition terminals. Telxon quickly became the largest customer of Telesystems.

Customers quickly realized the advantages of the new unlicensed offering and a migration began to take place, with the watershed event occurring in early 1991. Wal-Mart, now the world's largest company in terms of revenues, was then, as now, a company and one that aggressively leveraged new technology to further their leadership. Realizing how the unlicensed radios would enable it to have a common wireless infrastructure across all of its North American operations, Wal-Mart placed a staggering 30,000-piece order with Telxon, to be fulfilled by Telesystems. The order was to be fulfilled in six months' time and at a very low price.

Telxon quickly realized that the only way to meet the delivery and price terms was to make dedicated its supplier, and thus in early 1991, Telxon completed the acquisition of Telesystems SLW and completed the order. In 1999, Telxon spun off its radio group as Aironet Wireless Communications, which months later was acquired by networking giant, Cisco Systems.

While operation in the 900MHz band provided for a common infrastructure across the United States, Canada, and Australia, this band was limited in that it was not allocated for unlicensed operation in other parts of the world. To address markets outside these areas, manufacturers began producing radios that operated in the 2.4GHz portion of the frequency spectrum that was available for unlicensed operation across most of Europe and Japan—as well as in the United States, Canada, and Australia. In similar fashion to the 900MHz band, the 2.4GHz band presented vendors with the advantage of being able to repurpose components originally intended for use in European cellular phones that operated in a nearby licensed band. While 900MHz remained the most commonly used band in North America throughout the first half of the 1990s, 2.4GHz radios began to proliferate as license-free operation began to gain acceptance in Europe and Japan.

Operation in the 2.4GHz band had key advantages over the 900MHz band. By operating in an open band that was essentially common (there are some subtle differences in the frequency range from one country to the next), a manufacturer can build a single radio that, with some minor tuning, can be sold around the world, thereby providing for better economies of scale. Moreover, as license-free operation in North America became more popular, the airwaves at 900MHz became crowded with not just wireless LAN equipment but with the far more common cordless telephones as well. The 900MHz band began to be referred to as a "garbage band" due to all the interference that impacted wireless LAN performance and reliability. But, finally, it was the move toward standardization that sealed the fate of wireless LAN operation in the 900MHz band.

802.11: THE FIRST WIRELESS LAN STANDARD

Realizing the mutual benefit of defining industry standards for wireless LANs, in 1991 individuals representing a number of interested parties, including competing vendors like Telxon, NCR, Proxim Technology, and Symbol Technologies, first submitted a Project Authorization Request (PAR) to the IEEE to establish an interoperable standard for wireless LANs. As an international organization, the IEEE as a general rule drives toward standards that have worldwide applicability. This drove the newly formed group toward the 2.4GHz band and away from 900MHz.

By 1993, the foundation for a standard was in place, and in June of 1997, the IEEE 802.11 standard, more than six years in the making, was ratified. This first 802.11 standard provided for data rates of 1 and 2 megabits per second (Mbps), a rudimentary form of data encryption with the arguably misleading name Wired Equivalent Privacy (WEP), and transmission via both direct sequence and frequency-hopping technologies in the 2.4GHz band as well as over infrared light. The infrared aspects of this standard found little commercial favor and today represent little more than an historical footnote.

While WEP is still deployed, it has been roundly discredited as a viable means of securing traffic on a wireless LAN. As a compromise to satisfy the competing vendors represented in the committee, both frequency hopping and direct sequence spread spectrum were ratified as standards-compliant means of radio transmission. Operation in these two competing manners were, of course, not interoperable and indeed had the effect of interfering with each other and driving down performance when physically collocated. The effects of this compromise were wide ranging, resulted in substantial confusion, and are still being felt today, particularly as early adopters migrate to today's higher speed standards. Nonetheless, the first 802.11 standard marked the beginning of a whole new era and set the foundation for the next standard, 802.11b, which was ratified in 1999 and provides for an 11 Mbps data rate, approximately the same as standard Ethernet.

The details of 802.11b and associated standards, and what they mean to the networking professional, will be covered thoroughly throughout the rest of this book. By either 802.11 or Wi-Fi, the trade name now associated with the technology, wireless LANs are changing what it means to be well connected.

CHAPTER 2

A Summary of Common WLAN Standards

The issue of standards is one that many of us don't think about very often, yet it has been important to humankind for as long as people have been communicating with each other. Standards exist primarily to ensure a common basis and agreement for the form and function of the devices and services by which we are surrounded. Additionally, in modern times, standards are also used to help protect those who use products and services.

Standards also reduce the number of challenges with interoperability and information exchange. The more broadly adopted a standard is, the wider the market for a group of technology providers, with the most preferred standard being one that has been ratified on a global basis. It then follows that the more widely adopted a standard becomes, the greater the amount of synergy between technology providers and the marketplace they service. International standards, however, are far more difficult in practice than in theory.

Standards also define by law what certain values are, such as the foot, the meter, time, a gallon or liter of gasoline, and so on. Standards define what a specific device or service is or is not, and enable both technology and service providers to legitimately claim, use, and adhere to well-defined standards.

GLOBALIZATION OF STANDARDS

One of the earliest examples of a standard was the *cubit*, which was considered to be the length of a man's arm from his elbow to the tips of his fingers. In 8 B.C., this distance was widely agreed to be 17½ inches (although only nine years later it was generally agreed to be 21½ inches). By this standard, according to the Bible, Noah's ark (commonly believed to rest on Mt. Ararat in Turkey) was a relatively large vessel at 437.5 feet long by 72.9 feet wide by 43.75 feet high. Many other ancient records of measurements provide information regarding the size of buildings and the weights and measures used for commodities such as grain and currency.

The measurement of time is a very important standard, and the progress of technology has been directly linked to how well this resource is measured. Consider how the ancient traders and merchants of the Mediterranean engaged the owners of ships and caravans to coordinate the transfer of goods and money. It was common for either the ship's crew or the traders to wait for weeks or even months at a specified site to make their exchanges, because the standard of time used during that period was generally measured by the phases of the month or season. Predating this, navigation on the open ocean from the ancient Mediterranean world to the West could not occur until it was possible to measure time with an appropriate degree of accuracy and consistency.

Standards today have a tremendous impact on how we select and use products. In the United States, we are very familiar with the inch, the pound, the ounce, and the dollar, while most of the rest of the world is more familiar with the metric system and their native forms of currency. As the world continues to become a truly global community, many people have had to become fluent in the standards used in places far from where they work or reside.

Associated with this issue, the United Nations has been struggling with various countries for years in terms of which standard to use for mobile wireless communications, and it is only relatively recently that a world traveler could take their cellular phone from London, England, and travel to Singapore through the United States while using the same phone. This has far less to do with the use of a single standard than it has to do with manufacturers providing cellular phones that automatically switch between as many as three or four different modulation schemes and frequencies, and many people around the world own "dual mode" or even "tri-mode" phones for this specific reason. Standardization of these mobile wireless modulations makes it possible to build a cell phone in Norway that will function properly on three or more continents.

The definition of a standard can be entirely nontrivial. The even larger issue of *when* a standard is adopted is as important as the actual standard itself, as we live in a world where technology is conceptualized, developed, and deployed with rapidly decreasing amounts of time.

In the world of WLANs, we are fortunate to have certain fundamental standards that have been ratified at the global level, such as frequency, power, and time. A WLAN link that operates at 2.4GHz is equally understood and accepted in Japan, England, Canada, and the United States.

The 2.4GHz frequency is, in most nations, set aside for the purpose of having an unlicensed radio frequency system, and is probably the only frequency so well adopted, deployed, and characterized.

Further, since the idea of standardization for broadband, two-way WLAN usage is still somewhat new, regulatory groups, international bodies, and developing standards groups are struggling for control and authority to allocate and/or dedicate specific frequencies for particular uses in numerous countries.

Another issue not widely agreed upon on a global basis is that of *channelization*, which is how radios break up the amount of spectrum available into usable subsets for communication. Further, except for 2.4GHz, spectrum allocations vary widely from country to country in many cases, which makes it difficult for radio manufacturers and service providers to provide truly globally usable products, because they are commonly unwilling to design, test, and submit radios for local federal approval for every country that has a substantial market.

The lack of frequency and output power standards at the international level has forced some hardware vendors to adopt multiple products, designing specific RF units to work in allocated frequency bands for specific countries. This approach raises the cost of goods and inventories. Without this approach, countries with frequency bands different from the key revenue-generating superpowers, such as the United States, England, Germany, France, and Japan, are left without alternatives for broadband wireless.

This is one of the major reasons some companies have adopted architectures that allow indoor equipment, such as the routers and switches at each end of the radio links, to be independent of the carrier frequency, channelization, power requirements, and other settings that reside in the actual radios that operate the outdoor portion of the network. This approach still requires multiple outdoor units from one or more technology providers, depending on the specific country.

At this point, the technology does not exist, primarily for technical as well as financial reasons, that would enable *ultrawideband* microwave products that would cover multiple radio bands. Until the countries of the world and the governing bodies and regulators get together on frequency standards, there will be limited global acceptance of broadband wireless technology. The outlook for this general ratification is deemed unlikely as countries tend to rightly view spectrum as a national asset, which therefore should not be mandated by foreign countries. This is in part why the generally global adoption of 2.4GHz is a unique situation; and one that is being capitalized upon by radio manufacturers in order to increase the total addressable market.

EARLY TECHNOLOGY ADOPTERS VS. STANDARDS

In the open commercial market, the *early technology adopters,* commonly referred to as *early adopters,* are the first ones to adopt cutting-edge technology. They constitute the portion of the market that is willing to exchange the risk of using an unproven technology for a prospective gain on their competitors. The objective for them in some cases is to acquire as much market share as possible at the earliest date possible. In other cases, early adopters deploy cutting-edge technology on a bet that the overall cost of doing so will more than offset a particular problem. By accepting higher risk, new technologies can enable a competitive edge in both established and emerging markets.

Early adopters are generally very tolerant of the teething problems common to cutting-edge technology and are often selected as the first sites for equipment and technology trials. They also generally possess a higher level of technical savvy and experience and quite often employ unique enhancements to resolve some of the bugs that necessarily accompany relatively unproven technologies and solutions.

The early adopter market does not typically comprise the bulk of the market and is generally comprised of the smaller customers that want to give their larger or more adept competitors a run for their money and are willing to do so in part by adopting higher risk with their selected technologies. The bulk of a market opportunity for technology providers occurs later, after the early adopters have seeded the market with the latest technology and endured the significant growing pains and learning curves of leveraging an emerging technology.

These growing pains are usually fed back to the manufacturers to revise/improve/revisit their products to evolve better solutions that are (hopefully) made available to the risk takers first, who can (once again hopefully) enhance/extend the new providers a technology lead in the emerging market. If successful, or even apparently promising, larger companies will then follow suit in using the technology, which by then has generally been suitably debugged.

It is generally the larger companies that tend to require standards-based products, because this ensures several key issues for them:

- Technological maturity
- Stability of basic design
- Interoperability

Technological Maturity

Larger companies are generally not highly flexible or even fast-moving entities, even though they are now rapidly understanding that velocity in business has significant advantages in terms of being competitive, efficient, and, ultimately, profitable. Once they have begun to deploy a project based on a particular technology, they are very reluctant to retrieve deployments due to fundamental flaws in the design, because doing so is costly and time consuming. Their reluctance is based in part on the fact that there are financial and time costs associated with training and equipping their deployment teams for the new technology. In general, the larger the company, the later it deploys a new technology.

Stability of Basic Design

The stability of a technology is generally, but not always, related to its maturity. The exceptions to this include examples such as computer operating systems and other technologies that tend to grow by orders of magnitude during the technology life cycle. During the earliest phases of deployment, the fundamental design is more likely to change than during the middle phases of a technology's existence, which is where most of the major sales occur. During the latter phases of a technological life cycle, the design may again change substantially, or even be abandoned. Early adopters of technology are usually small enough and nimble enough to withstand the changes in the basic technology in terms of features, capabilities, scaling, migration, and interoperability.

Interoperability

Interoperability is defined in part as the ability for disparate elements to perform their functions with little degradation in speed, reliability, or maintenance. One of the most important issues the customers face in the deployment of new technology standards is that of interoperability with existing (often referred to as *legacy*) equipment. The larger customers have generally spent large sums of money deploying vast amounts of existing equipment featuring very high rates of interoperability. Of the many concerns large customers have, perhaps none is more important to them than assured interoperability.

Interoperability has long been a key metric for emerging technologies and a base requirement for incumbent operators, and this plays directly into one of the most important deliverables a standard provides. This is specifically why technologies are certified as "interoperable." The Wi-Fi certification from the Wireless Ethernet Compatibility Alliance (WECA) is an excellent example of this, even though, in practice, the degree to which equipment from different technology providers fully interoperates is open to some debate.

To be a bit more specific, it is one thing for a client adapter from one 802.11 provider to associate with the access point from another technology provider, but high levels of security are generally not consistently operable when equipment is purchased from disparate vendors. The 802.11i standard will help mitigate this interoperability problem, but it is this author's opinion that complete and full interoperability for maximum security measures will not occur any time soon relative to this writing.

HOW 802.11 AND OTHER STANDARDS ARE DEVELOPED

As stated previously, contrary to common understanding, standards occur in the mid to late phases of a technology life cycle, rather than in the introductory phase of getting a technology to a marketplace. In other words, standards generally follow widely deployed technologies, as opposed to the other way around. The order in which a standard occurs is generally as follows:

1. Introduction of new technology
2. Relatively high interest by developers
3. Deployment of technology to early adopters
4. Definition of standard by one or more technology providers
5. Establishment of standard by standards body
6. Ratification of standard by technology providers

The preceding order is that which generally reflects standards for the IEEE while some standards are essentially derived from the Requests for Comments (RFCs), which originate from the IEEE or other standards bodies such as the IETF. The input from these RFCs becomes de facto standards due to fairly wide adoption even though they do not always undergo the full standards process generally managed by the IEEE.

According to some individuals, most new technologies in the network industry are conceptualized and evolved by a working group, committee, or brainstorming organization. These groups comprise of members from multiple manufacturers who then take the in-process documents to their companies for internal development.

Introduction of New Technology

Companies are pushed to advance the state of the art in any technology. Cutting-edge technology is rarely compliant with any standard, and in many cases, standards don't exist for the newest of technologies. The introduction of a new technology may or may not occur with much advance notice to a marketplace, because some companies do not wish to reveal their development plans and jeopardize their opportunity to take advantage of the early adopters followed by general market adoption. This is particularly true when there is the possibility for a major shift in the capabilities available to the market. As a general rule, the bigger the shift, the more clandestine the technology development effort. Other technology providers (generally the largest ones) sometimes discuss their plans for providing a new technology openly, occasionally to discourage competition by having the mainstream marketplace delay purchases until their particular spin on the technology is made available, or when the development only enhances the existing product.

A new technology that is announced prior to its general availability is sometimes referred to as *vaporware* because, although the technology provider sometimes is willing to discuss the technology at length, the technology either is immature or, in some cases, does not even exist. If the company is a very large and well-known provider of technology, this can have detrimental effects on smaller companies, because the prevailing customer base may wait for the technology to be provided by a name-brand company who will ensure the technology is standards based.

It is common for a new technology to be provided by more than one company at a time, or to have several or more companies introduce a new technology within months of each other. The number of examples of this across many industries is fascinating to consider, because it seems as though completely unrelated technology providers develop the same new idea at virtually the same time without the slightest degree of collusion, cooperation, or even communication between them.

Relatively High Interest by Developers

A standard will not be developed unless sufficient interest exists among a relatively large number of technology providers or a few very large providers such as Cisco, General Electric, or Microsoft, which possess sufficient resources to reach the bulk of a market prior to a need for a standard. Indeed, a standard has little to no use if the technology is provided by only a single developer, largely because of the issue of interoperability.

While many cutting-edge technologies are developed by startups formed by employees of large companies that refused to pursue a promising technology, the size and number of the prospective technology providers must be taken into consideration. One example of this is the BlueTooth standard. At this writing, very few BlueTooth devices are on the market despite a considerable amount of press coverage over the last five or so years. While there are not an appreciable number of BlueTooth-standards–based products on the market right now, the level of interest is high for developing products that will incorporate the BlueTooth standard.

Deployment of Technology to Early Adopters

Cutting-edge technology is often deployed first to early adopters who have either had design input or formally expressed a willingness to use unproven technology. Part of the exchange for state-of-the-art technology often includes certain nondisclosure limitations on the part of the early adopter to not reveal product weaknesses or apparent displeasure with the performance of the equipment. Equipment is commonly, but not always, released in three phases: alpha, beta, and preproduction versions. After these phases, a version sometimes called *general acceptance* or *general availability (GA)* is released.

The engagement of early adopters is important because it enables the technology providers not only to determine how their equipment will perform in real-world conditions but also to have third-party users assist in the debugging process. There are also often nontechnology issues to be characterized, such as deployment practices, the training of deployment and network management personnel, and modeling how the system will alter existing traffic patterns, loads, and QoS mixes. Early adopters tend to be tolerant of technology bugs and other deficiencies such as the high cost of the initially released technology. Finally, early adopters tend to have small markets that are nevertheless statistically significant for the statistical analysis associated with characterizing how a new technology will perform.

Standards Definition by One or More Technology Providers

Following either limited or extensive field trials, one or more technology providers will work with standards bodies to define the standard. This is often accomplished by having personnel from various technology providers operate within the standards bodies in key positions. Commonly, the chairperson of a workgroup is a distinguished engineer from one of the larger technology companies. While the workgroups commonly comprise individuals from leading companies, this does not necessarily lead to a standard that is preferable to one vendor over another, because there are often checks and balances within the standards organizations to prevent this from happening, most particularly in the arena of voting, which is done by constituents from many companies.

Establishment of Standard by Standards Body

As it is common for multiple technology providers to develop a technology in parallel, it is also common for there to be more than one standard codified in parallel. Well-known examples of this include wireless Ethernet, which became the 802.11 standard, and the orthogonal frequency division multiplexing (OFDM) spreading technique, which has been codified into several standards, most notably 802.11a and 802.11g.

Sometimes standards emerge not from entities such as the IEEE or IETF, but rather from a consortium of technology providers such as the OFDM Forum or Wireless Ethernet Compatibility Alliance (WECA). Although these forums are not standards bodies, many are taken seriously by the market and technology providers because of their close relationship with the IEEE. In addition, forums like BWIF are generally comprised of some of the leading technology heavyweights such as Cisco. Forums also offer the advantage of access to open architectures.

One of the aspects of technology forums is that they tend to take less time to achieve consensus, possibly because they have less of a political legacy than some of the standards bodies. If no standard exists and a new technology has been introduced, waiting for full standardization entails the risk of a group of technology providers missing a market window. Importantly, forums allow groups of companies to band together quickly to begin voluntarily complying with a particular architecture and begin providing solutions that will interoperate seamlessly years before a ratified standard can be put in place. The consensus established at a technology forum has the same effect as a standard and commonly is utilized and ratified as a de facto standard prior to becoming a standard issued by entities such as the IEEE or EITF.

It is generally more common than not for a marketplace to have competing standards, and as the time required to develop and deploy new technologies decreases, the probability of competing standards increases. This is, to a large degree, why the concept of "a standard" can be somewhat of an illusion.

In a technological world where innovations are constant and occasionally revolutionary, the application of a standard is perhaps more greatly affected by how widely deployed a technology becomes than by which standards body ratifies the standard or when the standard is ratified.

Once in possession of a standards definition, the standards organization will commonly announce to the technology industry and market its intent to publish a standard. A period of time from three to six months is commonly provided for technology providers and the market in general to provide input to the proposed standard. A balloting process (detailed later in this chapter) commonly occurs next, wherein the standard is voted upon for ratification.

Once the standards organization has received input from the industry, or the period for comment has passed without substantial input from the technology providers or market, the standard is published and distributed.

In some cases, a technology becomes standard even though a considerable amount of the marketplace believes a different approach or standard would better serve the needs of the end users. Examples of this include the VHS versus Betamax standard for video cassettes, Macintosh (Apple) computers versus IBM (Windows), and, at the time of this writing, the several versions of DVD. VHS and Windows have dominated world markets not because they had superior technical merits, but rather by how a leading technology provider strategy was implemented.

Ratification of Standard by Technology Providers

Once the balloting process has been completed and the standard has been approved as written by one or more committees, the real work begins. The most important phase of the standards effort is when the technology providers decide whether or not to adopt the proposed standard. More importantly, the life and distribution of the standard depends on how much of the market adopts the new standard. Both of the authors of this book play a role at the largest provider of certain Internet elements, and it's fascinating to observe how fewer than 100 people will steer a major company's development, marketing, and sales resources to align behind a standard—or to not align these resources behind a standard. It is this very process that has more to do with whether a standard will even survive than how well thought out a standard is or the timing of the release of a standard.

There are many standards available in many industries, but the ones that are the most important are those that gain the greatest amount of mind share from technology providers and, following that, market share from the end users who pay for the standard-based equipment.

The release of a standard can take two years or longer, and then requires acceptance by an array of manufacturers, who then design their products in a compliant manner. A relatively large array of manufacturers is generally required in order to provide enough product to an open market, and the concept of getting a large number of independent and competing companies to agree to a standard is a time-consuming and challenging objective.

A number of successful standards initiatives relative to the Internet, LANs, and WLAN have emerged. Perhaps the best-known, understood, and widely deployed example is the Ethernet standard.

It's important to understand that the mere existence of a standard is no guarantee that every vendor must or will adhere to it. In the world of technology, there is generally no legal requirement for a company to provide a product in compliance with a given standard; they are completely at liberty to develop their own proprietary version of the standard. In general, however, most companies tend to adhere to standards, because this can reduce the cost of development, speed development, and maximize the addressable market.

Institute of Electrical and Electronics Engineers

The IEEE is an enormous organization comprised of both professionals and students, with over 350,000 members in approximately 25 countries. IEEE has an unspecified number of full-time employees, volunteers, and interns. Additionally, the IEEE utilizes the support of hundreds of employees of other companies and interested parties who meet in groups, chapters, and sections. Its effect on electrical engineering in general, the Internet, WLAN, and many other electronics disciplines cannot be overestimated. Few electrical engineering students the world over have not heard of this organization, and virtually every experienced engineer in the world has studied at least one IEEE paper at some point in their career.

Another way to identify the scope and impact of the IEEE is its dictionary, published in four- to five-year intervals and currently in its seventh edition. This edition contains over 35,000 technical terms relating to various electrical, computing, networking, and communications efforts from over 800 IEEE standards initiatives. Simply stated, the scope and output of this organization is vast.

The full process of either bringing a new standard into existence or updating an existing one is enormous and beyond the scope of a single chapter in a book. In summary, however, it involves various processes and phases of standards sponsorship, drafting, balloting, and committee review.

Further, the process is one of careful deliberation, in-depth discussion, and political wrangling worthy of the highest levels of most governments. These are international bodies that comprise members from many different countries and companies with varying viewpoints, agendas, and competitive concerns, and there is often energetic disagreement between committee members and the sponsors of standards. As a result, the completed standards often include compromises that don't wholly appeal to all interested parties.

Although there are other general practices exercised by other standards entities and forums, the following process is that used by the IEEE, and is entirely appropriate to summarize as part of a dissertation on standards, given the magnitude of this entity.

The following outline of how a standard is developed should be viewed as an ideal series of events that occur prior to the establishment of a standard—in many cases, there are iterations between the steps indicated:

1. Sponsor selection and duties.
2. Submit Project Authorization Request (PAR).
3. Approve PAR.
4. Organize working group.
5. Develop draft of standard.
6. Ballot draft of standard.
7. Approve draft standard.
8. Publish approved standard.

Sponsor Selection and Duties

The *sponsor* is the organization that assumes responsibility for the work of drafting the standards document and ensuring its timely passage through the various phases of deploying a standard. The IEEE retains ownership of the *technical* merits of the proposed standard, but it is the sponsor that shoulders the effort regarding the scope and technical content of the standard. The sponsor is generally an entity outside of the IEEE, while the IEEE *Standards Board* ensures that the proper rules and procedures for assembling and ratifying a standard are followed.

The bulk of the work is performed by an organization, not an individual. Once a standard has been conceptualized, the work of enabling a standard is accomplished by groups of individuals knowledgeable in the field in which the standard is being proposed. In many circumstances, working groups exist for new standards, but in the event no working group exists for a proposed standard, a working group is established by the IEEE through an invitation process.

The first step a sponsoring group takes is to become familiar with the various IEEE societies to determine if there is an existing committee or society that is familiar with the proposed standard. The IEEE has a large number of sponsors within various societies in the form of committees. A *society* is a group dedicated to a specific discipline, such as antennas or a modulation scheme. If the proposed standard comes within the scope of one of these committees, this is where the standards work begins. One would contact the

IEEE by e-mail or telephone to determine whether a certain society or committee would be appropriate for the proposed standard.

If no committee appears appropriate for a proposed standard, the group or person interested in the new standard would contact the IEEE's governing body for standards either by e-mail or telephone and make the request to a staff liaison to determine whether an existing committee would be interested in working with the sponsor in the new standard. In some cases, a standard would interest the members of more than one society, in which case the IEEE Standards Board has coordinating committees that exist to accommodate this type of development.

Submit Project Authorization Request

The PAR is a concise, three- to four-page document that indicates the new standard has been approved for consideration within the IEEE. This document is approved by the IEEE *New Standards Committee (NesCom)*, which is one of a number of the Standards Board's committees.

The PAR is a highly detailed document that usually conforms to a template provided by IEEE. It states the intent of the proposed standard, but is not a draft of the standard itself. While officially the IEEE doesn't recognize the work of a proposed standard until a PAR has been approved and logged in to the IEEE, it is common to have *study groups*, which are entities that guide the standards process and comprise various industry experts from an array of technology providers. Once a PAR has been approved, it must be completed within four years. If the standard requires longer than this period of time, an application for extension of time must be acquired from the NesCom.

Approve PAR

PARs are typically reviewed once a calendar quarter by the NesCom. The PAR is generally provided to the NesCom at least 40 days prior to review, and in most cases the committee offers feedback and input for improvement to the PAR. This is important, because the PAR details the scope and intent of the standard. Standards, even in their earliest phases, are embodied in living documents so that, as the standard matures and changes in detail, scope, and intent, the PAR is also updated in parallel.

Organize Working Group

Once the PAR has been approved by the NesCom, a *working group* is organized. The typical positions within a working group may commonly include the following:

- Chair
- Vice-chair
- Secretary
- Treasurer

- Technical editor
- Ballot coordinator
- International standards liaison—all the above bullets

The working group operates very much like a company board in terms of the agenda, and generally follows *Robert's Rules of Order*, which is a widely used standard for meetings and covers the manner in which the agenda is managed in terms of review of minutes, new business, old business, and so on. One of the key purposes of the working group is to ensure consensus among numbers of the working group relative to the standard; and the responsibilities of the officers are to ensure the work is moving forward at an appropriate pace and to ensure the interface with various committees and societies within the IEEE moves along smoothly. Like the PAR, the standard duration of a working group is four years, although this period can be extended.

Develop Draft of Standard

The draft of the standard is completed by the working group and is generally a complex and even daunting task. It is based on the PAR and begins with an outline. Because it is fairly common to have numerous authors of the draft, the coordination of the tone, content, and scope is done by the technical editor and officers of the working group.

From time to time, personnel from the industry affected by the standard may request a draft of the standard and may desire to provide input. Working groups commonly send copies of the standard's drafts to organizations and personnel outside the working group, but generally this is done in a manner such that the working group retains tight control of the draft.

Ballot Draft of Standard

Following the completion of a standard's draft, the work of sending it out for voting is provided through a process called *ballot work*, which takes anywhere from 30 to 90 days. The purpose of voting on a proposed standard is to ensure the greatest degree of consensus among those who will be affected by the standard, or if the balloting remains purely internal to the IEEE, to ensure that the greatest degree of consensus is achieved among the various committees. During the balloting process, the IEEE does not look for a unanimous agreement on the draft of a proposed standard, and in fact deems that a standard's draft has achieved consensus when 75 percent of the voters approve the standard.

There does not appear to be a single, uniform method for balloting, but in general, the ballot group is an active committee that exists exclusively within the IEEE. However, there are many examples of when the balloting is opened to a wide array of interested parties, both from within the IEEE and from the industries that the standard may affect. In the latter example, the working group may use various forms of media to provide notice to all interested parties.

The balloting group is generally made up of three types of groups: technology providers, end users, and other interested parties that may or may not be directly associated with the proposed standard. Ballots may be sent to the following entities:

- Corporations
- Government agencies
- Associations and societies
- Consultants
- Academic institutions
- User groups
- Other standards-development organizations

The working group will commonly achieve the best balance possible among the groups, with no company or balloting group comprising more than 50 percent of the entire ballots.

Of interest, the ballot for proposal of a standard includes an area in which the voter may provide either technical or editorial feedback with regard to the proposed standard. If the number of negative votes is substantial, the work begins of resolving the differences between the working group developing the standard and the voters. This negotiation can be the most time-consuming aspect of the entire process. After the working group has integrated the concerns from those casting ballots, the standard's draft is usually sent out once again for ballot.

Approve Draft Standard

Subsequent to the successful approval of the standard's draft through the balloting and comments process, the draft is then sent to a *Review Committee (RevCom)*, which reviews the entire process that has occurred to date with regard to the attempt to deploy a new standard. This review board is more focused on the process than the technical content of the draft and generally reviews the following items:

- Was the balloting group balanced?
- If the ballot was delegated to a subordinate committee, is there a record of that delegation?
- Was the ballot valid, with at least a 75 percent return and fewer than 30 percent abstentions?
- Did the ballot pass by at least 75 percent?
- Does the document match the title/scope/purpose of the PAR authorizing the work? (Note that title changes that are still within the PAR's scope and purpose are acceptable.)
- Was coordination with the required organizations achieved? Was coordination accomplished via the required method?

- Were all members of the balloting group given an opportunity to see all the outstanding negatives and the reasons why they could not be resolved?
- Were all members of the balloting group given an opportunity to change their vote as a result of changes made to resolve negative ballots?
- Are there any major technical or procedural oversights?

Once the RevCom is satisfied that the process has been compliant with the rules and procedures of the IEEE, it makes a recommendation for approval to the NesCom.

Publish Approved Standard

Prior to publication, there is still a considerable amount of work to be completed on the draft. Once the IEEE NesCom has approved the recommendation by the RevCom, the standard is then reviewed by a standards editor who ensures the standard is grammatically and syntactically correct in American English and ensures it adheres to the formatting as set forth in a document entitled *IEEE Standards Style Manual.* The editor does not alter the technical content of the standard, but in the event the editor finds glaring errors in formulas or other key elements of the draft standard, the editor will offer opinions that are then reviewed by the RevCom. If the RevCom approves the change, the completed document is then sent for publication. If the proposed changes do not make it past the RevCom, the changes may be incorporated into a subsequent revision of the standard or corrected through errata appendices.

The final review of the standard's draft is then performed by the working group chair or assigned delegate to ensure the edited and formatted version of the standard's draft remains consistent with the PAR and technical content of the draft.

Following this final review, the draft becomes a standard, that is then distributed through normal media channels both inside and outside the IEEE. Upon distribution, questions on the interpretation of the standard are common. Upon receipt of a request by the IEEE to interpret a standard, the request is sent to the working group and an interpretation is provided and distributed in a similar manner to the original standard. In some cases, the interpretations are cumulatively sufficient in scope that a volume of the interpretations is assembled and distributed. These interpretations do not alter the standard even upon discovery of an error, but they are important because the IEEE does not want issues with standards to remain unaddressed.

Wireless Ethernet Compatibility Alliance and Wi-Fi

WECA's mission is to certify interoperability of IEEE 802.11 high-data-rate products and to promote Wi-Fi as the global wireless LAN standard across all market segments. WECA is one of the groups leading the charge to refer to "802.11b" as "Wi-Fi" or *Wireless Fidelity.* There is also an emerging version of Wi-Fi for 802.11a, which will *not* be referred to as "Wi-Fi5", but rather, simply "Wi-Fi." But WECA is also trying to ensure that if you buy a product with the Wi-Fi badge on it, from any vendor, it will be compatible with other similar cards and, more importantly, with the access points with which it connects to the LAN or Internet at large, which also have the Wi-Fi logo.

Companies currently supporting this standards group include 3Com, Acere, Nokia, Apple Computer, Atmel, and Cisco Systems; currently, a total of approximately 150 companies. One of the distinguishing characteristics about WECA is that it is embracing and promoting a standard (802.11) as opposed to implementing a standard of its own. It is focused on a wide area of users, from business users, small and medium business (often referred to in the United States as "SMB"), highly utilized public areas such as airports, and hospitality venues such as hotels and convention centers, to the SOHO and residential user.

By comparison, HomeRF, a consortium of companies which focused primarily on the residential market for wireless devices, although it is interesting to note that WECA also works with the BlueTooth Special Interest Groups (SIGs), as the 802.11b frequency and the BlueTooth frequencies are similar and both use spread spectrum. The alliance between WECA and BlueTooth is intended to promote the ability for both protocols to operate in a common physical environment. While WECA devices will primarily connect PCs and printers, BlueTooth's intent is to primarily focus on smaller electronic items such as digital cameras, PDAs, and mobile phones, although there will certainly be BlueTooth devices installed in PCs.

At this writing, WECA is focused not only on the 802.11b standard and ensuring interoperability between products from different manufacturers, but also on the 802.11a standard, which operates at 5GHz. There is also a third working group at this writing, the 802.11g group, which is developing a high-speed standard with a carrier frequency identical to 802.11b although it utilizes OFDM as the spreading technique and the addition of QAM to the allowable modulation techniques.

It costs approximately $20,000 for a company to join WECA, and $100,000 to become a sponsoring company. Membership in WECA ensures a voice in the promotion and deployment of the 802.11 IEEE standard.

WECA recognizes that while both the 11b and 11a specifications utilize unique Layer 1 hardware, they share the same Layer 2 MAC protocol. It is the opinion of the authors of this book that the 802.11a standard is complementary to, as opposed to competitive with, the 11b and 11g standards. It is arguable that the 11g technology may become the most widely deployed and that 11b equipment will eventually be considered the "value line" among technology providers.

COMPETING WLAN STANDARDS

The following three competing WLAN standards currently exist, and there is some confusion and inaccurate information in the marketplace about the issue of a WLAN "standard." It's noteworthy that there is a considerable difference in the degree to which each of these standards has been adopted by not only the technology developers but the market itself.

- HomeRF
- BlueTooth
- 802.11

Proxim, through its constellation of cooperating companies, has established the HomeRF standard and has selected the residential market as its primary target, while the 802.11 standard has gone after the SMB, enterprise, and SOHO markets. IBM, with its BlueTooth market, has essentially pursued the commercial/retail market. HomeRF has placed products on the market with prices as low as $80 at Buy.com, while 802.11 equipment has been sold and currently is operating in more than 60 countries worldwide at prices ranging from $79 to $300 US (list) for a PCMCIA card, and from $150 to $1,000 US (list) for an access point. This enormous swing in pricing generally reflects the target markets; in other words, the very-low-cost equipment generally includes minimal security, low performance, and minimum levels of interoperability, and is intended for deployment where the radio is not required to operate as a sophisticated network element such as that found in commercial enterprises, the financial markets, and so forth.

BlueTooth has had perhaps the largest press buildup but by far the fewest number of devices in the marketplace, and it is virtually always integrated into another device such as a PDA or cellular phone. The long-standing target price for BlueTooth chipsets is $20 to manufacturers, who then sell to consumers.

The three competing WLAN standards are represented summarily in Table 2-1.

	HomeRF	BlueTooth	802.11b
Physical layer	FHSS	FHSS	FHSS, DSSS, IR
Hop frequency	50 hops per sec	1600 hops per sec	2.5 hops per sec
Max. transmitting power	100mW	100mW	800mW
Data rates	1- or 2Mbps	1Mbps	11Mbps
Max. number devices	Up to 127	Up to 26	Up to 256
Security	Blowfish format	0-, 40-, and 64-bit	40- and 128-bit RC4 TKIP MIC, SSN
Range	150 ft.	30 ft.	400 ft. indoors, 1000 ft. LOS
Current version	V1.0	V1.0	V1.0
Cost	Neither least nor most expensive	Least expensive	Most expensive
Physical size	Neither largest nor smallest	Smallest	Largest
Roaming outside of home	No	No	Yes

Table 2-1.   Competing Indoor RF Standards

The following are some notes regarding Table 2-1:

- 40- and 128-bit RC4 are not considered robust data security algorithms.

- 802.11 range of 1000 feet is at outdoor conditions, and is more likely to be an indication of the 802.11b standard. Indoor conditions are more difficult for these types of RF systems. Using an 802.11 bridge will enable much greater distances than when using an access point.

- 802.11 power output of 800mW is substantial.

- The maximum number of devices supported depends on the data rate per device.

- BlueTooth is currently heavily restricted by the FCC for power due to excessive spectral mask leaks. Optimal range for the revised version is estimated at 300 feet LOS, but at this writing is approximately 5 meters.

NOTE   Both HomeRF and BlueTooth are standards that are called *clustered*. This means that the companies that support the standard are clustered around the lead development company. In the case of HomeRF, the company central to the effort is Proxim, while IBM is the primary sponsor of BlueTooth. The constellations around each of these companies include channel resellers, which are groups that resell the products that use these standards, as well as silicon and other discrete electronics suppliers.

One of the key reasons for having a standard is so that equipment provided by an array of supplier A will work with the equipment of supplier B. The company that fostered the standard often stands to make considerable financial gain, because it often offers a key element or feature that is required as part of the standard. Large companies like standards-based products because they can often sell more product to a single customer, especially if the customer is a large one. Large customers like standards because they provide stability to the basic product designs and ensure interoperability as they both scale and migrate their networks.

It is important to note that only one of the three standards supports what can truly be called broadband, and that is the 802.11 standard. The authors make this claim because the 802.11 standard far outperforms the other two.. The 802.11 incoming standards will further this performance gap with the 54Mbps performance of the 11g and then 11a equipment.

There are two other major differences between the standards:

- Range
- Adoption rate by the market

The 802.11 Standard

As stated earlier in this chapter, the IEEE 802.11 standard should be viewed with an additional degree of granularity both because the general 802.11 standard has an array of variants and, perhaps more importantly, because it is the standard that has captured the mind share of the major providers of this technology and enjoys by far the largest amount of market share.

Table 2-2 provides a summary of the more prevalent versions of this standard, and a snapshot of each of them.

The IEEE adopted IEEE 802.11 in 1997, and it became the first WLAN standard. IEEE 802.11 as defined by the IEEE primarily controls Layers 1 and 2 of the OSI reference stack, which are the physical layer and the data-link layer (sometimes referred to as the link layer), respectively.

The 802.11 Media Access Control Layer

The MAC layer is a subset of the link layer, which is adjacent to the physical layer in an IP-based network. Layer 1 in an 802.11 network performs at least three essential functions:

- Serves as the interface between the MAC layer at two or more geographic locations. These locations are generally only a few hundred feet or less apart.

- Performs the actual sensing for the CSMA/CD events, which occur within the MAC layer.

- Performs the modulation and demodulation of the signal between two geographic points where 802.11 equipment resides. This modulation scheme can be either DSSS or FHSS.

Importantly, the 802.11 standard defines a *rate-shifting technique* that enables networks to reduce data rates as changes in distance, signal quality, and strength occur. IEEE 802.11b data rates may be as high as 11Mbps or as low as 1Mbps with DSSS modulation, while FHSS-modulated data rates are either 1- or 2Mbps. The

Standard	Carrier Frequency	Data Rate	Summary
802.11a	5.1–5.2GHz 5.2–5.3GHz 5.7–5.8GHz	54Mbps	Max power is 40mW in 5.1 band, 250mW in 5.2 band, and 800mW in 5.7 band (U.S.)
802.11b	2.4–2.485GHz	11Mbps	The most widely shipped standard at this writing
802.11d	N/A		Multiple regulatory domains
802.11e	N/A	N/A	Quality of Service
802.11f	N/A	N/A	Inter-Access Point Protocol (IAPP)
802.11g	2.4–2.485GHz	36- or 54Mbps	
802.11h	N/A	N/A	Dynamic Frequency Selection (DFS)
802.11i	N/A	N/A	Security

Table 2-2.   Table of IEEE Standards

standard also enables compatibility between 802.11a and 802.11b radios. The portion of an 802.11a network that uses 802.11b equipment will result in the lower data rates of the older standard.

The MAC layer is a sublayer of Layer 2 of the OSI stack and controls the connectivity of two or more points through an address scheme. Each laptop or access point has a MAC address. The IEEE 802.11 standard defines how this addressing works, along with how certain aspects of Layer 1 operate. This standard is similar in many respects to the Ethernet standard established by the same standards body. In effect, it defines the following:

- Functions required for an 802.11-compliant device to operate either in a peer-to-peer fashion or integrated with an existing WLAN
- Operation of the 802.11 device within the range of other 802.11 devices and how a client card would physically migrate from one access point to another
- MAC-level access control and data delivery services to upper layers of the network protocol stack
- Several physical layer signaling techniques and interfaces
- Privacy and security of user data being transferred over the wireless media

What makes a WLAN different from an Ethernet LAN is obviously the ability of users to roam from one point in the network to another, while remaining connected. This is the most important feature of a WLAN as well as the one that distinguishes it the most from an Ethernet LAN. The way that the 802.11 MAC operates under this standard is what allows the higher levels of the OSI stack to function normally. In other words, the MAC layer is the one that handles the mobility issues of an 802.11 network.

It is for this reason that an 802.11 MAC layer is forced to take on certain functionalities normally left to layers higher in the OSI stack such as the session layer (Layer 5), which controls session initiation and termination. In the 802.11 MAC standard, the flow of information is performed on a best-effort basis, which is also called *connectionless.* Connectionless links are those in which the receiving end of the link does not verify the receipt of data by the transmitting link. The technique used by the MAC layer is called Carrier Sense Multiple Access with Collision Detection (CSMA/CD), which is a technique that requires the transmitter to "listen" to the local environment to ensure there are no other transmissions in the frequency to which it is assigned. The actual sensing is performed at Layer 1, but the timing for the transmissions is controlled at the MAC layer.

CSMA/CD is a protocol intended to resolve transmission conflicts. As stated, the transmitter will determine if there is a transmission in the assigned frequency of an access point or client adapter. If a transmission is in progress, the access point or bridge will wait for a specified period of time, following which it will determine whether or not the radio channel is clear. The radios are programmed such that the timing between the attempts to determine whether or not a particular radio channel is clear is random. Some simple statistics are employed that state that the highest probability for a channel to remain in use is just after an attempt to transmit was halted because the radio channel was in use by another transmitter. It is for this reason that the time between attempts to transmit is randomly spaced. The amount of time between repeated attempts is often called *back-off time*.

In most 802.11 systems, however, the back-off time steadily diminishes until the transmitter determines there is an open channel. By having steadily diminishing but unequal time periods, a WLAN gains efficiency. It is easy to understand that network efficiency would suffer if all the radios on a common channel were to wait for an increasingly longer period. By having the radios listen for increasingly longer, though randomly selected, durations, the radios waiting to transmit traffic will wait the least amount of time.

In a best-effort architecture, there can be no guarantee that the data sent will be received successfully. One of the things an 802.11 system does to help ensure the successful receipt of information is to send the information repeatedly, which is called *chipping*.

One other function provided by an 802.11 MAC layer is that of security, which is typically handled at the presentation layer (Layer 6). The security measure compliant with this standard is Wired Equivalent Privacy (WEP), which is a method for handling keys and encrypting the data. See Chapter 11 on security for more information about WEP.

802.11b vs. 802.11a

At present, there are two types of high-rate RF products the 802.11 specifications, as ratified by the IEEE, cover. These are 802.11b and 802.11a. The 802.11g technology is still in development and likely will not be ratified until Spring 2003. While the 802.11a and 802.11b specifications were ratified by the IEEE on the same day in September 1999, products from the 802.11b technology were released to the market several years before the 802.11a and forthcoming (at this writing) 802.11g specifications. Table 2-3 illustrates the primary differences between the three technologies.

802.11a Summary Points

The following key points should be considered relative to the wide scope of issues on the standards as issued by the IEEE:

- Orthogonal Frequency Division Multiplexing (OFDM)
- Data rates supported: 54-, 48-, 36-, 24-, 12-, and 6Mbps
- Can "downshift" to lower data rates for longer range
- Will have greater average throughput in a mixed standard deployment (11b and 11g) than 802.11g since 802.11a has no backward-compatibility requirement
- Currently is only approved for indoor AP use in a handful of countries: Canada, Denmark, France, Japan, New Zealand, Singapore, Sweden, Taiwan, United Kingdom, and United States
- Effort underway to allow UNII-1 operation in certain European countries

	802.11b	802.11g	802.11a
Frequency	2.4GHz	2.4GHz	5.7GHz
OFDM	No	Yes	Yes
Non–Line-of-Sight	No	No	No
Data rates	11Mbps	54Mbps	54Mbps
Number of nonoverlapping channels	3	3	12

Table 2-3.   Snapshot Comparison of 802.11b and 802.11a Specifications

- Separate effort to allow 5.47-5.725GHz band to be used in United States and other countries, but is somewhat doubtful given that the U.S. military has expressed an interest in retaining this spectrum

- Long-term: Worldwide usage with adoption of Transmit Power Control (TPC) and Dynamic Frequency Selection (DFS) per 802.11h standard

- 5GHz band subject to less co-channel interference than 2.4GHz ISM band because there are presently far fewer devices like cordless phones in the same spectrum

The HomeRF Standard

The HomeRF standard is rooted in the Digital Enhanced Cordless Telephone (DECT) standard, and perhaps for good reason, because there are more than 200 million handsets that comply with this standard, from more than 100 suppliers worldwide. This also explains why the HomeRF standard is the only one that currently can carry toll-quality voice traffic, and in fact is taking the opposite migration path of 802.11 and BlueTooth, which is to go from voice to data.

It would seem clear that the intent of the HomeRF group is to provide an appliance that keys off a very large customer base of cordless phone users. Its intent seems to be to provide a central appliance that connects the devices within a home to the cordless phone to enable phone calls to and from the residence and then to provide broadband to the personal computer by interfacing a broadband connection within the home.

This is accomplished with an approach similar to 802.11, which is to have both MAC and physical layers of the OSI stack that comply with this standard. The HomeRF standard utilizes a combination of CSMA/CD for packet data and TDMA for voice and video traffic to optimize traffic flows on a priority basis.

The physical layer utilizes frequency shift keying (FSK) to supply variable bit rates of 800Kbps, and 1.6Mbps at 2.4GHz. There was an attempt to start up a second HomeRF standard called HomeRF2, which permitted data rates of 5- and 10Mbps, but, outside of Proxim, no other companies have invested in this technology. For HomeRF, bandwidth throttling is accomplished through the utilization of seventy-five 1MHz channels for voice and data channels at 1.6Mbps. The HomeRF2 standard uses fifteen 5MHz channels for 5- and 10Mbps data channels. The physical layer also features smart hopping to avoid transmission residency in channels that are heavily congested with interference.

Streaming media takes the top priority for transmission and is identified by application headers, while voice and data traffic takes up the balance of the bandwidth, again identified and based on application headers. The streaming media uses time and physical buffers to allow voice and then data traffic.

Of considerable interest, the HomeRF standard includes an impressive array of voice features such as call line ID, call waiting, call forwarding, and residential intercom. This is directly attributable to this standard's genesis in a telco voice standard.

For security, HomeRF uses 128-bit encryption augmented by the native security enhancement of an FHSS modulation at the physical layer. This combination should provide a high level of resistance to denial of service attacks, though the authors were not able to determine whether or not the keys are static or dynamic.

The BlueTooth Standard

While BlueTooth is indeed a WLAN standard, substantial confusion exists as to whether or not it competes directly with 802.11 and/or HomeRF. The sum of the matter is that BlueTooth does not compete directly with 802.11, and competes only in a peripheral manner with HomeRF. The primary reason is that BlueTooth is intended to be a standard with a nominal range of approximately one to three meters. Its intent is to connect laptop computers with cellular phones, PDAs with laptops and cellular phones, and so on. The secondary reason is that it is relatively speed limited at approximately 1.5Mbps—approximately one-tenth the speed of the 802.11b standard, and only a tiny fraction of the speed that will be afforded by the 802.11a and 802.11g standards.

The first versions of the BlueTooth specification were released in early 1999, with version 2 promised for release in 2002. This duration of time between the original specification's release and the second version's release could spell problems for the standard, especially as there has been a considerable amount of media exposure to BlueTooth 1, which was released in the mid-1990s. In other words, it took approximately four years for version 1 of the specification to be released, and an excessive delay in the release of BlueTooth 2 may erode the support base, because the supporting cast of engineers and companies may pursue other standards that are closer to release or are already on the market. At this writing, there are nearly 2,500 BlueTooth members listed in the Special Interest Group.

A company purchases the rights to use the BlueTooth standard at no cost. The design is a single chip, which is elegant, small, and has very low power consumption. This combination of features lends the design and the standard to certain applications, but is hardly a panacea for all broadband concerns.

While it does indeed approach the threshold of being a true broadband device, according to its home page, the maximum data rate is 1Mbps and is indicated as a gross data rate. Throughput should be expected on the order of approximately 750Kbps, depending on how much overhead is used for security and frequency-hopping management.

The BlueTooth standard has two strong points:

- **Size**   The form factor (size) afforded by BlueTooth enables it to be embedded in wristwatches, PDAs, and other small electronic devices where size is an important design criterion.

- **Power savings**   BlueTooth uses 30 micro amps, which is a very small amount of power. It uses a fraction of the power used by a standard wristwatch, and uses orders of magnitude below that used by cellular phones. This feature also plays very well to the industry, which often builds devices such as cordless headsets based on how much battery is required to provide a meaningful duty cycle (period of continuous operation).

In terms of security, BlueTooth has an encryption method, but it is not identified on its web page. It should be mentioned that an FHSS hopping scheme of 1600 hops per second and a very limited range of one to three meters would make it difficult to be eavesdropped upon from any distance.

If there is any negative aspect of the BlueTooth standard, it is that it has been the recipient of an enormous amount of hype. The BlueTooth Special Interest Group predicted in the mid-1990s that there would be over 200 million PCs with BlueTooth devices built into them as an original manufactured device by the year 2000. It turns out that what PC manufacturers are relying on are connections with speeds that are well in excess of that which BlueTooth can provide, in addition to transmission and reception ranges well beyond that which the BlueTooth standard provides at the time of this writing. This is why most major laptop computer vendors today supply products with an 802.11 option.

In fairness to the BlueTooth supporters, few BlueTooth-based products currently are on the market, mostly in the area of connecting cellular telephones to PDAs, keyboards and mouses to PCs, cameras to PCs, and the like.

Just prior to this writing, Microsoft announced it was backing away from the HomeRF standard. While the standard from which HomeRF is derived is very widely distributed throughout the world, it is the opinion of this author that the standard that undoubtedly is making the most rapid growth is 802.11.

In summary, the 802.11a and 802.11g standards promise 54Mbps of speed in conjunction with the virtually unanimous support by every major and minor WLAN vendors. These emerging standards will be built on a market fueled, at this writing, by worldwide sales in excess of $1 billion US for 802.11b. It is the prediction of the authors that HomeRF will go the way of Betamax as a competitor to 802.11. BlueTooth is not competitive to 802.11 because it addresses a different type of connectivity, that which may be termed "personal area network," which is generally limited in range to approximately five meters with low data rates. It will therefore become ancillary to the 802.11b/a/g standards because it will provide connectivity between users and their appliances, where the 802.11 standards will connect appliances to networks.

CHAPTER 3

Understanding Radio Frequency Fundamentals

In order to understand RF fundamentals, the first item to consider is electromagnetic energy, which is pervasive throughout the planet and intrinsically part of every electrical system. Every electrical system or device that carries electricity has an electromagnetic field.

The fundamental element of electromagnetism is the activity of electrons. Electrons are the particles that orbit around a nucleus of protons and neutrons. The essential art of RF is to get enough electrons to move in relative unison within, and local to, the transmitting antenna such that they have a detectable effect on electrons at the receiving antenna.

James Clerk Maxwell (Scottish theoretical physicist, 1831–1879) predicted that electric and magnetic fields move through space as waves. His theory was based on the following four concepts:

1. Electric lines originate on positive charges and terminate on negative charges.

2. Magnetic lines always form closed loops—that is, they do not begin or end at any specific point.

3. A varying magnetic field induces a magnetic force and therefore an electrical field.

4. Magnetic fields are generated by moving charges (currents).

Maxwell's scientific work is often considered among the most important of the nineteenth century. He supported these four concepts with a corresponding mathematical framework to prove two phenomena: electrical and magnetic fields are symmetric to each other, and by rapidly changing the electrical field, one can produce a magnetic field well beyond the electrical field.

Maxwell discovered that when an electrical field was rapidly changed, magnetic waves were sent through space much like waves generated by a stone when tossed into water. Importantly, he also calculated that these waves travel at the speed of light.

Also of considerable interest, Maxwell discovered that visible light, electrical waves, and magnetic waves have tightly linked relationships. His discovery that magnetic and electrical fields each generate the other is one of the greatest discoveries in science and has had a profound influence on later developments in science and industry.

Both magnetic and electrical fields are created when electrical energy is transferred from one point to another. It is this shift in energy that enables the phenomenon of magnetism and, by extension, radio frequency propagation. Therefore, to transmit information between two points, the energy must not be in a constant state; that is, it must change in either amplitude or frequency. Amplitude is the magnitude or strength of a waveform, while frequency is how often a complete wave passes a given point in space.

This change of energy is called *modulation*, of which there are many types, but all of which stem from changes either in amplitude or frequency. The issue of modulation will be treated more fully a bit later in this chapter.

The prevailing concept is that RF and electron behavior are inseparable, because any time you have an electrical current in place, you also have an electromagnetic field in place—and vice versa.

The full electromagnetic spectrum is considerable in scope, and the portion used for commercial wireless is a small subset of the available spectrum currently understood. Interestingly, the portion of the electromagnetic spectrum occupied by visible light (light perceived by human eyes) is less than 1 percent of what we understand as the total spectrum.

Electromagnetic fields affect conductors. Antennas are, in simplified terms, electrical conductors of a prescribed size and shape. To radiate a signal, the power from a transmitter must alternately push electrons into an antenna and then pull them out again. One *cycle* is one completed push and pull of electrons.

For each particular RF transmission and reception, there will be a certain number of cycles completed each second. This phenomenon is called *frequency,* and it occurs at very high rates. Table 3-1 indicates the relative cycles, or frequency, expressed in common terms. While there are no commercial terahertz radios at the time of this writing, there is experimental work being performed in this area.

For general reference—and there is a fair amount of misuse and disagreement on the terms—the entire radio spectrum is divided into large segments of frequency bands. The low bands, usually below 1GHz, are referred to as the RF spectrum. The band between approximately 1GHz and 10GHz is known as the microwave spectrum, and the band between approximately 10GHz and 100GHz is referred to as the millimeter wave spectrum.

Certain electrical components commonly found on printed circuit boards are relatively frequency dependent. Put another way, these components and circuits operate at higher levels of performance when carrying certain frequencies. By designing circuits and selecting certain components that are more responsive to specific frequencies and less responsive to other frequencies, circuit designers can improve that system's performance by a factor of 10 to 50 times.

Unit of Frequency	Symbol	Cycles per Second
Hertz	Hz	1
Kilohertz	KHz	1,000
Megahertz	MHz	1 million
Gigahertz	GHz	1 billion
Terahertz	THz	1 trillion

Table 3-1.   Units of Frequency

FREQUENCY BASICS

The concept of frequency is most easily understood through the analogy of the wave patterns created after dropping a pebble into a body of water, first considered in the context of radio frequency by Maxwell. The waves emanate outward with a specific shape from the point where the pebble entered the water. The waves weaken in energy as they move farther from the point the pebble entered the water, and they also change shape as they move away from the center. These waves are called *sine waves* because of their shape.

Sine waves depart a transmitting antenna in much the same manner as waves emanate from the point at which the rock enters the water. The number of times per second a complete sine wave departs from a transmitting antenna (or is received by a receiving antenna) is its frequency. The basic unit of time used in reference to this is "hertz" (refer to Table 3-1).

The broadband commercial wireless portion of the electromagnetic spectrum begins at about the 1GHz frequency and continues up through approximately 38GHz, though experimentation and product development for commercial wireless communications is being explored at 90GHz and higher. Currently, several countries are exploring the possibility of allocating (and auctioning) these upper-end millimeter wave bands. There is also a concerted effort by certain entities, including some of the networking giants like Cisco Systems, to ensure that a considerable amount of spectrum remains that will not require licenses.

Sine waves are "managed" in terms of amplitude, frequency, and phase. This management is known as *modulation,* which has a tremendous effect on data output and other key RF attributes. This "management" is accomplished through the execution of very specific engineering designs, which entail the selection of specific electrical components. When considered individually, these components are sometimes referred to as *discrete components,* or *discretes,* a term that typically refers to their unique electronic characteristics. It is important to note that *application-specific integrated circuits* (ASICs) commonly replace groups of discrete components in order to simplify design and reduce manufacturing cost and complexity. ASICs combine large numbers of discretes and circuits into a single component.

Discretes communicate with each other via electrical signals, which are typically transmitted over copper or gold paths that reside on a printed circuit board (PCB) or thin-film substrates manufactured from ceramics, depending on the frequency of operation. PCBs are complex in commercial radios and can have as many as 11 layers or more of conducting paths between the components. Commercial radios consist of a series of boards that are generally interconnected. By way of some oversimplification, connectors reside within the walls of the "box" that surrounds the PCBs; these connectors are used to connect the radio to other boxes such as power supplies that convert AC power to the DC power required by radios as well as other devices such as antennas.

Software is, of course, necessary to determine how some of the discretes interact with each other and how the user interacts with the box. Some of this software is fairly easy to modify, while other types of software reside inside certain types of discretes and cannot be altered without changing the component itself.

The characteristics of an RF wave are quite different at different points of the electromagnetic spectrum. Typically, the higher the frequency, the shorter the transmission distance for a given power and the greater the issue of multipath (covered later in this chapter). Conversely, for a given modulation technique, in general terms, the higher the frequency, the more data that can be transmitted in a given time. Modulation issues are also covered later in this chapter.

RF systems fall into two broad categories: wavelengths less than 10GHz (often referred to as microwave) and wavelengths greater than 10GHz (often referred to as millimeter wave). Each of them has certain advantages and disadvantages that pertain to cost, complexity, and the manner in which the waves propagate along a beam path. The differences are summarized in Table 3-2.

Since microwave wireless transmission equipment was first developed, manufacturers and operators have tried to mitigate the effects of reflected signals associated with RF. These reflections are called *multipath*. State-of-the-art commercial radio products not only tolerate multipath signals but, due to the repeatability of some multipath signals in the microwave band, can actually take advantage of them via techniques such as multiple antennas placed in two separate locations (though relatively adjacent to each other). This technique is often referred to as *antenna diversity*, or *spatial diversity*, which will be detailed at a point later in this chapter.

Power Transmission

RF transmission is an energy transfer process, although a highly inefficient one. Fortunately, very sensitive receivers offset this very low efficiency. A reception of one millionth of the signal sent by the transmitter is actually considered a good signal in terms of strength. A typical RF signal sent between two sites is often 10,000 times weaker than even that, yet, remarkably, it is quite usable, and indeed commonplace.

Characteristic	Microwave	Millimeter Wave
Frequency range	<10GHz	>10GHz
Cost	Less than millimeter wave	Higher than microwave
Complexity	Less than millimeter wave	Greater than microwave
Nominal range	5–20 miles	< 5 miles
Affected by weather?	Usually no	Usually yes
Typical use	Multipoint	Point to point
Multipath an issue?	Yes	Generally no
License required?	Usually	Usually

Table 3-2. Snapshot Comparison of Microwave Versus Millimeter Wave

The ratio of the power loss between two sites is called *path loss* or *free space path loss*. This refers to the energy that is lost during the time in which it is transmitted between two points. An important factor is that the path loss over a given path is typically constant regardless of the amount of power used at the transmitting site, so variations due to modulation are quite faithfully reproduced at the receiver. This factor should not be confused with the concept that the rate of loss over a given path is constant; rather, the total loss over a path is relatively constant for different levels of power or modulation types. Path loss through free space will occur at a rate different than that which occurs when a path is partially blocked.

Path loss is important to calculate because an RF link (often simply referred to as a "link") between two points must account for distances and obstructions between transmitters and receivers. An appropriate link design will provide parameters for *maximum allowable path loss*. If the proposed solution has a free space path loss in excess of the maximum allowable path loss, the system will lack appreciable bandwidth, have excess unreliability, or simply not work at all.

To overcome excessive path loss, you must increase the amount of power received at the receiving antenna. This can be accomplished in several ways. The most obvious is to increase the transmitted power to the limit set by the regulatory authorities. Other techniques include providing more directional antennas, increasing the gain (sensitivity) of the receiving antenna, or increasing the elevations of both the transmitting and receiving antennas to clear the obstructions causing the path loss. You can also, in some circumstances, use repeaters.

Because path loss numbers are typically orders of magnitude, they are typically expressed in a *decibel* (expressed as dB) scale, which is logarithmic. Simply stated, a loss of 3dB means that half of your transmit power has been lost. The common notation for expressing this loss is –3dB. Table 3-3 shows commonly used dB values.

The area closest to the transmitting antenna has two fields of energy that reside in the same space: an electrical field and a magnetic field. The field closest to the antenna is called the *induction* field. Outside of this field, the RF wave loses any identity from the original electrical field.

The RF wave then exists independently of the original current or voltage that created it, and it will continue to radiate through any space where there are no conductors

Factor of	dB
2	3
4	6
10	10
100	20
1,000	30

Table 3-3.   Decibel (dB) Values

or absorbers. When the wave comes near a conductor, some of the energy will be absorbed by that conductor and set up miniature copies of the currents and voltages that originally sent off the radiation in the first place. Again, these "copies" are so small that we use the dB scale to more easily express this change in strength. What does not change over time or during transfer through space is the original rate (frequency) at which the waves were sent.

However, in terms of such mobile systems as cellular phones or pagers, moving a receiver toward or away from a transmitter induces a phenomenon known as the Doppler effect, which changes the rate at which the waves are received. If the receiver is moving toward the transmitter, the waves are received at an increased rate; conversely, if the receiver is moving away from the transmitter, the rate at which the waves are received is reduced.

802.11 radio products accommodate the issue of roaming rather well in fact, and will continue to improve as the industry sees increasing amounts of latency-sensitive traffic such as voice and video over 802.11 networks. When signals are sent through a medium such as the atmosphere, the speed of the transmission is slowed slightly from the original transmission speed of 186,000 miles per second (again, the speed of light). An interesting physical phenomenon then occurs, which is that the frequency remains constant though the waves are slowed down. This is due to the fact that there are many more atoms in an atmosphere than in a vacuum.

Each atom along the beam path is affected by the electrons, which must forward the energy on an atom-by-atom basis. The more atoms, the more times the energy is transferred. As there is a miniscule loss of energy each time the energy is transferred from one atom to the next, the wave not only decreases in energy but also is slowed down in speed. The question that arises then is: How can the wavelength shorten and yet the frequency remain constant? The answer is perhaps best understood with a simple analogy.

Imagine you are standing next to a railway where cars are passing you at the rate of exactly one per second. If the train is moving at 60 miles per hour, each car must be 88 feet long. If the train passes you at 30 miles per hour, the cars must be 44 feet long to pass at the same rate. The slower cars would be half the length because they're traveling at half the speed.

This is, in effect, what happens to radio waves. When they pass through a medium such as atmosphere or water, the length of the waves shortens but the frequency remains the same. Some of the wavelength is converted to heat, which is the prevailing principle behind the microwave ovens we are so familiar with. Microwave ovens operate at a frequency of 2.4GHz, which is the frequency that has a particular reaction with water; that is, it excites the water molecules, which is another way of saying it heats water. It is the water content in foods that heats, which then heats the rest of the meal content.

The key point here is that as frequency is the most reliable aspect of RF radiation, it's the most accurate measurement of a signal in relation to others like amplitude, wavelength, and phase.

Frequency Bands

The U.S. government, like every other major government in the industrialized world, has set up groups of frequencies (bands) for use. There is no scientific or engineering reason for how these divisions are established, but the division and allocation of these bands is essential to the efficient and reliable use by the public.

Not all of the frequencies shown in Table 3-4 are within the scope of this book, but all are shown for reference and context. It's also important to note that, in general, some of these terms are no longer used. The wavelengths indicated are shown by general figures only (close estimates).

You'll note that these bands represent a 10:1 ratio of wavelength to frequency. Again, this is not driven by scientific or engineering principles; rather, it's an easy way to keep frequencies in blocks that are generally consistent with the way the carrier frequency propagates through the air.

SHF is also generally known as *millimeter wave frequency*, while UHF is also known as *microwave*.

Modulation

Any signal that can be translated into electrical form, such as audio, video, or data, can be modulated and sent over the air. Data, such as e-mail, is the easiest to modulate reliably, while video with voice is the most difficult for retention of fidelity to the original source.

Modulation is the technique of turning bits into something carried by the carrier frequency over the air. Carrier frequency has no intelligence; the modulated data carries the intelligence (data) between two points. *The carrier frequency of an 802.11b and 802.11g radio is 2.4GHz to 2.485GHz in the U.S.* There are no fewer than three ranges of carrier frequencies in the U.S. for the 11a standard, which are; 5.125GHz to 5.225GHz, 5.325GHz to 5.425- and 5.785GHz to 5.825GHz.

Band	Frequency Range	Wavelength at Lower End of Spectrum
Very low frequency (VLF)	0kHz–30kHz	100 km
Low frequency (LF)	30kHz–300kHz	10 km
Medium frequency (MF)	300kHz–3MHz	1 km
High frequency (HF)	3MHz–30MHz	100m
Very high frequency (VHF)	30 MHz–300MHz	10m
Ultra-high frequency (UHF)	300MHz–3GHz	1m
Super-high frequency (SHF)	3GHz–30GHz	100m
Extremely high frequency (EHF)	30GHz–300GHz	10m

Table 3-4.   Frequencies As Defined by the U.S. Government (Antiquated)

The purpose of commercial RF systems is to carry modulated waves of energy—that is, information. Earlier in this section, it was stated that it is the *changes* in amplitude, frequency, or phase that enable data to reside on a wave of radiated energy. Modulation is the difference between a steady-state RF signal (a signal that is nonchanging, referred to as a continuous wave [CW] tone) and one that carries information.

The selection of modulation schemes is based more or less on the compromise between maximizing bandwidth through high spectral efficiency and bit loss through complexity of scheme. Also, in general, the better the spectral efficiency, the worse the power efficiency, and vice versa. Simpler systems such as phase-shift keying (PSK) are very robust and easy to implement because they have low data rates. In PSK modulation, the shape of the wave is modified in neither amplitude nor frequency, but rather in phase. The phase can be thought of as a shift in time.

At lower frequencies (such as 2.4GHz), the selection of a modulation scheme is very important because there is inherently less bandwidth in general to work with than at higher frequencies such as LMDS uses (28GHz in the United States). The proper term with respect to this fundamental is *spectral efficiency;* that is, how to get the most out of the available bandwidth. The common term used for spectral efficiency is bits per hertz.

Numerous modulation schemes are available, and there is more than one issue to consider in regard to RF fundamentals. *Spectral density,* for example, is one of the key metrics for measuring RF link performance. This term refers to the number of bits sent out per complete sine wave or, in other words, one complete antenna cycle. To be more specific, if a transmitter were sending out data at 1Hz, there would be one complete sine wave per second; if it were transmitting at 1GHz, there would be one billion complete sine waves in the same interval, and so forth.

Spectral density is largely dependent on the selected modulation scheme. This section will assist the reader in understanding the pros and cons of various modulation schemes and the compromises associated with the use of various schemes.

Modulation Schemes

The objective of a modulation scheme is to transform ones and zeros into waveforms that can be transmitted and received by the carrier frequency of a radio link. The term *carrier frequency* has been used throughout this book, and though it is essentially unrelated to the issue of modulation schemes, it may be appropriate to use an analogy to better convey what it means. If you were using a printer, the carrier frequency would be the paper, and the modulated information would be the letters on the paper. Put another way, the carrier frequency does not in and of itself carry the information, but rather, the information is carried on this carrier frequency, hence the term.

By way of oversimplification, if you were able to take a very close look at a 2.4GHz sine wave that was departing an antenna used on an 802.11b radio, you would could see that while the general shape of the sine wave is such that one complete sine wave would depart the antenna at the rate of one every 0.0000002485 seconds. A close-up inspection with an oscilloscope would reveal that the actual shape of the sine wave would reflect changes in amplitude if the information was coded in AM, changes in phase if the information was coded in PM, or there would be be changes in frequency along the sine wave if the information was coded in FM.

Modulation, therefore, is the technique of turning bits into something that can be carried by the carrier frequency over the air. From the above paragraph, the reader can now understand that the carrier frequency has no intelligence; rather, it is the information which is modulated within the carrier frequency that carries the information.

At lower frequencies, such as the 2.4GHz spectrum used by 802.11, the selection of a modulation scheme is very important because there is inherently less bandwidth to work with than at higher frequencies such as LMDS (28GHz in the United States). The proper term with respect to this fundamental is *spectral efficiency*—how to get the most efficient use out of the available bandwidth.

There are many different modulation schemes; Table 3-5 contains a partial list.

All of the schemes shown in Table 3-5 are related to one of three fundamental types of modulation:

- **Amplitude modulation**   The output power of the transmitter is varied, while the frequency and phase of the sine wave remains constant.

- **Frequency modulation**   The output power and phase remains constant while the frequency is varied over a small range.

- **Phase modulation**   The amplitude and frequency remain constant but the phase within the carrier frequency changes over a small range.

Symbol	Modulation Scheme
AM	Amplitude modulation
FM	Frequency modulation
SSB	Single sideband
PM	Phase modulation
CCK	Complementary code keying
CW	Continuous wave (telegraphy)
PCM	Pulse code modulation
VSB	Vestigial sideband
BMAC	Type B multiplexed analog components
QAM	Quadrature amplitude modulation
DSSS	Direct sequence spread spectrum
FHSS	Frequency hopping spread spectrum
BFSK	Binary frequency shift keying
PBCC	Packet binary convolutional coding
QPSK	Quadrature phase shift keying

Table 3-5.   Various Modulation Schemes

The most common modulation schemes used for radios in general at the time of this writing are: BFSK (more commonly referred to as FSK), binary phase shift keying (BPSK), QPSK, and QAM.

The reader should note that a myriad of other types of modulation exist, however, they stem from either amplitude, phase, or frequency modulation schemes. Each of these modulation schemes represents an increase in complexity over the preceding one, from BFSK to various levels of QAM. BFSK will send a "one" with one frequency and a "zero" with another *frequency*. BPSK will send two states, a "one" with one phase and a "zero" with another *phase*.

QPSK gets more complex and has four states to represent either a 00, 01, 11, or 10, four phase states, all with the carrier wave retaining the same amplitude and frequency. Figure 3-1 indicates the "constellation," which is a collection of permitted maximum phase and amplitude combinations.

Where modulation becomes complex is with *quadrature amplitude modulation* (QAM_) which is a technique that modulates the carrier frequency in both phase and amplitude (using sine and cosine carriers that are 90 degrees apart).

Table 3-6 illustrates the fact that as the number of bits increases linearly, the number of phase/amplitude combinations increases exponentially, providing a very high spectral density at even 64QAM.

This means that with two amplitude values carried by a single carrier frequency, the link can carry two bits as opposed to a single bit, thereby having a higher *spectral density,* which means that more information is being carried for a given burst of energy (sine wave, or groups of sine waves) from the transmitter. Simply stated, the frequency

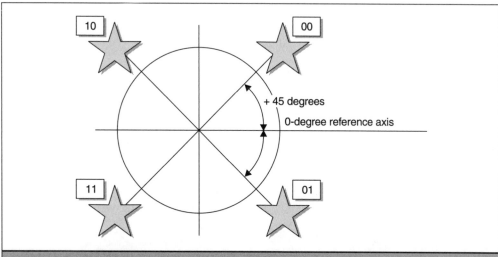

Figure 3-1.   The QPSK constellation

Amplitude/Phase Combinations	Bits Per Sine Wave
16QAM	4
32QAM	5
64QAM	6
128QAM	7
256QAM	8

Table 3-6.   QAM Versus Bits per Symbol

within the carrier does not change, but the amount of data transmitted increases as the modulation complexity increases. This is not without cost. As the modulation complexity increases, so does the probability of an error in the transmission. Errors in transmission mean mistaking a one for a zero or not being able to decipher the energy as either a one or a zero at the receiver. The metric for the relative amount of error is referred to as the bit error ratio (BER) which is a ratio of the unusable bits to the bits which can be demodulated.

The more latency sensitive the traffic, such as voice and video, the lower the bit error rate needs to be. State-of-the-art systems will see BERs from approximately 1×10^{-6} to 1×10^{-8}. Data links can operate satisfactorily with BERs from 1×10^{-3} to 1×10^{-6}. This means that *one* bit in $10^{\wedge8}$ would be in error.

The quality of the equipment becomes very important when using the more exotic modulation schemes. Quality of equipment refers not only to quality of manufacture but, more specifically, to inherent quality of design as well.

There are several trade-offs to be considered when deciding which modulation is most appropriate for a given environment, although within the 802.11 standard, there are provisions for *auto-rate negotiation* which is when the radios will automatically downshift to less complex modulation and spreading techniques in order to maintain higher levels of robustness.

Higher frequencies or greater distances tend to favor less complex modulations. Low signal to noise links with simpler modulation schemes generally work better and generally have a lower BER, all things being relatively equal. The trade-off for this simplicity is lower throughput.

Currently, a number of QAM modulation schemes are common. In the wireless arena, they range from 16 QAM for the 802.11a and the proposed 802.11g standards, up to 64QAM used in fixed wireless links. Today, 64QAM is more common for multichannel multipoint distribution service (MMDS) and U-NII band products, while spread spectrum techniques such as FHSS and DSSS are common to WLAN products, particularly IEEE–802.11b-compliant solutions

Currently, 64QAM is about as spectrally dense as the transmissions tend to be. It typically provides the best compromise between the ability to send a higher amount of traffic over a carrier frequency without incurring too much expense, complexity, and the time delay for processing, although radios using this modulation technique—none of which are currently part of the 802.11 standard—require very high amounts of processing power at the transmitter and receiver. Over time, QAM will, of course, move well beyond 256QAM as development teams improve stability and lower the cost of this type of system. Development is under way at this writing on 128QAM radios and beyond, but again, it will be a very long time off, if ever, that an 802.11-standards-based radio will use this type of modulation

In the cabled environment, QAM levels up to 1024 are being tested successfully, but it will be many years before the quality of the components is sufficient to make ultra-high-level QAM cost effective in the 802.11 world. Spectral density is especially important in the unlicensed bands like U-NII in the United States, where there are only 100MHz of spectrum allocated, and in general, all carrier frequencies below about 26GHz need more spectrally dense modulation schemes because they generally don't have as much spectrum as those found at 26GHz and above. Table 3-7 illustrates the amount of spectrum allocated in the United States for three of the more common bands.

The concept of cycles per bit leads into the concept of a *symbol,* which is a uniquely identifiable signal that contains a certain number of bits, as determined by modulation complexity. Individual symbols are distinguished by attributes such as duration, amplitude, frequency, or phase. The number of *bits per symbol* is one of the most common methods for determining spectral density. Four or more bits per symbol would normally be considered highly spectrally efficient, while one or two bits per symbol would be less spectrally efficient though still quite serviceable.

In the end, the selection of a modulation scheme is based more or less on the compromise between maximizing bandwidth and building in sufficient resistance

ISM (2.4GHz) 802.11b/g	83.5MHz
U-NII 802.11a	300

Table 3-7.   Spectrum Allocation in the United States for 802.11b/a/g

to interference. There is a very real distinction between high-end engineering teams whose primary mission is to develop a high-performance 802.11 product line and start-up companies that happen to provide an 802.11 link but tend to be far less sophisticated in their approach, especially when considering issues such as security, redundancy and resistance to interference. Most experienced electrical engineers can devise some sort of RF link between two devices, but it is an entirely nontrivial effort to produce commercially viable 802.11 radio links. Now more than ever, 802.11 radio must be considered as a network element as opposed to a radio that is tacked on to the Ethernet portion of the network.

Spreading Techniques

One of the more common mistakes we encounter while discussing radios is the confusion between modulation and spreading techniques. *The difference between a modulation technique and a spreading technique is that a spreading technique distributes the information over a number of channels, while a modulation technique modulates the information over* each *of the channels.* Direct sequence spread spectrum (DSSS), frequency hopping spread spectrum (FHSS), *code division multiplex access* (CDMA), and orthogonal frequency division multiplexing (OFDM) are examples of spreading techniques. *Coded orthogonal frequency division multiplexing* (COFDM) is the spreading technique used in 802.11a and 802.11g.

Direct Sequence Spread Spectrum and
Frequency Hopping Spread Spectrum

802.11 products utilize spread spectrum techniques. To legally operate in the 2.4GHz ISM spectrum in the United States and many other countries, a type of signal spreading must be used. There are two kinds of spread spectrum available for 802.11 and 802.11b: direct sequence spread spectrum (DSSS) and frequency hopping spread spectrum (FHSS). DHSS typically has better performance, while FHSS is typically more resistant to interference. Although OFDM is a technique for spreading the signal over a given bandwidth, it is not, by definition, a spread spectrum technique. The FCC is evaluating the specifics of the definition of spread spectrum. 802.11a and 802.11g use OFDM as their spreading techniques.

A commonly used analogy for understanding the concept of signal spreading (spread spectrum) is that of a series of trains departing a station. The payload is distributed relatively equally among the trains, which all depart at the same time. Upon arrival at the destination, the payload is taken off each train and collated. Duplications of payload are common to spread spectrum so that when data arrives excessively corrupted, or fails to arrive, the redundancies inherent to this architecture provide a more robust data link.

With DSSS, all trains leave in an order beginning with Train 1 and ending with Train N, depending on how many channels the spread spectrum system allocates. In the DSSS architecture, the trains always leave in the same order, though the number of railroad tracks can be in the hundreds or even thousands.

With the FHSS architecture, the trains leave in a different order; that is, not sequentially from Train 1 to Train *N*. In the best of FHSS systems, trains that run into interference are not sent out again until the interference abates. In FHSS systems, certain frequencies (channels) are avoided until the interference abates.

Interference tends to cover more than one channel at a time. Therefore, DSSS systems tend to lose more data from interference as the data is sent out over sequential channels. FHSS systems "hop" between channels in nonsequential order. The best of FHSS systems adjust channel selection such that highly interfered with channels are avoided as measured by excessively low bit error rates. Either approach is appropriate, and the choice depends on customer requirements, the selection criteria primarily involving a severe multipath or interfering RF environment.

Orthogonal Frequency Division Multiplex (OFDM)

Before we examine OFDM, a type of which is used in 802.11a and 802.11g radios, we should first consider the concept of *frequency division*. In a frequency division multiplexing (FDM) system, the available bandwidth is divided into multiple data carriers. The data to be transmitted is then divided between these subcarriers. Because each carrier is treated independently of the others, a frequency guard band must be placed around it, which is another way of saying that no other data will be carried on an adjacent frequency. This guard band lowers the bandwidth efficiency.

In some FDM systems, up to 50 percent of the available bandwidth is used for guard bands, which prevents their carrying data. In most FDM systems, individual users are segmented to a particular subcarrier; therefore, their burst rate cannot exceed the capacity of that subcarrier. If some subcarriers are idle, their bandwidth cannot be shared with other subcarriers.

In orthogonal frequency division multiplexing (OFDM), multiple carrier frequencies (or tones) are used to divide the data across the available spectrum, similar to FDM. In an OFDM system, however, each tone is considered to be orthogonal (independent or unrelated) to the adjacent tones.

One other key difference between OFDM and DSSS and FHSS is that while each of the channels sends energy in a *sequential* manner in FHSS and DHSS, in OFDM, all the energy is sent over all of the channels *at the same time*.

As shown in Figure 3-2, each tone is a frequency integer (one whole number) apart from the adjacent frequency and therefore no guard band is required around each tone.

Since OFDM requires guard bands only around a set of tones, it is more efficient spectrally than FDM. You can see how this works in Figure 3-3.

Because OFDM is made up of many narrowband tones, narrowband interference will degrade only a small portion of the signal and have no or little effect on the remainder of the frequency components.

OFDM systems use bursts of data to minimize ISI caused by delay spread. Data is transmitted in bursts, and each burst consists of a cyclic prefix followed by data *symbols*. For example, an OFDM signal occupying six MHz is made up of 512 individual carriers

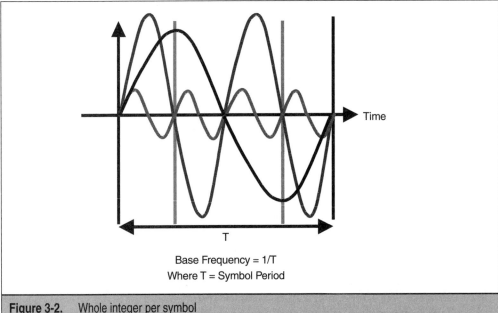

Base Frequency = 1/T
Where T = Symbol Period

Figure 3-2.   Whole integer per symbol

(or tones), each carrying a single QAM symbol per burst. As Figure 3-4 shows, the cyclic prefix is used to absorb late-arriving signals due to multipath (transients) from previous bursts. An additional 64 symbols are transmitted for the cyclic prefix. For each symbol period, a total of 576 symbols are transmitted, by only 512 unique QAM symbols per burst.

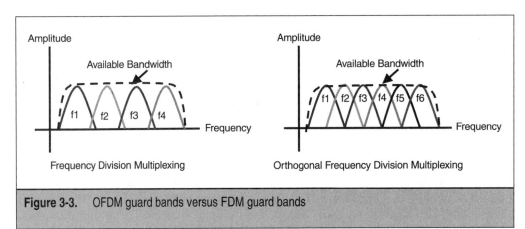

Figure 3-3.   OFDM guard bands versus FDM guard bands

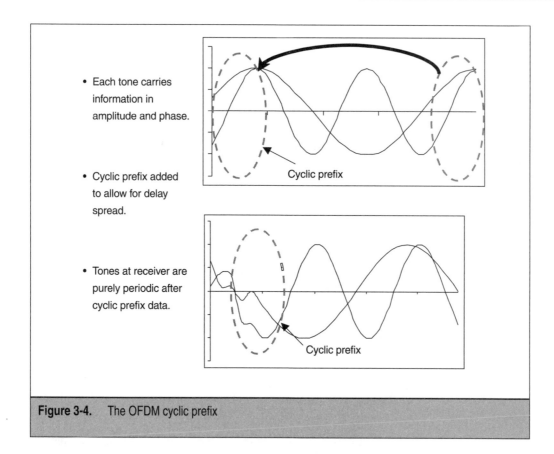

- Each tone carries information in amplitude and phase.

- Cyclic prefix added to allow for delay spread.

- Tones at receiver are purely periodic after cyclic prefix data.

Cyclic prefix

Cyclic prefix

Figure 3-4. The OFDM cyclic prefix

In general, by the time the cyclic prefix is over, the resulting waveform created by the combining multipath signals is not a function of any samples from the previous burst. Hence, there is no ISI. The cyclic prefix must be greater than the delay spread of the multipath signals. In a 6MHz system, the individual sample rate is 0.16 µsecs. Therefore, the total time for the cyclic prefix is 10.24 µsecs, greater than the anticipated 4 µsec delay spread.

Some OFDM systems only use QPSK for the modulation scheme. If 16QAM or 64QAM is used, then the amount of data transmitted significantly increases.

In addition to the standard OFDM principles, the use of spatial diversity can increase the system's tolerance to noise, interference, and multipath. Another way to visualize this is to think of a second antenna. Think of when you stop your car at a red light and the radio broadcast turns to static. To regain your broadcast signal, you move your car ahead a few inches to a few feet, which relocates your antenna outside of a void or null in the local reception area.

This is referred to as VOFDM, in which the *V* stands for "vector" and simply means that a second antenna is online along with the primary antenna; it does not refer to a dynamic movement of either the primary or secondary antenna.

CCK, PBCC and OFDM in 802.11

When we begin to review the technicalities of the 802.11g standard, it becomes important to know a bit more about the function of complementary code keying (CCK) and OFDM. It should be noted by the reader that as of this writing, the 11g standard has not been fully ratified by the IEEE, though it should be considered as reasonably mature and stable. With a modest element of risk that some of the finally ratified standard might deviate slightly from this content, it is anticipated that this risk is minimal.

The 11g standard is composed in part of *mandatory* and *optional* elements with regard to spreading techniques employed by equipment vendors. OFDM is a mandatory part of the 11g standard, and backward compatibility to 11b radios is also mandatory. Few experts in the IEEE are predicting this will not become an important part of the finalized 11g standard. This standard allows for both the CCK/OFDM and *packet binary convolutional coding*. The standard will require equipment vendors to include either the CCK/OFDM or PBCC/OFDM formats, but not both of them.

CCK is the basic modulation format for 11b and 11g radios, and it's a *single carrier* scheme, which is to say, it only operates over a very narrow range of frequency. As the reader will note per the summary earlier in this chapter, OFDM is a technique that sends information over *multiple-carriers in parallel*.

NOTE   For data rates at or below 11Mbps, CCK is generally viewed as an acceptable method for transmitting data. For data rates above that, OFDM is the format that enables the higher data rates of up to 54Mbps enjoyed by the users of both 11a and 11g.

The reader will recall that higher data rates for a given frequency and power output will more readily degrade over a given distance or time. The use of a more exotic modulation scheme, along with a more exotic spreading technique such as OFDM helps ensure the higher data rates do not incur excessive bit error rates. Indeed more exotic modulation and spreading techniques in and of themselves are more prone to degradation of bits for a given time/distance, but within the normal operating parameters for an 802.11 device, the use of the more exotic modulation and spreading techniques more than offset the inherent propensity for degradation because they provide far higher data rates for a given frequency and power output.

NOTE   It is important to note that the PBCC/OFDM and CCK/OFDM formats only affect the transmission of data rates in excess of 20Mbps.

Now, to clarify what the aforementioned information means, it's important to understand that 802.11 radios are termed *packet-based radios*. In part, this means that the 1's and 0's that represent information (the payload) always follow what are called the *preamble* and *header*. The preamble is a set of 1s and 0s that effectively "wakes up" all the radios within the collision domain (i.e., all the radios within range that will receive this information). The header provides important information that includes the duration in seconds of the payload that will immediately follow the preamble and header. The function of the header is important because upon receipt of this information, none of the other radios in the collision domain will attempt to transmit data; essential to ensuring that each radio *on a given channel* will not be interfered with.

The payload varies significantly in length from 64 bytes to just over 2000 bytes, and this duration is dependent on the data rate being used as well as the number of bytes being transmitted. *The preamble and header are sent using CCK modulation, and the payload at data rates in excess of 20Mbps will be sent via OFDM.* However, the vendor has the option to use OFDM in the preamble and header at the higher data speeds, which will reduce the overhead as an OFDM preamble is 16msecs in duration versus the much longer 72msecs for a CCK preamble.

NOTE   The more time that is used for transmitting the payload versus the preamble or header, the better the throughput for a radio, and this is one of ways that the radios such as those provided by Cisco outperform the lower-priced radios by other suppliers.

PBCC is a *single carrier method*, as is CCK, but employs more the more complex 8PSK versus the BPSK or QPSK for CCK and a convolutional code structure versus the more simple block code structure used by CCK.

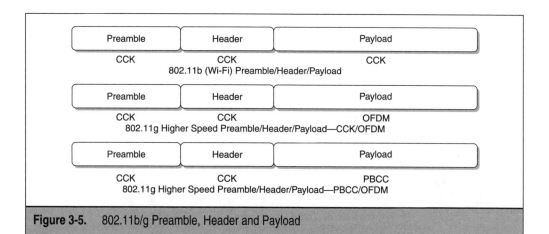

Figure 3-5.   802.11b/g Preamble, Header and Payload

One of the questions a sharp-minded 802.11 technologist should ask is, "Why would a manufacturer provide different schemes for the preamble/header and the payload?" The reason for this is rather elegant, which is that *the use of CCK in the preamble and header will enable both 11b as well as 11g radios to be alerted for an impending transmission.* Once the radios in the collision domain have been alerted, the transmission can occur at the much higher rates afforded by the 11g standard. Radios that operate at the 11b standard will engage the 11g radios and request that the data be downshifted to the lower 11b data rate.

This brings the potential for having 11g radios operate at the lower data rates of the 11b standard if there are any 11b radios within the collision domain of an 11g radio. This can be mitigated by separating the 11b radios from the 11g radios on a collision domain by the use of a unique SSID for each radio type, and of course ensuring that the root AP is an 11g device. For 11a radios, there is only one common speed (allowing of course for downshifting based on distance from the root AP). As long as the 11a radios have a relative common signal strength, they will receive the same high data rate. For collision domains where there are both 11g and 11b radios, specific configurations will be required to ensure that higher speed radios are not bogged down by the radios which operate only at the older 11b standard.

It should be noted that the PBCC format allows for a maximum data rate of 33Mbps while the CCK format allows for a much higher 54Mbps data rate.

Spatial Diversity

Spatial diversity is a term that refers to the concept of placing two antennas at a given distance apart for the same receiver. On virtually every system currently sold, spatial diversity is used only on receivers, not transmitters, as illustrated in Figure 3-6. It is expected, however, that spatial diversity will become standard at the transmitter end of each link before too long, because tremendous performance gains and increased geographic coverage will more than offset the additional cost for the extra transmit antenna. The technology surrounding the concept of multiple transmit and receive antennas is also referred to as *multiple-in, multiple-out,* or MIMO.

Diversity is based on the concept that a set of multipath signals arriving at a given receiver exhibits a definable and generally repeatable set of characteristics. If a second receive antenna is placed some distance away from the first (the minimum distance between the antennas depends in part on the frequency used), it will receive a second, unrelated, set of signals. If deployed properly, one of the two paths will exhibit a stronger signal than the other. A receiver can then either select and use the strongest signal from the two signal paths or combine the two paths for a composite signal. As stated previously, in the 802.11a and 802.11g systems, the OFDM technique is referred to as COFDM, where the C stands for "Coded," which means essentially that it is a specific version of OFDM ratified for use in the 802.11a and 802.11g radios.

A well-understood example of spatial diversity is when you stop your car at a red light and the radio broadcast in your car emits a great deal of static—or cuts out altogether. We have all moved our car a few feet (or even less than a foot in some

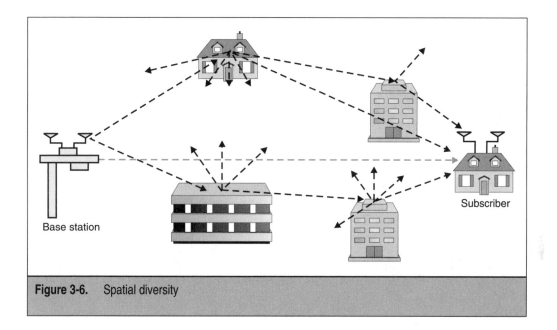

Figure 3-6.   Spatial diversity

instances) to regain the high-quality broadcast signal. By moving the car, you have relocated your antenna outside of a void or null in the local reception area.

Spatial diversity is a widely accepted technique for improving performance in multipath environments. Because multipath is a function of the collection of bounced signals, that collection is dependent on the location of the receiver antenna. If two or more antennas are placed in the system, each could have a different set of multipath signals. The effects of each channel would vary from one antenna to the next; therefore, carriers that may be unusable on one antenna may become usable on another. Spacing between the antennas is usually at least ten times the wavelength, and significant gains in the signal-to-interference plus noise ratio (SINR) are often obtained by using multiple antennas. Typically, a second antenna adds about 3dB in LOS environments and up to 14dB in non-LOS environments.

In comparing today's modulation techniques, OFDM combined with spatial diversity is a compelling technique to resolve multipath issues existing in highly obstructed environments, although the trade-off is at least a 20 percent rise in cost of goods sold for equipment, which can readily translate to a higher percent increase in retail price. Having said that, discounts on the order of 20 to 40 percent are reasonably common when purchasing an end-to-end network, and the extra cost of goods sold can be offset by the increased number of customers available through a greater *harvest rate*.

OFDM products used in obstructed environments provide key elements to enhance the harvest rate over systems that require a clear line of sight to operate. 802.11g and 802.11a customers may see upward of 30 to 40 percent additional coverage area for a given transmitter, which translates into a proportional number of users that can be accommodated within a single collision domain (WLAN). This reference to additional coverage area is not manifested in greater distance from the antenna but in accessing those areas closer in that are hidden to the traditional line-of-sight-only networks.

WLAN outdoor systems such as bridges therefore can also be deployed in dense urban environments where multipath is pervasive. No longer are point-to-multipoint systems limited to the macrocell models. Microcells similar to those for cell phones can be created. Instead of tall microwave towers, simple rooftop head ends can be used, and instead of macrocells with radii of approximately 10 to 20 miles, microcells with radii of 3 to 8 miles can be used. In general, OFDM allows the user to create simple, spectrally efficient, multipath-resistant, robust data communications links in areas where non-OFDM systems have had marginal performance.

In summary, the use of spatial diversity with OFDM greatly increases the 802.11g and 802.11a systems' tolerance of noise, interference, and multipath. Common throughout the microwave industry, spatial diversity has been used for years to reduce the impact from multipath interference. Spatial diversity is another way of stating "second antenna," which is used on the receive side of the transmission link only.

Multipath

Where the issues of advanced spreading techniques such as COFDM and spatial diversity come into play is in the attempt to resolve for *multipath interference*. As stated previously, radio systems fall into two broad categories: those using frequencies less than 10GHz and those with frequencies greater than 10GHz (referred to as millimeter wave systems).

A number of bands exist below 10GHz for high-speed transmissions ranging from the 2.4GHz band, to the licensed bands such as MMDS (2.5GHz) and include the unlicensed set of spectra referred to as the three U-NII bands in the 5GHz region. Bands below 10GHz can have propagation distances up to 30 miles in the United States, while millimeter wave products are generally limited to ranges of approximately five miles or less for the same relative modulation and power settings.

RF systems below 10GHz are generally unaffected by local atmospheric conditions such as rain and fog, and particulate from smog. These frequencies are generally not absorbed by objects in the atmosphere, but they are however, readily absorbed by vegetation. The energy used in these frequencies tends to reflect off various objects such as buildings, concrete, and water and thus result in a high amount of multipath.

Since the beginning of development of microwave wireless transmission equipment, manufacturers and operators have tried to mitigate the effects of reflected signals associated with RF. These reflections are called multipath. State-of-the-art 802.11 products not only tolerate multipath signals but can actually take advantage of them.

Multipath tends not to be an issue in millimeter wave frequencies, since most of the multipath energy is absorbed by the physical environment. However, when these frequencies are used in highly dense urban areas, the signals tend to bounce off objects like metal buildings or metalized windows. The use of repeaters can add to the multipath propagation by delaying the received signal.

It is important to understand that multipath from interference is much more of a potential issue in outdoor systems than indoor WLAN deployments mainly due to the fact that unless there is an appreciable amount of distance (or in other words, time), the *delay spread* between signals is not appreciable. The time between the first received signal and the last echoed signal is called the *delay spread.*

Multipath is the composition of a primary signal plus duplicate or echoed images caused by reflections of signals off objects between the transmitter and receiver. In Figure 3-7, the receiver "hears" the primary signal sent directly from the transmission facility, but it also sees secondary signals that are bounced off nearby objects. These bounced signals will arrive at the receiver later than the incident signal. Because of this misalignment, the "out-of-phase" signals will cause intersymbol interference or distortion of the received signal. Although most of the multipath is caused by bounces off tall objects, multipath can also occur from bounces on low objects such as lakes and pavements.

The actual received signal is a combination of a primary signal and several echoed signals. Because the distance traveled by the original signal is shorter than the bounced signal, the time differential causes two signals to be received. These signals are overlapped and combined into a single one.

In the example shown in Figure 3-7, the echoed signal is delayed in time and reduced in power. Both effects are caused by the additional distance the bounced signal traveled relative to the primary signal.

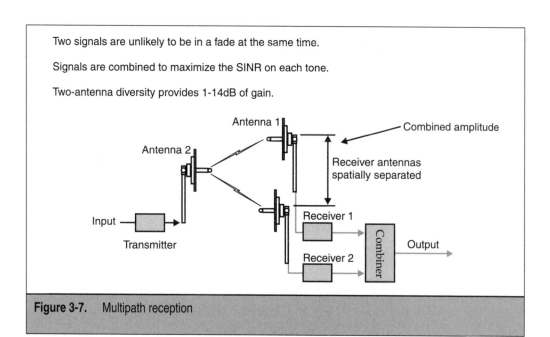

Figure 3-7.   Multipath reception

The greater the distance, the longer the delay and the lower the power of the echoed signal. One might think that the longer the delay, the better the reception would be. However, if the delay is too long, the reception of an echoed symbol can actually interfere with the primary signal by presenting a second burst of information. In some cases, where there may be no direct path for the incident signal in non-line-of-sight (LOS) environments, the "primary" signal may be small (lower in power) in comparison to other, secondary signals.

In analog systems, this multipath situation can be physically sensed, for instance, as a "ghost" image on your television. Occasionally, no matter how much you adjust the set, the image does not go away. In these analog systems, this is an annoyance. In digital systems, it usually corrupts the data stream and causes loss of data or lower performance. Correction algorithms must be put in place to compensate for the multipath, resulting in a lower available data rate.

In Figure 3-7, the echoed signal actually interferes with the reception of the second symbol, thus causing intersymbol interference (ISI). This ISI is the main result of multipath, and digital systems not designed to deal with it give up substantial performance and reliability.

In LOS environments with very short range, multipath can be minor and can be overcome easily. The amplitudes of the echoed signals are much smaller than that of the primary one and can be effectively filtered out using standard equalization techniques. In non-LOS environments, however, the echoed signals may have higher power levels or combine to have much stronger signals than the original signal because the primary signal may be partially or totally obstructed. In this scenario, resolving with equalization is more difficult.

In the previous discussions, the multipath occurs from stationary objects. However, multipath conditions can originate from mobile objects that initiate varying degrees of multipath from one sample period to the next. This effect is called *time variation*. Superior digital systems withstand rapid changes in the multipath conditions, referred to as "fast fading." In order to deal with this condition, digital systems need fast automatic gain control (AGC) circuits.

DUPLEXING TECHNIQUES

There are several fundamental ways in which a link has each end communicate to the other. They are represented in Table 3-8.

The most complex radio links are full duplex, and are not found within 802.11 radio product sets.

Type	Communication	Example
Simplex	One person at a time can use the link	Walkie-talkies
Half-duplex	The speaker cannot be interrupted by the other party	Speakerphones
Full-duplex	Both parties can transmit and receive in parallel; that is, the speaker can be interrupted by the other party	Broadband radio/telephone

Table 3-8. Different Duplexing Techniques

Error Control

There is a considerable difference between *error* detection and *error correction*. Both of these control issues are critical for network managers in determining and predicting how well their system will carry traffic reliably, especially low latency traffic.

Error detection is commonly referred to in terms of *bit error rate,* or BER, and is typically expressed in the form of a ratio; for instance, a value of 1×10^{-7} would mean that one bit in 10^{-7} bits transmitted would be in error. State-of-the-art systems have bit error rates of 10^{-8} for voice and 10^{-11} for data. These BERs are equivalent to those found in fiber optics systems and are therefore extraordinary.

There are a number of common error correction techniques; in all of them, the data is corrected on the receiving end of the transmission link, except when the data is retransmitted. The most common forms of error correction are applied such that a block of bits is sent along with the data in order to corroborate that all the data was sent satisfactorily.

Errors are introduced into the data from outside interfering sources such as other radios, multipath phenomena, other electronic equipment in the area, and even solar flares from the sun. Error-correction schemes enable the receiving end of a link to correct data to a very high degree. One way to accomplish this is with *parity bits*. With this method, the transmitted data includes a parity bit that ensures that the number of received bits is either odd or even. If a single bit is corrupted such that it can't be used, or the bit does not arrive at the receiver, the parity bit will notify other processing regimes that further correction, or retransmission of the data, must occur.

Of course, the system wouldn't request a retransmission if only a single bit out of thousands or millions was sent in error, but if the overall bit error rate was too high, the transmission could be re-sent (not for voice or video necessarily—although that is indeed doable with buffers—but fairly routinely for data transmissions that either go over a very long distance or involve very high data rates). Parity bit values depend on the types and quantity of the information sent over the link, and the receiving end of the link can repair the errors, live with the errors, or have the originating transmitter resend the information.

Cyclic redundancy check (CRC) is a common error-detection scheme that typically generates a value based on the result of a polynomial algorithm performed on the packet or frame header and data payload. The polynomial result is performed at the transmitter and then again at the receiver, at which point the CRC values are compared and should be identical.

OFDM includes an error-correction technique of *interpolation,* in which the data is corrected by interpolation based on the corrected values of training tones, which are equally spaced along the numbers of data carriers. In the United States, for example, the U-NII band has 1056 equally spaced training tones along each of the 100 MHz of U-NII spectrum.

This number of training tones is not a frequency-dependent issue but rather, the number of training tones is set by the operator. In an environment where there is a very high noise level, and consequently a low SNR, the number of training tones can be increased to improve the correction. However, as the number of training tones goes up, the number of carrier tones available to handle the actual information goes down. Therefore, a balance needs to be established between an acceptable amount of information throughput, an acceptable number of errors, and the number of training tones.

The receiver corrects the training tones to predetermined phase and amplitude settings. The data, which is evenly interspersed between the training tones, is also corrected for amplitude and phase. There is a relatively large number of training tones in the U-NII band (or any other band modulated by OFDM) in order to correct the narrowest amount of spectrum carrying data. Figure 3-8 shows the training tones evenly interspersed with the frequencies carrying data.

Forward error correction (FEC) is a correction scheme based on the concept of receiving multiple copies of the same bit and then having the system "vote" on the bit which is most likely correct. This scheme is indicated in Table 3-9.

Block interleaving is an error correction scheme that separates the "more important" bits and populates them among the "less important" bits. More important bits might be for a MAC address, for example, while a less important bit might represent some of the words in the middle of an e-mail message. Table 3-10 illustrates the concept of interleaving (E = bit error).

Bits	1	0	1	1	0
Transmitted channel-coded bits	111	000	111	111	000
Received bits (with errors)	101	100	011	101	001
Re-created original bit stream (error free)	1	0	1	1	0

Table 3-9.   Forward Error Correction

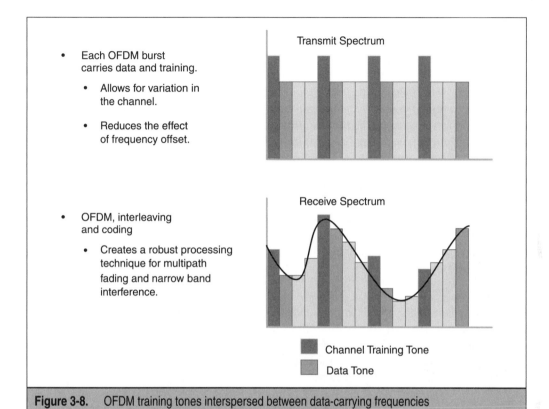

- Each OFDM burst carries data and training.
  - Allows for variation in the channel.
  - Reduces the effect of frequency offset.

- OFDM, interleaving and coding
  - Creates a robust processing technique for multipath fading and narrow band interference.

Figure 3-8.   OFDM training tones interspersed between data-carrying frequencies

Other error correction and detection schemes are commonly used, but these examples should be sufficient to demonstrate the concepts without requiring some

Data before entering transmitting radio	1	2	3	4	5	6	7	8	9	10	11	12	13
After interleaving but before transmission	13	6	8	1	11	3	7	12	4	9	5	2	10
Burst errors during transmission	13	6	8	1	11	E	E	E	E	E	5	2	10
Result after deinterleaving at the receiver	13	6	8	1	11	3	7	12	4	9	5	2	10

Table 3-10.   Example of Block Interleaving

degree of prior expertise in the subject matter and the use of mathematical formulas to adequately explain these other methods.

Antennas

There are several types of the most common antennas, but where possible, most companies deploy a parabolic type (dish) antenna when deploying a bridge over distances of a mile or more, as this antenna has the best performance and is most directional; however, while patch and omni antennas are the most common for indoor use, they also see duty outdoors where the ranges are typically at or under one mile.

Earth Curvature Calculation for 802.11 Bridges

Bridges that carry data over distances in excess of eight miles will require additional care and calculations. Since curvature of the earth causes bulges at the approximate rate of 12 feet for every 18 miles, Table 3-11 can be used to maintain line-of-sight status.

While observing these calculations, it's important to remember that this accounts only for earth bulge. Vegetation (such as trees) and other objects (such as buildings) must have their elevation added into this formula. A reasonable rule of thumb is 125 feet of elevation at both ends of the data link for a distance of 25 miles, but this should be considered an approximation only.

That which must clear the earth bulge and other obstructions is the Fresnel zone (pronounced "frennel"), which is the ellipsoid-shaped area directly between the antennas. The center area in this zone is of the greatest importance and is called the "first Fresnel zone." While the entire Fresnel zone covers an area of appreciable diameter between the antennas, the first Fresnel zone is considered as a radius about the axis between the antennas. A calculation is required to determine the radius (in feet) that must remain free from obstruction for optimal data transfer rates.

The industry standard is to keep 60 percent of the first Fresnel zone clear from obstacles. Therefore, the result of this calculation can be reduced by up to 60 percent without appreciable interference. This calculation should be considered as a reference only and does not account for the phenomenon of refraction from highly reflective surfaces.

Distance (Miles)	Earth Bulge (Feet)
8	8.0
10	12.5
12	18.0
14	24.5
16	32.0

Table 3-11.   Earth Bulge Table

CHAPTER 4

The RF Physical Layer

This chapter discusses what is known as Layer 1, or the Physical Layer, as it is referred to in the OSI Reference stack. It will cover the "physical" portion of the radio; in other words, the portion of the radio that you can touch with your hands. We'll review some radio basics, and more specifically, some 802.11 radio fundamentals as well as some of the more common modulation schemes in use today, and will also review the Media Access Control layer of today's 802.11 radio. We'll conclude this chapter with an overview of antennas, how they work, what kinds are most commonly used in 802.11 networks, and how they are differentiated, one from another.

THE RF PHYSICAL LAYER—LAYER 1

The authors of this work place a premium on the concept that today's WLAN equipment be considered as network elements, and not merely radios. Given that premise, it is appropriate to review the radio at both Layer 1, or *physical layer* (PHY) element, and at least one of the two subsets of Layer 2, called the *media access control*, or MAC layer, of the *OSI reference stack*.

By way of a quick refresher, OSI stands for "Open Systems Interconnection," and its reference model is a network architectural model accepted around the world. This model consists of seven layers, each of which specifies particular network functions such as addressing, flow control, error control, encapsulation, and reliable message transfer. The lowest layer, Layer 1 (also referred to as L1), is closest to the media technology, which in this case would be the radio, and is the focus for this chapter. The lower two OSI layers (Layer 1 and Layer 2) are implemented in hardware and software, while the upper five layers are implemented only in software. The highest layer (the application layer) is closest to the user. The OSI reference model is used universally as a method for teaching and understanding network functionality.

NOTE   The seven layers of the OSI stack are the physical, data-link, network, transport, session, presentation, and application layers, which you can memorize by using the mnemonic "**P**lease **D**o **N**ot **T**hrow **S**ausage **P**izza **A**way."

The Fundamental Radio Elements

The radios used in 802.11 feature three primary elements, regardless of whether the device is an access point (AP), PCMCIA, bridge, or other similar device:

- **Radio**   Generates and receives energy, which is sent to and received from an antenna.

- **Media Access Control (MAC) layer**   The layer which controls packet flow between two or more points in a network.

- **Antenna**   Available in a wide array of configurations, sizes, and performance levels.

This is an oversimplified explanation, but it will suffice at this juncture, and will allow us to focus on the basic elements of an 802.11 device.

The Radio

Recall from the last chapter that electromagnetic energy is pervasive throughout the planet, and indeed the universe, and is intrinsically part of every electrical system. Every electrical system or device that carries electricity has an electromagnetic field and vice versa. Recall also that the currency of electromagnetism is produced by the electrons that encircle all atoms. Thus, the primary function of a radio is to send information by altering the activity of electrons such that they move in relative unison within, and local to, the transmitting antenna in order to have a detectable effect on electrons at a receiving antenna. The associated activity at a receiver is to translate the change of state of the receiving antenna that is affected by the activity of the electrons in the local environment.

The radio itself is a very simple device, and a rudimentary version can be constructed with a 9-volt battery and a coin. If you short out the terminals with the coin, and do so near a common radio set in between AM stations, you'll hear the pop and crackle of static generated by the on/off contact between the coin and battery. If you tap the coin on the battery posts using Morse code, you'll have a fully functional radio! It won't have much range, but this demonstrates how simple the radio is as a device.

If you want to demonstrate a slightly more sophisticated version of this radio, you can hold one end of a machine file to one of the battery posts and attach a wire to the other post. When you run one end of the wire up and down the file, you'll see small sparks. You can also hear this with the same commercial radio referred to in the preceding paragraph. If you had enough voltage, you could hear the crackle in a receiver at a fairly appreciable distance, and in fact that's how the earliest radios worked, and is why they were called *spark coils*. This type of radio would work even today, but it would also knock out all radios in the vicinity of the spark coil, which is exactly why they're not legal to use today for commercial purposes.

One important item to note in regard to the fundamentals of how a radio works is that a radio works only when there is change in the state of the electrons at the transmitting and receiving antennas; this is what was accomplished in the previous experiments.

Today's radios use sine waves that are generated at the radio, because they carry a lot more information than a spark coil, and have far less tendency to interfere with other radios operating in the vicinity. But before we get into all of those details, let's examine the primary elements of a radio.

The 802.11 Radio

What sets the 802.11 radio apart from all other radios primarily is the way it interacts with other radios. IEEE has established a set of well-understood conventions, most of which have been readily adopted by the Internet equipment manufacturers. Many of the specific standards are still being written and ratified at this writing, and it's anticipated that the 802.11 standard will continue to evolve in many significant areas. What this chapter will help to clarify is the manner in which an 802.11 radio interacts with other radios within the same standard.

The 802.11 standard specifies the L1 elements of the radio; in other words, it specifies the *physical layer* of the radio, often referred to as the *PHY* layer of the radio.

Network Topologies

The 802.11 network has two different topologies, the *ad-hoc topology* and the *infrastructure topology*. Within each of these two topologies exists the *Basic Service Set (BSS)*, which consists of two or more *nodes*, sometimes referred to as *stations*. A node or station is an individual platform, such as an access point or a client card (for example, a PCMCIA or mini-PCMCIA card). A BSS has devices that recognized and work in concert with each other to minimize the number of collisions that exist within the domain of the BSS.

Ad-hoc networks are generally composed of two or more clients that are peers of each other, such as laptops or PDAs with 802.11 cards within them. Figure 4-1 illustrates an ad-hoc network.

An ad-hoc network is often referred to as an *Independent Basic Service Set (IBSS)*, with the word *independent* referring to the fact that there is no access point (AP) within this service set. Ad-hoc networks tend to be temporary and are used, for example, when two or more professionals from the same company wish to share files between their laptops or PDAs while at an airport.

The service set that is far more common within 802.11, and the one that has relatively permanent features, is the infrastructure network. While clients that reside within

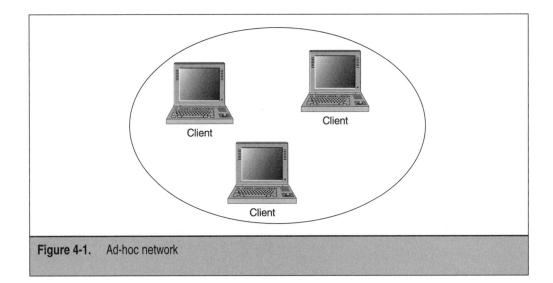

Figure 4-1.   Ad-hoc network

laptops, such as PCMCIA cards, tend to be quite mobile (or *nomadic*), the APs tend to be relatively permanent and one or more will provide connectivity to the network at large.

One may consider the AP as the base station to which all the clients refer, and in general it is the device that controls the traffic flow between the AP and the various clients; in other words, there is little to no client to client, or *peer to peer*, communication *in an 802.11 infrastructure network*. Figure 4-2 illustrates an example of an infrastructure network.

The appropriate reference for the clients and APs in an infrastructure network is Extended Service Set (ESS), because *this term* includes devices from more than one BSS and is typically connected by Ethernet over a distribution system such as an enterprise-wide LAN. The clients can roam between BSSs, thereby providing seamless connectivity for users while on their network.

DSSS and FHSS

The 802.11 standard has been widely adopted around the world, but there are some variants with respect to which frequencies are allowed in certain countries. The following table provides a snapshot of which frequencies are allowed in various countries:

Country	Allocated Spectrum
U.S.A., Europe, France	2.400GHz to 2.485GHz
Japan	2.471GHz to 2.497GHz
Spain	2.400GHz to 2.485GHz

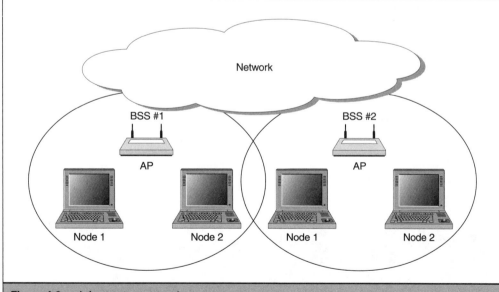

Figure 4-2. Infrastructure network

Do not confuse which *spectrum* is allowed in a country with which *modulation* or *spreading technique* is allowed for a given country.

The 802.11 standard allows for three variants of the PHY layer: direct sequence spread spectrum (DSSS), frequency hopping spread spectrum (FHSS), and infrared (which will not be discussed in this book). While the current 802.11b standard supports various data rates, and both FHSS and DSSS support 1- and 2Mbps speeds, the preponderance of manufacturers, if not all, currently sell equipment that utilizes DSSS as part of the 11Mbps speed found in the 802.11b standard.

The 802.11 DSSS standard calls for 11 channels in the United States, 13 in most ETSI-governed countries, and 14 in Japan. But because the spread spectrum energy covers as many as five different channels at a time, only three are nonoverlapping and (in the case of the U.S. 11-channel scheme) are identified as channels 1, 6, and 11. Figure 4-3 illustrates this concept.

As a practical matter, therefore, virtually all collision domains use no more than three APs, because there are only three nonoverlapping channels, and having the maximum amount of spectrum for a given transmission enables the highest speeds as well as a more robust link.

The number of APs should not be confused with the number of *clients* that can be used, because a single AP can service approximately 2000 clients, though not at the same time (because the usable bandwidth would have been long since used). Generally, the top-performing APs, such as those provided by Cisco, can accommodate as many as 256 clients at one time per AP, though this would not prove at all favorable in terms of access and performance. Further, with the range limitations of the devices, the amount

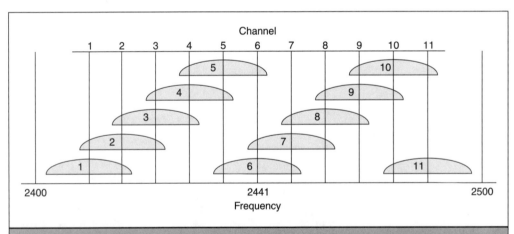

Figure 4-3.   The 11 radio channels in 802.11

of physical area normally required by 2000 users would prohibit associations between APs and clients. What is important to note here is that one would not normally put more than three APs in a single collision domain, as a nominal deployment would have them set on channels 1, 6, and 11, respectively.

NOTE   In summary, DSSS spreading technique works by taking the stream of ones and zeros that comprises the traffic and converting each of the individual numbers into a set of 11 numbers or "chips," known as a Barker code, or chipping sequence. Put another way, each group of 11 bits actually represents a single data stream bit. The chips (the 11 bits) are then modulated by one of a number of schemes and sent over one of the three nonoverlapping channels to a client or group of clients.

The 802.11 specification allows for less complex modulation techniques, such as binary phase shift keying (BPSK), which is used with one phase shift for each bit modulated to ensure maximum range is achievable; this speed would be limited to about 1Mbps. The next most complex modulation technique available is quadrature phase shift keying (QPSK), which encodes two bits of information in the same amount of spectrum as BPSK, though of course it has less range.

The most complex modulation technique used in 802.11b is called complementary code keying (CCK). CCK does not use Barker code; instead, it relies on a series of codes called *complementary sequences*. Sixty-four unique codes can be used to encode the individual bits in a data stream. In other words, up to six bits of data stream can be encoded, as opposed to the single one or zero used in the Barker scheme. The CCK code is then modulated with QPSK in 2Mbps to 11Mbps radios. Eight chips are then sent per symbol (sine wave), but each symbol encodes eight bits because of the QPSK modulation, which is then spread over the various channels by the DSSS spreading technique. This results in 11 megachips per second times the 1MHz of spectrum, which means the radios will use 22MHz of spectrum for each nonoverlapping channel. Therefore, to transmit 11 Mbps in the 802.11b standard, you'd send 11 megabits per second times 8 chips, which equals 11 megachips per second times 2MHz per QPSK-encoded channel, yielding 22MHz of required spectrum. Now, because it is still difficult to discern which of the 64 unique codes are being transmitted (even with today's processors), when range is added, or any element that degrades the quality of the link, one can see that it is prudent to use more than one modulation or chipping technique to ensure that the link remains usable.

PHY Layer Elements

The PHY layer has two sublayers, which are the *Physical Layer Convergence Protocol (PLCP)* and the *Physical Medium Dependent (PMD)*. The difference between the two is that the PLCP layer takes care of items like Barker and CCK encoding, along with the modulation techniques like QPSK and the DSSS spreading technique, whereas the PMD layer provides the interface to the MAC layer for carrier sensing via its *Clear Channel Assessment (CCA)*.

The PLCP consists of a 144-bit preamble that is used to synchronize the APs with the clients, to determine radio gain, and to establish CCA. This preamble consists of 128 bits for synchronization, followed by a 16-bit field consisting of the pattern 1111001110100000. This sequence is used to mark the start of a frame and is called the Start Frame Delimiter (SFD). The next 48 bits are collectively known as the PLCP header, which contains three fields: signal, service, and length and Header Error Check (HEC), which ensures the integrity of the header and preamble. The signal field indicates how fast the payload will be transmitted, which for 802.11b is 1-, 2-, 5.5-, or 11Mbps. 802.11g and 11a also include speeds up to 54Mbps. The service field is reserved for future use. The length field indicates the length of the ensuing payload, and includes the HEC 16-bit, which is performed by a cyclic redundancy check (CRC).

The PLCP is always transmitted at 1Mbps, because reliability and robustness of signal are given a premium and priority over speed. However, this header does impact the overall speed of a link, because 24 bytes of each packet are sent at 1Mbps. You probably have noticed at this juncture that no frame destination has yet been assigned. Because the 192-bit header payload is transmitted at 1Mbps, 802.11b is, at best, only 85 percent efficient at the physical layer.

While the radio internals handle the clocking, modulation, amplifying, spreading techniques, and so forth, the MAC layer is of particular interest to the 802.11 aficionado. By way of reference, other MAC layer controls are used in other networks, such as Ethernet and Token Ring, and the more seasoned readers of this book will recognize that the 802.11 standard has its MAC origins in the 802.3 Ethernet standard. The MAC layer is one of two sublayers of the data-link layer (or, simply, the link layer) and is responsible for controlling packet flow from one client to another across a shared channel like Ethernet or, in this case, 802.11.

NOTE   The primary function of the MAC layer is to ensure that packets/frames don't collide within a domain, such as a WLAN, by controlling access to the allocated and shared radio channels.

While often referred to as the "brains" of the WLAN because it controls packet flow, this MAC layer should only be considered as far as the radios proper, because many of the enhanced security protocols, such as the Extensible Authentication Protocol (EAP), that operate above and beyond the Wireless Equivalent Privacy (WEP) reside in dedicated servers and other "boxes" that reside on the network side of the WLAN. The 802.11, 11b, 11a, and 11g layers perform the tasks of carrier sensing, transmitting, and receiving of the 802.11 frames.

Carrier Sensing

Carrier sensing refers to the actual frequency, or radio energy, transmitted by an 802.11 radio that is received and recognized as native to the collision domain. Recall that information resides *within* the carrier wave. Therefore, the 802.11 standard uses a protocol, which is called *Carrier Sense Multiple Access with Collision Avoidance (CSMA/CA)* to ensure the number of collisions within a domain are kept to a minimum.

In CSMA/CA, an 802.11 platform such as an AP performs the following functions, and in the following order:

1. It listens on the desired radio channel (typically preset by the network management or deployment technicians).

2. If the channel is not carrying traffic, it is considered idle; at which point the AP or client sends a packet.

3. If the desired channel is busy, the transmitter that intends to send information waits until the current transmission stops and—this is important—then waits for a random period of time, called the *contention period,* that follows transmission from any transmitter. This allows every transmitter equal access to the radio channel set apart for a particular LAN. The contention period for DSSS systems is 20 microseconds. This allotment of time enables the transmitter and receiver to acknowledge successful receipt of information.

4. If the desired channel is free from traffic at the end of the transmission from another platform *plus the contention period,* the transmitter that has been awaiting transmission then begins sending information.

The 802.11 standard actually allows two forms of medium access (access to the desired radio channel), called *Distributed Coordination Function (DCF)* and *Point Coordinated Function (PCF).* DCF is a mandatory protocol within the 802.11 specifications, while PCF is an optional protocol used for latency-sensitive traffic like voice and video.

Before a node is granted access to the medium, it must transmit a value, called the *Network Allocation Value (NAV),* that is representative of how large a packet it wishes to send. A NAV is presented by every node that wishes to transmit information, and it indicates how much airtime the *previous* frame in the queue needs to complete. The NAV value must be zero before the node (AP or client) can send the next frame in the queue. Before the next frame in the queue is transmitted, the node calculates the amount of transmit time the next frame will require. When all the nodes in a collision domain receive the NAV, they use it for the basis of setting their transmission times.

One important element of the DCF protocol is *random backoff.* Random backoff timers are engaged if a node determines that there is already traffic on the channel it wishes to use. If the transmitting node has to wait for a clear channel, *it waits for a random period of time before attempting to access the medium again.* This ensures that multiple nodes awaiting transmission won't attempt to send their information at the same time, because the random backoff timers ensure that the waiting nodes are waiting for different amounts of time prior to transmission. The backoff timer is a highly effective, simple, and inexpensive method for reducing collisions within a single LAN (collision domain).

NOTE One peculiarity of the 802.11 specification is that nodes can't listen for collisions while sending data, because the node can't have its receiver on while it's transmitting.

One of the things the 802.11 specification does to help alleviate this condition is to have the receiving node send an *acknowledgement (ACK) packet* back to the transmitting device. This packet is sent if there are no errors in the packet; if the ACK packet isn't received by the transmitting node in a sufficient period of time due to interference or some other reason, the transmitting node will resend the packet.

When the WLAN is intended to carry low-latency-sensitive traffic, such as voice or video, the 802.11 specification allows for PCF, as stated earlier in this section. PCF grants access by a node after the root AP polls all the clients within a collision domain. PCF traffic is allowed in between DCF contention periods.

The Primary MAC Layer Functions

To help clarify what a MAC layer does, and to summarize the essential functions of the MAC layer, we will now consider the primary MAC layer functions:

- Scanning
- Authentication
- Association
- Security
- RTS/CTS
- Power save mode
- Fragmentation

Scanning

There are two types of scanning within the 802.11 protocol, active and passive. In this context, "scanning" refers to clients, such as PCMCIA cards and the like, seeking out APs, workgroup bridges, and so forth. Passive scanning is mandatory within the 802.11 protocol, and is accomplished by having the clients scan each of the available channels. This scanning is performed to find the optimal AP signal. Passive scanning is important, because many, if not most, 802.11 deployments have overlapping channels for the coverage of an area in order to ensure the highest levels of performance and ubiquitous coverage.

Signals called *beacons* are periodically broadcast by the APs, and the client cards receive them while scanning. The beacons include Service Set Identifiers (SSIDs), and other key information.

NOTE   The SSID is a password, such as the word "rodeo," assigned and distributed by the network administrator, that the APs will recognize upon receipt from the clients.

The client then locks onto the AP with the most favorable signal. The primary purpose of scanning is to ensure that the client associates with the most favorable AP in an area.

Active scanning is an optional protocol within 802.11 and is essentially the same process as passive scanning, the only difference being that the client sends a *probe frame* and all the APs within range respond with a *probe response*. The operative difference between passive and active scanning is that if a client is actively scanning, it does not wait for the regularly scheduled beacons sent by APs; in other words, the APs respond upon receipt of the active scan. While active scanning can provide a small advantage in terms of the time needed to identify the optimal AP with which to associate, it also requires additional overhead because of the recurring probe transmissions and corresponding response frames from APs.

Authentication

Authentication is the process whereby preapproved clients may join a collision domain. Authentication occurs prior to association, because it is during the association process that Internet protocol (IP) addresses are revealed by the AP and assigned to the client. The withholding of this information is mission critical in order to prevent *spoofing*, a security term that refers to the emulation of an authorized WLAN client or AP. This concept will be detailed in Chapter 12, along with the details of authentication.

There are two kinds of authentication within the 802.11 protocol:

- **Open system authentication**   Mandatory within the 802.11 specification. It is accomplished by first having the client send an authentication request with an SSID to an AP, which in turn responds with an approval or disapproval of authentication.

- **Shared key authentication**   The basis for the WEP protocol, which is widely recognized as a defeated security protocol (discussed later) for any WLAN used, but in particular for those used in small and medium business networks, on up to WLANs used in large and very large enterprises and campuses.

NOTE The snapshot summary of how WEP works is that a client sends a request for authentication to an AP, but instead of the AP responding with an approval or disapproval as with open authentication, it responds by sending *challenge text* into the body of the frame it uses to respond. Challenge text is really nothing more than text that is encrypted for the purpose of determining whether or not the client has the appropriate key to decrypt the text. Upon receipt, the client then uses its corresponding WEP key to decrypt the text, and then resends it back to the AP. Upon receipt of this challenge text, the AP decrypts it and compares it to the text originally sent to the client in response to the client's initial request for authentication. If the challenge text received by the AP matches correctly, the client is then sent an authentication frame, followed by the necessary IP address information of the AP and the IP address assigned to the client for that particular session.

WEP is considered defeated, in essence, because hackers have derived a way to acquire enough of the WEP key to construct an entire key. Once the hacker has the ability to provide the correct *hashing* of the challenge text, the WLAN network is generally unable to differentiate between a lawful WLAN resident or a hacker. Again, this authentication weakness will be detailed further in Chapter 12, in which you will receive further information on the 802.11i task force that has been set in motion to resolve this security issue with the emerging 802.1X protocol for security.

Association

After the authentication process has been completed, an association is initiated by a client card (such as a PCMCIA or the like) when it sends an association request frame containing SSID and supported data rates. The AP responds by sending an association response frame containing an association ID along with other information related to the specific AP, such as an IP address. Once the client and AP have associated, the authentication process then begins.

Security

With WEP, as previously outlined, the client encrypts the body, not the frame header, before transmission, using a WEP key. The AP decrypts the frame upon receipt, using the same key. The entirety of this section on MAC security will be detailed in Chapter 12.

RTS/CTS

RTS/CTS stands for Request to Send/Clear to Send. While the name itself makes fairly obvious what occurs in this aspect of the MAC layer, what is not well known about RTS/CTS is that the client users can set the maximum size for the frame length before this protocol will be used by the collision domain. As an example, if the user sets the maximum frame length to 1000 bytes, the client will use RTS/CTS on all frames that are 1000 bytes and larger.

NOTE   This protocol is quite handy when there are *hidden nodes*, two or more clients that don't detect each other's presence because they are out of range from each other.

The concept of a hidden node should not be confused with the inability of an AP to detect a client. An AP has to have a client in an associative state before traffic can be exchanged between the AP and the client.

RTS/CTS eliminates prospective timing problems for transmission between two clients that can't interact by RF. What specifically happens with the RTS/CTS protocol is that the client sends an RTS frame to an AP before transmission of a packet in excess of a preset threshold. The AP will then control the transmission time by sending a CTS packet to the client awaiting transmission. Upon receipt of a CTS packet at the client, the client then will include a duration value in the frame header. This duration value will prevent the AP from receiving packets from any other clients in the collision domain. The RTS/CTS protocol continues to exist as long as a client sends packets in excess of a preset size. It is important to note that each client can have unique packet sizes, though the upper limit for the standard is 2312 bytes.

Power Save Mode

The MAC layer provides the option of reducing power usage, which may be important where users have clients such as PCMCIA cards in laptop computers or PDAs. With the power save mode turned on, the client sends a message to the AP indicating that it will be going to sleep, which is accomplished by the status bit located in the header of each frame sent from the client. Upon receipt of the request to go to sleep, the AP then buffers packets corresponding to the client.

The default power utilization mode for clients is the Constant Awake Mode (CAM), which is essentially what it sounds like; the client remains in an awake mode constantly. However, if the user so chooses, they can go into a lower power mode, called *Polled Access Mode (PAM)*. However, even in sleep mode, the client must "awaken" periodically to receive from the AP a packet called a *Traffic Information Map (TIM)*, which is a notification to the client that there is traffic waiting at the AP. Once the traffic has been transferred from the AP to the client, the client will return to sleep. Because the client will not awaken at a random time, but rather at a very specific time, it will have a high statistical probability of not losing intended traffic. Depending on the volume of traffic, placing a client into PAM can save enormous amounts of power at the client.

The APs can be set to indicate traffic with a *Delivery Traffic Information Map (DTIM)*. The DTIM timer is always set to a multiple of the TIM timer and can be adjusted at the AP by the network administrator. By setting this value high enough, the clients will remain asleep for a longer period of time; however, the downside to this strategy is that it will reduce response time of the client, as it may be sleeping when a packet is sent to the AP for it.

Fragmentation

Fragmentation in the context of the 802.11 protocol refers to the ability of an AP to divide packets into smaller frames. This is most often done so that RF interference only wipes out smaller packets. Remember that a receiving device must send an ACK packet to the transmitting device to confirm that it received a packet successfully. It makes sense that some packets will be retransmitted. In such cases, the smaller the retransmission, the better the overall performance will be within a collision domain, because the other clients will not have to wait until the retransmission has been completed. Packet fragmentation also allows for increased amounts of clear channel time. Like the RTS/CTS protocol, the 802.11 standard enables the user to establish the maximum frame size threshold prior to the platform fragmenting the packet. If the user has set their fragmentation thresholds, no frame will be larger than the maximum allowable size set by the user.

In addition to collision avoidance and roaming, the MAC layer is also responsible for identifying the source and destination addresses of the packet being sent, as well as the CRC. Each node in an 802.11 network is identified by its MAC address, and in fact uses exactly an addressing scheme that is identical to that of Ethernet which is a 6 byte-48 bit value.

802.11 Roaming

The 802.11 standard provides for roaming of 802.11 clients among multiple APs, regardless of whether the "new" AP is transmitting on the same frequency as the prior one that was associated with the client. This is achieved through beacon frames from the APs, and the same principles of active and passive scanning from the clients remain applicable for the purposes of roaming.

When a client enters into a new collision domain, the first thing that has to happen is that the client must be made to operate on the same channel as the preferred AP. While the AP will be preset to operate on one of the available channels in the 802.11b specification, the client will acquire the channel used by the AP by scanning for a channel in a *channel sweep*. A channel sweep is where the client sweeps across the channels, and remains on each channel for a specified period of time to capture the signal radiated from the AP. In a *full sweep mode*, the full array of 11 channels (if the device is used in the United States) will be scanned, or the client may be configured to perform a *short sweep*, which is when the client will sweep only a selected set of channels, such as 1, 6, and 11 if the device is an 11b or 11g client. Short sweep selections are often based on which channels were used previously with the client. Once the channel has been acquired, the device will then authenticate and associate in the normal manner prescribed within the 802.11 standard.

NOTE   It is difficult to ensure the continuity of low-latency-sensitive traffic like voice and video while the user is mobile at pedestrian speeds with a client embedded into a PDA. While voice roaming is available through some 802.11 vendors, it is not ubiquitously available from all 802.11 equipment vendors currently, because they have not resolved the thorny issue of ensuring authentication while roaming from one AP to another.

Antennas

As stated earlier in the chapter, the essential art of RF is to get enough electrons to move in relative unison at the transmitting antenna such that they have a detectable effect on the electrons within the receiving antenna. Radio antennas perform two essential functions in RF:

- They greatly enhance the performance of a radio.
- They shape the radiated energy to the advantage of the user.

While the art of antenna design and theory has resulted in part in the publication of hundreds of books, most of them essentially are unreadable by the vast majority of humankind, primarily because an antenna has to be considered at the subatomic level to be truly understood. For this reason, the fundamental properties of this well-recognized but little understood device have not changed much over the years, and given their rather substantial use in today's world and in decades past, commercial antennas have not changed much in their performance or design. While the complexity of an antenna is such that it could glaze the eyes of even the most ardent enthusiast or professional, fortunately, the basics of an antenna are not hard to grasp.

Antennas are conductors, and, interestingly, although they are devices that handle magnetic energy, they are commonly composed of materials that are *nonaustenitic*, or nonmagnetic. For a material to be naturally magnetic (and not by virtue of running a current through a conductor such as copper), it must contain an appropriate amount of one of the only three known magnetic materials, iron, nickel, and cobalt. Such a material may not in and of itself be magnetic, but it will carry an electrical charge rather well, which is a property sufficient to radiate and capture RF energy. The reader will readily grasp the concept of electromagnets, which is to say that a conductor can and will become magnetic when a charge is sent through it.

The region close to the antenna is called the *induction field*. Outside the induction field is where the *radiation field* exists. There is a boundary layer between the two fields, but at this writing, the boundary layer remains relatively undefined, although there are important differences between the two fields. One difference is that while the energy within the radiation field moves in an outward direction from the source until it is absorbed, some of the energy within the induction field is returned to the circuit. The induction field is comprised of both magnetic and electrical energy in a relationship that is not fully understood. On the other hand, the energy within the radiation field is always a power flow of both electrical and magnetic forces, which are relatively well defined and understood.

As stated earlier in this chapter, when an RF wave comes near an antenna, some of the energy will be absorbed by that antenna. The antenna will then set up miniature copies of the currents and voltages that originally left the transmission source. Again, these "copies" are so small relative to the energy originally transmitted that we use the dB scale to more easily express this reduction in energy. While the amount of energy sent forth from the transmission source rapidly diminishes in amount, what does not change over time or during transfer through space is the original rate (frequency) at which the waves were sent.

Without an antenna, a radio would have only a tiny fraction of its ability to send energy over great distances, because the radio's printed circuit board has very limited means to store and then "push off" (transmit) a sufficient number of electrons to have a desired effect at a distant receiver. In a certain way, one may think of an antenna as a storage device; this is where the electrons produced by the radio are stored, and then transmitted.

As for a receiving antenna, one could use the analogy of either a catcher's mitt or perhaps a large ear. When a device is sufficiently large enough, it will absorb enough of the pattern of waves that have been transmitted. Again, this is a function that cannot be accomplished by the printed circuit board, which may be referred to as the radio proper. An antenna doesn't need to be very large to be quite effective. Omnidirectional antennas, typically used for indoor applications, are commonly only about six inches (about 15 cm) in length and 1/3-inch (about 10 mm) wide. Patch antennas for indoor use are generally on the order of six inches square and 1/5-inch thick.

The Isotropic Antenna

If you spend enough time studying radios, you'll come across the term *isotropic antenna* and its corresponding measurement *dBi*. In 802.1 radios, the radio circuitry puts out varying amounts of voltage to the antenna, which appears to the eye as a sine wave on an oscilloscope. The radiation field, therefore, also propagates a similar type of energy— energy that increases and decreases at any given point at which the energy can be detected. What is important, then, is to understand how much power is flowing to a given point in the area that is being radiated.

NOTE   The reader will recall that dBi stands for "dB isotropic"—the gain of an antenna over an antenna that radiates exactly the same amount of energy in all directions.

Whenever energy is transmitted, regardless of the type of energy, loss occurs. In the case of an 802.11 radio (or any radio), energy is lost at the circuit board because of *resistive losses*. Resistive losses can be readily understood as the resistance to the flow of electrons through a conductor. These losses result in the creation of heat from flowing of electrons, which reduces the amount of RF energy sent outward from the antenna. This loss is so predictable that the energy loss at the atomic (electron) level can be accurately predicted by measuring the amount of heat given off by the electrical components.

There are also losses in the induction field of the antenna because of the cycling of the alternating current or voltage at the antenna. Recall that the antenna is loaded with electrons, and then, alternately, the electrons are pulled out of the antenna. This is what sets up the desired sine wave, or alternating amount of energy in both the induction field (close to the antenna) and the radiating field (all the space away from the antenna that is wrapped around the induction field). As the electrons are loaded into the antenna, and then alternately pulled out of the antenna, there are resistive and other losses, the sum of which results in losses of efficiency. Put another way, not every single electron makes it efficiently into the antenna, and not every single electron is pulled out of the antenna during each cycle.

If not every electron makes it into, or out of, the antenna, then there are probably physical areas within the antenna at which more electrons will be loaded into, and pulled out of, the antenna. For this reason, the exact amount of radiation given off an antenna is not perfectly symmetrical. Make sure that you do not confuse this concept with gain, which will be covered later in this chapter. What is important to understand is that the number of electrons loaded into a radiation field is not symmetric over a given radiation field, which is often referred to as *energy density*. Those who design and deploy radios need to understand energy density to plan for optimal coverage of a WLAN space.

The rationale for an isotropic radiator is that it allows for a relatively easy calculation in regard to energy density. An isotropic radiator is a *theoretical antenna* because it is a radiating source that is perfectly symmetrical in its radiating field. Put another way, an isotropic radiator is one that has absolutely perfect performance—not a single electron is lost at any point of the alternating cycle in which electrons are loaded into, and pulled out of, the antenna.

Because real-world antennas do not provide radiation fields that are symmetrical, the actual field of the real-world antenna is measured against the theoretically perfect (isotropic) antenna, and this difference is stated in dBi.

Capture Area

The term *capture area* is one used relative to a receiving antenna. A receiving antenna shaped like a dish (parabola), where the area exceeds two or more wavelengths, behaves as if it were capturing all of the energy over a given two-dimensional area, which area is equal to the size of the antenna. However, in the case of an omnidirectional antenna, which is shaped more like a rod or stick, the capture characteristics are a bit surprising in that the conductor (the antenna) has an effect on the radiation field for some distance around the conductor. In the case of the omnidirectional antenna, the concept of simply assuming a two-dimensional coverage does not apply, and indeed the amount of area sampled by an omnidirectional antenna is not at all related to what might appear as a two-dimensional capture area adjacent to the antenna.

This energy is made available at the end of the antenna that connects to the radio circuit board, from which point the energy is translated into information via the various processes that occur within the radio circuitry along with the DSP circuitry.

Now let's take a look at some of the elements of an antenna that are transparent to the end user but rather important to the designers of 802.11 radios.

Dielectric Constant

The *dielectric constant* is a measurement of how well an antenna allows electrons to flow freely. The dielectric constant is always greater than one, because it is measured against a theoretically perfect radiating environment—a vacuum. The dielectric constant is relevant because if it's too high, the antenna will present a wavelength to the radio circuitry of something shorter than that normally associated with a frequency, such as the 12 cm normally associated with the 2.4GHz carrier frequency. This issue is particularly important in the selection of antenna coatings. A material that has a high dielectric constant has a high degree of *permittivity*. If an antenna is coated with a material with high permittivity, it will, for a given frequency, operate at a length shorter than the length normally provided as optimal. While this may appear to be something a design engineer could take advantage of, in particular when designing very small antennas for devices such as 802.11 PCMCIA cards or the even smaller mini-PCMCIA cards, the compromise is that the higher the permittivity, the greater the amount of energy that will be reflected *inside* the antenna before leaving it. This means that if an antenna has a coating with an excessively high permittivity, it will generally operate over a narrower amount of spectrum.

Voltage Standing Wave Ratio

Voltage standing wave ratio (VSWR) is a measurement of the impedance mismatch between the transmission line and its load. The transmission line includes the antenna and the cables and connectors. *Impedance* in the realm of antennas refers to the ratio of voltage to current on an antenna *at any particular point* of the antenna. This means that there are indeed varying amounts of impedance over the entire antenna. An antenna, its connectors, and the cable connecting the antenna to the radio circuitry must be closely matched for impedance.

Zero impedance would imply that all the materials between (and including) the antenna and the radio circuitry would not only be identical, but also be identical in temperature as material temperature affects conductivity. Impedance is measured in *ohms*, the unit of measurement used to characterize resistance. 802.11 radio components are generally designed such that the impedance is approximately 50 ohms. Connectors that are either in poor condition, or that have become damaged, worn, or as is the case most of the time, water-logged, or even if improperly designed antennas are used, the maximum power will not be radiated from the antenna. Often in these situations, the induction field is reflected back down from the antenna to the radio circuitry. The combination of the original sine wave sent to the antenna and the wave reflected is called the *standing wave*. Therefore, the ratio between these two waves is known as the *voltage standing wave ratio*, if measured in volts. This value is represented in order for engineers to describe how efficiently the antenna absorbs energy.

A VSWR value of 2.0:1 represents an antenna that has a power absorption rate of 90 percent, which is considered very good for an antenna likely to be used in an 802.11 WLAN. Most antennas have a VSWR value of 3.0:1, which represents a −6 dB loss. This is considered acceptable to good, because it means the antenna has a 75 percent power absorption rate. Another term commonly used to describe this phenomenon is called *return loss*. If 50 percent of the energy from the radio circuitry is absorbed by the antenna, and the other 50 percent is reflected back to the radio circuitry, the antenna would have a return loss of −3 dB.

Efficiency

Efficiency is similar to VSWR and return loss, but actually is a measurement of the total energy radiated from the antenna, compared to that which is induced by the radio circuitry. Again, per the previous section, an 802.11 antenna with an efficiency of 75 percent is quite good, and one with an efficiency of 50 percent is still quite acceptable. Note that antennas often perform at efficiencies less than advertised by the manufacturer, because they are measured in ideal conditions in tightly controlled laboratory settings. Fortunately, antennas available today from any reputable manufacturer are generally quite good.

Gain

Perhaps the best known of the technical terms used in regard to antennas, *gain* is simply a measure of how the energy is directed from an antenna. This expression is given in dB, and is a statement of the increased amount of energy that is found in the main lobe versus a theoretical antenna that has perfectly symmetric radiation in all directions. Gain is one of the most important functions of an antenna. The ability to shape the radiation field is very important relative to geographical coverage, whether this is in an office environment or for an 802.11 bridge with end points two miles apart.

NOTE   Antennas are basically one of two types: omnidirectional, such as a *dipole* antenna (sometimes also referred to as a vertical antenna), and directional (sometimes referred to as *high-gain* antennas). A dipole antenna is one that consists of two conductors that are placed end to end and are equal in length. Remember that as an antenna is one that accommodates alternating current (AC), it will of necessity require two conductors. While some people hold that there is technically only one kind of antenna (dipole), for the sake of clarification and simplicity, we will adopt the position that omnidirectional antennas are much closer in function to an isotropic radiator than a directional, or high-gain, antenna.

Omnidirectional antennas have gain also, if only for the reason that an isotropic antenna is theoretical, but more importantly, they're designed to optimize coverage in the physical area where clients are most likely to reside. Figure 4-4 represents what the typical coverage from an omnidirectional antenna might look like to the human eye if one could "see" the energy.

Another way to consider gain is to use the analogy of a flashlight that has an adjustable head. With this common type of flashlight, one can change the shape of a beam from wide to narrow. This is actually a good example of changing the "gain" of a flashlight. The same principle applies to antennas, although the amount of gain probably has a greater effect with regard to the detectable range of the energy (in other words, how far it will radiate in a useful manner from the source).

When discussing the concept of gain, it's important to note that real-world antennas, in particular those that are directional, have *lobes.* A lobe is the area in which the antenna radiates its energy. Gain is considered a description of the *main lobe,* which is the largest in size as well as the one with the greatest range from the transmitting radio. Gain is expressed in dBi, again, with respect to the ratio of the energy against that of an isotropic radiator. Gain is also expressed as dBd, in which the real-world radiation field is compared to that of a dipole operating in free space (an environment where there is no blockage of the energy). For comparison, 0dBd is equal to 2.15dBi.

On a practical front, it's a good idea to consider using an antenna that optimally shapes the field for your purposes, as opposed to increasing the power output of your 802.11 device. A very common gain increase for even a relatively low gain patch type antenna is 6 dBi. Consider that if you used only a 3dBi gain antenna, you'd double the amount of energy received at a given point in the area you are covering. The smaller antennas, such as those found on 802.11 PCMCIA cards, often have relatively low gain; for example, the Cisco Aironet PCMCIA external card has an antenna with 2.2dBi gain. At the maximum power setting, this will nominally provide a stated line-of-sight range of approximately 50 feet, though in practice it's probably well in excess of that with

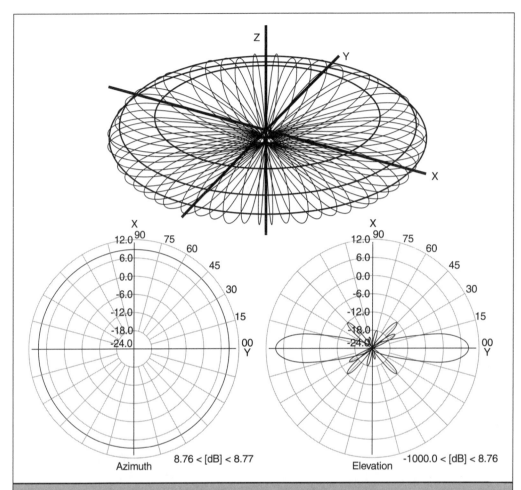

Figure 4-4.   Graphical representations of omnidirectional antenna coverage

usable signal quality. Equipment provided by other manufacturers will operate with varying, and generally lower, levels of performance.

NOTE   With regard to gain, transmit gain and receive gain are generally the same, because this is a function of antenna design as opposed to whether an antenna is actively radiating or receiving information, which is a relatively passive function.

Few if any 802.11 systems use separate antennas for transmitting and receiving energy, though it is common to see two antennas on an 802.11 device. This configuration is used for *receive diversity*, which is to say that capturing signals with two antennas usually results in one of the antennas receiving a slightly better signal. The device in most systems will simply select the antenna that has the stronger signal. Figure 4-5 illustrates the shape of a field that is nominally radiated from a directional antenna.

Polarization

The radiation field emitted from an 802.11 transmitter will have both an electromagnetic element and a magnetic element. In classical or traditional engineering representations, the electromagnetic element is referred to as the E field, and the magnetic field is referred to as the H field. Why the magnetic field is indicated as *H* is one of those mysteries in life; it's probably more useful to understand what it does than why it uses a certain naming convention.

NOTE Within a radiation field, both the E and H elements of the energy radiating from a source move in a direction that is *perpendicular* to that of the direction of the radiating field.

In Figure 4-6, the orientation of the E field (electrical), also called *vector,* is used to define the polarization of the energy. If the E field is oriented vertically, the radiation field is said to have *vertical polarization.* If the E field is oriented horizontally, the radiating field is said to have *horizontal polarization.* There is also a phenomenon known as *circular polarization,* which means that the E field rotates, but this is not generally a phenomenon associated with 802.11 radios. The theory of a circular rotating field is

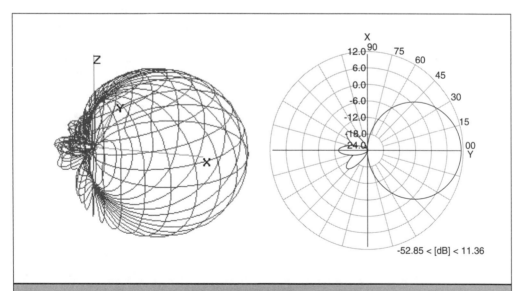

Figure 4-5. Graphical representations of directional antenna coverage

that it is less susceptible to interference. What is important to note about polarization is that both the transmitting and receiving antennas must have the same polarization in order to provide maximum performance of the radio link.

Beamwidth

Beamwidth is the measurement of how wide a lobe is at a point where it has one-half of the power originally transmitted (–3dB). What most people are not aware of is that the radiation field is quite dynamic. If you could watch a radiation field for a period of time, you'd see that it is somewhat similar to watching the aurora borealis, or northern lights (or aurora australis for the folks south of the equator). In other words, you'd see the radiation field moving. The point of this is that beamwidth is the measurement of the width of the radiation field at a given point. It is often referred to as the *directiveness* of an antenna and is defined as the *angle* between the two points of the radiation field of the main lobe, which are at one-half of the power originally transmitted.

Antenna Types

Consistent with the position that there are two main types of antennas, omnidirectional and directional, there is a fairly wide array of antenna types to be found in 802.11 deployments. These various types are summarized in Table 4-1.

The antennas listed in Table 4-1 should be considered representative of the types of antennas presently available for 802.11 deployment. There are a number of different types of coverage with regard to antennas; in other words, a company offering omnidirectional antennas will probably offer two, if not three, different models of this particular antenna, because not all deployment scenarios are the same. In some deployments, coverage close to the access point will be more important, and in other deployments, such as an outdoor deployment for campus networks, the desired area of coverage may be farther away from the access point or bridge.

While the radios at each end of a link must by symmetric in terms of the modulation and spreading techniques, they may well use different antennas, assuming the polarization is identical at both ends of the link. Both radios are mutually authenticated, which is to say that they must be granted authorization to become a member of a particular LAN. The issue of authentication and authorization will be covered in detail in Chapter 12, with regard to 802.11 security issues.

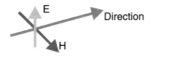

E field, H field, and direction of propagation

Figure 4-6.   Polarization-Energy Direction Versus Electrical and Magnetic Fields

Type	Nominal Gain	Coverage W×H (degrees)	Range	Primary Use
Omni	2.2 dBi	180×75	130 ft.	Indoors, generally from ceiling
Parabola	21 dBi	12.4×12.4	11 miles	Outdoor bridges
Yagi	13.5 dBi	30×25	2 miles	Indoor/outdoor medium-range directional connections
Patch	6.5 dBi	85×55	165 ft.	Indoor/outdoor unobtrusive medium-range antenna
Dipole	2.2 dBi	360×75	100 ft.	Indoor, typically used in a diversity configuration

Table 4-1.   Different types of antennas

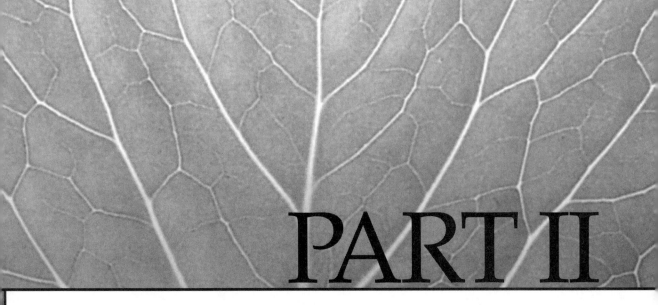

PART II

Designing Your Enterprise Wireless LAN

CHAPTER 5

Performance, Architechtural, and Interoperability Considerations

With most networking technologies, vendors frequently tout the performance and interoperability of their products. Customers are rightly on the lookout for a solution that offers high performance and complete interoperability. It's no exception with Wi-Fi: Customers demand performance and interoperability, and vendors are happy to provide it.

Deploying high-performance, fully interoperable LANs is not as simple as a vendor's brochure would suggest. And with Wi-Fi in particular, performance and interoperability are a matter of degrees. Technologies that are more mature or that operate over a more predictable medium like a cable, provide more absolute performance quantifications and interoperability guarantees . Maximizing Wi-Fi performance and providing interoperability takes a bit more involvement on the part of the network administrator than with Ethernet.

In this chapter, we'll detail the performance and interoperability considerations of Wi-Fi technology. Although each of these considerations will be covered in a separate section, it's important to bear in mind that all of these notions are interrelated. There tends to be a trade-off between performance and interoperability. A single vendor solution tends to provide the best performance in terms of features while a multivendor solution tends to degrade feature capabilities as the various elements operate at a lowest common denominator. Understanding this is key to a successful wireless LAN deployment.

This chapter addresses the current Wi-Fi technology, wireless LANs based on the 11Mbps 802.11b standard. In the following chapter, next-generation Wi-Fi gear based on the 54Mbps 802.11a and 802.11g standards will be covered. As 802.11a and 802.11g are similar in many regards to 802.11b, many of the performance and interoperability

What Is Wi-Fi?

Wi-Fi (pronounced "Why-Phy") is a trade name developed by an industry trade group called the Wi-Fi Alliance, the charter of which will be further detailed later in this chapter. Wi-Fi describes wireless local area networking products that are based on IEEE 802.11 standards and is meant to be a more user-friendly name in the same way that Ethernet and Token Ring are more user friendly than IEEE 802.3 and 802.5, respectively. Originally, Wi-Fi was meant to describe only 11Mbps–maximum devices that operate in the 2.4GHz portion of the frequency spectrum and that conform to the IEEE 802.11b specification. It was later decided that Wi-Fi should be expanded to include 54Mbps–maximum data rate products operating in both the 2.4GHz and 5GHz portions of the frequency spectrum that are based on the IEEE 802.11g and 802.11a specifications. Throughout this chapter, Wi-Fi refers only to the original IEEE 802.11b-compliant products. IEEE 802.11a and 802.11g will be discussed in Chapter 6.

considerations outlined in this chapter are applicable to the higher-speed technologies. In Chapter 9, the architectural considerations for Wi-Fi in the enterprise will be discussed. Network architecture does, of course, have a major impact on network capabilities and, ultimately, performance. This is even more the case with Wi-Fi, which, due to its radio-based nature, is by definition a shared-medium technology. Those who have architected a shared Ethernet wired network, something of a dying art given today's inexpensive Ethernet switches, know the major impact architecture can have on how well capabilities like security operate for the user.

WI-FI PERFORMANCE

"Performance" is an imprecise term that is nonetheless woefully overused in describing products ranging from razors to floor polish to wireless LAN equipment. As it relates to the latter, "performance" is a catchall word that is used to describe the maximum data rate of the device, the actual throughput that the device provides, and the range of the radio in the device. To make the notion of performance more meaningful, we'll examine each of these independently.

The Data Rates Supported by Wi-Fi

Although Wi-Fi LAN equipment is most commonly promoted as providing a maximum data rate of 11Mbps, it's important to note that the IEEE 802.11b specification that rests as the foundation for Wi-Fi actually supports a total of four data rates: 1, 2, 5.5, and 11Mbps. These data rates are all available on the same physical medium, specifically, an approximately 80MHz–wide portion of the radio frequency spectrum, starting at 2.400GHz, that is then divided into between 11 and 14 channels, depending upon the exact amount of spectrum allocated by various international government agencies. This band is available for use without a license throughout most of the world, the specifics of which are covered in detail in Chapter 7. The advantages and history of license-free operation are outlined in Chapter 1.

Although you cannot see, touch, hear, or feel this medium, it is as tangible and as concrete a means of sending data, voice, and video as is a copper wire or fiber-optic cable. With Ethernet, the physical medium remains the same as data rates increase or decrease—you can achieve data rates of between 1 and 1000Mbps on the same Category 5 copper twisted-pair cable. The same holds true for Wi-Fi; increasing or decreasing the performance of the wireless LAN is not a function of increasing or decreasing the size of the physical layer or changing the amount of bandwidth, but rather it's a function of the modulation type employed. In networking terms, this physical medium, whether copper, fiber, or radio frequencies, is referred to as the *physical layer* and represents the lower layers of the seven layers in the Open Systems Interconnection (OSI) reference model (covered in greater detail in Chapter 4).

The process of sending data from a digital device, such as a computer, over radio waves is the same as the process for sending data from a digital device over telephone lines. Because transmissions over most telephone lines and radio waves both are analog, a modem is required to convert the digital stream of 0s and 1s into an analog stream, a process known as *modulation.* A modem is also required at the receiving end to convert the analog stream back into a digital stream, a process known as *demodulation.* (The name "modem" is simply a truncation of the words *mo*dulation and *dem*odulation.)

The bases for the four data rates provided by the 802.11b standard are three different modulation types:

- Binary phase shift keying (BPSK) for 1Mbps
- Quadrature phase shift keying (QPSK) for 2Mbps
- Complementary code keying (CCK) for 5.5 and 11Mbps

One could reasonably question why, if faster is always better, the industry and the standards bother to support anything other than the CCK modulation type that provides for the fastest data rates. The answer comes down to a word: *range.* A brief description of each modulation type will help you to understand the interrelationship between modulation (and therefore data rate) and range.

BPSK Modulation for 1Mbps Data Rate

An analog wave can be measured in terms of its power, or *amplitude;* in terms of the number of waves per any given period of time, or *frequency;* or in terms of when the wave begins its cycle, or *phase.* By systematically varying these parameters, you can alter the encoding, and therefore transmission, of information.

Although at first glance it appears to be a collection of semantics, the name binary phase shift keying is actually fairly descriptive of how this means of modulation works; deconstructing this name is therefore helpful to understanding the process.

Binary indicates that in this type of modulation, the input to the process is simply either a 0 or a 1—as an example, unencoded digital data from a computer. With BPSK, only two states are possible: the 0 state or the 1 state, which, in digital terms, can be represented in a single bit of data. If the message you are transmitting is as simple as a yes or a no, an on or an off, a dot or a dash, the likelihood of that most basic message being received over even the most noisy carrier is increased relative to a more complex message. A binary modulation type, like BPSK, is the most basic, and therefore the most robust, modulation type. However, sending a given amount of data using this basic modulation type also takes a greater number of transmissions than using a more involved modulation type. As the most basic modulation type, BPSK is the modulation type for the 1Mbps base data rate specified by the 802.11 standard.

As the name suggests, BPSK uses changes, or *shifts,* in the start times of a wave to indicate which of the binary states are being encoded, or *keyed.* Each frame of data sent begins with a preamble that sets the baseline for the transmission and precedes actual information being transmitted. During the handshake process between the sending and the receiving stations, the devices are synchronized such that a common baseline is established. Changes from this baseline, or shifts in *phase,* are then used to signal that a change is made from the transmission of a 0 to a 1 or from a 1 to a 0. Here again, using changes in the start time for a wave is a very robust means of encoding data; unlike changes in amplitude, which can be obscured by radio noise, shifts in phase are discernable by the receiving device even in high-interference environments.

Because BPSK is the most robust of all the modulation types specified by 802.11 (if data encoded by BPSK won't get through, nothing will), it is the modulation type used for all frame headers regardless of which modulation type is used for the information payload.

QPSK Modulation for 2Mbps Data Rate

Quadrature phase shift keying is a variation on the BPSK theme. As the name suggests, it still uses shifts in phase to encode the data stream. This data stream, however, is not simply binary states of either 0s or 1s, but rather a set of four states (thus the *quad* in quadrature). This is represented not in a single bit, as in BPSK, but in two bits resulting in four states: 00, 01, 10, and 11. These four states are then encoded based upon changes in the start times for the waves. Because four states are twice as many as two states, QPSK provides 2Mbps performance, twice that of the 1Mbps performance provided by BPSK.

Naturally, discerning four shifts in phase rather than just two requires a relatively clearer signal. The frame header, which again is sent in BPSK, indicates which modulation type will be used for transmitting the payload. The sending station will attempt to transmit the payload using higher-order modulation types like QPSK to increase the data rate. If an inordinately large number of errors results when the payload is being sent via the higher-order modulation type, the sending station will fall back to progressively more simple, and therefore more robust, modulation types on the resends until the frame is received with an acceptable number of errors. This process of *rate shifting* provides for an automatic means of maximizing the data rate when conditions such as noise and distance allow. By the same token, it provides for maximum reliability even as noise and distance increase, albeit at the expense of network performance. BPSK and QPSK are the two modulation types specified by the original IEEE 802.11 standard ratified in 1997.

While 1 and 2Mbps represent acceptable levels of performance when sending relatively small amounts of data, as is typical in vertical applications like bar code scanning and numeric transactions, they tend to be quite insufficient to support more performance-intensive applications like those found in office environments. Stated another way, the original 802.11 standard—while well suited for the long-range and low data-rate requirements of retail, warehousing, manufacturing, and similar environments—is ill suited for the shorter range and high-performance requirements of office environments. As such, the wireless LAN industry moved quickly to bring forth an extension to the original standard—the 11Mbps 802.11b standard, which was developed and ratified in just two years from the original 802.11 standard, which took a full six years to develop and ratify.

CCK Modulation for 5.5 and 11Mbps Data Rates

The modulation type used for 802.11b is complementary code keying, which provides for both 5.5Mbps and a maximum data rate of 11Mbps. CCK is a far more involved modulation type than BPSK or even QPSK. Indeed, to achieve the higher data rates, devices compliant to the 802.11b standard modulate the signal with both BPSK and QPSK *as well as* CCK. With BPSK, the radio starts with a two-bit data stream; with QPSK, the radio starts with a four-bit data stream. CCK follows this exponential pattern by starting with an eight-bit data stream to achieve the 11Mbps data rate, and dropping back to a four-bit stream when conditions dictate to achieve a 5.5Mbps data rate.

Naturally, a transmission that is modulated twice will require a clearer channel than a transmission that is modulated just once. Similarly, the longer, eight-bit stream will require a clearer channel than bit streams that are one or two orders of magnitude shorter. It follows that 802.11b represents a trade-off between performance (defined as data rate) and range. All other things being held constant, there is an *inverse relationship between the data rate and range:* as the data rate increases, range decreases.

Rate Shifting

The term *rate shifting* refers to the ability of a device to dynamically and automatically change between the various speeds, or rates, at which data is transmitted. To get the best of all worlds, the 802.11b standard allows for rate shifting from CCK back to the 802.11 QPSK and BPSK modulation types. Again, the frame header is modulated via BPSK to maximize the likelihood of receipt. The sending and receiving stations negotiate the maximum starting data rate possible through a handshaking process, ideally settling upon 11Mbps using CCK. This data rate negotiation process is a dynamic one; the negotiated data rate is subject to change as conditions change.

The process whereby a data rate is established or reestablished is based upon the number of errors received when a packet is sent at a certain data rate using a specific modulation type. If the number of received errors passes a certain vendor-specified threshold, the Wi-Fi device will take action. First, a Wi-Fi client will search across all channels in the 2.4GHz band for an access point that provides a stronger signal, and therefore the likelihood of a correspondingly smaller number of transmission errors. If the client device finds an access point with a stronger signal, it will associate itself with the access point providing the stronger signal and thereby either establish or maintain the highest data rate possible. If, however, the client is unable to find an access point that provides a stronger signal, it will begin the process of rate shifting. This automatic process uses progressively less complex, and therefore more robust, modulation types that will result in fewer errors, greater geographic coverage, and a lower data rate.

At a conceptual level, you can view the relationship between range and data rate to have a structure sort of like the structure of a wedding cake (see Figure 5-1). At the base, the diameter of the coverage area is greatest but the data rate is also the lowest. Moving to the second level, the diameter of the coverage area decreases but the data rate increases. The third and fourth levels, representing 5.5 and 11Mbps, respectively, have correspondingly decreasing diameters and higher data rates.

In general, errors are caused by interference, sometimes caused by competitive sources of radio energy, and at other times caused by the phenomenon of *multipath,* the convergence or cancellation of energy from a native radio. Interference is a fairly

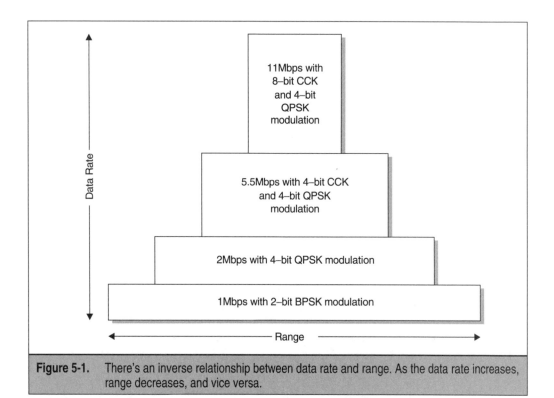

Figure 5-1. There's an inverse relationship between data rate and range. As the data rate increases, range decreases, and vice versa.

intuitive concept. Indeed, as listeners of commercial broadcast radio, we're likely to hear it on a regular basis. Interference is primarily other transmissions or emissions of radio energy that are at or near the same frequency as the sending and receiving devices—for Wi-Fi products, this means energy produced around the 2.4GHz frequency range. Some common sources of 2.4GHz interference, and the architectural means for working around them, will be covered in Chapter 9.

The specific ranges associated with each data rate and modulation type are subject to wide variations that are dependent upon environmental and radio design considerations (which will be covered in detail later in this chapter).

What Really Matters: Throughput

Having outlined the various data rates supported by the 802.11b standard that underlies Wi-Fi, and the modulation types that provide for these data rates, it now seems appropriate to advise, or at least remind, you that data rates have minimal relevance to the speed at which a file is sent from one point to another. The data rate represents the speed at which the entire packet, inclusive of transaction overhead, travels. Additionally, the data rate does not take into account transmission errors that are serious enough to result in a resend but not frequent enough to result in a shift to a lower data rate. Finally, the notion of data rate is applicable to the whole of the transmission medium, not to the individual user who is sharing this medium with all other users in the same cell or collision domain. In this section, we'll drill down from data rate into the throughput subset to gain a deeper understanding of real-world Wi-Fi performance and the various means of measuring it.

Overhead vs. Payload

With spacecraft, the cargo that is intended for destinations beyond the earth represent a tiny fraction of the total weight and mass of the rocket as a whole. Rather, the great majority of the bulk is *overhead*, the means to get the cargo where it's supposed to go. The satellite, experiment, or astronaut *payload* is a very small percentage of the total vehicle. Similarly, with Ethernet (whether 10Mbps Ethernet, 100Mbps Fast Ethernet, or the latest Gigabit Ethernet and 10Gbps variants) the data "cargo" is but a portion of the whole packet. Thankfully, the ratio for Ethernet is reversed from that of space vehicles: With Ethernet, the great majority of the packet, well over 80 percent, is the actual data being sent, with the rest comprising a relatively efficient packet header.

The ratio of transaction overhead to payload for Wi-Fi wireless LANs falls between spacecraft and Ethernet, although far closer to Ethernet. This should come as little surprise as the IEEE 802.11b standard for Wi-Fi is closely modeled on the IEEE 802.3 standard for Ethernet. The great majority of the throughput difference between Wi-Fi and Ethernet is due to the fact that the process of data transmission over radio frequencies is inherently more involved than transmission over a wire. Accordingly, a greater percentage of the whole data packet is taken up by transaction processing overhead, leaving less of the data rate remaining for actual data. To make the point, 10Mpbs Ethernet is considerably faster than 11Mbps Wi-Fi.

The specifications for these controlling functions that allow for data transmission and account for this overhead are, for the most part, defined within the Media Access Control (MAC) portions of the 802.11 standard. This MAC portion corresponds to the second layer (often referred to as Layer 2, or the data-link layer) of the OSI model, and is the layer immediately above the physical layer. The 802.11 MAC is applicable to all physical media and modulation types supported by the standard. This being the case, and all other things being held equal, the ratio between overhead and payload remains essentially constant as data rates increase. Rare, however, are the times when all other things are held constant. Rather, a multitude of things impact the throughput, which is the *actual* performance of the wireless LAN, including interference, multipath propagation, the means of medium access used, fragmentation thresholds, Request to Send (RTS) thresholds, short versus long headers, encryption, and the selection of vendor. We'll examine each of these in this section.

Interference

As was outlined in the previous section, the errors and resends caused by interference can result in a roam or shift to a lower data rate. However, for a Wi-Fi device to roam or rate shift, a relatively large number of errors must occur. Stated another way, a Wi-Fi device will maintain the same association or data rate while receiving errors until such time as the vendor-specified error threshold is reached and a roam or rate shift is initiated. Prior to this threshold being reached, the device will continue to resend packets. These resends have the effect of driving down throughput—the data rate remains the same, but the actual performance is diminished. Oftentimes, there is little difference between poor throughput at a higher data rate and good throughput at a lower data rate. As such, while shifts in data rate appear as a step function, abruptly dropping from one data rate to the next (from, say, 11 to 5.5Mbps), a decline in throughput tends to be a smoother curve.

Multipath Propagation

Multipath propagation is a specific type of event that can either prevent the receiving device from receiving sufficient levels of energy or, in certain cases, provide a type of energy convergence that greatly enhances the quality and amount of energy received at the receiving device. As a radio signal moves out, or *propagates,* from a sending device, it encounters various environmental obstacles, beginning with the medium of the atmosphere. Some of these obstacles act as barriers, absorbing the energy and effectively stopping the signal. Other types of obstacles reflect the signal in the same way as a mirror reflects light and creates a secondary image or a canyon wall reflects sound and creates an echo. In radio terms, these reflections or echoes are duplications, or *multiple paths,* of the same propagated signal.

The most commonly cited material that causes multipath propagation is metal. Metal can be found in walls. Obvious examples are the metal walls of airplane hangers and warehouses. A less obvious example is the steel reinforcing bars (rebar) found in concrete walls. Chain-link fences can, in certain circumstances, provide a highly effective barrier to radio energy. Filing cabinets and metal-backed whiteboards are common fixtures in most offices and amount to mirrors for radio waves. Certain types of tinted glass found in modern building windows have a high metal content and result in reflection, and with relatively low angles of incidence, are an excellent source for bouncing radio energy. Some materials can provide a relatively dynamic effect with regard to multipath, such as relatively smooth concrete that is wet. This same surface will produce dissimilar amounts of multipath when wet or dry.

You can actually observe the effects of multipath propagation on a television set receiving a broadcast signal. The "ghost images" that are all too common with broadcast television are the result of the television receiving, and then displaying, multiple versions of what started as a single signal. For Wi-Fi, these duplicate signals aren't ghost images, but "ghost signals," multiple versions of the same signal received at slightly different times. These duplicate signals mix in the radio and form a distorted signal that cannot be properly decoded into the data stream. This causes data to be resent. These additional transmissions take time, which decreases throughput.

Wi-Fi radios do, however, have the ability to identify some reflected signals as being duplicates and ignores them. However, radios are capable of making this duplicate packet identification only for a given period of time. This period of time is referred to as the *delay spread,* which is measured in some hundreds of nanoseconds and varies from manufacturer to manufacturer. The greater the delay spread, the longer the period that the radio can identify (and ignore) a duplicate signal and therefore not drive down performance though unnecessary processing. Not all vendors quote a delay spread period on their specification sheets. In general, the higher the delay spread number, the better the throughput, particularly in environments subject to a high degree of multipath propagation, although for indoor applications, this tends to deviate very slightly given that the energy travels at approximately the speed of light.

Medium Access Method

The most efficient means of transmitting on a network is a system whereby all devices have the ability to access the medium (transmit) when they need to, provided that they first sense the medium (listen) before they speak (send). In networking terms, this is referred to as Carrier Sense Multiple Access (CSMA). This access method was first popularized by Ethernet and is a well accepted and understood protocol. With Ethernet, added to CSMA is a means of detecting collisions or uncompleted transmissions, resulting in a complete protocol known as CSMA/CD (Collision Detection), which was first standardized in the 1970s as IEEE 802.3.

The 802.11 and Wi-Fi 802.11b standards borrow heavily from 802.3. The Distributed Control Function (DCF), far and away the most common means of medium access for Wi-Fi networks, is based on CSMA. However, due to the fundamental differences between a copper wire and radio frequencies, Ethernet-like collision detection is not possible. Rather, a wireless-specific protocol, Collision Avoidance (CA), is added to CSMA. When operating in DCF mode, which is based upon CSMA/CA, a device first senses the medium before transmitting. If that device encounters another device already transmitting, it will back off and wait to reattempt the transmission. To increase the likelihood that the next time it senses the medium it will be clear, the amount of time each device waits to sense again is generated on a random basis. The sending station will continue this process until it receives back an acknowledgement packet, or *ack*, from the destination station indicating that the packet has been received successfully.

Clearly, collision avoidance and the inherent random backoff periods and acknowledgements result in increased overhead relative to more simple collision detection—this is but one of many factors that result in a lower ratio of overhead to payload for Wi-Fi than for Ethernet.

One of the benefits of CSMA, and a principal reason for its success as a medium access method both for the dominant wired and wireless LAN technologies, is that it maximizes the performance of limited bandwidth. The protocol "empowers" each station on the LAN to send data when needed without a waiting for its turn, as is the case with Token Ring or with centralized polling protocols. The downside of this very democratic approach is that it is most fundamentally applicable to sending data—all stations on the LAN, and therefore all their traffic, are treated with equal priority. While this works well for data such as an e-mail message, a spreadsheet file, or web traffic, it tends not to work well when sending traffic with low *latency* requirements, like voice or video. A telephone call, for example, would sound choppy if the sending station lost its access to the medium while another station sent a packet or two of an e-mail message.

To address this, and to allow a CSMA LAN to carry data traffic as well as voice and video, various means of assigning priority, and thereby providing for some level of quality of service (QoS), have been developed both for wired and wireless LANs. All these approaches modify CSMA to varying degrees. The various standardized and proprietary means of providing QoS will be detailed in Chapter 12. In this discussion of performance, suffice it to say that because QoS requires greater overhead than the very efficient CSMA, the performance of the overall LAN will be reduced when any means of providing QoS is applied—it has the effect of increasing the performance of some stations and some packets at the expense of others.

Measuring Throughput

The keys to conducting a comparative analysis of the throughput provided by various Wi-Fi devices is to have a consistent environment and measuring tool that best approximates the real-world environment and requirements of the wireless LAN. The fact that Wi-Fi devices are fundamentally radios complicates the establishment of a consistent environment insofar as the amount of ambient interference can vary over relatively short periods of time and therefore vary throughput during the test cycle. When measuring throughput, it's advisable to find a facility that's not subject to noise around the 2.4GHz band from devices like cordless phones, microwave ovens, Bluetooth devices, and existing Wi-Fi LANs. At the same time, it's best to find a facility made from construction materials similar to those of the real-world facilities and one that has a similar floor plan.

A variety of tools for measuring network performance are available, with differing levels of depth and price points. TcpSpeed from Maximized Software (www.maximized.com) provides a base-level throughput test designed mostly to check wide area connections but applicable to wireless LANs as well. The price is right—it's a freeware download from the Maximized web site. An even more basic way of measuring throughput is to simply send File Transfer Protocol (FTP) "puts" and receive FTP "gets" of various sizes, and use utilities included with most operating systems to measure the transit time for each. Far and away, however, the most widely accepted tool for measuring throughput is NetIQ's (www.netiq.com) Chariot utility. Formerly from Ganymede Software, Chariot enables the evaluator to model traffic that is more similar to real-world traffic, inclusive of applications, SMTP (e-mail) traffic, HTTP (web browsing), and even Voice over IP (VoIP). This flexibility makes Chariot the hands-down favorite of independent testing laboratories and the review labs at various industry trade publications. The throughput measurements quoted in most trade publications' comparative reviews tend to be arrived at through Chariot testing.

Fragmentation Thresholds and Throughput

The 802.11 standard specifies that the size of a payload may range from 256 to 2312 bytes. Naturally, LAN traffic including audio and video files, presentations, and even relatively small web pages is far larger than 2.3 kilobytes (KB). These data packets must therefore be broken up into smaller chunks, or *fragments.* The larger the fragment, the greater percentage of the whole packet, inclusive of overhead, the payload will represent. As such, in general, the larger the fragment, the better the performance, because less bandwidth will be used for overhead. Most manufacturers by default set the fragmentation threshold to the maximum of 2.3KB.

Since the fragmentation threshold is defaulted to the largest possible fragment, it is by association set to the largest possible overall packet size, inclusive of both overhead and payload. You must remember that throughput is not so much about how many packets get sent, but rather how many packets are received—not all packets are received successfully. *The likelihood of a packet being received successfully is inversely proportional to its size*—over an inherently noisy medium like unlicensed radio frequencies, the larger the packet, the more likely it will be garbled by interference to the point that it cannot be read successfully by the receiving station.

In general, however, throughput is maximized when the packet size (defined by the fragmentation threshold) is maximized. In particularly noisy environments, throughput can be improved by decreasing the size of the packet, by decreasing the fragmentation threshold. Fragmenting a packet divides it up into smaller packets at the transmitting radio, sends it in several smaller packets across the RF, and reassembles it to its original packet content at the receiving radio. This smaller packet size causes the overall timeframe for each smaller packet being transmitted to be shorter, and therefore provides less opportunity for the packet to be corrupted by interference on the RF.

A classic example of a noisy environment is an airport, in which a large number of wireless devices commonly are in use. As Wi-Fi LANs become more popular, and as other devices that operate in the unlicensed 2.4GHz band (like cordless phones and Bluetooth devices) increase in number, almost any environment can become relatively noisy. This suggests that the optimization of throughput through adjustment of fragmentation thresholds is both a process of fine tuning through trial and error and a dynamic process that should be monitored periodically as the amount of noise and a particular environment changes. Understanding the impact of fragmentation thresholds and adjusting them when needed can provide a substantial improvement in throughput.

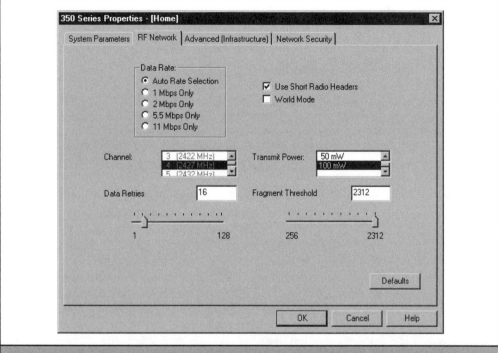

Figure 5-2.   Fragmentation thresholds can be manually set for the best possible throughput in varying environments.

Request to Send (RTS), Clear to Send (CTS), and Throughput

With wired CSMA LANs, you can assume that the sending station can hear all other stations with which it shares the common medium. With wireless LANs, you can assume only that all client devices (such as PCs and bar code scanners) can hear the access point and that the access point can hear all client devices. You *cannot* assume that all client devices can hear each other. There are a variety of reasons for this.

Suppose that a client device is at its maximum range and it is oriented at the 9 o'clock position relative to the access point in the center of the watch dial position. Suppose that another client device is similarly at its maximum range and is oriented at 3 o'clock on the opposite side of the dial. Both clients can hear the access point, but neither can hear the other. Another example is where clients are obstructed from each other by an object that is impenetrable to radio waves, such as the lead-lined walls that surround x-ray rooms in hospitals. This is referred to as the "hidden-node" problem. The problem is that the carrier sense portion of CSMA doesn't work when clients are hidden from each other and the clients will therefore access the medium simultaneously (send at the same time). This will create relatively large amounts of interference and drive down throughput.

The 802.11 standard addresses the hidden node problem with an optional feature called Request to Send/Clear to Send (more commonly, RTS/CTS). With RTS/CTS enabled, client devices (that potentially cannot hear their peers) first ask permission to send a data packet from the access point—the only device known by definition to be able to hear all other client devices on the network. The client does this by sending a relatively small RTS packet, which is encoded via BPSK modulation. The access point replies to the RTS packet with a CTS packet if it knows that no other station is sending at that time.

If the sending device is told to "standby," it'll wait for a specified period of time before sending another RTS packet. If the sending device is told to standby repeatedly, it will then send RTS packets at what are called random backoff intervals. The intent of this feature is to statistically enhance the probability of receiving a CTS packet from the receiving device. As shown in Figure 3, the data packet sizes that trigger the initialization RTS/CTS packets can be adjusted to best fit application and environmental requirements.

A commonly held misconception in 802.11 is that the clients that report to a root access point will all operate at the slowest speed selected by the clients. All clients can receive at the same speed, and in many, if not most, deployments, various speeds are utilized by various clients, mostly due to range and interference. In 802.11, specifically due to CSMA, both the slower- and faster-operating clients will have to wait until they receive a CTS packet. Once they receive this packet, the clients closer to the root device will normally operate at a faster speed on a per-packet basis, even though they might not be able to transmit while waiting for a slower-speed client to complete its transmission.

If other stations are sending, the access point does nothing at all and the client device that needs to send a packet will continue sending RTS packets until it receives a CTS packet in response, indicating that no other client is sending. The client will only then begin a transmission, ensured by the access point that the medium is indeed clear to send. As a brief aside, RTS/CTS is also under consideration as a means of allowing for mixed environments of Wi-Fi and upcoming 802.11g clients to interoperate without mutual interference. This topic will be covered in greater detail in Chapter 6.

In short, RTS/CTS is a fairly elegant way to solve the hidden node problem that is particular to wireless. It layers a means of centralized control atop the basic CSMA model. In so doing, however, it not only solves the hidden node problem but also introduces an entirely new packet type to the 802.116 traffic and another layer of overhead. In other words, there is a performance penalty paid when RTS/CTS is enabled. In summary, it should be enabled on an as-needed basis, because in the absence of hidden nodes, RTS/CTS introduces unnecessary overhead.

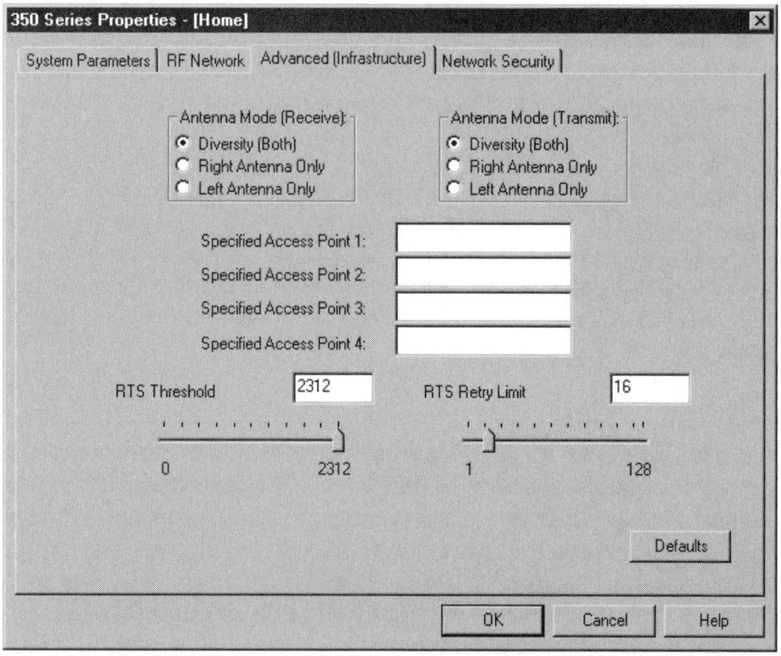

Figure 5-3. With some vendors, RTS thresholds can be set to varying packet sizes. The default tends to be the largest packet size possible, which is a good place to start.

In general, RTS should be enabled in the following scenarios:

- In deployments that are architected such that client devices are often at their absolute maximum transmission distance. In deployments where there is a greater density of access points to allow for higher data rates through CCK modulation, there is a decreased need for RTS/CTS, because the clients have a greater likelihood of being within listening range of each other. (More on architecting for higher data rates is provided later in this chapter.)

- In environments with a relatively large number of physical barriers that are impenetrable to radio frequencies. The classic example is the lead-lined walls of x-ray rooms, but any wall or similar divider within a given facility will block signals to varying degrees. (This topic too will be covered later in the chapter.)

The decision to enable RTS/CTS is not a binary one. Most Wi-Fi vendors that support RTS/CTS also allow the user to set the threshold (quantified in terms of packet size) at which an RTS packet will be sent first. In other words, because RTS and CTS packets are themselves overhead in some scenarios, it may be beneficial to simply send smaller packets and run the risk of simultaneous transmission without going through the RTS/CTS process. Similar to setting fragmentation thresholds, there is regrettably a fair bit of trial and error associated with this process.

The Short Header Option

The 802.11b standard includes an option to use a short header. This option decreases the size of the synchronization portion of the frame's overhead from 128 bits to 56 bits. While this represents a decrease by half, remember that this is but a small fraction of the total frame, inclusive of overhead and payload. Still, to optimize throughput, the short header option should be enabled, when available, in almost all cases. As it is an option, it is not guaranteed to be provided by all Wi-Fi vendors. Moreover, when provided, it cannot be guaranteed to be turned on by default. Consulting your vendor's documentation or searching through the device's setup software will indicate whether the short header option is available and how to control its on/off status. The only scenario where the short header option should not be enabled is in a mixed environment of 802.11- (1- and 2Mbps only) and 802.11b-compliant devices. As 802.11 devices were only produced circa 1997 through 1999 and in relatively small quantities, it is increasingly less likely that 802.11 devices will be present in a contemporary Wi-Fi LAN.

Encryption and Throughput

An option to the 802.11 standard provides for a fairly rudimentary level of security called Wired Equivalent Privacy (WEP). While one can argue whether this ambitious name is a misnomer, whether WEP really does make a wireless connection as secure as a wired one, this currently is the only ratified and interoperable encryption standard within 802.11. A new extension to the 802.11 standards, 802.11i, is in process and already vendors are beginning to release products that are compliant with the draft form of the standard. Wi-Fi security considerations will be covered in greater detail in Chapter 11; here, we will outline the impact security has on throughput.

Both WEP and the upcoming 802.11i standard provide for a means of *packet encryption* to secure the wireless link. With WEP, the keys used to encrypt these packets are static—they remain the same until someone manually changes them and the encryption key is shared by, and common to, all users on the LAN. With 802.11i, the encryption keys are dynamic; they are changed out on a regular basis, the frequency of which is specified by the network administrator. These keys are particular to the individual user, and it's important to note that the user will generally gain more security from increasing the rate at which the keys change as opposed to having a longer key that remains in use for a longer period of time.

While these two systems provide two very different levels of security and scalability, their impact on performance is essentially the same: *Encrypting and decrypting packets require processing power and bandwidth, which drives down throughput.* This is not to say that you should forego security to improve performance, because, in most cases, the trade-off is a reasonable one. Rather, you should be aware of this fundamental issue and plan for it.

The best way to plan for this is to select a vendor that plans for it as well. The processing required for encryption can be done by the processor on the device into which the radio is installed (host-based processing), such as the processor on an access point, the processor on a laptop, or, to make the point, the microcontroller on a bar code scanner. Encryption processing can also be done on the radio itself if that particular vendor chooses to incorporate an *encryption engine* into the radio's MAC.

When doing encryption processing on the host, the degree to which performance is degraded varies based upon the processing power of the various host processors and the processing loads that they are otherwise handling. Nevertheless, empirical testing with benchmarking tools (see measuring throughput) tends to report an approximate 25 percent reduction in performance when encryption processing is done on the host. When encryption processing is done on a radio-based encryption engine, there is less variance in the degree of performance degradation since this processor is dedicated to nothing but encryption processing. The reduction in throughput is also far less dramatic, averaging approximately 2 percent, a negligible amount that will essentially go unnoticed in real-world applications.

It's important to note that the encryption engine is dedicated both in terms of encryption processing being its only function and in terms of it being specifically designed to process a particular *encryption algorithm.* Today, encryption engines are designed to process the RC4 algorithm that is the foundation for WEP and the draft 802.11i standard. The 802.11i task group is currently considering the inclusion of a next-generation and more robust encryption algorithm called the Advanced Encryption Standard (AES) in its specification as an alternative to RC4.

AES is a U.S. Federal Information Processing Standards (FIPS) standard and specifically refers to FIPS Publication 197, which specifies a cryptographic algorithm for use by U.S. government organizations to protect sensitive, unclassified information. Security experts generally agree that this standard will rapidly be adopted on a voluntary basis by many commercial entities and Wi-Fi vendors.

An encryption engine that is designed for RC4 will provide no throughput benefit if packets are encrypted via AES. Various vendors, typically those that provide an RC4 encryption engine, are in the process of developing an encryption engine for AES. The need for this is even more acute than the need for an RC4 encryption engine, as AES requires a greater amount of processing than RC4. It is, however, possible that early vendor support for AES will be via host-based processing, resulting in a substantial trade-off between throughput and the additional security provided by AES relative to RC4—particularly when an RC4 encryption engine is available.

A common alternative to running either WEP or 802.11i security is to set up a secure, encrypted "tunnel" via a virtual private network (VPN). The overall advantages and disadvantages of this approach will be outlined in Chapter 11. With particular regard to throughput, VPNs have a fairly substantial impact. Most VPNs today use either the DES or 3DES (Triple DES) algorithm—not RC4. As such, even in the presence of an encryption engine, all processing will take place on the host. Because DES and certainly 3DES require a greater amount of processing to encrypt and decrypt packets than does RC4, the throughput degradation associated with running a VPN will exceed the throughput degradation when running RC4 (WEP or 802.11i) in the absence of an encryption engine. Here again, the degree of degradation will vary depending upon the performance of these host processors and their processing load, but in relative terms, the degradation in throughput will be greater when using a VPN than when using WEP or 802.11i. This difference is even more pronounced when VPN throughput is compared to WEP or 802.11i with encryption engine assistance.

Presuming that responsible network administrators will take security precautions inclusive of packet encryption, the selection of the means of encryption—whether host-based WEP or 802.11i, encryption-engine-assisted WEP or 802.11i, or a VPN—has a substantial impact on throughput. Naturally, vendor specification sheets and marketing literature for their Wi-Fi products typically do not provide a level of detail that includes information as to the presence or lack of an encryption engine and the algorithms supported. Additional research, inclusive of gathering data from third parties like industry trade publications, is necessary to understand the wide variations in *encrypted* throughput between products from different Wi-Fi vendors. Additionally, the decision to forego WEP or 802.11i security in favor of a VPN should not be made without first factoring in the impact encryption via a VPN will have on throughput relative to other solutions. Choice of encryption can have a major impact on throughput that will be noticed by Wi-Fi users.

The Bottom Line

As has been discussed throughout this chapter, numerous things can affect throughput, ranging from the environment to the choice of vendor to the way you configure various settings. Still, while it's a difficult question to answer with any degree of exactitude, it's not unreasonable to simply ask: "About how much throughput can I plan for?" The answer is that when operating at an 11Mbps data rate and transferring "typical" office network traffic like web browsing, e-mail, and attached files, throughput ranges from a low of around 4.5Mbps to as much as 6.5Mbps. In general, regardless of the data rate, you can expect that Wi-Fi throughput will be about half that of the data rate.

Vendor Selection and Throughput

The IEEE 802.11b specification defines the data rates for Wi-Fi devices. There is not, however, any 802.11 specification that defines a minimum level of throughput; indeed, as this section title suggests, throughput can and does vary greatly from manufacturer to manufacturer. This variance can be accounted for by the vendor's decision to support or not support options to the standard, like RTS/CTS or short headers, as well as the inclusion of features like an encryption engine in the MAC. The choice of other main components, like the base-band processor (otherwise referred to as a physical-layer controller or modem) or the radio chip set itself, goes a long way toward determining what level of throughput is possible. But even past all this, the throughput provided by a vendor can come down to design decisions that are difficult, if not impossible, for an end user to identify. The quality and performance of esoteric components like filters, oscillators, and amplifiers, the thickness of printed circuits boards, and the skill of the design engineer can all have an impact on throughput. None of this would be detailed in a specification sheet that a vendor releases to the public.

Given this, an end user is best advised to view a vendor's device as a closed system or black box and examine the output of the system. That is, an individual reviewing Wi-Fi offerings from various vendors should focus on the throughput provided, not the manner by which it is provided. Complicating this review is the fact that the majority of vendors don't report throughput in their documentation, and even if they did, the results would be subjective and suspect to the point of being essentially useless.

Rather, an end user should compare throughput values from various vendors only in *relative* terms. Various computer and networking trade publications, on a regular basis, conduct "round-up" or "bake-off" reviews of leading vendors. Quantified measurement of Wi-Fi throughput almost always accompanies these reviews. This measurement typically takes place in a controlled laboratory environment where the technician can hold constant external factors such as server and PC models, test software, interference, transmission distance, and testing methodology that can have a great impact on the measured throughput. To make the point, it is interesting to observe the wide variance in reported throughput for the exact same product from one review to the next.

In addition to trade publications, independent laboratories also conduct throughput testing and make the results available for a fee. They will additionally conduct custom testing, albeit for a greater fee. Given, however, the fairly large body of up-to-date data available from trade publications at newsstand prices, it is typically unnecessary to go to these extremes.

CAUTION   Vendors occasionally contract for comparative testing with "independent" third-party testing laboratories and publish the purportedly unbiased results. This data should be considered to be as objective as a vendor's specification sheet or similar marketing literature—not necessarily untrue, but certainly selected and delivered such that it puts that particular product in the best light possible.

While gathering comparative laboratory data from various independent sources is certainly better than looking only at product literature or doing no research at all, the best data is real-world data. The throughput for a Wi-Fi LAN is far more subject to situational variances than the throughput for a wired LAN. Environmental factors, including building materials, building design, particular architectures, and ambient interference, can all impact the throughput of a Wi-Fi device, which will vary on a vendor-by-vendor basis. In short, the most applicable comparative testing is the testing that is done in-house in a controlled environment that best approximates the real-world environment into which the Wi-Fi LAN is to be installed.

Going the Distance: Range

With wired Ethernet, the answer to the question of range is a fairly absolute one. As a matter of specification, you can locate an Ethernet client as far as 100 meters from a hub or a switch. Individuals, understandably, look for a similar specification with Wi-Fi or at least an absolute distance quantification from their vendor. Although there is no minimum specification for the distance from access point to client, the vendors typically provide not just one but as many as four range specifications. Vendors often quote the maximum distance that a client will maintain an association at 11Mbps in an "office" environment, at 11Mbps outdoors, and at 1Mbps both in an office and outdoors.

All of this information helps to get some approximation of how far you can expect to maintain a connection at a couple of data rates. It would be all the more helpful if these quoted range estimations were accurate.

The range for a Wi-Fi device is very dependent upon environmental factors, which is significant particularly for enterprise Wi-Fi deployments: Office environments can vary a great deal in terms of design and construction materials, which have a substantial impact on range. However, the distances quoted in a specification sheet represent the range achieved in as few as a single location.

There are, however, more objective measures that will allow you to make more meaningful comparisons when reviewing vendor specifications. In this section, we'll discuss transmit power, receive sensitivity, antenna gain, antenna diversity, and cable loss, all of which are elements that contribute to the range of a given Wi-Fi device.

Transmit Power

Transmit power is the most easily understood element of all the parameters that impact range. As listeners of broadcast radio, we know that some stations have stronger signals than others. College radio stations have little transmit power and, as such, are difficult to receive across town or even across campus. On the other hand, "pirate" radio stations with transmitters outside the jurisdiction of regulatory bodies like the FCC can blast their signal staggering distances by employing far more transmit power than allowed across the border. Transmit power can be thought of in very colloquial terms as the volume at which a radio can speak. The greater the transmit power, the louder the voice, and the greater the distance that the voice can be heard (all other things being equal).

While broadcast radio stations measure their transmit power in millions of watts (megawatts) and their signals travel tens of miles in all directions, Wi-Fi devices are measured in thousand*ths* of watts or milliwatts (mW) and their signals travel tens of feet.

A Wi-Fi silicon chipset will include, in addition to a MAC and PHY chip, a radio front end, which is typically referred to as an RF front end and a transmitter final. This collection of chips that makes up the transmitter and final typically provides for some level of transmit power in and of itself. Although it varies from chipset vendor to chipset vendor, contemporary chipsets provide for approximately 30mW of transmit power. Some vendors choose to add an additional component called a power amplifier (PA) to their design. This chip does just as its name implies—it increases the transmit power, albeit at the price of adding a small amount of cost to the design and increasing the amount of power consumed by the radio. With a PA, transmit power is typically increased to 100mW. All other things being equal, a 100mW radio transmits further than a 30mW radio, although not nearly by a factor of three as the numbers might suggest.

In addition to milliwatts, there is an alternative unit of measure for transmit power, one that is less used and not as easily understood, but one that better allows transmit power to be put in proper context of being just one element that defines range. This unit of measure is decibels (dB), which is more commonly associated with measuring sound—indeed, it's just another wave in the frequency spectrum.

Decibels express not just a power rating, but also the ratio of power or voltage in terms of gain or loss. Units are expressed logarithmically. dB is not an absolute value, but rather is the measure of power loss or gain between two valves. For example, –3dB indicates a 50 percent loss in power, and +3dB indicates a doubling of power. The rule of thumb to remember is that 10dB indicates an approximate increase (or loss) by a factor of 10; 20dB indicates an approximate increase (or loss) by a factor of 100; and 30dB indicates an approximate increase (or loss) by a factor of 1000. Gain or loss is expressed with a + or – sign before the number. Because antennas and other RF devices/systems commonly have power gains or losses that vary by multiple orders of magnitude, dB is a more easily used expression. For wireless LANs, dBm decibels relative to 1mw of power is the most common unit of measure.

The formula to convert transmit power in mW to transmit power in dBm is as follows:

Transmit Power (dBm) = 10 * log[Transmit Power (mW)]

In the real world, few people take the time to run this formula. Rather, it is more common to refer to a chart or memorize some common conversions:

Transmit Power in mW	Transmit Power in dBm
100	20
50	17
30	14
20	13
10	10
5	7
1	0

Receive Sensitivity

The notion of receive sensitivity is a bit more involved than transmit power. While transmit power can be thought of as being the volume at which the radio speaks, receive sensitivity can be thought of as how sharp the radio can hear. Receive sensitivity is a measurement of the weakest signal a radio can successfully receive and demodulate. Clearly, these abilities are equally important, because with a Wi-Fi radio, there is a continual requirement to both send and *receive* transmissions.

Receive sensitivity is measured in decibels just as transmit power can be. Think of a dB scale just as you would a thermometer. The value of 0 does not indicate nothing, or the absence of some value (such as $0), it is simply a placeholder (–10 degrees still has some value of heat). In radio power, both for transmitters and receivers, 0 is equal to 1mW or .001W. Likewise, a negative dBm reading such as –10dBm has an actual value of .0001W or .1mW as the minimum power value that a receiver can "hear." Receive sensitivity is typically measured in negative decibels. Because packets encoded with different modulation types have differing receive sensitivity requirements, receive sensitivity is data-rate dependent—as the data rate increases (as more stringent modulation types are employed), the receiving radio requires a stronger signal. So, while a radio may provide a receive sensitivity of –85dBm at 11Mbps, it could successfully demodulate a weaker signal, say –94dBm, if transmitting at just 1Mbps.

Ambient noise and signal strength can be quantified in terms of negative decibels as well. This ambient noise or interference is referred to as a *noise floor*. If the noise floor value exceeds the value of the received signal, the signal is lost in the noise and is not received. The difference between the noise floor and the signal is referred to as a *signal to noise ratio (SNR)*. For example, if the noise level in a facility is –125dBm (a relatively quiet facility) and the signal strength is –63dBm, the SNR would be 62dB, a very good SNR. On the other hand, in a fairly noisy environment with a noise floor at a much higher –80dBm with a fairly weak signal of –90dBm, the SNR is a negative number, the noise floor exceeds that of the signal, and the signal is unreceivable—the noise is "louder" than the signal. Naturally, the noisier the facility, the shorter the range. Many vendors specify the SNR necessary for properly receiving and decoding a signal for a given data rate. For 802.11 radios operating at 11Mbps, an SNR value of 10 to 20dB is common.

In much the same way as vendors choose to include a power amplifier to increase the transmit power of a radio, vendors can also choose to include a low noise amplifier (LNA) to improve receive sensitivity. So again, even vendors using the exact same chipset can provide for differing levels of receive sensitivity due to their individual design choices.

Antenna Gain

Almost as overlooked as receive sensitivity in terms of its impact on range is antenna gain. For an amplifier, "gain" is the ratio of the output amplitude of a signal to the input amplitude of a signal. This ratio is typically expressed in decibels. For an antenna, "gain" is the ratio of its directivity in a given direction compared to some reference antenna. The higher the gain, the more directional the antenna pattern.

When using a common unit of measure such as dB for transmit power, receive sensitivity, and antenna gain, it's plain to see that the gain of an antenna easily adds as much to the range performance of a system as can improvements to the radio itself, such as PAs and LNAs. Indeed, antenna gain is applicable to both the transmission and the receipt of a signal; changes in gain will have an equal effect on both sides of the link.

While the subject of antennas is treated in detail in Chapter 4, an antenna is specifically designed for a particular portion of the radio frequency spectrum with antennas designed for Wi-Fi systems tuned, of course, to the 2.4GHz band. While transmitting antennas are energized with the loading and release of electrons in a highly prescribed manner, receiving antennas are fundamentally passive devices that receive radio energy over a specific range of frequencies. It's important to note that most radios incorporate antennas that perform both transmission and reception. One of the other key functions antennas provide is that of gain, which in a basic sense is the ability to transmit and receive energy over a limited set of directions. With a perfectly theoretical antenna, a signal will radiate equally in all directions. This spherical *coverage pattern* is referred to as being *isotropic*.

A perfectly isotropic radiator does not exist in the real world; all radiators will have some degree, however small, of *directionality*. Nonetheless, the idea of an isotropic radiator is important in that it is the theoretical benchmark to which antennas can be compared. An isotropic radiator has no directionality and no antenna gain. Antenna gain is typically quantified in dBi (decibels compared to an isotropic radiator). Alternatively, antenna gain can be quantified in dBd, its gain in decibels relative to a common antenna type called a dipole, which itself typically has a gain of 2.14dBi. To convert from a dBd value to a dBi value, simply subtract 2.14 from the dBd value.

The ideas of gain and directionality are inexorably linked, and there is a direct inverse relationship between the two. As antenna gain increases, directionality, which is measured in degrees in terms of horizontal and vertical beamwidth, decreases. For example, an omnidirectional antenna, one that provides for a 360-degree horizontal beamwidth and something less than a 360-degree vertical beamwidth (the so-called donut-shaped coverage pattern), achieves its greater horizontal transmit and receive distance (its gain) by redirecting sideways energy that would have otherwise been going up and down.

There are a variety of antennas, each of which provides different trade-offs between gain and directionality, as outlined in Table 5-1. More information on the applicability of these antenna types to different enterprise deployments will be covered in Chapter 9.

Antenna Diversity

Simply put, a diversity antenna system is one that has two antennas, or two antenna elements attached to a single RF device, most commonly the receiving device. The type of diversity most commonly used with Wi-Fi LANs is spatial passive diversity. The purpose of having two antennas is not to double the gain, as indeed only one of the two diversity antennas (as used in the 802.11 arena) is ever operational at any given time. Rather, a diversity antenna system, inclusive of dual antennas and a radio capable of taking advantage of them, is designed to physically position the antenna in the best possible place to receive an incoming signal.

Antenna Type	Coverage Pattern	Approximate Horizontal Beam Width	Approximate Gain
Omnidirectional	Omnidirectional	360 degrees	Between 2 and 12dBi
Patch	Hemispherical	Between 60 and 80 degrees	Between 3 and 9dBi
Yagi	Directional	Between 20 and 40 degrees	Between 10 and 15dBi
Parabolic dish	Narrow beam	Between 10 and 20 degrees	Between 20 and 28dBi

Table 5-1. You can choose from a variety of Wi-Fi antennas to achieve different combinations of gain and beamwidth.

Diversity antennas for Wi-Fi devices are optimally spaced approximately four and a half inches from each other, approximately the same as the physical length of a radio wave with a frequency of 2.4GHz. Diversity antennas spaced closer than the length of the wave to be received will still provide benefit, albeit to a lesser degree. Having two antennas spaced apart from each other on a static device like an access point and selecting between the two based on the quality of the received signal has the same effect as repositioning a single antenna on a device like a car that is capable of movement. This, by the way, is also why it is far more important to have a diversity antenna system on an infrastructure device like an access point or a mounted antenna than it is on a mobile device like a laptop or PDA—either of the latter devices can be nudged a bit one way or the other to improve a signal. Besides, only a very small space between the antennas can be provided for on small form factors like PCMCIA cards. Similarly, diversity antenna systems are less important when all devices are static, as would be the case with an access point that is serving only desktop PC clients—the antennas can be optimally positioned and will remain in proper place.

The Bottom Line on Range

Similar to Wi-Fi throughput, determining range with any degree of exactitude is difficult due to vendor and environmental impact on it. Nonetheless, it's reasonable to look for an approximation, a range of ranges. A "typical" office environment, one that is relatively open and obstructed mostly by partial cubicle walls only rather than complete floor-to-ceiling walls, is the usual kind of facility used to make range approximations. Additionally, enterprise users of Wi-Fi tend to be more concerned with range approximations at the 11Mbps data rate than at the lower data rates more applicable to vertical market applications. Range approximations tend to be based upon the most standard antenna type, a 2.2dBi dipole antenna (sometimes referred to as a "rubber duck") that provides an omnidirectional coverage pattern. Based upon all of this, a fair range approximation is between 90 and 150 feet, with products from most vendors being closer to 90 feet than to 150. For "budgetary purposes," figure on about a 100-foot coverage radius. Remember, "Your mileage may vary."

Cable Loss

As will be detailed in Chapter 9, it is often desirable to have access points located in an easily accessed, centralized, and secure location (like a wiring closet) and then "cable out" to an antenna located in a place such as the middle of a ceiling that is both optimal from a radio perspective and difficult to reach from a human perspective. The convenience, elegance, and aesthetics of this mode of deployment come at a cost in terms of range.

Antenna cable for Wi-Fi devices is typically thick coaxial cable, similar in appearance, flexibility, and cost to the cable used for 10Base5 "Thicknet" Ethernet or cable television. Antenna cable is available from a variety of manufacturers, each of whom provides cable with differing loss characteristics. This cable loss is expressed in terms of dB per foot or a similar loss-to-distance ratio. Although manufacturer specifications vary, antenna cables are commonly divided into "low-loss" and "ultralow-loss" categories, with the former allowing for a loss of approximately 6.7dB per 100 feet and the latter a loss of about 4.4dB per 100 feet. From this, you can see that a long cable run, even when using ultralow-loss cable (which is more expensive and less flexible than low-loss cable) can easily negate most or even all gain provided by the antenna to which it's connected. A more detailed discussion of the pros and cons of using a centralized location of access points and remotely cabled antennas will follow in Chapter 9.

INTEROPERABILITY

With a technology like Ethernet, the idea of interoperability is fairly well understood and binary. Products from different vendors either work together or they don't, and far more often than not, they do interoperate. This is a function of the relative maturity of the standard, the completeness of this standard in terms of the functions demanded by customers (and provided by vendors), and the nature of the wired medium that it uses. The IEEE 802.11b standard that underlies Wi-Fi, unlike the IEEE 802.3 standard that underlies Ethernet, is far from mature and less than complete. Add to that the reality that transmission over radio waves is a more nuanced process than transmission over wires.

Still, you can and should expect that some level of interoperability exists between the more than 70 vendors who today are shipping over 300 different products compliant with the 802.11b standard. With Wi-Fi, interoperability is more a matter of degree than it is an absolute. Here are some reasons why:

- **The 802.11 standards have numerous options.**   Features discussed in this chapter, such as short headers, RTS/CTS, and even WEP encryption, are options to the standard. A vendor can rightly hold itself up as being fully compliant without providing these optional features. Due to the bidirectional nature of data communications, you must have either the same vendor or different vendors who support that particular option on both sides of the link to take advantage of the optional feature.

- **Numerous features demanded by enterprise customers are not yet standardized.**   In a perfectly interoperable world, one that in networking terms is approximated by Ethernet, all features required by all enterprise customers would be fully standardized and therefore fully interoperable. As detailed more completely throughout this book, various key features like QoS, scalable security, power management, and roaming have yet to be fully standardized. In the absence of a standard, and to respond to customer requirements, vendors deliver prestandard or proprietary implementations that do not provide for any degree of interoperability.

- **The legacy of wireless LANs is that of single-vendor solutions.**   Wireless LANs existed for more than a decade before the first standards were ratified in 1997. Businesses, products, and reputations were built during this period by providing a complete, albeit vertical market, solution from a single vendor. Changing this mindset is difficult—it is far quicker and certainly less frustrating for a vendor to simply deliver a feature required by a customer without first agreeing to the implementation of the feature with a collection of competitors. Proprietary systems also tend to be more profitable on a per-unit basis than systems that allow for the free substitution of components from competing vendors. In short, while all vendors publicly voice their support for standardization and the resulting interoperability, their actions sometimes speak louder than their words. This is particularly the case during periods of rapid market growth where a vendor can enjoy the rare confluence of high per-unit profitability and increasing unit volumes.

Despite all of these factors, you can expect a basic level of interoperability between vendors. Wi-Fi products from different manufacturers can be expected to work together, albeit not as well as products from the same vendor will work together. A multivendor system will tend to provide lesser throughput and range than a single-vendor system. It will provide for fewer security options and other features such as differentiating voice packets from data packets.

The Wi-Fi Alliance

No other organization has done so much to further the goal of complete interoperability of devices based on 802.11 standards as the Wi-Fi Alliance. Originally known as the Wireless Ethernet Compatibility Alliance, the group is responsible for the term "Wi-Fi" (which is meant to be a truncation of Wireless Fidelity) and, more importantly, independent testing to verify interoperability.

Founded in August 1999 by 3Com, Aironet Wireless Communications (now part of Cisco Systems), Harris Semiconductor (now Intersil), Lucent Technologies (later Agere and now part of Proxim Technology), Nokia, and Symbol Technologies, the Wi-Fi Alliance has grown to more than 150 members. Hundreds of products, ranging from bar code scanners to embedded modules, from residential gateways to enterprise access points, have successfully passed Wi-Fi interoperability testing and earned the right to carry the Wi-Fi label. This ensures customers of at least a base level of interoperability. Wi-Fi testing, currently conducted at the Agilent Technologies Interoperability Certification Lab, is fairly stringent. It's a testament to the challenges of designing a wireless LAN device that communicates via radio waves that vendors frequently fail testing and have to modify their products to meet the standard.

A customer implementing a multivendor Wi-Fi network is well advised to demand that all devices in the LAN have passed interoperability testing and verification and have received the Wi-Fi logo.

CHECKLIST

There's certainly a lot to understand when optimizing the performance and interoperability of your Wi-Fi wireless LAN. A complete knowledge of this is desirable, but often not practical. Here are some key points to remember:

- ☐ Trade-offs between performance and interoperability exist. Single-vendor networks tend to provide the best performance.

- ☐ Performance is an imprecise term. Data rate, throughput, and range have a lot more meaning and practical implications.

- ☐ The 802.11b standard for Wi-Fi products supports four data rates, 11, 5.5, 2, and 1Mbps.

- ☐ Throughput is what really matters when assessing network speed. It varies, based on a number of different factors. Still, you can roughly approximate Wi-Fi throughput to be about half that of the applicable data rate.

- ☐ There's an inverse relationship between data rate and range: As range increases, data rate decreases, and vice versa. A number of factors impact range.

- ☐ Interoperability between Wi-Fi devices is a matter of degree, not an absolute. All vendor features are not supported by other vendors. The Wi-Fi Alliance, with its test and certification programs, provides an assurance of a base level of interoperability for certified products.

CHAPTER 6

802.11a and 802.11g: High Performance Wireless LAN Standards

When the first products based on the 802.11b standard (then in draft form) began shipping in 1998, they were touted as providing an "Ethernet-like 11Mbps data rate." This statement was in the strictest sense true and, by associating the new technology with the established and well-respected Ethernet, a good marketing message as well. Referring to Wi-Fi as having an Ethernet-like 11Mbps data rate does, however, gloss over some inconvenient truths:

- 10Mbps Ethernet is faster than 11Mbps Wi-Fi. As discussed previously, the overhead associated with the 802.11b standard exceeds the overhead for 802.3 Ethernet, resulting in better throughput for 10Mbps Ethernet than for 11Mbps Wi-Fi.

- Today, most wired connections are switched, not shared. In addition to having a lower aggregate throughput than Ethernet, Wi-Fi is by nature a shared medium with the aggregate data rate divided among the number of users associated to a particular access point, essentially a wireless hub. With the advent of inexpensive, easy-to-manage Ethernet switches, it is today far more common for an individual client to be attached to a switched, rather than a shared, port and enjoy an Ethernet connection dedicated to just that user's requirements.

- Ethernet is largely obsolete. Even by the time Wi-Fi products began to ship, the 10Mbps standard had been largely supplanted by Fast Ethernet, the 100Mbps successor standard. While 10Mbps Ethernet still constitutes a substantial portion of the installed based, new (switched) connections to the client desktop are almost exclusively 100Mbps Fast Ethernet—if not 1000Mbps Gigabit Ethernet— the successor to Fast Ethernet.

The point is that users compare wireless performance to the performance of a typical wired connection. They will rightly perceive that Wi-Fi is at least a generation and an order of magnitude behind the predominant wired standard. The good news, however, is that in much the same way as wired technologies have moved forward, wireless standards too have been developed to provide a level of performance more in keeping with user's performance requirements and expectations.

The 802.11a and 802.11g standards are two *complementary* standards that provide for as much as a 54Mbps data rate—not quite Fast Ethernet, but substantially greater than 802.11b and much more applicable to today's (and tomorrow's) enterprise performance needs. As the letter *a* suggests, the ratification of the 802.11a standard actually predates the 802.11b standard (by approximately a half hour as it turns out). While the 802.11a standard has been ratified since 1999, it was only in late 2001 that the first 802.11a-compliant products first appeared on the market. 802.11g is estimated by the IEEE to be ratified in early 2003, with vendors developing products based upon the draft standard.

In this chapter, we'll detail the incremental differences between these standards and 802.11b, compare and contrast the two standards, outline which of the standards are best suited for particular applications, and, finally, show how on a practical level the standards are merging into a single high-speed offering that provides the best of all worlds.

ORTHOGONAL FREQUENCY DIVISION MULTIPLEXING

Like 802.11b, 802.11a and 802.11g provide for more than just a single data rate. Although they commonly are referred to as 54Mbps technologies, in fact, 802.11a and 802.11g provide for a variety of data rates. Indeed, the mandatory, or basic, data rates defined in the 802.11a standard are 6, 12, and 24Mbps—the highly touted 54Mbps data rate is an option. The reason for providing this selection is the same as for 802.11b—there's an inverse relationship between data rate and range, and the lower data rates specified in both 802.11a and 802.11g allow users to select the trade-off between the two that is most appropriate for their particular application.

Orthogonal frequency division multiplexing (OFDM) is a means of transmission and is the main point of commonality between 802.11a and 802.11g. Although there are options within the 802.11g draft standard that allow for alternative transmission types, it is widely believed that these alternatives will be little implemented and even more rarely deployed. As was detailed in Chapter 4, OFDM is a means of transmission that is particularly well suited for transmission over radio frequencies. OFDM is a transmission technique, just like Code Division Multiple Access (CDMA), which is used by certain kinds of mobile telephones, or direct sequence spread spectrum (DSSS), the means of spread spectrum transmission specified by 802.11b and used by 11Mbps Wi-Fi devices.

OFDM is fairly robust in terms of interference and multipath distortion and makes efficient use of a given amount of spectrum—more efficient use than DSSS. At first glance, *orthogonal frequency division multiplexing* appears to be little more than a collection of buzzwords, so deconstructing the term can help you to gain some level of understanding. With OFDM, a given range of *frequencies,* such as the 200MHz band located in the 5GHz portion of the radio frequency spectrum, is *divided* into separate channels, or *subcarriers.* When transmitting, these separate, or *orthogonal,* subcarriers are joined together, or *multiplexed.*

For both 802.11a and 802.11g, varying types of modulation are employed, each encoding an increasing number of bits per transmission to achieve higher data rates. As outlined in Chapter 5, the greater the number of bits encoded, the clearer the signal must be for the transmission to be successfully received and demodulated. Indeed, the receive sensitivity specified by 802.11a is between –82 and –65dBm, which, as outlined in Chapter 4, is a significantly stronger signal than that commonly received by 802.11b devices. With OFDM as applied to 802.11a and 802.11g, the higher orders of modulation, and associated data rates, pick up where 802.11b leaves off:

Data Rate in Mbps	Modulation Type	Number of Bits Encoded
6	BPSK	1
9	BPSK	1
12	QPSK	2
18	QPSK	2
24	16-QAM	4

Data Rate in Mbps	Modulation Type	Number of Bits Encoded
36	16-QAM	4
48	64-QAM	6
64	64-QAM	6

Note that with 802.11a and 802.11g, the binary phase shift keying (BPSK) and quadrature phase shift keying (QPSK) modulation types used for 802.11b are again employed, encoding one and two bits, respectively. However, with 802.11a and 802.11g, when using BPSK modulation, the data rate achieved is not 1Mbps, as is the case with 802.11b, but rather 6 or 9Mbps (depending upon the rate at which the encoding takes place). The difference between a 1 and 6Mbps data rate is attributed to the greater efficiency of OFDM relative to DSSS. Similarly, with 802.11a and 802.11g, QPSK modulation yields not the 2Mbps data rate as is the case with 802.11b, but rather 12 or 18 Mbps when transmitting via OFDM as specified by 802.11a and 802.11g.

Instead of using the complementary code keying (CCK) modulation type, as specified by 802.11b for higher data rates, 802.11a and 802.11g specify quadrature amplitude modulation (QAM), which encodes via both changes in phase (as is the case with BPSK and QPSK) and changes in amplitude. Remember from Chapter 5 that when encoding a single bit, two possible messages, or *symbols,* are possible (0 or 1). When encoding two bits, four symbols are possible. Working the exponential progression of this, when encoding four bits, 16 symbols are possible, and when encoding six bits, 64 symbols are possible. Thus, 16-QAM encodes four bits and provides for either 24 or 36Mbps data rates, depending upon the rate of encoding, and 64-QAM encodes six bits and provides for either 48 or 64Mbps data rates, depending upon the rate of encoding. As is the case with 802.11b, increases in data rate are achieved by modulating an increasingly larger number of bits, not by increases in bandwidth. And, as a greater number of bits are

PBCC: A Standard Skipped

Early versions of the 802.11g draft outlined an implementation of OFDM that was different from the implementation used by 802.11a. Even earlier versions of the draft defined the use of phased binary convolutional coding (PBCC), which is a nonimplemented option within the 802.11b standard. As the draft 802.11g standard reads today, the mandatory aspects of the standard include an implementation of OFDM that is identical to that of 802.11a. This is a major benefit for vendors, who can now better leverage existing 802.11a development directly to 802.11g. It also benefits users in that it leads to lower costs and earlier availability, and, as will be discussed in greater detail later in the chapter, allows for a more streamlined dual-band radio. The earlier 802.11g-specific implementations of OFDM and PBCC have both been relegated to options to the standard are expected to be little implemented by vendors and little deployed by users.

encoded (particularly a greater number of bits than are encoded by 11Mbps Wi-Fi devices), the price paid for the higher data rates provided by 802.11a and 802.11g is figured in terms of range.

DIFFERENT BANDS, DIFFERENT BENEFITS

While 802.11a and 802.11g share a common means of transmission and modulation, the similarities essentially end there. 802.11a is defined as operating in various bands within the 5GHz portion of the radio frequency spectrum (the specific bands varying on a geographic basis due to local regulations for unlicensed operation). 802.11g, meanwhile, operates in exactly the same 2.4GHz band as does 802.11b. These different bands provide very different benefits for each of the technologies, and also result in differing shortcomings and resulting implementation challenges.

When the wireless LAN industry began the transition from 900MHz to 2.4GHz in the mid-1990s, many underestimated the challenges associated. While the benefits of operation in 2.4GHz relative to 900MHz were well understood (international operation and a greater number of available channels), the peculiarities of 2.4GHz tended to be less well defined by vendors. The same, of course, holds true for the transition from 2.4GHz to 5GHz operation. Understanding the aspects of this is key to arriving at an appropriate strategy for migration to 5GHz.

The 5GHz Band

In the most general of terms, the benefits and drawbacks associated with operation in the 5GHz portion of the frequency spectrum are not a matter of the laws of physics but rather the laws of a force nearly as powerful as the physical universe: governmental regulatory agencies. That said, the 5GHz waveform does provide some advantages and disadvantages relative to the 2.4GHz waveform.

As was mentioned in Chapter 5, to the degree that microwave ovens transmit (leak energy that should be going into food or at least staying inside the oven), they transmit in the 2.4GHz band. This begs the question: Why is it that microwave ovens are tuned to 2.4GHz? The answer is that 2.4GHz waves are optimally captured by water. Microwave ovens cook by trapping these waves, which creates heat and thereby heats up a burrito. Tuning microwaves to transmit waves at a 2.4GHz frequency makes these devices as efficient as possible.

As almost any high school student knows, the human body is over 90 percent water, making human beings just as efficient at stopping a 2.4GHz wave as is the aforementioned burrito. A 5GHz wave is about half the length of a 2.4GHz wave. These shorter waves tend to pass through water with less attenuation than the longer 2.4GHz wave. While this might be something of a disturbing thought (the safety aspects of wireless LANs will be detailed in Chapter 7), what it means is that in areas with a high density of people, such as a stock trading floor, devices like 802.11a wireless LANs that operate at 5GHz will tend to have an advantage in terms of signal propagation and resulting range over devices like 802.11b wireless LANs that operate at 2.4GHz, the same general waveform as that of a microwave oven.

The relatively shorter 5GHz wave that provides the advantage previously outlined also leads to a principal disadvantage of 802.11a relative to 802.11b. The aforementioned scenario not withstanding, *an inverse relationship exists between wavelength and range.* This relationship should not be considered to be linear—although the 5GHz wave is approximately half the length of the 2.4GHz wave, one should not assume that this will alone cut range in half. Still, the relationship is absolute and significant. Additionally, the shorter 5GHz wave tends to be captured to a greater degree than the 2.4GHz wave by common building materials like concrete and drywall. The 5GHz wave is more prone to create multipath propagation than is a longer, 2.4GHz wave. All the issues associated with the relatively shorter 5GHz wave, coupled with the range implications of higher data rates, lead one to conclude that with 802.11a relative to 802.11b, there is a sort of "double whammy" on range.

The specific regulatory aspects of international operation in the 5GHz portion of the frequency spectrum will be detailed in Chapter 7. However, given that the regulations that pertain to 5GHz operation are so central to the benefits and drawbacks of 802.11a, they will be outlined generally here.

802.11a operates in unlicensed bands in exactly the same way as 802.11b and earlier 900MHz systems operate in unlicensed bands. That is, there are no restrictions on the types of devices that operate in these bands, provided that they all conform to a common set of rules. The 900MHz portion of the spectrum was initially used by wireless LANs and then, far more commonly, by cordless telephones. Although these devices all complied with applicable regulations, they acted upon each other as interferers, mutually degrading performance and usability. Ultimately, the wireless LAN industry essentially abandoned the 900MHz band and migrated to the 2.4GHz band.

Initially, the wireless LAN industry essentially had sole use of the 2.4GHz band (unless one counts microwave ovens as transmitting devices). Eventually, however, the band became crowded with an increasing number of 802.11 products, the possibility of an explosion of Bluetooth devices, and 2.4GHz cordless telephones. The attractiveness of the 2.4GHz band to manufacturers, license-free operation on an international scale and the resulting worldwide marketability for 2.4GHz devices leads to a central problem for the 2.4GHz band—overcrowding. This in turn leads to a principal advantage of 802.11a—because it operates in the more pristine 5GHz band, it has less interference from other devices.

802.11a products themselves are relatively few in number. Bluetooth operates in the 2.4GHz band, and only a few 5GHz cordless telephones currently are on the market. The point is that although today the 5GHz band is relatively "clean," there are no restrictions on this band that don't apply equally to 900MHz and 2.4GHz. Over time, the 5GHz band could become equally crowded with interference-causing devices.

In many countries, a larger portion of the frequency spectrum has been allocated for unlicensed operation in 5GHz than in 2.4GHz. As an example, in the United States and other countries that subscribe to FCC regulations, a total of 300MHz has been set aside for unlicensed operation. The 802.11a specification is designed to take advantage of 200MHz of this allowance. This compares to the 83 MHz set aside in 2.4GHz, which is used by both 802.11b and 802.11g. 802.11a devices allocate this 200MHz into eight channels, each of which is 25MHz wide, which compares to the three 22MHz–wide non-overlapping channels used by 802.11b and 802.11g.

There are two main advantages to having a greater number of channels to work with, the specifics of which will be detailed in Chapter 9. These advantages come down to channel reuse and capacity. Understanding that in enterprise deployments, more than one access point is typically installed in a given area, it follows that the greater number of channels to select from, the easier it is to architect a wireless LAN such that no two adjacent access points are set to the same channel. This is important in that the traffic from devices in overlapping cells set to the same channel results in mutual interference, which drives down performance. With just three channels in the 2.4GHz band used by 802.11b and 802.11g, this represents a shortcoming that complicates deployments. With eight channels typically available in the 5GHz bands (depending upon local regulations), channel reuse is rendered a non-issue for 802.11a.

The availability of a greater number of channels not only makes wireless LAN architectures more straightforward, but also provides greater network capacity. Because wireless LANs are, by their very nature, a shared medium, with each client vying for access to the medium, the greater the number of users contending for a given amount of bandwidth, the lesser the performance on a per-user basis. One means of addressing this issue (which will be discussed in greater detail in Chapter 9) is to divide a given number of users across a larger number of media. In Ethernet terms, this means dividing users into a larger number of *collision domains* through increasing network segmentation and the liberal use of Ethernet switches. The terminal state for this process is switching to the desktop whereby each client has its own segment, resulting in but a single user in a given collision domain.

With wireless LANs, switching is today an impossibility, as the technology's physical layer is radio waves. If, however, one takes the definition of switched Ethernet to be a state where there is a single user per collision domain, one can come to approximate "switched wireless" and thereby approach the performance advantages inherent in a switched architecture. With wireless, channels stand in for switched segments. Therefore, the greater the number of channels, the greater the number of segments across which a given number of users may be divided. As the number of users per channel or collision domain approaches one, the architecture approaches a switched architecture. For the purposes of illustration (and putting aside the issues of physical deployment and user count, detailed in Chapter 9), the following table lists the capacity for the various standards, which is derived by multiplying the maximum data rate by the number of channels:

Standard	Maximum Data Rate	Number of Channels	Capacity
802.11b	11Mbps	3	33Mbps
802.11g	54Mbps	3	162Mbps
802.11a	54Mbps	8	432Mbps

Again, this is an oversimplification that doesn't take into account the difference between data rate and range. Nor does it take into account the physical or financial practicality of architecting either an 802.11g or 802.11a wireless LAN for 54Mbps performance given the fairly limited range. It is not meant to suggest that a single user could enjoy a dedicated "pipe" providing a 432Mbps data rate. What it does illustrate is that the number of channels available has a huge, multiplying impact on capacity, and that (as a matter of arithmetic) channels have as great an impact on network capacity as the data rate.

In theory (not necessarily in practice), an 802.11a wireless LAN could be architected such that each of eight users is associated with a dedicated access point, each of which is set to one of eight channels. These lucky users would each enjoy a dedicated segment capable of providing up to a 54Mbps data rate. Multiplying the number of channels (eight) by the maximum data rate (54Mbps) and then dividing by the user count (eight) yields 54Mbps—roughly analogous to a switched 54Mbps segment. With 802.11g, these same eight users would share three access points, each set to one of three available channels, each of which is capable of up to 54Mbps. Multiplying the number of channels (three) by the maximum data rate (54Mbps) and then dividing by the user count (eight) yields 20.25 Mbps—a significantly smaller amount of bandwidth.

While the regulatory aspects of operation in the 5GHz bands have a positive effect on channel reuse and capacity, they have a negative effect on range. Again, these regulations vary on a geographic basis, which will be detailed in Chapter 7. Still, there is enough commonality with respect to 5GHz regulations around the world to assert in general terms that the laws of various regulatory bodies, coupled with the laws of physics, severely impact the range of 802.11a devices when compared to 802.11b and even 802.11g devices.

As was detailed in Chapter 5, transmit power is one of the characteristics of a radio that can impact range. In general terms, the greater the amount of transmit power, the greater the range of a device (although with the current generation of 802.11a radios, increased transmit power can have the counterintuitive effect of decreasing range when modulating at 64-QAM, due to the greater transmit power distorting the signal to the point of transmission failure). Given the laws of physics that work against range in 5GHz relative to 2.4GHz, a reasonable person would assume that regulators would allow for greater transmit power in the 5GHz ISM bands than in the 2.4GHz ISM bands. A reasonable person would, of course, be wrong.

Rather, although transmit power allowances vary depending upon geography and the specific band in the 5GHz portion of the spectrum, transmit power allowances in 5GHz are *less* than they are in 2.4GHz. While it is common for 802.11b devices operating in the 2.4GHz band to feature as much as 100mW or 20dBm of transmit power, FCC regulations that apply to the portion of the frequency spectrum used by the bottom four channels of 802.11a restrict transmit power to no more than 40mW or 15dBm. Just when transmit power is needed most to compensate for relatively shorter wavelength and more involved modulation types, regulatory bodies restrict its use.

As was also detailed in Chapter 5, antenna gain and antenna coverage patterns have a huge, but often less well understood, impact on range. It was illustrated that antenna gain can have as great an impact on range as transmit power or receive sensitivity. Here again, at least with respect to the many countries that subscribe to FCC regulations, governmental bodies have impacted range and complicated installation. Whereas in 2.4GHz, one can select from a variety of auxiliary antennas attached to the transmitting device either directly or via a cable, in at least a portion of the band used by 802.11a, the regulatory mandate is that the antenna and the transmitting device must be "integral."

Manufacturers are obligated to sell only 802.11a products (which utilize the bottom four channels) that have antennas directly attached to, and not removable from, the device itself. Given inventory considerations, among others, this means that while a manufacturer may provide a dozen or so differing antenna types for 802.11b devices operating in the less restricted 2.4GHz band, they are likely to offer no more than one or two different antenna types for 802.11a devices that operate in part in the more restricted band. The option of centrally locating access points and cabling out to a remote antenna is removed, as is the option of providing the device a protective enclosure.

Naturally, in addition to restricting transmit power and antennas to only integrated types, the FCC has restricted antenna gain as well. At the maximum transmit power of 40mW or 15dBm, antenna gain when using the bottom four channels of 802.11a is restricted to no more than 6dBi of gain. To put this all into perspective, the combination of transmit power and antenna gain (effective isotropic radiated power, or EIRP) for the bottom four channels of 802.11a is restricted to 21dBi. For 802.11b *and 802.11g* devices that operate in the 2.4GHz ISM band, the EIRP limitation is 36dBi—and remember that this scale is logarithmic, not linear.

The Bottom Line on 802.11a Range

One must always place a number of caveats on any estimation of range, particularly with a relatively new technology. Physical environment, choice of vendor, and network architecture will always impact range. Still, users look for some range estimate, often for budgetary purposes. In indoor office environments that are fairly open, and assuming omnidirectional antennas, one can expect something on the order of a 60-foot range of coverage when transmitting at the maximum 54Mbps data rate. When transmitting at the 6Mbps minimum data rate, indoor range can be expected to be around 170 feet. As was mentioned before, your mileage may vary.

Finally, as was suggested, FCC regulations do allow for higher transmit power, higher antenna gain, and auxiliary antennas in the upper four channels used by 802.11a devices. At this point in the early days of the evolution of 802.11a products, however, only a few manufacturers are delivering products designed for exclusive use on these less restricted upper four channels. These devices sacrifice one of the principal benefits of 802.11a—the relatively large number of channels and resulting increased capacity and simplified channel reuse. Most vendors typically provide a single 802.11a product line, one that must comply with the "lowest common denominator" of regulations, meaning devices with integrated, nonremovable antennas with no more than 6dBi of gain. Some vendors do provide the option of higher transmit power when the access point is set to the upper four, less restricted channels—an improvement but one that complicates network architecture. The specifics of the worldwide regulations for 802.11a devices will be covered in Chapter 7, while a discussion of wireless LAN architectures, inclusive of those for 802.11a devices, will be covered in Chapter 9.

Higher 802.11a Data Rates than 54Mbps?

Well yes, sort of. Some manufacturers of 802.11a devices provide a "Turbo Mode" option that provides for 72 or even as much as 108 Mbps data rates. The attractiveness of this is obvious—even at 54Mbps, wireless LANs are still significantly behind common wired data rates, to say nothing about the shared (verses dedicated) aspect of wireless LANs. These vendors achieve this through a process of "channel binding," where two channels are essentially multiplexed, providing the aggregate data rate of these two channels. Binding two channels, each providing a 36Mbps data rate, yields 72Mbps, and binding two channels providing the 802.11a maximum data rate of 54Mbps yields 108Mbps (and enables the manufacturer to tout data rates greater than those of Fast Ethernet!). Although there is some benefit to channel binding, the benefit is more limited than one would expect at first blush, for several reasons:

- You sacrifice half the 802.11a channels, because you're binding together two channels, resulting in a total of four channels (in FCC countries). This brings the number of available channels down to nearly that of the 2.4GHz band.

- Channel binding is *not* part of the 802.11a specification, meaning that by implementing this feature, you lock yourself into a single-vendor solution in terms of both access points and (worse) all client-side radios.

- The design of the 802.11 MAC (that's common to 802.11a, b, and g) is such that after approximately 54Mbps data rates, the ratio between data rate and throughput begins to change. While at data rates up to 54Mbps, throughput tends to be approximately half the data rate (or around 26Mbps, depending upon how it's measured), after 54Mbps, increases in throughput begin to approach zero. To quantify, the highest amount of throughput one can possibly expect, even when set to the 108 Mbps Turbo Mode, is 30 Mbps—well less than half the 108 Mbps data rate. The throughput one can expect at 72 Mbps is approximately 26Mbps, which can be achieved with a single channel when set to the standard and interoperable 54Mbps data rate.

Thus, users will have to decide if, for their particular application, the modest benefits of Turbo Mode outweigh the costs in capacity and interoperability.

The 2.4GHz Band

Simply put, the benefit of 802.11g is higher performance with backward compatibility. As discussed previously, 802.11g uses the same transmission type and modulation as 802.11a and therefore supports the same data rates. In addition, the draft 802.11g specification also mandates that 802.11g devices support the DSSS transmission type and the BPSK, QPSK, and CCK modulation types of 802.11b. This requirement, coupled with the fact that 802.11g operates in the same 2.4GHz frequency band as 802.11b, provides for this backward compatibility.

802.11a proponents have tried to hold up 54Mbps 802.11a as a successor technology to 11Mbps 802.11b in much the same way that 100Mbps Fast Ethernet was a successor technology to 10Mbps Ethernet—essentially replacing the technology in a short period of time. The analogy has a central flaw: One of the key benefits of Fast Ethernet is its backward compatibility to Ethernet, allowing customers to migrate to the technology at their own pace with a mixed (and interoperable at the 10Mbps data rate) environment of Ethernet and Fast Ethernet devices. Indeed, today, more than five years after the introduction of Fast Ethernet, it's not uncommon at all to find legacy 10Mbps Ethernet devices in use in otherwise Fast Ethernet LANs.

802.11a does not support the 802.11b transmission type and modulation and operates in a wholly separate band from 802.11b. It therefore does not provide for backward compatibility to 802.11b. To overstate the point for the sake of illustration, 802.11a is to ATM as 802.11b is to Ethernet, rather than 802.11a is to Fast Ethernet as 802.11b is to Ethernet. That is, 54Mbps 802.11a does indeed provide a relatively high data rate, just as 155 Mbps ATM does. ATM did not, however, supplant Ethernet, as many proponents of the technology claimed it would. And one of the principal factors for this failure of ATM to go mainstream is a lack of backward compatibility to Ethernet.

Instead, Fast Ethernet, a technology that provides a slower data rate with less throughput and no deterministic protocols for quality of service, became the successor standard to Ethernet. Although there were a number of factors behind this, backward compatibility was principal among them.

As 802.11g operates in the 2.4GHz band, all the physics and essentially all the international regulations that apply to 802.11b apply to 802.11g. With 802.11g available today only as a draft standard and with no products actually shipping, it's difficult to discuss with absolute accuracy a real-world operating factor like range. That said, the known factors that apply and that require only a small leap of faith suggest that 802.11g range will be greater than that of 802.11a. Because it transmits in 2.4GHz, 802.11g takes advantage of the relatively longer waveform and, as such, will carry further than the 5GHz 802.11a waveform, all other things being held equal. All other things are not, however, held equal. Although they vary around the world, 2.4GHz regulations (detailed in Chapter 7) generally allow for greater transmit power than what is allowed for the 802.11a 5GHz bands. Moreover, the same relatively high antenna gain allowed for 802.11b devices is allowed for 802.11g devices.

With 802.11g, and unlike 802.11a, there are no inconvenient and limiting restrictions as to antenna and device integration. Just as with 802.11b, one can select from various antenna types (refer to Chapter 5) and either connect them directly to an access point or place them remotely, connecting to the access point via a cable. Because 802.11g operates in the same portion of the frequency spectrum as 802.11b, *802.11g uses the exact same antennas as 802.11b*. This means that although 802.11g is a new technology, indeed one that is not yet even shipping, it will launch with a very complete and varied line of antennas available, one that was built up over the course of years for 802.11b and even earlier 802.11 devices. This also means that users may well be able to leave in place 2.4GHz antennas and cables already installed for 802.11b and simply replace 802.11b access points with 802.11g access points, which significantly reduces the cost of an installation in terms of both labor and equipment costs.

Along with the key feature of backward compatibility, however, comes the key drawback of 802.11g. Because it operates in the same 2.4GHz band as does 802.11b, it is subject to the capacity and interference shortcomings of 802.11b. The 2.4GHz band allows for just three channels, as opposed to the eight 5GHz channels available in many countries. The 2.4GHz band is crowded (and getting more crowded by the day) with 802.11b devices and cordless telephones and potentially with Bluetooth devices. Some, particularly those who are partisan to 802.11a, have sneered that the 2.4GHz

What about HiperLAN2?

Although 802.11a has been maligned by at least one party as being the wireless analog to ATM, the technology that really best fits this analogy is HiperLAN2. This high-speed wireless standard operating in the 5GHz portion of the frequency spectrum enjoyed the support of leading technology companies like Ericsson, Motorola, Nokia, Panasonic, and Sony. The powerful European regulatory body, ETSI, specifically designed regulations with HiperLAN2 in mind and to the detriment of 802.11a. Nevertheless, as a wireless LAN technology, HiperLAN2 is essentially dead. A few vendors have gamely displayed prototypes and have tried to position it as a consumer technology, but HiperLAN enjoys little support by the wireless LAN community. Although one can debate the reasons for this, most would agree that they include the fact that it was relatively difficult to implement, based in large part on—ATM.

band is a "garbage band" littered with radio interference. A high-speed technology, and the increased adoption that it promises, can only further this.

Although 802.11g (as defined by the draft standard) uses the same means of transmission as 802.11a and provides the same data rates, it is likely that, in practice, it will not provide for as great throughput as 802.11a. This is understood to be the case even holding aside the issues of interference in the 2.4GHz band, which of course would result in decreased throughput due to transmission errors and associated retries. Because the draft standard requires 802.11g radios to interoperate with both other 802.11g radios and 802.11b radios, they must assume some legacy 802.11b definitions—when operating on a mixed 802.11b and 802.11g environment when interoperating 802.11b with other 802.11g radios. As an example, the draft 802.11g standard calls for packet resend intervals that are based on 802.11b intervals, which are longer than the intervals required when transmitting via OFDM. Naturally, the 802.11a standard, which supports only OFDM, calls for only the shorter resend interval and therefore provides for better throughput.

A Dual-Band, Tri-Mode Solution

Throughout this chapter, the benefits and the drawbacks of both 802.11a and 802.11g have been discussed. Some benefits are common to both the technologies—both share OFDM transmission, which yields far higher performance than 802.11b, although to varying degrees. Due to the inverse relationship between data rate and range, both 802.11a and 802.11g will provide lesser range than 802.11b, although 802.11g is understood to likely have a slight range advantage relative to 802.11a.

RTS/CTS and "Hidden" 802.11g Nodes

In Chapter 5, the Request to Send/Clear to Send feature was discussed, outlining how this system added a level of centralization to the otherwise decentralized CSMA/CA media access protocol. It's assumed that an access point can hear all clients but that all clients cannot hear each other. This applies when clients are separated from each other by physical barriers like walls. It also applies when clients are separated from each other by barriers like different generations of technology.

Assume that an access point is compliant to 802.11g and therefore can hear both 802.11g and 802.11b clients. Assume further that there is a mixed cell with both 802.11g and legacy 802.11b clients associated to the same access point. The 802.11g clients can hear each other as well as the access point and therefore will not transmit simultaneously—they'll sense the media before sending and hear other 802.11g clients. The 802.11b clients can hear other 802.11b clients and the access point (which communicates with the 802.11b clients via DSSS) but not 802.11g clients, which send traffic to the 802.11g access point via OFDM. The 802.11g clients are, in effect, hidden from the 802.11b clients. Technically speaking, this is the same hidden node problem as is generated by physical barriers. The RTS/CTS solution to the hidden node problem is therefore an applicable solution to the problem of mixed 802.11b and 802.11g client cells.

But a great number of the advantages and disadvantages of the technologies are complementary. 802.11a, operating in the relatively large and pristine unlicensed 5GHz bands, provides a large number of channels and resulting capacity and, for at least the foreseeable term, relative freedom from other interfering devices. 802.11g, supporting legacy devices through backward compatibility, protects the investment users have made in 802.11b devices and allows for a much smoother migration path to higher data rates that can be implemented incrementally and as resources and budgets allow. Table 6-1 outlines the complementary advantages and disadvantages of the technologies.

Through a combination of both 802.11a *and* 802.11g, you can achieve the best of both worlds, one that maximizes capacity, allows for backward compatibility, and delivers the benefit of performance on the user's schedule, not the industry's schedule.

Vendors are aware of this. Dual-band (supporting both 2.4GHz and 5GHz operation), tri-mode (supporting 802.11b, 802.11a, and 802.11g) devices are well understood by the industry to represent the "promised land" for 802.11 wireless LANs. Regrettably, the combination of 802.11*b*, 802.11*a*, and 802.11*g* spells out B-A-G, leading to the almost inevitable reference to this fully integrated device as being the "bag" radio—it is, however, no worse than popular industry references for other acronyms, like "skuzzy" for SCSI and "gooey" for GUI.

The architecture of both 802.11a and the current 802.11b radios discussed in Chapter 5 allow for the fairly rapid development of a dual-band, tri-mode radio. The 802.11 media

	802.11a	802.11g
Performance	**Advantage:** OFDM only, 5GHz band, and lack of mixed cells provides better throughput	Disadvantage: Support for the legacy standard, mixed cells, and operation in potentially crowded 2.4GHz band likely to result in slightly less throughput than 802.11a
Capacity	**Advantage:** With eight channels, 802.11a provides for a theoretical aggregate capacity of 432Mbps (54Mbps multiplied by eight channels)	Disadvantage: With just three channels, 802.11g provides for a theoretical aggregate capacity of 162 Mbps (54Mbps multiplied by three channels)
Range	Disadvantage: Shorter wavelength and regulatory restrictions on transmit power and antenna gain work against 802.11a range	**Advantage:** Although 802.11g will not provide the same range as 802.11b due to higher data rates, the physics and regulations in the 2.4GHz band allow for greater range than when operating in the 5GHz band
Interference	**Advantage:** 802.11a wireless LANs operate in the relatively large and as yet uncrowded, unlicensed 5GHz bands	Disadvantage: The 2.4GHz unlicensed bands are relatively small and becoming crowded with wireless LANs, cordless telephones, and potentially, Bluetooth devices
Migration	Disadvantage: Operating at 5GHz and supporting only OFDM transmission, 802.11a provides no backward compatibility to 802.11b devices	**Advantage:** By operating in the legacy 2.4GHz band and supporting DSSS, 802.11g provides the key feature of backward compatibility to 802.11b
Installation flexibility	Disadvantage: FCC regulations that apply to the bottom four 802.11a channels restrict vendors to integrated, nonremovable antennas only	**Advantage:** Just like 802.11b, auxiliary 2.4GHz antennas, either directly connected or connected to cables, are allowed for 802.11g
Worldwide operation	Disadvantage: Operation in FCC countries and Japan, but uncertainty in Europe	**Advantage:** License-free operation on an essentially worldwide basis

Table 6-1.   In summary, the advantages and disadvantages of 802.11a and 802.11g are complementary. Both technologies can be deployed to achieve maximum benefit.

access controller (MAC) is common to all 802.11 technologies. The function of the physical layer controller (PHY) is essentially to modulate and demodulate, and is, at a conceptual level, indifferent to the transmission frequency of the radio front end to which it interfaces. The 802.11b PHY supports DSSS transmission and BPSK, QPSK, and CCK modulation types. The 802.11a PHY supports OFDM transmission and BPSK, QPSK, and 16- and 64-QAM modulation. The point here is that the 802.11g PHY is essentially a combination of the 802.11b and 802.11a PHY functions and, as such, does not require an extra physical layer, requires only incremental development effort, and promises to hit the market in a fully fledged state. 802.11b and 802.11g share the same 2.4GHz radio front end with 802.11a, requiring a dedicated 5GHz radio front end.

Integrating all of these functions is not simply an academic discussion. Rather, the development of a single radio capable of supporting 802.11b, 802.11a, and 802.11g is today the common goal of more than two dozen competing silicon developers. As interim steps, dual-band radios that support 802.11a and 802.11b and single-band dual-mode radios that support 802.11g and 802.11b are expected to be available in the first half of 2003. Dual-band, tri-mode radios, the "bag" radios, that support all three standards are expected in the marketplace in the second half of 2003. The capacities provided by these technologies are as follow:

- **802.11a/802.11b dual-band, dual-mode radios**   54Mbps maximum data rate multiplied by 8 channels equals a capacity of 432Mbps, and 11Mbps maximum data rate multiplied by 3 channels equals 33Mbps for a combined capacity of 465 Mbps

- **802.11b/802.11a/802.11g dual-band, tri-mode radios**   54Mbps maximum data rate multiplied by 11 channels equals a capacity of 594Mbps

These expected developments actually closely parallel the developments of other transmission technologies. In the early days of both radio and television, both industries occupied a single portion of the frequency spectrum, the AM band (for amplitude modulation between 535kHz and 1605kHz) and the VHF band (for very high frequency intermittently between 54MHz and 216MHz), respectively. This is similar to the single, 83 MHz–wide, 2.4GHz band used by 802.11b and, going forward, 802.11g.

As the demand for more varied radio content and better quality sound increased, the radio industry set to work to both increase their frequency allocation and introduce an alternate means of transmission. The FM band from 88 to 108MHz (as you know from your radio dial) was added using frequency, rather than amplitude modulation, allowing for a whole new set of radio stations, all providing far better quality sound than the AM band. Similarly, as the television industry grew, it too received an additional spectral allocation, the ultra high frequency (UHF) band, intermittently from 470MHz to 806MHz, allowing for a larger selection of reruns, syndicated talk shows, and cartoons. For a time after these new additional bands were allocated, it remained common for manufacturers to provide both singe-band receivers (AM radios and VHF televisions) and, at a higher price, dual-band AM/FM radios and VHF/UHF televisions.

Ultimately, the once premium dual-band receivers became the standard, and it became nearly impossible to even purchase the more limited single-band devices. During the migration process, field upgrade kits were common, allowing users to add FM support to their radios and UHF support to their televisions. Over time, dual-band support became the user expectation, and the price premium for dual-band devices evaporated as the technology matured and economies of scale developed.

With dual-band, tri-mode radios, the wireless LAN industry delivers investment protection through backward compatibility and a total of 11 high-speed channels for the maximum in capacity and ease of deployment. Incremental steps like single-band 802.11a and 802.11g radios deliver much of these benefits, albeit with greater architectural challenges (which will be detailed in Chapter 9). While 802.11b represented a watershed for the Wi-Fi industry and first made wireless LANs practical for the enterprise, the soon-to-be-available "bag" radio takes the industry, and the expectations of users, to a whole new level.

CHECKLIST

There are a number of considerations to make when selecting the best high-speed Wi-Fi technology for your particular application. Here are a few things to keep in mind:

- ☐ 11Mbps data rates are insufficient for many applications, particularly when transmission overhead is relatively high and the medium is shared.

- ☐ OFDM is a relatively efficient means of transmission, providing higher data rates over similar sized channels.

- ☐ 802.11a operates in the 5GHz portion of the radio frequency spectrum, which has advantages like greater capacity and less interference and disadvantages like relatively short range and regulatory restrictions on antennas.

- ☐ 802.11g operates in the same 2.4GHz band as 802.11b and thereby provides backward compatibility but with lesser capacity than 802.11a.

- ☐ The combination of both technologies into a single dual-band radio is being pursued by a number of vendors and provides the best of both worlds.

CHAPTER 7

Understanding the Regulatory Environment

One of the principal attractions of Wi-Fi is that no license is required to operate the devices in the 2.4GHz or, in the United States and a growing number of countries, the 5GHz band. "Unlicensed," however, does not mean "unregulated." Indeed, to degrees that vary on a country-by-country basis, Wi-Fi is subject to a variety of regulations that impact range, scalability, portability, product safety, and a range of other factors that impact the overall usability of the technology.

In this chapter, the rules and regulations that impact the unlicensed operation of *intentional radiators* are discussed. Although this chapter places a relatively large emphasis on FCC regulations, we recognize that Wi-Fi is an international phenomenon, and thus present the regulations of various other countries for enterprise users who travel internationally and operate Wi-Fi devices in areas subject to varying regulations. This chapter defines the applicable regulatory authorities and their areas of jurisdiction and outlines their regulations for both the 2.4GHz and, to the extent that unlicensed operations are allowed, the 5GHz bands. The differences between regulations applicable to the 2.4- and 5GHz bands are highlighted. Finally, the practical, operational impact of these regulations on Wi-Fi users is described.

THEY'RE HERE TO HELP: THE REGULATORY AGENCIES APPLICABLE TO WI-FI

"Hello, I'm from the government and I'm here to help" is often held up as a fundamental untruth and is a fairly consistent laugh-getter. In fact, though, various regulatory bodies have played a key role in driving the popularity of Wi-Fi. Regulatory agencies have had the foresight to allow for license-free operation and, by coordinating their efforts, have provided some level of worldwide commonality. They have applied and enforced regulations that have furthered, rather than hindered, the usage of these bands. In short, absent the cooperation and even leadership provided by various regulatory bodies, the Wi-Fi we know today would be an impossibility.

Regulatory Domains

There are approximately 200 countries in the world today. As sovereign states, each has the authority to create and enforce regulations that are unique to its country. Indeed, a few (thankfully, only a few) countries have put forth regulations on Wi-Fi that are particular only to themselves. The great majority of countries chose to adopt a common set of regulations from another (typically larger) country. A collection of typically adjoining countries that share a common set of regulations is referred to in the 802.11 specification as a *regulatory domain*. Table 7-1 defines the current regulatory domains for Wi-Fi products.

Regulatory Domain	Geographic Area
Americas or FCC (U.S. Federal Communications Commission)	North, South, and Central America, Australia and New Zealand, various parts of Asia and Oceania
Europe or ETSI (European Telecommunications Standards Institute)	Europe (both EU and non-EU countries), Middle East, Africa, various parts of Asia and Oceania
Japan	Japan
China	People's Republic of China (Mainland China)
Israel	Israel
Singapore*	Singapore
Taiwan*	Republic of China (Taiwan)

*The regulations of the Singapore and Taiwan regulatory domains for wireless LANs are particular to these countries only for operation in the 5GHz band; for operation in 2.4GHz, Singapore and Taiwan fall into the ETSI and FCC domains, respectively.

Table 7-1. Current Regulatory Domains for Wi-Fi Products

Note in Table 7-1 that the great majority of the world falls into two main regulatory domains, the FCC and the ETSI domains. Other countries that have a governmental tradition of "doing things their own way" commonly also have particularly acute defense issues and tend to put these considerations above the convenience and cost savings associated with simply adopting the regulations developed by another country (as is the case with FCC adoption) or an international standards-setting body (like ETSI).

Since being a "member" of a regulatory domain is completely voluntary, membership can and does change on a fairly frequent basis. As examples, until 2001, France and Singapore shared a coincidentally common set of regulations for 2.4GHz operation, which they independently abandoned at different times, each then joining the ETSI regulatory domain (France actually allows the manufacturer to ship the ETSI channel set, but still only allows usage of a subset of the spectrum). On the other hand, Israel was once part of the ETSI regulatory domain but, after additional spectra was required by its military, became a unique domain providing a subset of spectra relative to the ETSI allocation.

As suggested in the footnote to Table 7-1, countries have differing positions on 2.4GHz and 5GHz operation, which leads to slightly different regulatory domains for each band—Singapore and Taiwan are unique regulatory domains for 5GHz operation, there is no 5GHz regulatory domain for China, and the 5GHz ETSI domain is in a great state of flux both in terms of membership as well as the regulations themselves. For these and other reasons, it's best to discuss rules and requirements for the 2.4- and 5GHz regulatory domains as separate topics.

Unintentional Emissions

This chapter focuses on the intentional emissions of Wi-Fi devices—that is, the radio energy that they release to transmit data. In addition though, virtually every electronic device also unintentionally releases (leaks) some level of energy that can impact the operation of other devices or even represent a health hazard. These *unintentional emissions* are subject to regulation as well. In the FCC regulatory domains, the amount of allowable unintentional release falls into two categories. FCC Class A regulations allow for a higher amount of emissions and is applied to devices designed for operation in industrial, office, and similar commercial environments. FCC Class B is a more stringent standard that applies to operation in residential environments as well as commercial environments representing a superset of the two.

A similar set of dual standards exists in the ETSI domain, which is referred to as CEPT and is proscribed in EN-55022. It too has a Class A for commercial use and a Class B for residential operation, although CEPT Classes A and B do not map exactly to FCC Classes A and B in terms of emissions allowances and the definition of environments.

A central benefit of Wi-Fi is that it allows users to safely gain connectivity in a variety of environments: their home, their office, or even in hotels, airports, coffee houses, and other public areas. Wi-Fi client adapters are therefore subject to the more stringent FCC Class B compliance. Wi-Fi infrastructure devices such as access points and bridges are static and can therefore be designed with a particular operating environment, residential or commercial, in mind. Ironically, the higher-performance, higher-cost access points designed for operation in the enterprise are subject to a more forgiving emissions standard than their lower-cost counterparts designed for installation in the home. This is why it's typical for enterprise Wi-Fi access points to be FCC Class B certified even though it's not an absolute requirement—it shows a generally higher level of quality. When it comes to unintentional emissions, *B* stands for better.

The FCC Regulatory Domain

The Federal Communications Commission was established by the Communications Act of 1934, a New Deal–era law that established the federal government as the steward of the radio frequency spectrum in the United States. The frequency spectrum was, and is, viewed as a public asset, the use of which is subject to government regulation. The great majority of the frequency spectrum is allocated to licensed use—operation in these *licensed bands* is restricted to the license holder. In return for this exclusive use of a particular band, the licensee is obligated to follow FCC regulations (although the requirements of the military tend to supercede those of the FCC), pay a fee, and, in many cases, "act in the public interest." This is why a local television broadcaster can, for example, broadcast without competition on Channel 4 but is required to air free public interest advertisements (typically in the wee hours of weekday mornings). While operation in unlicensed bands does not require any formal licensing process, it still obligates the user to follow regulations.

The set of FCC regulations that apply to Wi-Fi operation in both the 2.4GHz and 5GHz bands is a subset of FCC Part 15 regulations, which apply to a broad range of devices, including personal computers as well as radio and television receivers. The vendor community, including television and radio networks, PC and consumer electronics manufacturers, and Wi-Fi device providers, plays an active role in defining and proposing new or altered FCC regulations. The public at large (and affected industries in particular) have the opportunity to provide feedback to the FCC prior to new rules taking effect by responding to a Notice of Proposed Rule Making (NPRM). It is through NPRMs and other, less formal processes that new proposed rules are refined to balance the needs of often competing constituencies. Within the Part 15 regulations, three separate frequency bands, 900MHz, 2.4GHz, and Unlicensed National Information Infrastructure (UNII), are defined as being available for unlicensed industrial, scientific, and medical applications. Table 7-2 outlines the characteristics of these frequency bands.

Although they are all within the Part 15 regulations, different rules apply to each of the bands. The 900MHz band is populated mostly with cordless telephones, pre-standard wireless LANs, and other devices other than Wi-Fi. As such, we'll focus on the 2.4- and 5GHz bands.

The 2.4GHz Band

The principal attractiveness of the 2.4GHz band is that it is reserved for unlicensed operation not only by the FCC but by other regulatory agencies as well, meaning that it is unlicensed throughout most of the world. Relative to the regulations for 2.4GHz in other parts of the world and relative to the FCC's regulations for the 5GHz bands, the rules of operation in the FCC 2.4GHz band are fairly unrestrictive. The regulations define operation for frequency hopping spread spectrum (FHSS) systems like legacy

Band	Common Name	Frequency Range	Common Use
900MHz	900 "meg"	902- to 928MHz	Early wireless LANs, cordless telephones
2.4GHz	Two-four or 2.4 "gig"	2.400- to 2.4835GHz (83.5MHz wide)	802.11b and 802.11g Wi-Fi wireless LANs, Bluetooth, cordless telephones
UNII-1	Eunnie-one	5.15- to 5.25GHz (100MHz wide)	Indoor wireless LANs
UNII-2	Eunnie-two	5.25- to 5.35GHz (100MHz wide)	Indoor and outdoor wireless LANs and short-range wireless bridging
UNII-3	Eunnie-three	5.725- to 5.825GHz (100MHz wide)	Long-range outdoor wireless bridging

Table 7-2. The FCC designates various portions of the radio frequency spectrum for unlicensed operation and sometimes specifies or suggests uses for these bands.

wireless LANs, cordless telephones, and Bluetooth devices and further define operation for direct sequence spread spectrum (DSSS) systems like Wi-Fi. Originally, this was to the exclusion of ODFM-based systems like 802.11g Wi-Fi, but this has since been modified to allow for these higher-performance systems operating at 2.4GHz. Compliance with the great majority of these regulations is more the responsibility of the vendor community than that of the user—manufacturers provide compliant systems and the user simply operates them as intended.

Note that it's the vendor's responsibility to provide a compliant *system* rather than simply a compliant *product*. For example, when an access point or client adapter incorporates antennas, and the user has no way of attaching a different type of antenna, then the system is the product. On the other hand, if an access point has an antenna connector, the manufacturer must certify not just the access point but the access point with all possible combinations of antennas. The user can then choose from among these possible antennas and still deploy a compliant system.

The following regulation within the FCC Part 15 rules, Subpart C, Subsection 15.203, is intended to better define what "all possible" antennas means:

> "An intentional radiator [remember, that's a radio in government-speak] shall be designed to ensure that no antenna other than that furnished by the responsible party [the vendor, for example] shall be used with the device. The use of a permanently attached antenna or of an antenna that uses a unique coupling device to the intentional radiator shall be considered sufficient to comply with the provisions of this section."

To comply with this regulation, manufacturers typically modify an industry-standard connector such that it becomes "unique" to them, and not generally available from other sources. For example, Cisco Systems modifies an industry-standard threaded navel connector (TNC) by reversing the polarity of the coupling to result in an RP-TNC connector. Other manufacturers make similarly easy-to-replicate modifications, leading to a third-party connector industry that is both healthy and understandably low profile. It is therefore fairly easy to obtain third-party antennas with connectors that will fit with industry-leading access points.

It is not a violation of FCC rules to attach third-party antennas to a Wi-Fi device. Working in cooperation with the manufacturer of the intentional radiator, the antenna vendor—whether the antenna manufacturer itself or a distributor of the antenna—can certify the system (all the access points they want to attach to and all the antennas that they want to attach) for FCC compliance, making them, not the manufacturer, the "responsible party." This is a large, costly, and time-consuming regulatory burden and the motivation to "cut corners" is certainly present. For users, the most prudent course is to simply obtain antennas from the same manufacturer that provides the access point. Failing that, one should ask to see compliance certification for their particular access point or client adapter when obtaining a third-party antenna.

Having established that the access point and antenna system are compliant, the primary area users should then be concerned with is staying within transmit power limitations. This is primarily only a concern with point-to-point and point-to-multipoint bridging products, which are often *based* on Wi-Fi devices but are not, strictly speaking, access points or client devices.

The FCC limits the total of radio transmit power and antenna gain less any cable loss to no more than 36dBm or 4 watts. This Effective Isotropic Radiated Power (EIRP) allows for a fair bit of flexibility on the part of the user and the manufacturer but is placed into effect by the FCC and other regulatory agencies around the world to ensure that the vendor does not provide equipment that will radiate an excessive amount of energy into a given space. For example, any of the following radio, antenna, and cable scenarios are within FCC compliance:

- 20dBm (100mW) transmitting device with a directly connected 2dBi dipole (standard "rubber duck") antenna; 20 + 2 = 22dBm, < 36dBm

- 20dBm (100mW) transmitting device with a directly connected 5dBi omnidirectional antenna; 20 +5 = 25dBm, < 36dBm

- 20dBm (100mW) transmitting device with a directly connected 13dBi Yagi antenna; 20 + 13 – 2 = 31dBm, < 36dBm

On the other hand, the following scenario is out of compliance:

- 20dBm (100mW) transmitting device with a 21dBi dish antenna connected by 25 feet of cable that provides about 2dBm of loss; 20 + 21 – 2 = 39dBm, > 36dBm

Note from the preceding examples that with most any type of antenna designed for wireless LAN applications, the user is in little danger of exceeding FCC EIRP limitations. Only when you design a system that uses high-gain, narrow-beam antennas, such as parabolic dish antennas that are designed for point-to-point bridging applications, do you have to consider either reductions in transmit power or the introduction of cable loss to maintain compliance. Simply put, if you use unmodified Wi-Fi devices, maintaining compliance with FCC EIRP limitations should be of little concern.

While the FCC's regulations for antennas are fairly restrictive, they pale by comparison to the FCC's regulations for external amplifiers. An *amplifier* is a powered device that attaches between the radio and the antenna and introduces extra power into the system, thereby increasing total power density to a given space. While the FCC allows for the sale of individual antennas, it specifically forbids the sale of external amplifiers as stand-alone devices. External amplifiers can be purchased only as part of a kit that includes the intentional radiator, the antenna, any cable required, and the external amplifier. These kits must be certified for FCC compliance as a complete system. Many have observed that the FCC takes a dim view of amplifiers in general due to the potential they provide for abuse. By way of illustration, note the completeness of the following from subsection 15.204: "…no person shall use, manufacture, sell or lease, offer for sale or lease (including advertising for sale or lease), or import, ship or distribute for the purpose of selling or leasing, any external radio frequency power amplifier or amplifier kit intended for use with a Part 15 intentional radiator."

The Professional Installer Exemption

There is an exception to the FCC's antenna connector requirement that is open to fairly broad interpretation: "…this requirement does not apply to intentional radiators that must be professionally installed." This exemption was intended to provide those who install more complicated wireless systems, like long-range broadband fixed wireless systems, with the flexibility they need. The meaning of "must be professionally installed" is a subjective one and the definition of "professional installer" is not provided. Broadly defined, a professional installer is anyone who receives any compensation for any installation; there is no professional licensing or certification. Understand, however, that if one holds oneself up as a professional installer and exercises this exemption, they become the "responsible party." As the responsible party, noncompliance with FCC regulations makes them subject to fines and even imprisonment.

The flexibility afforded the professional installer is intended to allow them the design flexibility to shape antenna coverage patterns that at the same time allow for maximum power density—and, of course, do so in a manner that will not adversely affect human or animal life forms. There are two considerations the professional installer includes as part of their customer installations.

- Applying maximum power density to a specific antenna or area is far from the accepted norm. Indeed, a considerable amount of radio interference comes from "native radios"—radios belonging to a specific network. Frequency planning mitigates this to a large extent, but the experienced professional installer will have long since realized that custom installations use the *minimum* power necessary to provide suitable link margins and performance.

- The professional installer tends to shape beams no wider than absolutely necessary in order to provide suitable link margins, which in turn help provide suitable reliability and performance. This means that the experienced professional installer won't send energy where it does little good; in other words, anywhere not near a receiving antenna.

Having offered these two considerations, it is always wise to not stand in front of or near an antenna any longer than absolutely necessary if you are not fully cognizant of what the operational parameters are of the antenna.

The regulations go on to clarify that kits inclusive of the intentional radiator are allowed, but still the subsection continues to read like a lecture. For the great majority of Wi-Fi applications, all the gain a user requires can be obtained through antenna selection—an external amplifier is unnecessary. To a slightly lesser degree, the same can be said for bridging applications. In general, the user is well advised to simply avoid external amplifiers, especially if they are not provided as a certified element that is part of the 802.11 components being purchased.

Although the FCC allocation for the 2.4GHz ISM band is defined as being from 2.4- to 2.4835GHz, Wi-Fi devices operating in that band work in terms of channels. The 802.11b and 802.11g specification defines the available channels in the FCC band for use in the United States as follows:

Channel ID (MHz)	Frequency
1	2412
2	2417
3	2422
4	2427
5	2432
6	2437
7	2442
8	2447
9	2452
10	2457
11	2462

The preceding results from the 802.11b and 802.11g specifications misleadingly suggest that the user has 11 channels available in the 2.4GHz band. Of course, this is not the case. As indicated previously, the user actually has no more than three *nonoverlapping* channels. For Wi-Fi transmission in 2.4GHz, a minimum of 22MHz of bandwidth is required. As shown in Figure 7-1, these 22MHz–wide channels extend 11MHz off the center point of the channel in either direction. The only available channels of these 11 that allow for 11MHz in either direction without interfering with another channel or

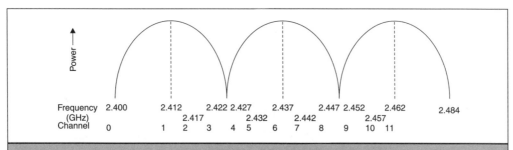

Figure 7-1.   Although the 802.11b and 802.11g specifications define 11 channels in the FCC 2.4GHz ISM band, only three are nonoverlapping and therefore usable.

extending beyond the allocated frequency (exceeding the side bands) are channels 1, 6, and 11. Although there is no legal restriction on architecting a wireless LAN with fewer or greater channel usage, it is typically best to use all three channels, no more, no less, to take best balance capacity and reliability. This will be further detailed in Chapter 9.

The 5GHz Bands

As indicated in the Table 7-2, the FCC has allocated three unlicensed bands in the 5GHz portion of the frequency spectrum that are collectively known as Unlicensed National Information Infrastructure (UNII) bands. (For reasons that are not intuitive, the FCC insists upon putting a hyphen between the *U* and the *N*, resulting in U-NNI, a convention that virtually all other parties have had the good sense to ignore.) Each of the three bands is 100MHz wide. UNII-1 is located at 5.15–5.25GHz, UNII-2 at 5.25–5.35GHz, and UNII-3 at 5.725–5.825GHz. Notice that the UNII-1 and the UNII-2 bands are contiguous and are indeed treated by 802.11a as being a continuous swath of spectrum 200MHz wide, more than twice the size of the 2.4GHz ISM band. As discussed in Chapter 6, this results in a key benefit for 802.11a—the 200MHz wide UNII-1 and UNII-2 bands are divided up into eight *nonoverlapping* channels, each 25MHz wide.

As Table 7-2 indicated, each UNII band is intended for a different use. As unlicensed bands, these intended uses are not themselves part of the regulations; rather, the regulations are designed to promote the intended use to the detriment or at least inconvenience of other uses. The UNII-3 band is intended for long-range point-to-point and point-to-multipoint wireless bridging and may only be used outdoors. (The UNII-3 band and its usage will be detailed in Chapter 14.) Although the UNII-1 and the UNII-2 bands are contiguous and are treated as a single band by most 5GHz Wi-Fi devices, they have very different regulatory limitations.

UNII-1

The UNII-1 band is intended for indoor wireless LANs, with use outdoors prohibited by the regulations. Of the three UNII bands, UNII-1 carries with it the most restrictive set of regulations. Unlike the 900MHz and 2.4GHz bands and all other UNII bands, UNII-1 requires that the antenna and the intentional radiator be integral devices; the use of connectors, antenna cables, and auxiliary antennas is simply prohibited. Antenna gain is limited to no more than 6dBi. In addition to the antenna restriction, transmit power is limited to 50mW at peak or 40mW nominal, the normal operating state. The resulting EIRP limitation for UNII-1 is 22dBm, which compares to 36dBm for the 2.4GHz band (remember that the decibel scale is logarithmic). The result of these restrictions is that all devices, inclusive of 5GHz Wi-Fi products, offer relatively shorter range and fewer installation and coverage pattern options.

UNII-2

The UNII-2 band is intended for wireless use for both indoor applications and short-range outdoor applications. To facilitate this, the regulations allow for connectors and the use of cable and auxiliary antennas. The EIRP limitation is 29dBm, a lot more than UNII-1 but not nearly the 52dBm allowed in the UNII-3 band intended for *long-range* wireless bridging. Transmit power is limited to no more than 250mW when a 6dBi antenna is used and may be reduced to accommodate higher gain, more-directional antennas while staying within the 29dBm EIRP limitation.

Few people are actually using UNII-2 in the manner for which it is intended. Indoor wireless bridging is today a fairly niche application. The UNII-3 band, with far greater transmit power and antenna gain allowances, is preferable for outdoor wireless bridging. Rather, the UNII-2 band is treated by the Wi-Fi community as being a less-restrictive extension of the UNII-1 band. The result of this is that some vendors of 802.11a-compliant devices will allow for higher transmit power in the upper four (UNII-2) channels than they do in the lower four (UNII-1) channels. The physical nature of the antenna connector restriction results in 802.11a access points and client adapters that adhere to the more restrictive UNII-1 regulations—even though half their operating channels are in UNII-2, they still have integrated antennas to allow for operation in the bottom four UNII-1 channels.

Health and Safety Regulations

Under the National Environmental Policy Act of 1969, the FCC was required to *evaluate* the effects of RF exposure on the human body. Today, the FCC and regulatory bodies around the world have provided guidelines and some absolute limits on RF energy. The FCC has based its rules around guidelines put forth by the American National Standards Institute (ANSI), the Institute of Electrical and Electronics Engineers (IEEE), and the National Council on Radiation Protection and Measurements (NCRPM). These nongovernmental expert organizations have put forth the notion of a specific absorption rate (SAR), which is a measure of the rate at which the body absorbs RF energy, expressed in watts or milliwatts per kilogram (W/kg or mW/kg). The absorption of most any energy like sunlight, radiation or radio energy can lead to cellular damage that can result in cancer. Based on the nearly four decades of research by these organizations and others, the FCC has restricted the maximum allowable SAR for portable devices, including cellular telephones, cordless telephones, and Wi-Fi equipment.

The SAR limitation for "occupational or controlled exposure" (at work) is 400mW/kg when the whole body is exposed and 8W/kg when only a portion of the body is exposed. For general or uncontrolled exposure, the limitations are 80mW/kg for the whole body and 1.6W/kg for partial exposure. Telephones are subject to partial body exposure because they contact the body at the head and, when on a holster, the waist. Wi-Fi adapters are similarly subject to partial body limitations because they tend to be installed in devices that contact the body at the hand, in the case of a PDA, or the (gulp) lap, in the case of the laptop. The FCC is good enough to point out in its Bulletin 56 issued in August 1999 that the eyes and the testes are particularly vulnerable to damage from RF energy.

Wi-Fi devices fall far below even the uncontrolled partial body exposure limitations. Cellular telephones, on the other hand, tend to come much closer. To illustrate, the popular Nokia 5160 telephone delivers a SAR of as much as 1.14mW/kg. The Motorola StarTAC delivers a SAR of as much as 1.32mW/kg. The maximum transmit power of the Nokia telephone is 497mW, with the Motorola device having a maximum transmit power of 495mW. It's also important to note that cellular telephones have a continual mode of operation, and during a typical conversation the device is frequently both transmitting and receiving.

Wi-Fi devices range in transmit power from between 30 to 100mW or anywhere from one-fifth to one-fifteenth the transmit power of the cellular devices in the preceding example. They tend to transmit less power than a cellular telephone; as an example, sending 100MB of data would typically take under three minutes on a 802.11b-compliant Wi-Fi LAN, while cellular telephone conversations can (and do!) stretch into hours. Although laptops can be operated in the location that their name suggests, it is just as typical for them to be located atop a shielding desk.

In short, while users should be concerned about the health and safety considerations of Wi-Fi operation, they should also be aware that years of research have been conducted in this area and the findings of this research have been incorporated into the applicable regulations. Wi-Fi devices deliver a fraction of the transmit power of a typical cellular telephone, leading to an SAR that is a fraction of that delivered by the cellular device, and the differing usage patterns of a Wi-Fi device lead to far less exposure time than would be typical for a cellular telephone. While many debate the safety of cellular telephones, it is undisputable that Wi-Fi devices pose a very small fraction of the health issues that are rightly or wrongly associated with cellular telephones.

The ETSI Domain

Unlike the FCC in the United States, the European Telecommunications Standards Institute (ETSI) is more of an advisory body than a regulatory body. Although, as a result of the European Union, pan-European regulations are becoming more common, ETSI makes recommendations to individual countries who typically adopt them exactly as recommended but have the freedom to make changes before instituting them as regulations or to simply ignore the recommendations.

Those who have done business in Europe or who have even traveled there will be little surprised that ETSI recommendations and the resulting regulations are more detailed and indeed more restrictive when compared to the "freewheeling ways" of the FCC. For the sake of illustration, the following table outlines regulations that apply to Wi-Fi operation in the ETSI regulatory domain:

Regulation	Description
EN 55022	Line Conducted
EN 1000-4-2	Electrostatic Discharge
EN 1000-4-3	RF Field Immunity (80MHz to 1GHz)
EN 1000-4-4	Electrical Fast Transient
EN 1000-4-5	Surge/Transient
EN 1000-4-6	Line Conducted Immunity (150kHz to 80MHz)
EN 1000-4-11	Voltage Transients
EN 6001-3-2	Power Line Harmonics
EN 6001-3-3	Voltage Flicker

The restrictive nature of the ETSI regulations is best exemplified by the limitations of transmit power in the 2.4GHz band. To illustrate, the FCC allows for 4 watts EIRP in the band, or 36dBm. ETSI allows for no more than 100mW EIRP, or 20dBm. While most Wi-Fi transmitters come nowhere near 36dBm, the 20dBm restriction does have an impact on range when operating under ETSI regulations. Most 802.11b, and presumably upcoming 802.11g radios, will provide transmit power between 30- and 100mW. With a 30mW (15dBm) radio, ETSI EIRP limitations restrict antenna gain to no more than 5dBi. Antennas connected to 100mW (20dBm) radios in ETSI countries can have no gain at all—the transmitter must be "dialed back" to a lower transmit power to allow for any antenna gain and therefore selection of coverage pattern and beam width. The result is that some antenna types like Yagis and many patches are not allowed in ETSI countries without substantial transmit power reductions. Other antennas may be used, but their use is limited more toward redirecting RF energy than increasing range, because any range gain on the antenna will be cancelled out by the reductions in transmit power necessary to stay within the overall EIRP limitations.

On the other hand, ETSI does provide for a slightly wider 2.4GHz band than does the FCC. Using the same 802.11-defined channelization as is applied to the FCC band, the result is a total of 13, not 11, channels. As was mentioned previously, the number of these channels has little practical meaning—it's the number of *nonoverlapping* channels that matters. Regrettably, the number of nonoverlapping channels possible with either 11 or 13 802.11-defined channels is exactly the same—three. In other words, the slightly greater width of ETSI's 2.4GHz band relative to the FCC's 2.4GHz band has no real-world benefit.

The 5GHz band in the ETSI domain best illustrates the recommendatory and not regulatory nature of the body. The ETSI-recommended band is a very wide one, stretching from 5.15GHz (the same point in the spectrum as is the start of the FCC UNII-1 band) all the way to 5.7GHz, the great majority of the 5GHz band and far more than what is allowed by the FCC. In exchange for this wide swath of spectrum, the ETSI recommendation mandates the inclusion of two features not found in 802.11 products, dynamic frequency selection (DFS) and transmit power control (TPC). Tellingly, DFS and TPC are

Operation in Multiple Domains: 802.11d

In today's globalized world, Wi-Fi users often roam from one regulatory domain to another. It's not unheard of for a business person to travel from, say, Cleveland in the FCC regulatory domain to Paris in the ETSI domain and from there to China and Japan, each of which has its own particular set of regulations. This brutal business trip is made all the worse because the Wi-Fi user would have to bring four Wi-Fi adapters, one for each regulatory domain, and swap them into their laptop depending upon the country.

Recognizing this, the IEEE 802.11 group set up a specific task force to develop a means whereby a client radio could operate in multiple regulatory domains while still maintaining regulatory compliance. These efforts came to fruition in June 2001 with the ratification of the 802.11d standard for Multiple Domain Operation.

The standard is based upon the presumption that the access point in a Wi-Fi network is within regulatory compliance. It specifies the manner in which the access point advertises in its management packets (beacons and probe responses) the regulatory domain to which it's compliant.

For client devices, their typical mode of operation is to be configured for compliance with a particular regulatory domain and actively scan for an access point to associate with by transmitting probes. If, however, the configuration is inconsistent with the regulatory domain in which it is operating, these probes represent noncompliant transmissions and subject the user to penalties. When set to multiple-domain mode, the client device is configured to only *receive* incoming management packets. Upon receipt of a beacon from an 802.11d-enabled access point, the client will read the management information and from that discern the regulatory domain to which that access point is configured. The client will then adopt these configurations and only then begin the process of association and operation. Note here that the client device still has a base regulatory domain configuration, which is necessary when operating with an access point that does not support 802.11d or when the client is in ad-hoc mode and operating directly with a peer client without an access point at all. Note also that by passively, rather than actively, scanning and then reconfiguring itself, the amount of time to associate when operating in multiple-domain mode will be slightly longer than when operating in standard mode.

The main problem with 802.11d is not the aforementioned minor shortcomings. Rather, the main problem is that, to date, only a single vendor, Symbol Technologies, has adopted this useful standard. If a few Wi-Fi industry luminaries were perhaps detained for a couple of days in a foreign jail, the issue of noncompliant operation might get a bit more attention.

two functions handled quite well by the HiperLAN 2 specification, a technology that was advocated to the exclusion of 802.11a by Europe-based companies, like Nokia, Ericsson, and Siemans.

The idea behind DFS is that an 802.11 infrastructure device would first listen to the whole of the frequency band available to it and then automatically assign itself to the least congested channel available. The initial requirement behind DFS is that in Europe, portions around the middle of the 5GHz band are assigned to military use, largely for radar systems. The thinking is that by listening first before automatically selecting a channel, the access point and its associated clients would not interfere with incumbent users of the band in situations where they are co-located. In addition, the availability of the feature would simplify any enterprise installation, because the devices themselves would automatically optimize their channel reuse pattern (more information on channel reuse and the issues associated with a high-density deployment of access points is provided in Chapter 9).

TPC is a notion borrowed from the cellular telephone industry. As has been discussed previously, the transmit power of the access point and the client adapter can be set by the user to allow for different coverage area sizes and, in the case of the client, to conserve battery life. The problem is that these are static settings and no exchange of information regarding transmit power occurs between the client and the access point. As an example, an access point can be set to a low 5mW transmit power to minimize cell size, which is useful in areas with high user density (and therefore correspondingly high access point density, as will be discussed in Chapter 9). The clients will, however, be "blasting away" at whatever their previously assigned and static transmit power setting is. They'll likely be using far more transmit power than is required to maintain association with the access point that is sending out a relatively weak signal. The result is unnecessary RF energy emanating from the clients, which raises the overall noise floor, limiting range and performance for all Wi-Fi devices in the same general physical and radio frequency location.

With a relatively high population density, you can see how TPC would be of greater interest to those in Europe than those in less densely populated parts of the world. With transmit power control, the client device dynamically adjusts its transmit power such that it uses only enough energy to maintain association to the access point at a given data rate. The result of this is that the client contributes less to raising the overall noise floor, allowing for more densely deployed high-performance Wi-Fi LANs. It has the additional benefit of providing longer battery life on the client device, as less power is used by the Wi-Fi adapter.

Naturally, neither DFS nor TPC has been incorporated into any Wi-Fi device to date. The technical complexity of implementing these functions suggests that their implementation on a standardized, interoperable basis could stretch into a matter of years. The IEEE has formed a task group, 802.11h, specifically to put forth a standard for both DFS and TPC that will apply to the 5GHz band (to meet regulatory requirements). The result is that if the individual countries that tend to adopt ETSI recommendations were to adopt the requirement for DFS and TPC, users in these countries would be excluded from the performance and scalability benefits of 802.11a technology.

Instead, the normally monolithic ETSI regulatory domain is crumbling on this particular issue and, on a country-by-country basis, alternative regulations are being proposed and adopted. At the time of this writing, the situation is too fluid to predict a final outcome. What is understood, however, is that in general terms, a smaller portion of the 5GHz band with lower transmit power restrictions than would otherwise be allowed for will be provided. This smaller, lower-power band will not require DFS or TPC.

In some countries, there is a requirement for a much more easy to implement "static" frequency selection, whereby a manufacturer is obligated to randomly assign (and therefore evenly distribute) default channel settings on access points. Other countries provide for higher transmit power allowances if TPC, which is easier to implement than DFS, is provided. Note that the smaller bandwidth allowances map to the FCC's UNII-1 or, depending upon the country, UNII-1 and UNII-2 combined bands—either four channels or eight channels. Note as well that for some countries, the maximum transmit power is not too different from the power allowed by the FCC for the lower-power UNII-1 band in particular. The upshot of this development is that it tends to decrease the industry's urgency to implement DFS and, to a lesser degree, TPC, even calling into question the eventual availability of these functions.

Country	Frequency Band (GHz)	Maximum Transmit Power EIRP with TPC (mW)	Maximum Transmit Power without TPC (mW)
Austria	5.15–5.25	200	200
Belgium	5.15–5.35	120	60
Denmark	5.15–5.25	50	50
France	5.15–5.25	200	200
Germany	5.15–5.25	50	50
Ireland	5.15–5.35	120	60
Netherlands	5.15–5.25	200	200
Sweden	5.15–5.25	200	200
Switzerland	5.15–5.25	200	200
United Kingdom	5.15–5.35	120	60

The Japanese Regulatory Domain

Unlike the FCC and ETSI regulatory domains, which cover a multitude of countries, the regulations of TELEC, the Japanese equivalent of the FCC and ETSI, have been adopted only by the body's home country. In general terms, the TELEC regulations are more restrictive on transmit power than even ETSI but provide for a larger swath of bandwidth. The TELEC regulations are not based upon a specific power limitation but rather a limitation that is based upon the amount of bandwidth available. For Wi-Fi products, this is 10mW per 1MHz EIRP. The upshot of this is that 2.4GHz Wi-Fi products are limited to no more than 30mW of transmit power with up to 6dBi of antenna gain, or no more that 50mW with a 0dBi antenna. To install higher-gain antennas like Yagis, transmit power must be reduced to 5mW, which largely negates any range increase resulting from the higher antenna gain. Like the ETSI 2.4GHz band, the slightly greater width of the band provides for little practical benefit; while 14 802.11-defined channels are available, only 3 of these 14 are nonoverlapping.

For 802.11a operation, TELEC has taken a similar approach to that of Denmark and Germany; that is, only the 100MHz wide band from 5.15- to 5.25GHz is available, with fairly stringent restrictions on total transmit power.

Other Regulatory Domains

In addition to the FCC, ETSI and Japanese regulatory domains, other smaller regulatory domains exist. Due to the size of their respective markets, they are treated here in summary fashion. Each of these sets of regulations covers just its single home country.

For 2.4GHz, the Israeli regulatory domain is a subset of the ETSI regulatory domain, allowing the same transmit power and antenna combinations as ETSI but only seven channels. This is about half the channels allowed by ETSI, resulting in only two nonoverlapping channels rather than three. Israel does not currently allow for unlicensed operation in the 5GHz band.

The Chinese regulatory domain follows FCC bandwidth allowances in 2.4GHz but has other restrictions on transmit power and antenna types. Like Israel, China does not allow for unlicensed operation in 5GHz.

Singapore follows ETSI regulations for 2.4GHz operation but, like many countries in Europe, departs from ETSI regulations for 5GHz. Taiwan follows FCC regulations for 2.4GHz but restricts operation to the equivalent of the UNII-2 band for 5GHz.

Over time, these countries may find it beneficial to adopt the rules of a larger regulatory domain, because fielding products specific to a single country tends to increase their price and decrease their availability.

CHECKLIST

While the onus to maintain compliance with applicable regulations is in large part on Wi-Fi vendors, it's important for those who deploy and use Wi-Fi equipment to have at least a base understanding of these regulations. Even within a specific geography, one can operate off-the-shelf Wi-Fi equipment in a noncompliant manner. The potential for noncompliance grows as you move from one geographic area to another, which is very consistent with a mobile technology in an increasingly globalized world. Here are a few points to remember:

- [ ] A regulatory domain is a collection of countries that subscribe to a common set of regulations. The great majority of countries in the world fall into two main regulatory domains: one that subscribes to the regulations of the FCC, and one that subscribes to Europe's ETSI. The Americas and parts of Asia are in the FCC regulatory domain. Europe, Africa, most of the Middle East, and parts of Asia fall into the ETSI domain. There are other, single-country regulatory domains, like Japan, Israel, and China.

- [ ] Regulations apply to both intentional radiation as well as unintentional radiation, which is another term for electromagnetic leakage. In the FCC and ETSI regulatory domains, Class B approval means that the device leaks less energy and causes less interference than a Class A device.

- [ ] The FCC regulations that apply to Wi-Fi products for the 2.4GHz band tend to be less restrictive than the regulations for the 5GHz bands. Greater transmit power is allowed as well as less restrictive antenna regulations.

- [ ] Wi-Fi devices adhere to the same FCC health and safety regulations that apply to devices like cellular telephones. Wi-Fi devices transmit a fraction of the power that cellular phones do and, as such, deliver a fraction of the energy absorbed by the human body. Additionally, Wi-Fi devices tend to transmit for shorter durations than cellular telephones and are often shielded from the user by a desk or table. In short, Wi-Fi devices are understood to be far safer than cellular telephones.

- [ ] The ETSI domain has more restrictive transmit power regulations than does the FCC for 2.4GHz operation. ETSI's requirements for DFS and TPC in the 5GHz band have caused individual countries to put forth regulations that do not call for these features, thereby allowing for earlier deployment.

- [ ] 802.11d is a ratified but largely unimplemented standard that enables Wi-Fi devices to automatically adjust their channel and power settings to meet regulatory compliance.

- [ ] Other, smaller regulatory domains tend to be subsets of the FCC and ETSI domains in terms of channels and maximum transmit power. An exception to this is the Japanese regulatory domain, which restricts transmit power based upon a ratio of allowed power over a given amount of bandwidth.

PART III

WLAN Equipment and Component Selection

CHAPTER 8

Selecting the Right Wireless LAN Equipment Components

Now that you have decided to add a wireless system to your network, you need to determine where to start and what products you need to use. Throughout this book, we've discussed how Wi-Fi LANs provide the enterprise with overall productivity improvements, based on user mobility and resulting improvements in organizational and individual efficiency. All of this, however, is based on selecting the proper components that will support the desired and needed applications, mobility, ranges, security, and other network features. As network administrators rush to integrate wireless LANs across enterprise networks, they often underestimate and oversimplify the technology.

A properly selected and installed Wi-Fi LAN can provide a dramatic increase in productivity at the individual level, which in the end affects the bottom line for the company. However, selecting the wrong components can just as easily result in a system that the users hate, because of its arcane access and use rules, or a system that causes the network to become unbearably slow, insecure, or extremely unstable.

This chapter discusses the various features and functions available in WLAN products, as well as the issues and features that you should consider so that you are able to scale the network in the future and accommodate technological migrations such as that from 802.11b to 11a and 11g. The 802.11 elements that most likely will change are authentication and encryption. You have to be prepared for expansion and continued growth, because once users experience a well-deployed WLAN, they will demand nothing less.

DEFINING THE WLAN REQUIREMENTS

The first step in designing any network is determining the end point—the users' needs. For a WLAN, this includes defining the coverage area. Before you can determine *what* you need, you have to decide *why* you need it. Mobility is most often the reason for implementing a wireless network, although mobility should not be confused with the ability to provide uninterrupted connectivity with the LAN. So, early in the planning stage, you must determine the key points at which users will reside, as well as the most common paths between the primary locations for gathering, such as conference rooms, the offices of key personnel, development labs, and so forth. Critical to this process is having a good diagram of the facility showing what the WLAN needs to cover.

You also need to determine the minimum speeds required by users. Toward this end, you must have a description of the applications that the users run. Of course, every network engineer will say that each user needs 100Mbps, just as in a wired switched network. But wireless is not a switched medium. It is a shared medium. Therefore, not all applications will truly fit well into a WLAN system. From our understanding of network traffic, we know that network use is in fact very "spiky"—a user requests a download (low speed required), which is followed by the actual download (greater speed required). The opposite is true when uploading documents. Because traffic loads tend to be spiky, the network design requires a fraction of the available bandwidth formerly thought of as mission critical. This does not mean that high-speed networks of 100Mbps and even gigabit rates are never needed—the minimum amount of speed required generally increases over time as more users access a LAN.

It is unlikely that all users in a LAN will use the same device. Thus, you need to determine whether users need specialty devices on the wireless system, such as print servers, bar code readers, PCI cards, PCMCIA cards, or perhaps even wireless IP phones. If so, you need to decide whether to procure all the devices from the same vendor or different vendors. This decision could be very important, due to vendor interoperability issues. Keep in mind that the weakest link in the chain—the weakest LAN element (or the least experienced network administrator!)—determines the LAN's maximum level of performance, stability, and security.

Migrations of the Technology

You need to determine the technology you will use for your WLAN. Over the past several years, different WLAN technologies have been available. This chapter starts by walking you through the migration path, to emphasize some of the key issues you need to consider when selecting your WLAN components. These different systems include Wireless LAN Interoperability Forum (WLIF) systems, 802.11 frequency hopping (FH) systems, 802.11 direct sequence (DS) systems, 802.11b systems, wide-band frequency hopping (WBFH) systems, and 802.11a systems. So, how do you determine which one is right for you?

Proprietary Systems

To avoid repeating mistakes made by others in the past, let's spend a few minutes reviewing some key points in WLAN product evolution. In the beginning, all WLANs were very vendor-specific and proprietary systems. Data rates of available WLAN products approached 1Mbps, and radios were based on the 900MHz ISM band. The availability of standard form factors was limited to access points, ISA cards, and, to a lesser degree, PCMCIA cards. For PCMCIA cards, the overall power consumption of the WLAN client was high, reducing available battery runtime, which therefore limited the degree to which a user could be truly untethered from an AC power source.

The main use of these early WLANs was for retail and warehouse systems, primarily to do barcoding and inventory control. The required bandwidth for such application was (and in many cases still is today) comparatively low. This type of system typically had one to five users as well as a low overall transaction rate, so the limited availability of bandwidth generally was acceptable.

One issue with the early 900MHz WLAN was the limited number of countries that allowed the use of this type of equipment. The 900MHz band could not be used in Europe and most of the Asia Pacific and South American countries. However, companies such as Ford Motor Company and IBM wanted a system that could be used in all of their corporate locations, and since 900MHz could not be used, they pushed for a more widely acceptable solution.

In part for these reasons, the 2.4GHz ISM band became the band of choice for innovative WLAN vendors. With 2.4GHz systems, the speed increased to an average of 2Mb (One WLAN company, Breezecom Technologies, even pushed this limit to 3Mb). The 2.4GHz technology was permitted in more than 60 countries at that time, and between the higher speed and global availability, WLANs started moving into more mainstream networking.

Standards-Based Systems

There was still one drawback: interpretability among products. There was no standard, and therefore WLANs were all proprietary and single-source products. As is the case today, most large users wanted to avoid a single-vendor implementation because, in part, they wanted to ensure equipment availability, prompt service, and full support in the event the vendor that sold them the equipment became unavailable or provided poor service. Indeed, some companies that chose to implement early WLANS ended up with a proprietary system that only worked with a single vendor's product line.

One of the other risks of a single-vendor implementation was the possibility that future scaling, or expansion, would be impossible. If the vendor dropped the product line (which has happened on more than one occasion) or, worse, went out of business, the client was left with a system that it could not expand or update, and in some cases could not even continue to get support for. This meant only one thing—R&R, or rip and replace. The industry and the IEEE saw a need to compile a standard for WLANs to follow that would allow interoperation across vendors' platforms. The result was the formation of IEEE 802.11. Even though it was six long years before the IEEE completed the standard, the promise of standards-based products (and therefore interoperability) has had a tremendous impact on the adoption of 802.11 equipment by customers both large and small.

In lieu of any completed industry standard, one company (Proxim) tried to develop an industry de facto standard, known as Wireless LAN Interoperability Forum (WLIF). This was based on the Proxim Frequency Hopping radio that provided a maximum data rate of 1.6Mbps in the 2.4GHz band. Many of the Proxim partners and customers joined the WLIF and this was a dominant force in the WLAN for several years, even with the limited bandwidth available with the WLIF standard.

When the IEEE completed the 802.11 standard in 1997, it caused even more confusion. The standard actually supported two different RF implementations, FH and DS, which were totally incompatible. This caused some users, again, to not know what to install. There was a "religious war" between FH and DS vendors, similar to the VHS versus BETA technology war in the videotape arena. This confusion also prompted many possible WLAN users to wait to install because they did not know which path to follow, FH or DS.

The new 802.11 systems had data rates defined up to 2Mbps, but the data rate advantage over the WLIF format was minimal, and therefore took a little while to catch on. The main advantages were that it was an *industry* standard (unlike WLIF, which was a standard clustered around a single company) and was intended to (and in many cases did) provide interoperability. However, many issues arose with trying to get vendor A to work with vendor B, and users had to take the word of their possible vendors as to interoperability. This again stalled the event of widespread WLAN adoption.

By the time the 802.11 products were starting to take hold in the industry, users were screaming for higher data rates. Two years later, the industry made a huge jump to 11Mbps with the completion of the 802.11b standard and the introduction of 11Mbps products based on the standard. As 802.11b devices started to become available, users still had some skepticism about interoperability among vendors. The main reason that Wi-Fi certification was started was to provide users the secure feeling that vendor A's products would have a minimum degree of interoperability with vendor B's products.

The Demise of FH

The 802.11b standard, and the supporting Wi-Fi certification, was defined for *only* direct sequence. This immediately put a dark cloud over the FH systems. The advantages of higher data rates with 802.11b and certified interoperability quickly overcame any advantage even the craftiest marketing person could dream up for FH, and new installs of FH products slowed.

This caused a quick response by one WLAN company, Proxim, which resulted in a push to develop a higher-speed FH system. Proxim petitioned the FCC for a rule change to allow a new FH system, and then introduced WBFH technology. This moved FH to a data rate of 10Mbps. The problem was that Wi-Fi, IEEE, and companies like Microsoft and Cisco made it known that they would not support the new technology, the result of which was very little implementation ever being done using WBFH.

Today's Products

With all the changes in technology, there was still much confusion in the industry regarding what was the best technology, what was interoperable, and what was upgradeable. With 11Mbps, and certified interoperability being available under the 802.11b standard, WLIF, FH, and WBFH all but became extinct. This basically meant users had a single choice of technology, 802.11b. Thus, the industry again had a de facto standard, but this one was widely adopted across the industry, and that had interoperability among different vendors products.

As mentioned earlier in this book, the most recent advancements in WLAN are 802.11a and 802.11g technologies, both of which offer data rates up to 54Mbps. Interoperability certification from the Wi-Fi alliance will be available for both. The 802.11a products started hitting the market in 2001, and 802.11g should be available in early 2003.

Defining Your Technology Requirements

Now that we have narrowed it down to three technologies (802.11a, b and g), which way do we go? Well, since 802.11g is not expected to be available until early 2003, we will focus on 802.11a and 802.11b, with the understanding that upgrading to 802.11g will be an option in 2003. But before we can decide which technology to use, we first must answer more questions. As you move forward in your decision, you should make a list and define the answers to the following questions:

- What are the present applications that will be used and what is their bandwidth requirement per user?

This question is vital. If you plan to use the network for simple network connection and average office type applications (MS Office, e-mail, web browsing, database access, and so forth), the bandwidth of a normal 802.11b system will probably be sufficient (depending on the answer to the following question).

- What is the average and maximum density of WLAN users in any given coverage area and will this density increase over time?

You need to determine how many users will be in a given area, both on a routine basis and on a maximum-user basis. For the average office application (listed in the preceding description), you can get reasonable performance with 10 to 20 users per 802.11b access point. For small-transaction applications with a low bandwidth requirement, such as a stock trading floor or barcoding, the number of users per AP can increase dramatically. Remember that the aggregate throughput (not data rate) of an 11Mbps 802.11b system is about 5.5 to 6Mbps aggregate per AP.

- What future applications are being considered, and what is their expected bandwidth requirement?

The answer to this may determine whether you need to move today to a higher-speed broadband wireless system or if you can wait to upgrade in the future. If you decide to use 802.11b today (based on answers to these questions), yet need to migrate to higher bandwidth at a later date, the ability to add 5GHz is one possibility (again pending your answers). Another possibility is to upgrade the 802.11b APs to 802.11g when available, and use 802.11g clients for the more bandwidth-intensive applications. Either solution permits slow migration and investment protection, because you can continue to use your existing 802.11b clients for the lower-bandwidth applications. Looking forward approximately 12 to 18 months will help guide you in this portion of the preplanning process.

- To what physical areas do you plan to provide WLAN access?

If you are looking for maximum coverage, then 802.11b systems will provide the best solution. If you are looking to cover both indoor and outdoor areas, you must use 802.11b, or limit the use of 802.11a systems to the upper four channels (UNII 2) for outdoor usage, along with the lower power output setting of UNII 1. The lower channels of the 802.11a (UNII 1 channels) are for indoor use only.

- Do you plan to use the WLAN for portable VoIP connections, and if so, how many concurrent VoIP connections will be used in any given AP coverage area?

This could also be a stumbling block if you are trying to install 802.11a today. As of the writing of this book, the available 802.11-based phones are limited to 802.11 DS and 802.11b systems. If you need the bandwidth of 802.11a for other applications, and still desire to install VoIP wireless phones, your best solution is a dual-band AP, which provides an excellent method of separating VoIP and data traffic (aside from using VLANs), although another satisfactory architectural approach is to use separate virtual collision domains, called *virtual local area networks,* or *VLANs* (see Chapter 10). Present 802.11b APs and 802.11b phone systems will carry four to seven concurrent calls. Add data to this and the number of calls decreases. The 802.11b phone vendors are making major improvements to their products, so ask the vendor for guidance on the number of calls, the overall bandwidth, and so forth that you need.

- Do the APs need to be placed in the ceiling or in secure out-of-sight locations?

This is a critical issue. In public access sites, schools, healthcare facilities, and other public places, the APs are usually kept out of sight and external antennas are used both for aesthetic reasons and to protect the equipment from vandalism and theft. If this describes your situation, you need to determine whether you somehow can mount them in an area that will not hinder the antenna performance or need external antennas. Remember that the UNII 1 band (part of 802.11a) requires that the antenna be an integral part of the 802.11a radio, so external antennas are not permitted. APs that combine both UNII 1 and UNII 2 also require antennas that are attached by the manufacturer, so antenna selection requires some forethought. In some cases, mounting above the ceiling tile might work, but you need to ensure that air conditioning ducts, electrical conduit and other cable trays, and lightning fixtures will not hinder the antenna performance. In most cases, this is not an acceptable location to put the antenna, and hence 802.11a is probably not a good solution.

Another issue with placing APs in the ceiling may be plenum ratings. The *plenum* is the area above a room where heating and air conditioning run. Fire regulations require that the materials used in that area do not contribute poisonous gases or excessive flammability in the event of extreme heat or fire. Many local regulations require that the equipment placed above ceilings meet certain fire and smoke regulations. Check with the local authorities to determine what these regulations are, and verify that at a minimum the device meets the UL2043 standard.

- Who will determine the client radio vendor—users or administrators?

If the WLAN client devices will be determined by the IS staff, this is not an issue (in most cases). However, if the users themselves may decide what client device they will use, this can complicate the product decision. Consider an educational facility in which both students and facility will be using the WLAN. The faculty members will likely get their devices via the network administrator; however, the students will be bringing in their Linksys, D-link, Microsoft, or other WLAN card that they bought at the local store. With the limited availability of 802.11a cards today, and the abundance of 802.11b cards, this makes the decision easier. Also, many computers today come with built-in 802.11b radios and integrated antennas. As of this writing, there are no available PCs with built-in 802.1a radios, and since the antenna is integrated into the computer (and antennas are frequency sensitive), you cannot exchange the 802.11b radio for an 802.11a radio. If there will be an array of client devices, interoperability will be a greater issue, which means you'll want to select an AP with the greatest degree of proven interoperability, such as the 350 or 1200 series APs from Cisco.

One other item to consider is that as 802.11a becomes more prevalent in the marketplace, and availability and cost come into line with 802.1b devices, users will demand support of these as well. For this reason, a dual-band AP may be the best strategy for future growth.

- What types of client devices will be used on the WLAN?

Do you need specialty devices, such as bar code scanners, wearable computers, PDAs, cash registers, location-finding devices, and so forth? If so, you need to determine, with the help of the device vendor, whether these devices can support 802.11a, and either Cardbus interfaces or mini-PCI interfaces. As 802.11b is only 11Mbps, a PCMCIA interface to the radio is perfectly acceptable. However, if you're moving to 802.11a (or 802.11g), you need

Cardbus support or mini-PCI support, because a PCMCIA interface is not fast enough to provide 54Mbps of data rate.

- What are the regulations governing use of IEEE 802.11 in this region?

As explained in the 802.11a section of this book, there are still many countries that do not permit 802.11a systems. Other countries require the use of dynamic frequency selection and automatic power control (both of which are part of 802.11h) for 802.11a, or other 5GHz radio systems.

Other regulatory issues, like EIRP limits, frequency allocation, and antenna limitations, can come into play, as well. Even 2.4GHz has many different regulations from country to country. You need to check the local approvals and regulations for the countries the systems are to be used in. The last thing you want to do is choose a technology or product line, install it in half of your facilities, and then find out you have to use some different system in the remaining facilities because what you selected is not permitted. You can avoid much of this problem by selecting a vendor that provides this technology on the open world market, as opposed to a vendor that does not do any exporting of this technology. You'll also want to ensure that the security assets you purchase are appropriately configured, and legal, to export; again, this will be greatly alleviated if you select a vendor that routinely ships this technology to many countries around the world.

- Will anything in the building construction interfere with the RF signal?

You need to determine whether the facility is built such that RF will penetrate into the necessary areas, or whether you require special antennas to get coverage in certain areas. Remember that 2.4GHz signals will penetrate standard construction easier than 5GHz signals. A good practice is to actually do some on-site testing with both technologies to verify performance in your typical environment.

- Does the facility employ any other 2.4 or 5GHz equipment such as Bluetooth systems, cordless phones, microwaves, wireless security cameras and alarms, and so on?

If other systems are installed, and being actively used, this may be a reason to choose one technology over another. However, it may also simply require your attention during the site survey and installation to be certain the interference is kept to a minimum. Many times this can be achieved by proper placement of APs and antennas.

Selecting Necessary WLAN Services

Now that you have considered the preceding questions and determined the technology you want to use (or hopefully have a good idea about what you want), you need to determine what other functions will be important to your installation. Previous chapter have discussed VLANs, QoS, and security, and it is important that you understand the issues that some of these services and their support (or, in some cases, lack of support) will cause. This will also be an important part of choosing the proper WLAN products.

VLANs

VLANs are a relatively new feature in many of the WLAN products on the market and are detailed further in Chapter 10. A VLAN provides the ability to separate traffic over the RF. In the past, this had to be done at the switch, and for every VLAN, you needed a separate WLAN system.

Why would you want VLANs over the wireless? One example is for guest traffic in the enterprise system. Typically, a security system is set up on the WLAN for the "normal" corporate users. When guests arrive, giving them access to the network is not necessarily easy (or even desired), because passwords and accounts need to be set up, and these visitors may change on a day-to-day basis. By using VLANs, you can provide one VLAN for users that incorporates certain security modes (PEAP, LEAP, EAP-TLS, WPA, and so forth) and permits access to the corporate network, and provide a separate VLAN for guest users with static WEP, or perhaps no WEP at all. This VLAN would funnel the guest user only to certain network areas or perhaps even just the "dirtynet" for Internet access only. With the use of VLANs, both types of users can share the same AP.

If you plan to carry voice traffic over your WLAN equipment, you probably also want to configure your WLAN equipment such that all the voice traffic is carried over dedicated VLANs, to ensure that the low-latency traffic (voice in this case) is not competing with data that has less latency.

Quality of Service

QoS is a service that is necessary if you intend to support VoIP, and also if you want to differentiate traffic by port, application, or user. Until the IEEE 802.11e task group completes the standard for QoS, you will need to verify that the WLAN product you choose supports the QoS modes for the VoIP devices you select.

IP Subnet Roaming

IP subnet roaming is an issue that also requires some planning. While the whole intention of wireless is to be portable and mobile, you need to realize that it is *part* of the wired network. In fact, the AP is really at the edge of the network. The switch (or hubs in older days) used to be considered the edge of the network, but now it has been moved out to the AP. If you plan to install five APs, keeping them all on the same subnet is not a problem. However, if you are installing 2,000 APs across many campus buildings, it might be very difficult (and very undesirable) to keep them all on the same subnet, especially if you include low-latency-sensitive traffic over the same subnet.

If you move from one subnet to another, you will drop any IP connections that are presently running, and unless there is some method for a release-and-renew function for IP addresses, you will not have IP connectivity. Mobile IP was developed several years ago to handle these issues. Through the use of home and foreign agents on the infrastructure, and a special IP stack on the client, a client can move across subnets, without ever changing the client IP address. (A detailed description of Mobile IP is beyond the scope of this book.) The problem, however, is that this requires two things: support for Mobile IP on the infrastructure, typically in the routers, and, more importantly, a *different* IP stack on the client that supports the mobile node functions of Mobile IP. This is not something most IS and desktop support personnel want to dive into unless they have experience with larger networks.

A newer scheme, Proxy Mobile IP (PMIP), provides a solution. PMIP uses intelligence on the AP to proxy the IP address for the client, replacing the need to change the client IP stack to support mobile node functions. This allows *any* client IP stack to be used. If you have a large campus, or one where roaming is the norm, this is one feature you may want to investigate on the products you are considering.

Security

Security is a major concern. This book provides a complete chapter on this topic, so we will keep our discussion here to a minimum. You need to make sure the security solution you select and the products you select are compatible, keeping in mind again that you will have no higher level of security than the least sophisticated device on your network. An example would be a healthcare facility in which the patient-records application runs on standard laptop computers that support many different versions of security (PEAP, LEAP, EAP-TLS, WPA, and so forth), but the pharmaceutical application requires barcoding, and the barcode scanners may or may not support the same security solution. So, take care to select products that support the security method that you have chosen.

Load Balancing

Other features such as load balancing and hot standby in APs are also items to be considered. Most of the higher-end enterprise-type APs support these functions, but in some cases may require your attention to how they are configured. However, many of the lower-end products (products targeted for the SOHO markets) that IS professionals may be inclined to evaluate (based on pressure from upper-level management to lower costs) do not support these types of services.

Interoperability

Interoperability is also a concern when you are selecting products. Make sure that any product you select is Wi-Fi certified. This at least provides some basic level of interoperability testing and certification. Also be aware that there are several different Wi-Fi certifications, such as 802.11a, 802.11b, security, quality of service, etc. The packages of newer Wi-Fi certified products include a certification compliance label, which lists the features supported by the product (802.11a, 802.1b, WPA, QoS, and so forth).

HARDWARE SELECTION OF THE ACCESS POINT

There are several different designs of APs out there, both in physical form and in architectural form. Selecting the proper form factor can be critical to your implementation as well as your management support, overall cost, security, and reliability. Let's look at the two major different architectural implementations.

First let's consider an intelligent Access Point architecture, as depicted in Figure 8-1.

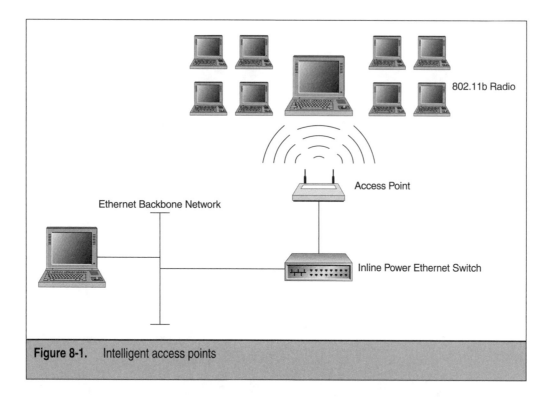

Figure 8-1. Intelligent access points

In this architecture, the AP has a fair amount of processing power, and maintains intelligence at the edge of the network. It ties directly into the network, and is an independent AP, not reliant on any other server or controller on the network (other than Ethernet connectivity) to maintain communication to the wireless clients. If one AP fails, only that one AP is affected, and all other devices continue to operate normally. The downside to this approach is that, in large installations, it usually requires some management server (for example, SNMP manager) to provide adequate support, configuration, and management. However, if the product is chosen so that its management requirements can be incorporated into the WLAN management system already in use, integration of management is very easy and efficient.

Intelligent Access Points are also the easiest to install. You can add an AP anywhere you need, and scale simply by adding more APs. There is nothing else on the network (providing you have Ethernet ports available) to add as you increase the AP population.

Now let's examine the architecture of a WLAN that utilizes Access Points with very little intelligence, and a central controller, and as shown in Figure 8-2.

In this style of WLAN system, the intelligence is removed from the AP and moved to the central controller on the network. In some systems, this setup can be easier to manage, because the management and configuration are handled by a single controller. All traffic coming into the AP flows into the controller, which handles authentication, security, configuration files, and so forth. The problem is that this is a single point of failure. If the controller fails, every AP that is controlled by that one controller also fails.

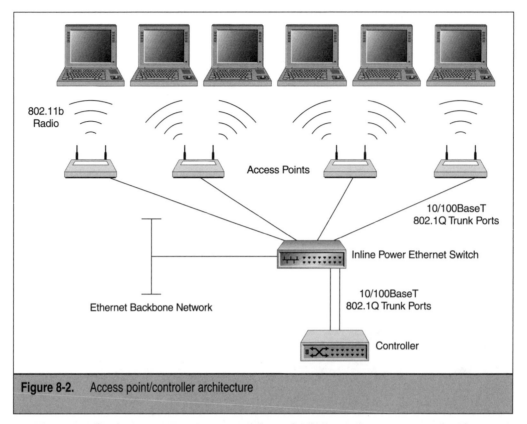

Figure 8-2. Access point/controller architecture

The controller has some maximum number of APs it supports or controls. If you are only installing two APs, then the cost of the system goes up drastically, because you have to buy a controller to support just two APs. However, if the controller can support up to as many as 25 APs, then the cost of a single controller is spread out over 25 devices, and it becomes more in line with an intelligent AP design cost.

In systems with 2000 APs, you need a number of controllers (generally, four controllers per 100 access points), and you also need a management station to manage the controllers. Again, this adds complexity to the overall WLAN system, but will be anticipated in a network large enough to require that many access points.

Single or Dual Radio Architecture

Most APs were designed to support a single-radio platform—one radio per AP. Some APs were provided with dual PCMCIA slots so that a second radio could also be operated. At the time of introduction, these were actually intended to provide a migration path from 900MHz to 2.4GHz. You could put one of each radio into the AP and have support for both bands, as you migrated away from 900MHz. However, there were some vendors that promised double the bandwidth with the architecture by using two of the same radios in the AP. However, this actually introduces a problem called *receiver desensitization,* causing poor performance of both radios (see sidebar).

Receiver Desensitization

Every radio receiver has a specification that defines the ability of the receiver to "hear and understand" some minimal signal strength. This is called receiver sensitivity or receiver threshold. This value represents the lowest signal that a radio can receive and still recover the information or data from the signal. In the case of most 802.11b WLAN radios, this is on the order of –80 to –85dBm (the lower the number, the smaller the signal). The typical 802.11b transmitter has a transmit power of +15 to +20dBm (or 100dB stronger than the receive threshold).

Because some cross-talk may occur between the different channels in the 802.11 band, the receiver incorporates filters and circuitry to reduce interference from other channels in the same band. With the 802.11 chip sets that are available on the market, about the best filtering (reject certain RF energy) that you can do, even at opposite ends of the band, is perhaps 65–75dB. This means the signal level coming out of a transmitter set to channel 1 is 15–20dBm at channel 1, but at the frequencies at channel 11, it is 65–75dB lower, or –50dBm to –60dBm. This value is stronger than the minimal signal level of the receiver by at least 20dBm. As shown below, if the AP radio on channel 11 is trying to receive a signal from a distant client, and the signal level is near the minimal receiver threshold, the energy present in the channel 11 area, transmitted from the channel 1 transmitter only a few inches away, will have a stronger signal level and mask out the desired signal from the actual client. This effectively reduces the coverage area of one channel any time the other radio is transmitting.

This issue can result from placing two single-band APs in close proximity. There should be, at minimum, approximately 5 feet between any two antennas attached to different 802.11b radios to provide adequate separation and receiver performance.

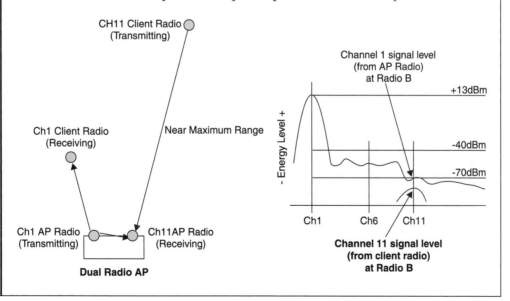

A number of dual-band APs have come on the market over the last year. These were designed with the intention of providing support for both 802.11b and 802.11a simultaneously. This architecture can be used to migrate from one technology to another or to simply add bandwidth by permitting some users on one technology and other users on another technology. However, because these architectures have different specifications and ranges, you must consider a few items at the network design stages. If you want the cell sizes the same for both technologies, you will have to adjust power levels or antenna selections appropriately.

AP radios come in several flavors. In some cases, they are internal, and not accessible to the outside. In the case of many low-end products, this means the antenna is also internal, providing minimal possible antenna configuration. In others cases, the radios can be plugged into the AP, providing upgradability. However, the style of radio interface may present two issues. First, it must have the ability to be secured to the AP, or it stands the chance of "walking away." Secondly, for 5GHz, the antenna selection may be limited (remember, the antenna has to be part of the radio for indoor use). For 2.4GHz, if the form factor is a PCMCIA card, this means external antennas will have to use a very small cable and connector, providing an easy failure point. If external antennas are desired, you should consider an AP that utilizes antenna connectors such as a TNC, SMA, or N connector (or some variation of one of these).

Upgradability is another issue. If you plan to move to a system supporting both 802.11a and 802.11b (or 802.11g), you should consider an AP that supports both devices in the same package. This helps to keep down installation costs, as well as wired infrastructure costs (every extra AP costs an extra wired switch port). If you plan to start with 802.11b and move to either 802.11a or 802.11g, you want to make sure the AP utilizes a Cardbus or mini-PCI interface, rather than a PCMCIA interface for the radio, and supports upgrades to the desired path.

Upgrading can also be an issue for older AP platforms. If an AP was designed to handle the 100Mbps Ethernet and one or two 802.11b radio cards (11Mbps each), the processor will support 122Mbps of data just fine (100 + 11 + 11). However, if the radios are upgraded to one 802.11a and one 802.11g, both supporting 54Mbps, then the AP needs to have enough processing power to support 208Mbps of data (100 + 54 + 54), plus the overhead of QoS, security, VLANs, or other services you want to turn on.

Inline power is a feature supported by many vendors today, and can save a tremendous amount of installation cost. Inline power also comes in several flavors and architectures. Presently, an IEEE committee (802.3af) is working on making Power over Ethernet (PoE) a standard. The standard is expected to be finalized late in 2002.

There are several ways to implement PoE. To apply power to the Cat 5 cable, you can use an Ethernet switch to provide this power, or you can use some power injector, which is inserted into the Cat 5 cables between the network and the AP. Some APs have an internal circuit to separate the power and Ethernet signals. Other vendors provide a power injector, as well as a power splitter. The splitter goes at the AP end, and has the circuitry to separate the Ethernet from the power. The splitter then has two output cables, one for Ethernet and one for power.

If you plan to power your AP from your network switches, you should investigate the power options of the switch (does it support 802.3af, or some other vendor's specific scheme?) as well as the AP to be sure they are compatible. Also be aware that some switches may not have enough power to support dual-band APs, resulting in the need to use a power injector or a third-party power module.

SELECTING THE CLIENT PRODUCT

Because most of the network features reside in the AP (at the edge of the network), there are many fewer items to consider on the client side. The biggest question to consider is what type of clients will be required, and who controls the client selection.

First, let's look at issues regarding the type of client. As mentioned earlier in this chapter, not all devices have been migrated to support 802.11a. This can be one crucial factor in the technology decision. But you must also consider interoperability, for not only the basic 802.11 side, but also things like security and QoS. Many of the specialty client devices on the market today do not support the wide range of features that are supported by the standard WLAN NIC-type devices. There are even some devices that still operate under DOS environments, severely limiting their feature support. For this reason, you should first select the features that are needed for your system, and then go in search of the client devices. In cases where you may have no choice but to use some of these "featureless" client devices, you may want to use VLANs to segregate traffic and help keep the main network secure.

Next, let's look at who controls what clients are used. If this is an education-related or public network, the network administrator typically has minimal input on the client side and is limited to a statement like "802.11b Wi-Fi compliance is required." While this seems fine at first, it has a major effect on the design of the network, because not all clients' radios are created equal.

Some radio vendors provide a very typical transmitter power of 15dBm (30mW), while others provide a higher transmitter power of up to 20dBm (100mW). Using a 100mW AP end with a 30mW client card results in nonsymmetrical performance (remember, this is a two-way communication path). The client can hear the AP, but the AP cannot hear the client.

If you are installing a 100mW, higher-end AP into the system, you want to set the power levels of the AP to be comparable to the lowest-power client card. This provides the best overall performance from *all* client devices.

Some client devices support several devices over a single radio connection. This is known as an Ethernet client, minibridge, or workgroup bridge. The idea behind this device is to provide RF connectivity for some small number of wired devices. As an example, consider a hospital nursing station that has three or four wired computers at the desk. Rather than pulling three or four cables (or even a single cable) to the desk, you can install one of these Ethernet clients, add an inexpensive hub, and attach all the devices to the hub. The devices will all access the network via the singe radio device.

Another example is a mobile crane in a shipping port. Such a crane likely has more than one computer device, and therefore requires more than one radio device and corresponding antennas (since the crane is comprised nearly entirely of metal, the antennas has to be remote and placed outside the crane operator's suite or computer closet). By using the Ethernet client, all the network devices in the crane can be funneled to a single radio and one antenna.

For desktop-style computers, or other devices that require PCI cards, two main styles of devices are offered today, the main difference being their antenna options. In one case, the PCI card is really a PC card-to-PCI converter, and a standard PC is used. This means that the antennas are typically attached and remote antennas are not available. The second style of PCI card is one that offers an external antenna, with the ability to mount the antenna remotely.

So, what is the difference between the two styles? Examine the situations where your computer is the type that you put on the floor under your desk, and your desk is steel, or perhaps the computer is in a point-of-sale device, such as a portable cash register, that gets mounted under the mobile cart. These typical installations can have a major effect on the ability of the antenna to transmit or receive properly, unless the antenna can be located in an open area.

SUMMARY

As this chapter points out, you need to ask yourself a lot of questions when selecting WLAN products. It is not as simple as picking a Wi-Fi-certified AP, or choosing one based solely on cost. Doing so will probably result in a system that is far less productive and useful than desired. You should take special care in this selection process to ensure you can support all users, applications, and features, as well as future growth.

One question that many people have when considering all the different technologies and features is, "Should I wait until all the standards are completed?" Asking this question is similar to asking whether you should wait for that faster computer to come out before you buy one. In either case, answering yes means you will probably never get a WLAN or a computer, because just as a faster computer will always be in development, the standards and WLAN products will continue to evolve.

Will you have control of what client devices are used on your WLAN? If you are an educational facility, for example, you may not, as students will purchase their own client devices. This means you need a system that supports a wide range of vendors' devices that are generally available to the students. Also, some type of tested interoperability between these devices would be required. The same is true if you plan to buy some specialty devices, such as IP phones or wireless print servers, that are only available from specific vendors, and are not available from the same manufacturer as the access points.

PART IV

Integrating WLAN into Your Network Infrastructure

CHAPTER 9

Wireless LANs
in the Enterprise

As discussed in Chapter 1, early forms of wireless LANs have been available since the mid-1980s. Standardized and interoperable WLANs have been shipping since 1997, and Wi-Fi products have been available since 1999. Despite this and the more than $1 billion spent worldwide annually on 802.11 products at this writing, WLAN deployments in the enterprise are still in their earliest days. Today, to the extent that WLANs are found in the enterprise, they tend to be limited deployments in places like conference rooms, cafeterias, and, naturally, the senior executive floors. Indeed, WLAN proliferation into vertical markets like retail, manufacturing, and warehousing greatly exceeds enterprise adoption. As evidenced by the sheer number of low-cost, easy-to-install Wi-Fi products available at computer retailers and catalogers, proliferation of wireless into residences and small offices is growing rapidly—in fact, far more quickly than into enterprises. Today's enterprise deployments are almost experimental in nature, as enterprise IS (information services) professionals, managers, and staff gain familiarity with WLANs and come to understand how they can best integrate Wi-Fi into an overall enterprise information infrastructure.

In this chapter, we define enterprise WLAN deployments, making, at the functional level, a distinction between enterprise deployments and small office/home office (SOHO) deployments. We discuss the approach an enterprise typically takes when deploying a WLAN. We also outline the steps enterprise IS professionals should take to maximize the likelihood of a successful initial deployment, including a physical assessment of the facilities in which wireless is to be deployed (the site survey) and the capacity planning needed to provide the enterprise-level performance demanded by users. Given that in the enterprise an existing wired LAN already exists, we discuss how IS professionals best can integrate Wi-Fi into this overall infrastructure, where wireless adds a vital mobility element to a network and where it might be a replacement or alternative to more traditional wires. We also discuss how you can best leverage existing network management tools and practices from the wired world to most expediently bring a similar level of management to the WLAN.

A theme throughout this chapter is that 802.11 equipment should be considered a highly integrated network element, rather than simply tacked onto a LAN, whether the network is in the home office or resides within a large enterprise.

WHAT IS THE ENTERPRISE?

First and foremost, the *Enterprise* is, of course, a series of starships, all captained by dashing leaders and crewed by a pan-galactic collection of Federation officers. Having said that, a definition of the enterprise as it relates to WLAN deployments is probably more germane to this book. Like the *Enterprise*, many enterprises are large, consisting of, at minimum, hundreds of individuals, all of whom are users of the organization's information infrastructure in some fashion. While many of these users may be located in a single headquarters building or campus, the enterprise is typically geographically distributed, with users scattered across a region, a continent, or even around the world.

The fact that a user may be working out of a spare bedroom thousands of miles from the enterprise headquarters makes that user no less an enterprise user—indeed, it is these sorts of users who often most challenge IS professionals.

NOTE The average 802.11 sale to enterprises consists of three to five access points, because most enterprises worldwide are small businesses rather than the more widely publicized large corporations.

Certainly, large commercial entities around the world are considered to be enterprise-level organizations. The more expansive definition is one that includes any large organization with a common purpose where individuals are engaged in specific, complementary tasks—including managing the enterprise information infrastructure. By this definition, larger governmental entities on the city, county, state, and provincial level as well as on the national level are "enterprises." Similarly, school systems, whether public or private, are enterprise organizations.

Stated another way, an enterprise is any organization that reaches the size at which it requires a dedicated staff of one or more IS professionals. The charter of this staff, no matter how small, is to make certain that the information infrastructure meets the needs of the organization and enables it to meet its goals—ideally, better than competitive organizations. And to remain *competitive*, leveraging new technologies to its advantage is a requirement for any organization, whether in the private or public sector. Wireless LANs are an excellent example—perhaps the best example available today—of an information technology that can have dramatic impact on the efficiency and effectiveness of an organization. Not surprisingly, IS professionals around the world are increasingly being charged with installing Wi-Fi, often on a trial basis with small pilot programs but with a mind toward a ubiquitous enterprise-wide deployment.

A SOHO Wi-Fi deployment presents few of the challenges associated with an enterprise deployment. As discussed in Chapters 5 and 6, the range of Wi-Fi devices, varying from a low of 60 feet to over hundreds of feet, is more than sufficient to cover even the largest of homes and small offices—even at the highest possible data rates. Indeed, if a home is so large as to require more than a single access point to achieve full physical coverage, it's likely that the owner has the wherewithal to hire an IS professional to manage the installation. The number of users in a SOHO environment tends to be fairly limited. While it's true that users of a SOHO LAN use the LAN to access other local computers, it is far more typical for users on a smaller LAN to access data from across the WAN, which can be cable, DSL, or even dial-up. This sets their performance expectations at fairly modest levels.

The enterprise is, of course, a completely different story. Typical corporate, governmental, and educational facilities, by their multistory nature alone, require more than a single access point to cover the entire building. In campus settings, the requirement can even be extended to include not just complete and reliable in-building coverage, but also WLAN availability between buildings. This opens up a whole host of challenges not found in SOHO deployments including *roaming* and *channel reuse* that will be discussed further in this chapter.

In larger enterprises, users have come to expect a level of network performance that is consistent with a wired network, one that is often switched, providing dedicated bandwidth that is typically rated at 100Mbps—and occasionally faster. Given this level of expectation, the IS professional's challenge is to provide the freedom and flexibility of wireless with performance and security that approximates that of the wired network.

In short, an enterprise is a relatively large organization with a common goal. The organization is typically in some form of competition with organizations with similar goals and, as such, employs information technology (among other tools) to gain competitive advantage. As such, the deployment of Wi-Fi in an enterprise presents challenges not found in other sorts of deployments and substantial consequences when things don't go quite as planned.

WI-FI DEPLOYMENT IN THE ENTERPRISE

Like any large project, the first step is to set goals and then formulate a plan to meet those goals. Although the specific goals of an enterprise's Wi-Fi deployment will vary, there is a constant: to deploy a Wi-Fi network in designated areas that provides reliable coverage and delivers the expected level of performance without compromising corporate security. Although this sounds simple, as the saying goes, "The devil is in the details."

Designating Areas

Rare are the cases in which a large enterprise chooses to deploy a Wi-Fi network across the whole organization in one fell swoop from initial deployment. There are a few reasons for this. Obviously, finding the budget for what can be a significant financial undertaking can be quite difficult. Responsible financial planners tend to take more of a "show me" approach, requesting first that a pilot program be run to assess the expense and resource drains of the project, the veracity of the budget estimates, and the return on investment.

Additionally, IS professionals recognize that Wi-Fi has a learning curve (as is typical with any new technology), and running a limited deployment provides valuable on-the-job training. Finally, as was discussed in Chapter 6, Wi-Fi is a technology undergoing rapid change, and organizations have concerns, unfounded or not, that the product they deploy will lock them into a soon-to-be-obsolete technology.

The great majority of enterprises instead initially opt for a limited WLAN deployment. There are different criteria by which these deployments can be limited, as described in the following sections.

Limiting Deployment to Only Where It's Needed Most

This strategy is based on the assumption that when laptop users are in their base area, such as an office, cubicle, or desk, they access the network via a wired connection, either by plugging directly into an Ethernet jack or through a docking station. Therefore, the Wi-Fi deployment is limited to places people tend to congregate *away from their desks,* in areas like conference rooms and smaller meeting rooms, cafeterias, classrooms, auditoriums, lobbies, and other similar public areas. For many enterprise organizations, this strategy meets the "80-20 rule"—it deploys WLANs in the 20 percent of places where 80 percent of it will be demanded.

What this strategy doesn't take into account is the fact that people are unpredictable and the places where they meet to collaborate are not always where the building's architect envisioned. Information is exchanged (and required from the network) in a variety of places: leaning up against a coworker's cubicle, in the smoking "lounge" outside, in the hallway. . .wherever.

This unpredictability continues to increase as enterprises more commonly issue laptops (as opposed to desktop computers) and as more than data is being transferred. Also, the growing popularity of personal digital assistants (PDAs) and devices such as bar code scanners and 802.11 handheld phones, and the associated demand for them to be just as connected as a laptop, drives demand for a more ubiquitous wireless infrastructure, because people use PDAs and similar devices in more places than they would a full laptop.

Similarly, as organizations begin to use the Wi-Fi infrastructure to provide local voice support, the user expectation is that coverage will be as complete as for their cellular telephone—only more reliable. For other organizations, deploying Wi-Fi "only" in the classrooms and auditoriums is tantamount to a full deployment. If a limited deployment in kindergarten through twelfth-grade schools, colleges, and universities is desired, another means of limiting the deployment is necessary—leading us to the next strategy.

Limiting Deployment to One Building at a Time

In campus environments, particularly those campuses where different buildings or groups of buildings have differing charters, it's common for Wi-Fi to be rolled out on a building-by-building basis. This is a very typical model in a university where, for example, the business school deploys WLANs in its building and then supplies Wi-Fi client adapters to (or mandates their purchase by) all students who use that facility.

Often, the financial structure of a university plays a role in the choice of this strategy. Using the business school example again, the business school may have the budget autonomy to fund an initiative to deploy Wi-Fi without the involvement of the university's central organization, and may be able to rely on outside sources of funds such as alumni associations and local business partnerships.

Sometimes, a single-building deployment is accomplished even without the involvement of the central IS organization, although this is more common, not surprisingly, in an engineering school than in a business school. The central drawback to this approach is that all but a few students and even some faculty spend their academic days in more than a single building or group of buildings. This is all the more true of new matriculates—the very ones who are receiving the first client adapters.

Experience has shown that once WLANs are deployed in a single building, the expectation is set that it should be similarly deployed across campus, in classrooms, cafeterias, and unions, and even in the dormitories. As discussed in the next section, this unmet demand can have very real ramifications for the whole of the IS infrastructure.

Limiting Deployment to Temporary Buildings and Workgroups

In this model, Wi-Fi is deployed not so much for the mobility it provides the user, but rather for the mobility it provides the *infrastructure*. In today's dynamic economic environment, it's common for organizations to rapidly increase and decrease in size. It's also common for groups of people from different groups and even locations to be brought together on a temporary basis for a specific project. This phenomenon has fostered the creation of the term *networks in motion*. Enterprise organizations sometimes deploy a Wi-Fi network to meet these challenges.

With a temporary building, there's little economic sense to installing Ethernet cable throughout a building, or the far more expensive option of trenching for either Ethernet or fiber optics, only to soon leave it behind. Often, a temporary building has a copper plant in place that supports a telephone system, but the cabling is insufficient for modern information networks. Temporary cabling solutions with cable exposed hanging from ceilings, between buildings, or duct taped to walls present an unprofessional appearance and potential safety hazard inconsistent with most enterprise organizations' standards. A Wi-Fi network can be deployed far more rapidly throughout a building than a traditional network infrastructure and with far less expense. When it's time to vacate the building, the network infrastructure can be easily packed up and redeployed at the next location.

Temporary workgroups present challenges similar to those of a temporary building and are similarly well suited to a Wi-Fi deployment. Again, Wi-Fi networks can be rapidly deployed in areas like cafeterias, gymnasiums, tents, and the like that are designated for a temporary workgroup, including emergency or disaster relief organizations, or for business continuity purposes in the event of a local disaster. WLAN deployments greatly mitigate the "spaghetti problem" of Ethernet cable being run to individual workstations. Wi-Fi equipment can easily be easily deployed—and redeployed.

It is these sorts of installations in the enterprise that drive a significant portion of the demand for client form factors, such as USB and PCI, that are designed for desktop, rather than laptop, PCs. Industry data shows that these form factors account for as much as a quarter of all client adapter unit sales, suggesting that the deployment of Wi-Fi LANs for temporary buildings and workgroups is more common than is immediately intuitive.

Limiting Deployment from the Outside In

Enterprise organizations report that, on average, around 30 percent of all branch offices and/or their personnel will relocate over the course of a single year. This presents major challenges for enterprise IS staff—handling network additions and moves is a costly and time-consuming exercise in any event, but performing them on a remote basis in a branch office presents an even greater challenge.

While the smaller size of a branch office tends to decrease the need for the mobility Wi-Fi provides to the user, the remote and dynamic nature of a branch office (the so-called "extended enterprise") *increases* the applicability of a WLAN. As is the case with a temporary building, a branch office building or office suite tends not to be owned by the enterprise itself. Granted, this arrangement usually is in the form of a longer-term lease rather than a simple rental agreement, but the temporary nature of the relationship is fundamentally the same and there are commonly additional complications with negotiating infrastructure changes to a rented or leased facility.

Wi-Fi LANs, particularly in smaller facilities, can be remotely installed by the IS staff by providing direction to a local contractor or even an enterprise employee, which decreases or even eliminates the need for travel to remote locations. And again, when the lease term expires, the WLAN portion of the network infrastructure is portable and reusable, not buried in the walls of someone else's building.

Security Alert: The Consequences of Unmet Demand

With inexpensive, easy-to-install residential versions of Wi-Fi readily available to end users through computer retailers, consumer electronics stores, catalogers, and the Internet, Wi-Fi has been installed in many homes. This exciting market is discussed further in Chapter 10. This dynamic also has implications for the enterprise.

It's instructive to briefly review the way in which PCs entered the enterprise. Few IS staffs in the early 1980s took the initiative to deploy PCs to enterprise users. Rather, it was far more common for them to battle the proliferation of the devices until it became apparent that the fight could not be won. Enterprise IS had typically deployed a centralized and secure information infrastructure based on mainframes and minicomputers with simple "dumb" terminals deployed on the desktop. It was at the departmental and even individual level that PCs began to enter the enterprise. Users demanded the freedom and flexibility of a PC, a demand that was unmet by all but the most forward-thinking IS organizations. With PC prices falling to within the reach of departmental and individual expense budgets, it became possible to bring them into the enterprise without the involvement, or sometimes even the knowledge, of the IS organization.

The same dynamic today is playing out with Wi-Fi. Users are increasingly familiar with the benefits of Wi-Fi, often having experienced them firsthand in their homes. Whereas early PCs barely fit into departmental and individual budgets, residential versions of Wi-Fi access points can be purchased for a few hundred dollars, an amount that causes little scrutiny in most enterprises. The small size of Wi-Fi access points allows them literally to be hidden from view under a box or behind a desk, and installation is about as easy as plugging them in to an available and ubiquitous Ethernet jack.

As alluded to previously, in the absence of an enterprise IS-sanctioned Wi-Fi infrastructure, users will create their own. The problem with this grass-roots infrastructure is that individual users tend to pay little heed to the management and security requirements of the enterprise IS infrastructure. And, with an unsecured access point attached to an Ethernet port broadcasting a signal that passes easily through walls, the situation is tantamount to installing an Ethernet jack in the parking lot. Not only is the Wi-Fi network unsecure, but by attaching to an Ethernet jack that itself has no authentication mechanism, it opens access to the whole of the enterprise network, both wireless *and* wired.

This dynamic is likely to expand over time. More and more, "Wintel" laptop manufacturers—those providing devices based on Intel x86 architecture and Microsoft Windows operating systems—are providing embedded Wi-Fi adapters with their products as low-cost options. Apple Computer has been providing embedded Wi-Fi since 1999 with great acceptance. Many expect more than half of all Wintel laptops to ship with embedded Wi-Fi by the end of 2003. With departments within the enterprise rather than the central IS organization often being responsible for end-user device purchases, many choose embedded Wi-Fi in their laptops. The users of these increasingly ubiquitous Wi-Fi-enabled devices will be looking for the infrastructure needed to make this feature useful—and, as a matter of fact, most laptop vendors are happy to sell a low-cost access point with the laptop. Those who have been around networks and computers long enough recognize that the very same thing happened with the inclusion of modems and then Ethernet ports on PCs. No brand-name PC or laptop is sold, or at least used, without one to three different data access devices such as modem, Ethernet port, PCMCIA slot, and now built-in WLAN clients.

The point is that, as happened previously with PCs, the proliferation of Wi-Fi into the enterprise likely is inevitable—not from the top down, and not as an organizational initiative, but rather from the grassroots up. This occurs on a worldwide basis, from military sites to Wall Street to the smallest print shop. Wi-Fi is a disruptive technology, a revolution. IS professionals can be in the vanguard, deploying a Wi-Fi network that is as manageable and as secure as the wired LAN, or they can let the coming wave crash over them.

In Chapter 11, we detail how you can find rogue Wi-Fi networks and provide a variety of strategies for deploying a secure WLAN. While policing the enterprise and rooting out rogue networks is a prudent short-term tactic for maintaining network security, the more strategic and long-term means of addressing the current and increasing number of rogue access points is simply to preempt the incentive for individuals to deploy them by deploying instead an enterprise Wi-Fi network. After all, when was the last time someone snuck a PC into work?

Capacity Planning

Having defined a deployment strategy, the next step in the process should be to define what level of WLAN service you need to provide to the Wi-Fi users. Wireless LANs are, by their nature, a shared-medium technology. An access point establishes a coverage area or cell that provides an *aggregate* amount of throughput that is shared by all the client devices within that cell, associated to that access point. In Ethernet terms, a coverage cell is a collision domain. With Ethernet, you can define the precise number of client devices within the collision domain by choosing how many ports on an Ethernet hub will be used. With WLANs, there are, of course, no physical ports; you use the size and shape of the coverage area as a means of limiting the number of users who typically are associated to that particular access point. The means by which you can decrease (and indeed increase) the coverage size of an access point is covered in the next section on coverage planning.

With Ethernet, capacity planning is an absolute: the number of users connected to a single hub is the same as the number of users in the collision domain (assuming the hub is on its own switched segment). With Wi-Fi, on the other hand, the number of users can vary greatly as they enter and exit the coverage area. Additionally, with transmission over radio waves, throughput is subject to variation as transitory factors such as interference that decrease throughput present themselves in the coverage area. As such, capacity planning for WLANs is an approximation.

The central question that needs to be answered is: "How much throughput should, on average, be provided to each user of the Wi-Fi LAN?" Naturally, different types of users have different average throughput requirements. Warehouse and retail workers with bar code scanners have very modest throughput requirements. Office and classroom users transferring e-mail, browsing the Web, and exchanging the occasional word processor document, spreadsheet, or presentation file have greater, yet still relatively modest, throughput requirements. Finally, those transferring high-resolution graphics and layouts, CAD (computer aided drafting) files, and x-ray and other medical images have very large throughput requirements. Because the question of average-per-user throughput is essentially a division problem, one can affect either the divisor or the dividend to achieve the same quotient. The following are a few illustrations:

- **Stockroom associates with bar code scanners** For these sorts of devices, 25Kbps provides more than enough bandwidth per user. 802.11b-compliant WLANs provide approximately 5Mbps of aggregate throughput when set to an 11Mbps data rate, and provide approximately 500Kbps of throughput when set to a 1Mbps data rate. The maximum number of users per access point set to 11Mbps would be 200, with the maximum number when set to 1Mbps being 20. Few warehouses and retail locations have more than 20 associates performing bar code scans at a single time within the same collision domain. In this scenario, the goal would be to provide physical coverage in all areas where scanning is performed with as few access points as possible—capacity is not a real issue in this scenario. As an aside, hybrid devices that serve both as bar code scanners and cordless telephones are becoming increasingly popular in these markets. The need to support voice as well as data complicates this scenario considerably and will be covered in Chapter 12.

- **Students accessing a university intranet site while in a lecture hall**   While the Hypertext Transfer Protocol (HTTP) is fairly efficient, the transfer of graphics-rich web pages requires a substantial amount of bandwidth, say 300Kbps, for an acceptable user experience. This requirement becomes all the more onerous when, as part of an instructor's presentation, many students might access the WLAN at nearly the same time. With an 802.11b-compliant Wi-Fi access point providing about 5Mbps of aggregate throughput, the number of users per access point should be about 17. For a class of 85 students (not uncommon at the university level), this translates to a need for five access points in the room, which presents channel reuse challenges, as discussed in the next section. Alternatively, if the technology deployed is 802.11a or, when available, 802.11g, the aggregate throughput when set to a 54Mbps data rate will be on the order of 25Mbps, resulting in the provision of the same 300Kbps of throughput with a single access point. In this particular scenario, the very high density of users sitting in lecture hall desks renders the relatively limited range of 802.11a (and, to a lesser extent, 802.11g) a nonissue, as the single access point should be capable of covering most lecture halls, which themselves tend to be very open indoor facilities.

- **Office users transferring files**   With presentation files, spreadsheet-based financial models, and even some word processing documents going well beyond 1MB in size, office workers (for whom time is, after all, money) often demand WLAN performance that compares to the switched wired connection they typically have on their desktop. For these users, their per-user throughput requirements can easily be a half a megabit per second, and ten users to an 802.11b access point may well be the right number to budget. Here again, if it's an 802.11a or 802.11g access point with approximately five times the aggregate throughput, 50 users could occupy the same coverage area and enjoy the same average per-user throughput—to the extent that 50 users could occupy the coverage area provided by shorter-range high-performance access points. Today's office cubicles are small, but not *that* small.

Naturally, the operational capacity at any given point in time is not entirely the decision of the IS department. First, defining the level of performance users can expect often requires negotiations with representatives of the user community. Remember, too, that these are the same users who have grown accustomed to a switched 100Mbps wired connection their desktop. IS professionals know that the utilization of this connection is well less than 10 percent for the great majority of users. Nevertheless, it's not uncommon for users to want both the freedom of wireless and the level of performance that they think they need.

End-user decisions, or at least their decisions in conjunction with the decisions made by laptop vendors, also play a role in operational capacity. As discussed in the sidebar earlier in this chapter, it is becoming increasingly common for laptops to be offered with Wi-Fi radios embedded directly into the device—and for laptop purchase decisions to be made at the departmental level, not by the IS organization. The antennas for these radios are themselves embedded around the laptop's display. As discussed in Chapter 5, antennas are specially designed to transmit and receive radio energy within a certain frequency band. With design cycles for laptops of approximately a year and a half, most antennas embedded in today's laptops are tuned to 2.4GHz, the frequency band of 11Mbps 802.11b, not the 5GHz band of 54Mbps 802.11a. The irony is that the laptops with wireless embedded that are demanded by users and departments complicate the ability of the IS department to provide them with the performance that they think they need.

It is, by the way, typical for 802.11b Wi-Fi networks to be deployed for 11Mbps coverage areas. Given their relatively short range of 802.11a at their maximum data rate of 54Mbps, it is more typical to plan for one of the lower supported data rates that provides for greater range—although the newness of the technology makes generalizations like this difficult.

The principal way to increase per-user throughput is to decrease the number of users contending for the aggregate throughput provided by the access point. This limiting of users is typically accomplished by decreasing the size of the coverage cell. Two major implications arise from this.

The first is that it doesn't come free. The obvious implication of decreasing the coverage area of an access point is that more access points are required to cover the same given physical area. Doubling the amount of throughput provisioned for each user doubles the cost of the access points and the deployment thereof.

The second implication is that deploying for higher per-user throughput can simplify deployments—or complicate them. As discussed in Chapter 1, the legacy environments for WLANs are similar to those described in the earlier stockroom example—a relatively low density of users with low bandwidth requirements. Accordingly, the physical planning for WLANs focuses on achieving coverage in all required areas with the fewest number of access points possible. After all, as recently as 1999, access points cost more than $2000 each, while leading performance devices today are approximately one third of that price. Deploying for high per-user throughput eliminates the need to optimize access point range.

You must also consider that the cost of deploying an AP includes the labor cost and, commonly, the cost of deploying additional Ethernet cable and access to AC power (although APs exist that do not require separate lines for power and data). High transmit power, receive sensitivity, and antenna gain are unnecessary when limiting the number of users in the collision domain through *decreased* cell size.

A high density of access points does, however, present other problems. Not all vendors provide features like transmit power control settings that are designed to decrease coverage area. Antenna attenuators that decrease the gain of an antenna, and therefore cell size, can be expensive and are only a possibility when using antennas with connectors. Finally, when spacing access points close together, channel reuse problems become more acute, particularly in the narrow 2.4GHz band that allows for just three nonoverlapping channels.

Coverage Planning: The Site Survey

In the first chapter of *Baby and Child Care,* his seminal book on child rearing, Dr. Benjamin Spock famously started with, "Trust yourself, you know more than you think you do."

The idea was to reassure concerned and even frightened first-time parents that they should trust their intuition when raising their children. After all, parents had managed to raise their children before instruction manuals and trained professionals existed. Parents then and now draw upon their experiences, their intuition, and the advice of other parents. With all that said, in some more challenging situations, parents look to professionals for guidance and assistance. And indeed, as Dr. Spock has told you, they buy and read books on the subject.

Today, faced with deploying a WLAN, IS professionals in the enterprise are a little like first-time parents, competent and effective people confronted with a new and unfamiliar challenge. IS professionals are typically well versed in *wired* network architectures, the tools designed for managing the *wired* LAN, security policies that presume physical ports, and, of course, even the bend radii for various types of fiber-optic and coaxial cable. All of which, at least at the surface, have little to do with Wi-Fi.

On the other hand, IS professionals, like anyone else living in an industrialized country in the twenty-first century, have a lifetime of experience with radio waves. We watch television and listen to AM/FM radio. We might have even had a CB radio (although typically we choose not to admit it). Walkie-talkies, pagers, cell phones, baby monitors . . . we've grown up with radio and we live with it still. We know intuitively that radio waves go through walls but that the signal is weakened when they do; that subtle movements and changes in position can have a huge impact upon how well a signal is received; that a signal gets weaker as it gets further from its transmitter; that when two signals are at similar frequencies, they can interfere with each other; and that, just as visible waves of light can be blocked, creating shadows, radio waves can be blocked, causing a signal to disappear as we drive through a tunnel. Trust yourself, you know more than you think you do. This is not to say that an IS professional should lumber into a Wi-Fi deployment unaware, or that there's no difference between a wired and a WLAN. Rather, it's meant to point out that performing the tasks that are specific to a Wi-Fi network, and that are necessary for a successful deployment, can all be learned and that you probably have a bigger head start than you think.

If the goal of capacity planning is to provide users with what they need, the goal of coverage planning is to provide them with what they need *where* they need it. This relates back to the various deployment strategies—some areas will be designated for

WLAN deployment and others will not. Coverage planning is often referred to as a *site survey*, a process whereby an individual or group gathers data and then makes specific recommendations as to the types of access points, antennas, and other equipment to be installed and the specific locations for these installations.

A site survey takes into account the design of the building and its construction materials (ascertained through blueprints and floor plans as well as direct examination), the traffic patterns within the facility, the sorts of barriers likely to be encountered in the facility, the range and coverage pattern capabilities of the access points to be used and the flexibility of those capabilities, the technologies (802.11b, 802.11a, or both) and resulting throughput channels available to them, and, of course, the capacity plan.

When Is a Site Survey *Not* Necessary?

Before answering the question, first let's better define the term *site survey*. In the most elementary sense, a site survey is a simple look around a facility before placing an access point. In a home, it can be a matter of choosing on which bookshelf to place the access point. In the more extreme cases, a site survey can take days and require you to hire experienced and trained professionals who tend not to work cheaply, and who provide the network administrator with a large binder full of information about WLAN network element placement. For the purposes of this question, we define a site survey as requiring the services of someone specially trained in doing them, which tends to mean hiring a consultant or a reseller of WLAN and other network hardware.

Frankly, those with long-time experience with WLANs sometimes tend to overemphasize the need for a site survey, probably more so in SOHO environments than in a larger enterprise network where network unreliability readily converts to operational inefficiencies and lost profits and revenues. The tendency of some WLAN professionals to over-optimize a site survey may result from their experience in challenging applications like retail locations, warehouses, and hospitals. Naturally, these are some of the earliest adopters of WLANs and the types of installations industry veterans have a great deal of experience with—to the exclusion of more recent enterprise adopters that are generally less challenging environments for WLANs. Another possibility is that there is a fairly lucrative market for the professional services needed for what are sometimes unnecessary site surveys.

As a general rule, if a single access point can cover a facility and provide the per- user throughput required, and the facility has no server, a site survey is unnecessary. Remember that even 802.11a access points, which provide less coverage than their 802.11b counterparts, provide an approximate 50-foot coverage radius at their 54Mbps maximum data rate. With an omnidirectional antenna providing a circular coverage pattern, the resulting coverage area is 11,000 square feet. With an 802.11b access point with a 100-foot coverage radius, the area grows to more than 30,000 square feet.

The point is that even 11,000 square feet is larger than most homes, most small offices, and most branch offices. Assuming these facilities are made with standard building materials like wood, drywall, and plaster for interior walls and don't have an inordinate number of interior fixtures like file cabinets and whiteboards that are unfriendly to radio waves, they can typically be covered by a single access point. Even in situations where more than one access point is needed either for capacity purposes or to cover the corners or recesses of the facility, their placement is fairly intuitive. Remember that even the 2.4GHz band provides for three channels. You can place as many as three access points in a facility (it's good practice to keep them at least ten feet apart to avoid interference) without any concern for interference between the devices.

In short, even in situations where up to three access points are required to cover the facility, you may well be able to dispense with a formal site survey. This isn't to say that you should indiscriminately install access points without thinking; it means that with a little planning, study, and common sense, you can successfully deploy your Wi-Fi LAN.

Internal and External Building Design

"They just don't build 'em the way they used to" is a common refrain heard regarding buildings. Hallmarks of buildings from the first part of the twentieth century and before are brick or even stone external walls, plaster and lath internal walls stretching from floor to ceiling, and high plaster ceilings. In North America at least, buildings from the postwar era are a very different story. Exterior walls generally are thinner, predominant construction material for interior walls is drywall, open spaces separated by cubicles are more common, and larger windows and suspended ceilings are the norm.

Although people can and do decry the perceived decline in building quality, the newer buildings are a lot more friendly to Wi-Fi installation. In general, the more dense the construction material, the more it prevents RF energy from passing through it. This matter of energy loss is referred to as *attenuation*. Wood, drywall, cubicle walls, room partitions, and the like have a relatively high amount of air in them, whereas brick, cement, stone, and thick plaster walls have less air in them, and also tend to be thicker. Metal, such as the exterior metal walls of a warehouse or hanger, or even the metal studs used today for interior walls instead of wood, presents a special problem because it not only stops a signal, but reflects it, creating the multipath propagation discussed in Chapter 5.

Understanding the effect various building materials have on radio energy makes for a good starting point when surveying the facility to be covered. Through either blueprints or, better still, direct physical inspection, you should familiarize yourself with the types of construction materials found in the facility.

- Avoid planning for penetration through exterior walls, as they typically degrade a signal to a large and unpredictable degree. This makes the resulting exterior coverage area variable in performance and reliability. If an exterior coverage area is desired (as is often the case with university and corporate campuses), antennas should be installed outdoors specifically for these coverage areas.

- Plan for little attenuation when installing an access point in an open office environment, like the types populated with cubicles.

- When installing a Wi-Fi LAN operating in the 2.4GHz band, plan for penetration through most interior walls, including those made from drywall, plaster, and even cinderblocks, although they provide increasing levels of attenuation. The metal studs often found in interior drywall in commercial buildings can introduce a level of unpredictability and multipath when at a high angle of incidence to the transmitter. The 5GHz waveform of 802.11a Wi-Fi LANs is absorbed and distorted by common materials to a greater degree than is the 2.4GHz waveform, due to the differing length of the waveforms. With a physical length of around two inches, the 5GHz wave is about half the length of the 2.4GHz wave, causing it to deteriorate more extensively as a function of time and as a function of coming into contact with structural elements. Generally, you can plan for penetration through drywall and plaster but typically not through cinderblock when working in the 5GHz band. Note, however, that the relative newness of 802.11a results in a much smaller body of empirical installation data in the world of WLAN.

- While you can plan for coverage through walls that are *partly* made of metal, you cannot assume penetration through all-metal walls. Indeed, due to the multipath-inducing properties of metal, you should plan around them.

The operative words here are "plan" and "assume." That is, this is just the first step in the process, which is then followed by an actual physical verification of these assumptions. The documentation of these assumptions is usually a site plan in which provisional access point placements are made to a copy of the building's floor plan. This is a very useful and arguably indispensable tool for implementations. It is also useful for establishing a budget, as you can get a fairly accurate estimate of the number of access points, antennas, cables, and other accessories needed at this stage. A compass, set to the correct scale of the floor plan, is ideal for estimating omnidirectional and hemispherical coverage areas.

As shown in Figure 9-1, in the 2.4GHz band, three nonoverlapping channels are available for 802.11b and, when available, 802.11g. If a facility can be covered with three or fewer access points, co-channel interference is not a problem, which significantly simplifies a deployment. A single access point, and certainly three, will cover contemporary office floors, which tend to have only partial cubicle walls rather than floor-to-ceiling walls, which tend to attenuate RF energy and reduce coverage.

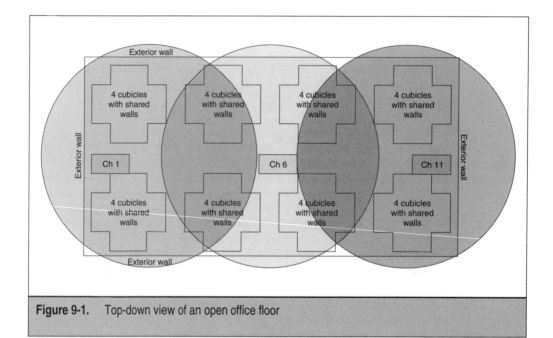

Figure 9-1. Top-down view of an open office floor

Retail stores and warehouses are among the more challenging environments for RF coverage, as shown in Figure 9-2. Depending upon elevation, material selection, and angle relative to the transmitter, shelved merchandise can very effectively block RF energy from one row to the next. The metal shelves themselves reflect RF energy and create multipath propagation, which drives down performance. An effective strategy for deployment in these facilities is to use patch or Yagi antennas to direct the RF energy in a tight beam down the rows, thereby covering the areas associated with inventory control and minimizing the reflections from the metal shelves.

The propagation characteristics of the 2.4GHz waveform allow for penetration through walls made of many types of building materials—even the cinderblock walls often found in primary and university classrooms. An 802.11b and likely an 802.11g access point with an omnidirectional antenna placed against a wall can often cover two classrooms. Given the high user density consistent with classroom environments, the per-user throughput provided by this deployment could be quite low. With only three nonoverlapping channels available, the isolation of cells set to the same channel becomes an issue. Note that the coverage area provided down the corridor overlaps slightly with a classroom coverage area set to the same channel. In more densely deployed environments like this one, minimizing co-channel interference rather than eliminating it entirely can be the goal.

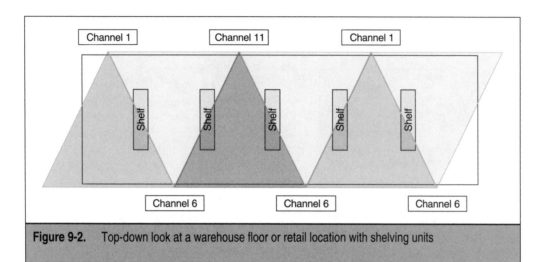

Figure 9-2.   Top-down look at a warehouse floor or retail location with shelving units

The 5GHz waveform is attenuated by common building materials to a greater degree than the 2.4GHz wave. Whereas a 802.11b access point can be installed such that it covers more than a single room, the coverage of an 802.11a access point more typically is limited to a single classroom—particularly when constructed of materials like brick or cinderblock. Given the high user density consistent with classrooms, this characteristic can actually be beneficial in that it helps to limit the cell size and thereby provides for a higher level of per-user throughput. Note that the eight channels available in the UNII-1 and UNII-2 bands combined decrease, if not eliminate, channel reuse concerns. Even with a very large number of access points deployed, the large number of channels (coupled with the more limited cell size) allows for a deployment with no overlapping cells set to the same channel, thereby eliminating any performance-degrading co-channel interference.

Some objects and building materials are essentially impenetrable to radio waves of any frequency, as shown in Figure 9-3. Elevator shafts with a large amount of steel and, to an even greater degree, the x-ray rooms with lead-lined walls that are commonly found in hospitals are best planned around. 802.11b access points with omnidirectional antennas can cover a number of examination rooms while this same type of access point, installed in the x-ray room, covers just that room. Patch antennas with a wide-angle coverage pattern can be used to fill in areas not covered by omnidirectional antennas. Note that while the three available channels in the 2.4GHz band are a limiting factor, access points can be deployed such that full coverage can be achieved without any overlapping cells set to the same channel.

Multistory structures like office towers, hospitals, and university classroom buildings introduce a third dimension to coverage planning. The 2.4GHz waveform of 802.11b

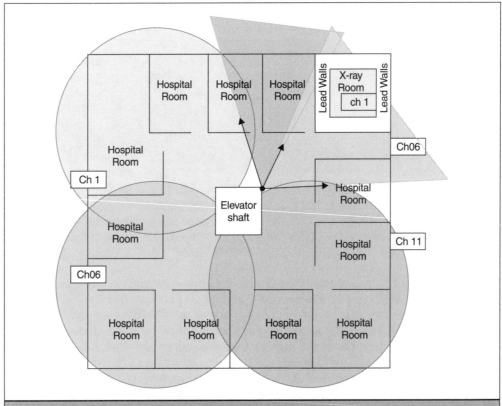

Figure 9-3. Objects and building materials that are impenetrable to radio waves of any frequency

and, when available, 802.11g will pass through both walls and floors. The 5GHz waveform of 802.11a will pass through both as well, but to a lesser degree. For 2.4GHz Wi-Fi LANs in particular, you must avoid overlapping cells on the same floor and on adjacent floors. Even with only three channels, this can be achieved through careful three-dimensional planning.

Placement Options

Choosing the best locations for access point and antenna placement involves a number of different and sometimes competing factors. Optimal locations from a propagation perspective may be aesthetically or economically unacceptable. Budgetary constraints may result in access points with suboptimal range and reduced antenna options. Every building is going to present different parameters suggesting different placements, but some general rules do apply.

Roaming

Strictly defined within the Wi-Fi standards, *roaming* is the process whereby a client can move from the coverage area of one access point to the coverage area of the next access point. As discussed in Chapter 5, this is accomplished through a client-side process of scanning for available access points and, if better performance can be had when associated to another access point, disassociation followed by association with the other access point. Roaming can, however, also be thought of as the means by which you can scale a Wi-Fi deployment to cover an area of almost any size. Indeed, as will be discussed in Chapter 14, Wi-Fi deployments covering entire towns and neighborhoods are already in place, with citywide deployments within the realm of technical possibility.

You should consider the infrastructure to be a web of interconnected access points that, in the aggregate, provide complete, uninterrupted coverage. Roaming is the capability that allows a client to "view" access points in the same manner. That said, the process of roaming is neither perfect nor instantaneous. Frequent roams increase the possibility of noticeable performance degradation, particularly when running latency- sensitive traffic like voice and video. And, of course, each "coverage area" is actually an access point that costs money. Given this, you should minimize the number of roams necessary to cover the required area by maximizing the cell size of each access point—within the context of the capacity plan.

Ceiling placements tend to work best. By placing access points or antennas on or above ceilings, circular cells that maximize the coverage area of the access point can be set up with omnidirectional antennas, the most common type available. Placement on the ceiling gets access points and antennas away from people, minimizing intentional or unintentional contact. Some access points can be hidden above suspended ceilings (see the sidebar on plenum considerations) with only antennas visible, a positive feature from both aesthetic and theft-deterrence points of view. Even access points with nonremovable antennas and plastic cases can sometimes be mounted on ceilings.

When working with access points with connectors that support auxiliary antennas, you have some flexibility in terms of access point placement. Access points can be remotely located in places like wiring closets that provide for centralized management and theft protection. On the other hand, as discussed in Chapter 5, substantial loss in gain results from cable runs. This cable loss can negate any gain provided by the antenna. In facilities with suspended ceilings, it's more typical to place an access point designed for these locations (see "What Is the Plenum?" sidebar) near the antenna than it is to suffer the cost and cable loss associated with remote access point placement.

Ceiling placement allows the RF energy to radiate down to the floor below and, in some cases, can even provide a "bonus" coverage area on the floor above. Access points may be placed in ceiling centers or, if more than a single access point is necessary for coverage or capacity, spaced at intervals that in the aggregate provide for full coverage (refer to Figure 9-1).

Mounting access points on desktops or, better still, on the top rails of cubicles provides benefits similar to ceiling mounts. This sort of installation is common when working with lower-cost access points that are ill-suited to ceiling installation or when an installation is likely to be temporary.

What Is the Plenum?

The National Electric Code (NEC) defined in 1999 the *plenum* as being "...a compartment or chamber to which one or more air ducts are connected and that forms part of the air distribution system." In other words, the plenum is typically the space above a suspended ceiling where things like heating and air conditioning duct work runs and overhead lights are installed, an area that's ideal in many ways for the placement of Wi-Fi access points.

Because of the types of things installed in the plenum, it's an area that is subject to fire codes. In the event of a fire, this area is ideal for the spread of flames and, more to the point, noxious fumes and poisonous gasses, which are a far greater cause of fatalities in fires than flames themselves. The types of materials you can put in the plenum are therefore restricted.

Because the plenum is subject to *local* fire and building codes, there is no one national or international standard for what types and amounts of materials are acceptable for placement in the plenum. Indeed, some municipalities define the plenum to include not only the space above a suspended ceiling, but also an area extending some number of inches *below* the suspended ceiling. Still, you can make choices that maximize the likelihood of steering clear of problems with the local building inspector or, much worse, creating a hazard in your workplace.

Although there is no universal standard for plenum rating, there is a very good substitute. Underwriters Laboratories has developed a standard, UL2043, titled "Fire Test for Heat and Visible Smoke Release for Discrete Products and Their Accessories Installed in Air-Handling Spaces." This test, and resulting compliance to the standard, does not address the toxicity of the fumes released when the device is burned; rather, it addresses the rate at which they burn and the quantity of energy released and then ignited. Still, if a product is certified to UL2043, it's a good bet it'll meet with local building codes. Cisco Systems, www.cisco.com, is alone in certifying selected access points to this standard.

Absent UL2043 certification, the rule of thumb is to avoid access points with plastic cases for placement in the plenum. Anyone who's burned a model airplane or unfortunate army man knows that plastic burns and, when it does, releases dense black smoke and a variety of harmful gasses. On the other hand, if a device has a metal case, it'll most likely be acceptable for placement in the plenum. Even devices with a small amount of plastic, such as connectors, labels, and "rubber" feet, tend to be acceptable. In addition to Cisco, other vendors like Enterasys, Proxim, and

Symbol Technologies provide metal-cased access points or access points with plastic cases that can be removed to reveal an inner metal case.

In short, when installing an access point above a suspended ceiling, make sure it has either UL2043 certification or a metal case.

In buildings where ceiling mounting is impractical, would represent an unacceptable disruption to normal operations, or is considered to be aesthetically unpleasing, wall mounting is an increasingly popular option. With omnidirectional antennas installed, 2.4GHz Wi-Fi access points mounted on walls can often cover two rooms. For 5GHz Wi-Fi devices, the attenuation associated with the waveform through walls eliminates the two-room option. For either 2.4- or 5GHz Wi-Fi access points, patch antennas can be used that direct the RF energy from the wall across the room. By placing multiple access points on walls, complete coverage from wall-mounted units can be achieved in all but the largest rooms.

The Physical Site Survey

With a capacity and coverage plan complete, you can test your assumptions. Now is the time to actually place access points and selected antennas in their provisional locations and test for coverage. In the same way that an actual product can be very different from its data sheet, a building can be very different from its floor plan. And signal propagation in practice can be inexplicably different than it is in theory—this is, after all, radio. So, before buying equipment and permanently installing it, it's very wise if not mandatory to do test installations at most, if not all, of the provisional locations defined during the coverage planning process.

NOTE   A key thought to remember is that not even the most experienced RF engineers will trust their eyes as to what *should apparently* seem to work in the realm of RF propagation. While you can have indicators and even a reasonably developed instinct for how a radio will perform in a certain location, the longer you are in this industry, the more careful you tend to become about acting on the assumption "I can't imagine it wouldn't work just fine in this room." A second interesting thought is that the trend now for high-value networks is to occasionally repeat the site survey, because the general tendency for networks that use 2.4GHz, and many other frequencies, is degradation of the radiating environment over time due to co-channel interference (someone else in the vicinity also broadcasting in the same frequencies), adjacent channel interference, or the alteration of the physical environment. Perhaps one of the best examples of this is in the financial markets in New York City, where site surveys are completed *on a weekly basis* just to ensure one other very important item—the absence of rogue equipment.

The frequency and scale of your site surveys dictate to a degree how comprehensive your site survey toolkit should be. There are, however, some basic tools that you should have that will make this process easier and more effective.

First, at minimum, is a vendor-provided site survey tool. Most Wi-Fi vendors provide site survey tools of varying capabilities with their client adapters utilities. As shown in Figure 9-4, a site survey utility reports the access point to which the client adapter is associated. It reports the strength of the signal and the resulting data rate supported as well as the ambient noise level. Some site surveys incorporate what amounts to a ping test to measure the number of IP packets lost during a transfer. You'll want to ensure through your site survey efforts that you have not only good signal *strength*, but also good signal *quality*. This is important for a number of reasons, not the least of which is that you can consider installing an access point at a location where a good amount of RF energy in the correct frequencies is received but, for various reasons, will not carry an appropriate ratio of recognizable bits to degraded bits.

As part of your capacity plan, you will have established the required data rate to be provided by the access points and the location and number of users for a given access point. With a site survey tool, you can ascertain not only the associated data rate but also the reliability of that data rate by taking into account more qualitative data. like

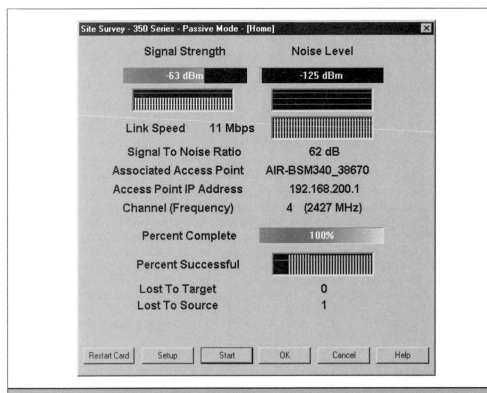

Figure 9-4.   Site survey utility report

signal strength and packet loss. As shown in Figure 9-5, some site survey tools report a subjective level of the signal quality, such as Excellent, Good, Fair, and Poor, either in lieu of, or as an option to, the decibel scale, although most experienced WLAN professionals prefer that the tool simply report back the raw data. As discussed in Chapter 5, the signal-to-noise ratio (SNR) is a useful metric for assessing the reliability of the link at a given data rate. As an example, at 11Mbps, it is typical to provide for a link margin of at least 10dBm.

For the Serious Site Survey: AirMagnet

Most Wi-Fi client adapters come complete with a site survey tool that reports basic information, such as the data rate, signal strength and quality of the associated access point, the ambient noise floor, and the resulting SNR. Some provide other rudimentary but useful tools. For many site surveys, these tools may be all that's needed for a successful deployment. And since they come free with a client adapter, the price is certainly right.

More advanced tools may be in order for more involved site surveys, or for those who do a lot of site surveys or need to integrate their 802.11 equipment at the highest levels of network integration. In the freeware category, NetStumbler, www.netstumbler .com, is designed as both IS professionals a site survey tool and, as per the NetStumbler web site, "overly curious bystanders" and "drive-by snoopers" as a means to "pick up ladies." The site is worth checking out if for no reason other than entertainment value. The principal function of NetStumbler is to search the airwaves for access point beacons and then display them. In the hands of a hacker or someone looking for free access to the Internet, it can be dangerous. On the other hand, it can be useful to the IS professional to check for unprotected and rogue access points (more on security in the next chapter) or as a tool for checking multiple AP coverage. NetStumbler supports a variety of client adapters and runs on most Windows desktop operating systems and Windows CE.

The most full-featured site survey tool is AirMagnet, www.airmagnet.com, from a company of the same name. AirMagnet runs exclusively on Windows CE, meaning that it's designed for operation on a PDA such as a Compaq iPaq. Although PDAs make ideal devices for site surveys due to their small size, their 16-bit PCMCIA interface (rather than 32-bit CardBus) limits current support to 802.11b and not 802.11a client adapters. To describe AirMagnet as a site survey tool is a bit of an injustice, because the full scope of this tool includes a variety of capabilities for security and performance monitoring—indeed, the product has been described as a "Swiss army knife for wireless LANs." For site surveys, it provides detailed information on the whole RF environment plus packet-level data in a helpful graphical format. All this functionality comes at a price, $2495 to be exact. Still, professionals require professional tools, and for the right people, AirMagnet could be the right product.

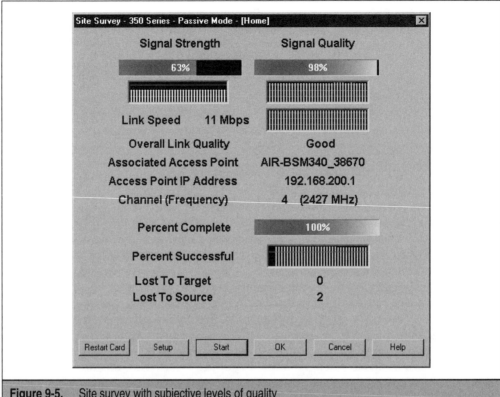

Figure 9-5.   Site survey with subjective levels of quality

In addition to site survey software, other tools are necessary for a site survey. Since you'll be placing access points or antennas in temporary positions and may need to make a few adjustments until the optimum location is found, you need a quick yet sturdy means of mounting the devices to a variety of surfaces that also enables you to remove them without damaging the surface they are attached to. For some surfaces, duct tape (naturally) works, although it has the tendency to remove paint. An increasingly popular alternative to duct tape is to use zip ties, which can be used in areas where the access point will reside upon fairly new paint, or on top of a wallpapered surface.

Once you have identified access point installation locations, you need some means of marking these locations. Firms specializing in site surveys sometimes use small flags with their company logo on them—they're effective for marking locations as well as advertising their company. Brightly colored tape works just as well but without the commercial benefits. Finally, you need a tape measure or, better still, a measuring wheel for recording distances.

An important item to remember when performing a larger site survey as well as smaller site surveys is to record the location of the APs in some manner that will make sense a year later both to you and, even more importantly, to other individuals.

Documentation of where APs are located is a very important item because you'll need that documentation for future reference as you build out your 802.11 network, as well as for troubleshooting and security purposes. One of the most indispensable tools for a site survey is a small camera, which is used to record the actual AP along with some wider angle shots of where it is deployed. Obviously, a digital camera is an even better asset than a camera that uses film. Veterans of site surveys will tell you that the first indicator of a professional installation (after how well the 802.11 elements perform) is how well the deployment is documented.

You have to take into account the differing capabilities of the client devices that will be using the wireless infrastructure once it is deployed. Client adapters from different manufacturers can vary by as much as 5dBm in transmit power. Different client-side form factors allow for different antenna gain, which adds further variance to client capabilities as a whole. In areas that likely will include different types of clients, you're well advised to plan for the lowest common denominator, the client types with the lowest capabilities.

Naturally, if the access points you'll be working with support external antennas, you should have a variety of antennas with you to try out allowing you to select the one that provides the best coverage for that particular installation location. In general, you'll want to have at least two omnidirectional and two patch antennas, each with differing amounts of gain in order to determine the optimal AP configuration. Variable or rotary attenuators are small devices that connect between the antenna and the access point and allow you to reduce (typically in 1dBi increments) the gain of a given antenna. This allows you to carry a smaller number of antennas and to approximate the range of lower-gain antennas. While this is a convenience, it doesn't take into account the larger beam width associated with lower-gain antennas, which could result in some unexpected results when the actual antennas are installed. In short, attenuators can be useful but are not necessary for most site surveys.

For the convenience of both the site surveyor as well as those in the facility when the site survey is being conducted, a battery pack is a useful addition to the site surveyor's toolkit. Temporarily running access points off of DC battery power saves you from long extension cord runs from AC outlets to the provisional access point locations. Extension cords running along floors and up to ceilings are unsightly, inconvenient, and even present a safety hazard, and in some cases, the site survey is performed before there is local AC power installed, such as in new buildings or highly renovated floors within a building. The complication is that battery packs specifically designed for site survey use with access points tend not to be readily available off the shelf. Added to this is the reality that differing access points run off of different voltages, ranging from a low of 12VDC to as much as 48VDC. One source for access point battery packs as well as other site survey tools is TerraWave Solutions, at www.terra-wav e.com.

WI-FI MANAGEMENT IN THE ENTERPRISE

After you have deployed a Wi-Fi LAN, it needs to be managed just as a wired LAN has to be managed. It is in this area that significant differences in capabilities between low-cost access points and those designed for the enterprise become most apparent. The management capabilities of lower-cost offerings assume the deployment of a relatively small number of devices and, accordingly, provide little in the way of large-scale manageability. The management interface is typically limited to the browser, with no command-line interface (CLI) available—a very real complication if you prefer to write scripts to automate tasks for a large number of devices. Similarly, lower-cost devices often don't provide the Simple Network Management Protocol (SNMP) support required for operation with network management software (NMS) like Hewlett-Packard's OpenView and Computer Associates' Unicenter that is used with wired networks.

Maintaining the Infrastructure

Given the relative newness of, and the rapid rate of change in, the Wi-Fi industry, it's common for vendors to provide software upgrades as frequently as on a quarterly basis. These software upgrades can provide bug fixes, new features, refinements to existing features, and the standardized implementation of features previously released as proprietary offerings. In short, it's typically in the user's best interests to increase the functionality of their Wi-Fi infrastructure by upgrading the firmware. This means that you'll be performing software upgrades on a frequent basis across the whole population of deployed access points.

Access points developed specifically for enterprise deployments provide the management features necessary for the deployment of large numbers of devices. Like wired enterprise switches and hubs, they typically provide not only a browser interface but also a CLI, which enterprise IS professionals often find to be more efficient and more conducive to scripting, partly because it enables them to cut and paste commands from one element to another, or an array of others. The browser interface on enterprise access points tends to provide far more features designed for enterprise scalability than devices designed for SOHO deployments. While the vendors of lower-cost access points focus their efforts on ease of use, enterprise access point vendors offer features like the ability to replicate a single access point configuration across all other access points, the ability to download a firmware upgrade or configuration file from a centralized server that the access point is directed to by a link provided by a BOOT-P or DHCP server, and the ability to rekey passwords and SSID information.

In addition to the CLI and browser interface, enterprise access points provide a similar and increasing level of SNMP support that IS professionals would expect from wired LAN infrastructure devices. The management information bases (MIBs) provided by enterprise access points can be compiled by the same NMS that enterprises use to manage the wired LAN. This allows IS departments to leverage both their monetary and training investment in existing NMSs as well manage the wired and wireless network as it should be—a seamless and cohesive unit.

Regrettably, little of the remote management capabilities found with access points are found with client adapters, even client adapters provided by vendors focusing on the enterprise. Although emerging enterprise architectures are designed to require less frequent client-side configuration changes and firmware upgrades, the need to perform these tasks is both very real and will occur on at least an annual basis. The task is further complicated by the need for user involvement, remote locations, and the greater number of clients relative to access points. Although some solutions are available today (see the sidebar "Mobile Manager from Wavelink"), there are few client-side management capabilities provided by hardware vendors and third parties to address the need for client-side management.

Mobile Manager from Wavelink

Although you can manage your WLAN using traditional network management software like HP's OpenView or CA's Unicenter, there is a product available specifically designed to manage WLANs. Mobile Manager from Wavelink Corporation, www.wavelink.com, supports access points from leading enterprise vendors like 3Com, Cisco, Intel, Proxim, and Symbol Technologies.

Mobile Manager, and the more feature-rich Mobile Manager Enterprise, can be used to automatically detect the installation of new access points on the network using SNMP. Once detected, you can send predefined configurations to all the access points, which saves you from having to manually configure each device one at a time. After you install Mobile Manager, it can be used to monitor the WLAN, providing individual access point utilization data, failure alerts, and a general log file. Mobile Manager can be configured to send alerts via pager and also to other NMSs, better integrating the WLAN with the wired LAN. While these sorts of capabilities are available from vendors like Cisco and Symbol (indeed, Wavelink collaborated with Symbol to develop its WMNS management system), Wavelink provides the ability to manage an access point environment with products from two or more companies.

Although management software like Wavelink is very useful in configuring not only a large number of APs but also APs sourced from multiple vendors network administrators and purchasers of 802.11 equipment should keep in mind that not all APs have the same level of sophistication, ease of management, reliability, and security. The 802.11 standard ensures that the radio itself, and the MAC layer will conform a minimal level of functionality and interoperability but it by no means ensures that all 802.11 equipment is created the same.

Mobile Manager works in conjunction with Wavelink's Avalanche, a product that provides similar management capabilities to client devices. With Avalanche, firmware upgrades and configuration changes can be made on a global basis across the RF and to the individual clients without any end-user intervention. However, Avalanche is expensive, putting this very useful capability out of the reach of even many enterprise organizations.

For enterprise deployments, Wavelink and other wireless-specific NMSs that may come to market are worth consideration.

Monitoring the Infrastructure

As is the case with maintenance, there are considerable differences between lower-cost devices intended primarily for SOHO use and 802.11 devices intended for enterprise deployments. Enterprise access points provide detailed association lists and logs so that IS professionals can be continually aware of the user and bandwidth load on each device; indeed, one of the key differentiators between 802.11 access points used in larger enterprise organizations compared to those used in small deployments is the amount of resolution a network administrator has available for these devices. In the same way that the site survey verifies and helps to refine the coverage plan, ongoing monitoring of access point traffic allows you to verify and refine the capacity plan. On enterprise access points, this status data is available through the CLI, the browser, or, via a compiled MIB through general and wireless-specific NMSs.

CHECKLIST

In this chapter, we focused specifically on the unique nature of Wi-Fi deployment in the enterprise. We defined the enterprise and outlined the various Wi-Fi deployment strategies that enterprises are using. We discussed capacity planning, coverage planning, and the need for a site survey. Finally, the chapter covered the types of management capabilities provided by differing access points. Some key points follow:

☐ For the purposes of this chapter, the enterprise is defined as being not only large commercial entities but also relatively large educational and governmental institutions—essentially, any organization of a scale that requires a dedicated IS organization.

☐ There are various ways that enterprises go about deploying WLANs. Some deploy Wi-Fi only in the areas where it is perceived to be needed most, like conference rooms and other public spaces. Campus-based organizations, such as universities, may deploy one complete floor or building at a time. For some enterprises, initial Wi-Fi deployments are used only for temporary workgroups or for buildings that are to be occupied on a short-term basis. Finally, geographically distributed enterprises will first deploy Wi-Fi in remote locations, like branch offices.

☐ A Wi-Fi LAN is, by its very nature, a shared-medium technology, where all users associated to an access point share the aggregate throughput provided by that device. Capacity planning entails planning for the maximum number of users per cell to provide on average a reasonably predictable per-user throughput. Different applications, from retail to classroom to office deployments, tend to call for differing levels of per-user throughput. Since collision domains are restricted by limiting the coverage area provided by an access point, any capacity planning is more of an approximation than an absolute.

☐ The very different nature of facilities calls for different coverage plans. Various building materials, floor plans, and internal structures have effects on RF propagation characteristics, which in turn are different for the 2.4- and 5GHz waveforms. There are various coverage strategies associated with different types of facilities, including offices, classrooms, and warehouses.

☐ Different placement options for access points are available. Ceiling mounts are the most common and generally provide for the largest coverage area, with a circular, omnidirectional coverage pattern. Ceiling placement can also result in coverage in the floor above, which may be intentional or unintentional, but in either event must be measured and accounted for. Wall mounting is an increasingly popular option since installation tends to be less disruptive to operations and less aesthetically obtrusive.

☐ The site survey is an absolutely necessary step for enterprise deployment. For smaller deployments, this can be a relatively informal process. For larger deployments, it can be quite involved and require a degree of training and experience, and a reasonable probability of the use of highly experienced professionals. For any site survey, software, temporary mounting abilities, measurement tools, and documentation are required. For larger or frequent site surveys, more advanced software and additional tools like attenuators and battery packs are desirable.

☐ Having deployed an enterprise Wi-Fi infrastructure, there is an ongoing need to maintain and monitor the LAN, and the need for recurring site surveys and ongoing network maintenance, management, and documentation increases proportionally with the scale of the deployment, along with the required level of security. It is in these areas where the differences between lower-cost access points and enterprise access points become particularly apparent. Lower-cost devices typically provide for only browser-based management designed for small-scale deployments, and are not manageable in large deployments because of the requirement to manipulate each device. Enterprise access points provide for management via the CLI, the browser, and NMSs through the SNMP. Enterprise access points are increasingly providing the same features found in wired switches and routers and they better provide for the scalability required in the enterprise.

CHAPTER 10

Wireless LANs in Small, Branch, and Home Offices

In this chapter, we review the fundamental WLAN components to be used in small office/home office (SOHO) deployments. This is an essential issue to cover for three reasons. First, this has been the fastest-growing 802.11 market sector in the industry over the past 12 months or so. Second, in the office environment, the WLAN equipment more or less magically appears on your desk and in your laptop; there may be some inconvenience to you while the network technicians are setting up your work area and your laptop, but in general, the evaluation process has long since been concluded, and you can simply use the equipment. The third reason to review these WLAN components is that if you're going to purchase this equipment, it'll probably be the first time you've ever handled or even seen an access point, omnidirectional antenna, or PCMCIA card, and you'll probably be purchasing it in a consumer electronics store in which the salesperson likely knows little more than you do about the equipment.

THE PRIMARY ISSUES TO CONSIDER WHEN SELECTING 802.11 EQUIPMENT

You need to address several issues for a SOHO deployment. Generally, these issues are the same as those faced by network administrators and technicians at medium- and large-size businesses, with a few exceptions. For a small office, you do not have to manage a large number of wireless devices, and you'll need to install new versions of software much less often because the software on this type of deployment is generally more stable than in larger enterprises, if only because the larger enterprises must respond more often to security and management enhancements.

The following are the primary issues you'll confront when selecting 802.11 elements for a SOHO deployment:

- How will the WLAN be used?
- Who will use the WLAN?
- What protocol—11b, 11a, or 11g?
- How many access points?
- Which vendor will you select for the access points and client adapters?
- Which antennas will you select for the access points and client adapters?
- What security protocol will you use?
- Self-installation or professional installation?
- Who will you call if the network goes down?
- Where will you acquire training for the devices for deployment and use?

This list may seem daunting at first, but this chapter will help you to ensure that you have addressed all of these important issues *before* you spend any hard-earned money on equipment.

How Will the WLAN Be Used?

Before you set foot in a consumer electronics store, or look any further online for which equipment to purchase, you need to determine how your WLAN will be used. Essentially, you need to decide whether you'll use it simply for data, which is what virtually all 802.11 equipment users do, or for data and low-latency-sensitive traffic like voice and video. Very few SOHO users carry voice or video traffic over their 802.11 elements, so we'll not spend a lot of time on that issue in this chapter. That type of usage is much more prevalent for larger enterprises in which, for example, a lot of video is used for training, or highly mobile users cover relatively large areas, such as the retail floor space and parking lot at a Wal-Mart or for campus security.

In any event, for voice, the user (mostly in large office settings) likely will consider an 802.11 phone, such as the Link phone from SpectraLink or the 7920 from Cisco Systems. These devices require a call manager and the ability to prioritize the voice packets over data packets. With the SpectraLink phone, for example, this is done with its Netlink SVP server. With the Cisco 802.11 phone, this is handled with its Call Manager software, which resides at the 3900 series Catalyst switch. Configuring a WLAN for voice traffic also requires some additional configuration efforts, and possibly more detailed traffic management, but other than that, the bulk of the 802.11 elements will remain the same.

Again, as this is rarely an architecture used in small offices, we'll not explore this capability further. Virtually all small offices, whether in a home, a retail location, or a small commercial office building, carry only data over their 802.11 elements, so let's take a look at the other issues regarding the selection of equipment in this type of deployment.

Who Will Use The WLAN?

There is one other possible item to consider with regard to usage, which is whether or not you want users other than those in your family or company to access the network through your 802.11 hardware. Allowing this type of access is not prevalent in home office deployments, with the exception of those intrepid souls who offer freenets. A freenet is comprised of one or more 802.11 access points without security implementations, which are intended for use by anyone within the radio range of the device. When deployed at small businesses or condominium or apartment complexes, there is sometimes a sign placed outside the facility indicating the presence of free Internet access. In commercial settings, however, the company may want to allow contractors or other visitors to connect to its home office or other Internet sites. This can be readily accomplished by using virtual LANs (VLANs). As an example, with a Cisco Systems 1200 access point, you can establish up to 16 VLANs, which, as you'll recall, is a virtual collision domain. By setting aside one of the VLANs on your site for unsecured use, you can allow users to access the Internet while at your site with their own 802.11 client adapter. Figure 10-1 shows an example of a VLAN.

The advantage of a VLAN in this format is that by increasing the efficiency and speed of a contractor or other small office-related visitor being able to connect with their home servers you reduce the time and expense of having them at the small office

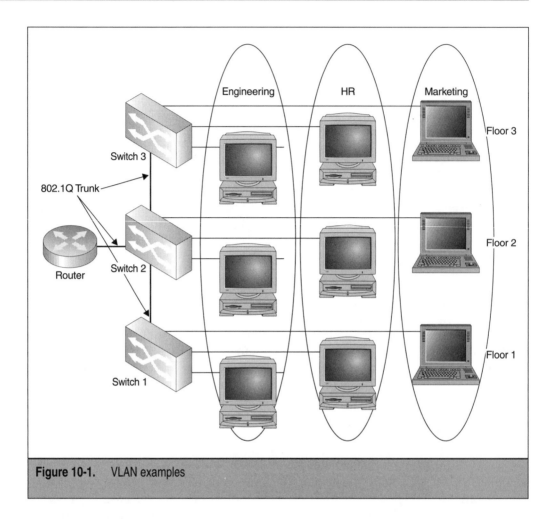

Figure 10-1. VLAN examples

premises. Maintenance work at power plants is a classic example of this advantage, and as the traffic belonging to the contractors or visitors does not mingle with the home office LAN, there are obvious and advantageous security measures that remain in place.

One other item to consider is whether or not you wish to allow users to enter your site by providing freenet access (which requires a strong belief in the goodness of humankind). This decision will not have much impact on the selection of WLAN equipment, because this is more of a configuration issue.

Which Protocol—11b, 11a, or 11g?

This is where the equipment selection becomes more interesting. As stated earlier in this work, most SOHO deployments operate very well with the 802.11b protocol. The speeds are more than sufficient for almost all uses, and unless you're getting more than about 25 people using the same AP, you probably won't need the additional speed of an 802.11a WLAN. Further, 11a devices currently require enormous amounts of power, which can affect those operating either laptops without an AC cord or PDAs. Another key factor is that 11b prices are dropping rapidly, for such reasons as increased production demand, the availability of the 11a option, and the impending availability of the 11g option.

At Cisco Systems, which has approximately 35,000 employees (including the authors of this book), virtually all of the WLAN infrastructure is on 11b, and it works very well. In larger rooms where more than 25 people are situated, an additional AP is simply added. Both authors have been in many company meetings with 100 or more people, all using 802.11b, and it works more than sufficiently for speed, coverage, and reliability. Eventually, Cisco will probably migrate to 11g, but that won't be for several years, because swapping out existing hardware is not a trivial matter, although it will be easier to migrate to the higher-speed standard in places where dual-band APs are installed.

Essentially, for all but a few small offices, the 11b protocol will work just fine. Also, you can plan to migrate to the 11g standard in a few years and still retain and redeploy your 11b equipment, as the 11g standard is backward compatible.

How Many Access Points?

Cisco is the number-one Wi-Fi equipment provider for the enterprise market, and this provides an interesting and very broad-based statistical analysis of, among other things, how much equipment is purchased, on average, for a given site. In previous fiscal years, Cisco sold approximately $218 million worth of 802.11 equipment—and yet the average deployment was less than five APs. Again, the rule of thumb used by Cisco with its equipment is to have up to 25 users for a common AP on the 11b standard. While you can certainly have many times more than that number associated with a single AP, experience proves that using this number of users works quite well and the authors suggest this as a good starting point for your SOHO deployment.

Thus, most SOHO deployments require only one or two APs, and as many client adapters as there are platforms in which to install them. In many cases, users swap a single PCMCIA card between their iPAQ and laptops, and this is an economical way to keep costs down while retaining the same degree of connectivity.

Which Vendor to Select for Access Points and Client Adapters?

The selection of a client adapter is pretty straightforward; it is primarily a matter of which platform the client adapter will reside on. If it's a desktop computer, then you'll probably be installing a PC card; a laptop with a PCMCIA slot requires that form factor; and so on. It's also pretty straightforward to select an AP over a workgroup station or base station, as the extra cost for an AP provides more flexibility and ease of use. Connecting two outdoor locations requires a bridge or an AP configured in the bridge mode.

Vendor selection is a bit trickier. If there's one well-learned lesson in network equipment, it's that "cheapest ain't always cheapest." Network equipment is a prime example of getting what you pay for. While we don't necessarily recommend that you spend the maximum amount of money for equipment, we know through much experience that if you do your homework and understand what you need, as well as how the equipment from various vendors generally operates, you'll be able to reduce a very considerable amount of frustration in your life with regard to your network.

It's also important not to confuse the rapidly decreasing cost of PCs with the cost of networking equipment. The number of PCs on the planet is far greater than networking equipment, although both industries have plenty of competition. The point is that even if you can purchase a good PC for approximately $600, this does not mean an appropriate price for an AP should be one-third or less of that; again, the premise of getting what you pay for is very true with 802.11 equipment.

According to the research company Dell'Oro, Cisco Systems is the largest single provider of 802.11 equipment for the enterprise market, as shown in Figure 10-2.

There can be little doubt that an Internet equipment company that spends approximately $3 *billion annually* on research and development has a pretty good handle on what technologies are required to ensure the right balance between security, cost, performance, and reliability. The 802.11 equipment from Cisco has won every performance and security shootout performed by such major magazines as *PC Magazine* in May of 2002 and up to the time of this writing. Cisco equipment is not the least expensive equipment on the market, but when you have a mission-critical job to perform and you have precious little time to complete it, you won't be thanking yourself for saving money if your WLAN freezes.

The following seven key areas must be considered when selecting an 802.11 equipment vendor:

- Performance
- Reliability
- Interoperability
- Security
- Networking knowledge
- Financial stability
- Cost

Performance, security, and reliability are three of the most important assets when choosing 802.11 elements, and networking equipment in general. In 2002, *PC Magazine* awarded Cisco the Editors' Choice award for the enterprise class for its Aironet 350 access point. The summary of the competition, in which there were approximately 20 competitors, can be viewed at www.pcmag.com/article2/0,4149,50515,00.asp. The summary comment for the Aironet equipment from this test states, in part, "Price, performance, and security are key with the Cisco Aironet 350 Series; they were the deciding factors as we selected it for our Editors' Choice."

Interoperability is also important, especially as the network becomes larger, because more often than not, two or more vendors have supplied 802.11 equipment. In part this is because the network administrators commonly purchase their first deployments of 802.11 equipment under the assumption that because the various vendors all supply equipment which complies with the standard. Interoperability is something that occurs in degrees; to

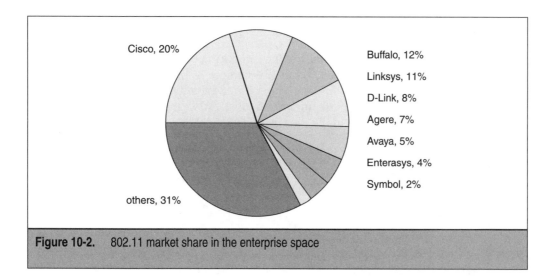

Figure 10-2. 802.11 market share in the enterprise space

be Wi-Fi-certified, a vendor needs to demonstrate only the most rudimentary level of interoperability. One of the times when network administrators learn firsthand that there are varying degrees of interoperability between equipment vendors is when they attempt to configure a WLAN for a particular level of security, or configure to a security protocol.

For interoperability, again, Cisco Systems' Aironet equipment is widely-regarded as the most interoperable 802.11 equipment. The reason, in part, is that the radios have the most sensitive receivers and the best performance, and Aironet is the only equipment on the market that has all the available security methodologies. It's important to remember that the WLAN will only be as secure as the weakest security-bearing element in the chain. Further, when the radios themselves don't operate at the highest levels of performance, links tend to operate less reliably; in other words, two poorly-performing radios will not have the same range, reliability, and performance as two of the top-performing radios. Indeed, a surprising range of performance, reliability, and security features exists across the 20 or so providers of 802.11 technology.

At this point in the book, you are well aware of the premise that the WLAN equipment must be considered as fully integrated network elements, not merely radios tacked onto an ether line. For this reason, Cisco must be considered a preferred vendor for this equipment by virtue of its networking pedigree. No other 802.11 vendor has anywhere near the networking experience as Cisco, which is evident from the key metrics provided in this chapter.

Financial stability of the vendor is key when you're selecting the source for your components. You should consider not only the issue of longevity, but also key issues such as the amount of research and development invested in the products. While the authors of this work don't profess to be economic analysts, the fact that Cisco has, at this writing, no debt and more than $20 billion in cash on hand should not be discounted when considering whether or not the company will continue to exist for the next 20 years, and how much investment the company will make in 802.11 and its associated technologies, such as LAN switching.

While pricing is not the primary metric for comparing 802.11 network equipment, it is still a factor that cannot be ignored. Table 10-1 compares the price of equipment from the major vendors. Naturally, pricing is nothing if not dynamic, so you should acquire updated information when you perform your analysis. Also, this list should not be considered comprehensive in terms of the varying elements available from each of the major vendors.

Manufacturer	Product	Part Number	List Price
Agere Systems	World PC Card–Gold	888 441 556	$119
Agere Systems	USB Client–Gold	848 623 856	$169
Agere Systems	AP-500 (Integrated PC Card Radio)	848 587 838	$495
Agere Systems	AP-200	700 017 505	$199
Agere Systems	Remote Outdoor Router (ROR-1000)	848 591 111	$1,345
Agere Systems	Central Outdoor Router (COR-1100)	848 591 152	$1,695
Alvarion	PC Card	PC-DS.11–811708	$155
Alvarion	AP-DS.11 Indoor	AP-DS.11B–811701	$575
Alvarion	Remote Bridge	RB.DS11–811500	$1,595
Alvarion	Remote Bridge	DS.5800–811640	$2,345
Alvarion	Base Unit	DS.5800–811642	$2,650
Buffalo	Wireless LAN Card	WLI-PCM-L11G	$119
Buffalo	USB Client	WLI-USB-L11G	$179
Buffalo	AirStation Standard Model (Router)	WLA-L11G	$249
Buffalo	AirStation Pro	WLA-AWCG	$549
Cisco	350 Series PC Card	AIR-PCM352	$169
Cisco	350 Series Access Point	AIR-AP352E2C	$749
Cisco	1200 Series Access Point	AIR-AP1200	$850
Cisco	1200 Series .11b Mini-PCI	AIR-MP20B-A-K9	$149
Cisco	1200 Series Access Point with .11b Mini-PCI	AIR-AP1220B-A-K9	$999
Cisco	1200 Series .11a Radio Module	AIR-RM20A-A-K9	$499
3Com	3Com Workgroup Bridge	3CRWE83096A	$349
3Com	3Com AP 8000	3CRWE80096A	$749
3Com	3Com AP-6000	3CRWE60092A	$499
3Com	3Com AP-2000	3CRWE20096A	$199
3Com	3Com Building-to-Building Bridge	3CRWE90096A	$1095
D-Link	PC CardBus Adapter	DWL-650+	$90
D-Link	802.11a Wireless PC Card	DWL-A650	$170

Table 10-1. Price Comparison of Products from Major 802.11 Vendors

Manufacturer	Product	Part Number	List Price
D-Link	802.11a Wireless Access Point	DWL-5000AP	$399
D-Link	5 GHz/2.4 GHz Dual Band Wireless Access Point	DWL-6000AP	$499
Enterasys	High Rate PC Card	CSIBD-AA-128	$149
Enterasys	R2 Wireless Access Platform (PC Card sold separately)	RBTR2-AA	$1349
Enterasys	Access Point 2000	CSIWS-AA	$849
Enterasys	R1 Wireless Access Point	RBTR1-AX	$399
Intel	PRO/Wireless 2011B LAN PC Card	WPC2011BWW	$112
Intel	Access Point	WSAP5000	$449
Intel	Pro/Wireless 5000 LAN Dual Access Point	WDAP5000	$649
Linksys	Instant Wireless Network PC Card	WPC11	$128
Linksys	Wireless Ethernet Bridge	WET11	$190
Linksys	Instant Wireless Network Access Point	WAP11	$220
Linksys	Instant Wireless PC Card	WPC54A	$210
Linksys	Instant Wireless Access Point	WAP54A	$500
Proxim	PC Card	8342-05	$149
Proxim	Access Point	8551-05	$595
Proxim	Access Point	8570-05	$695
Symbol	Ethernet AP	AP 4131-1050-WW	$899
Symbol	AP 4121 Access Point	AP-4121-1050-US	$999
Western Multiplex	Tsunami 10BaseT Wireless Ethernet Bridge	31190-41A1/41A2, 31145-41A1/41A2	$6,995

Table 10-1.   Price Comparison of Products from Major 802.11 Vendors *(continued)*

While it may seem readily apparent that we are major proponents of Cisco Aironet equipment, it's fair to state that other vendors also provide good equipment to the SOHO market. The Orinoco (now Proxim) AP-500 is a good example of a decent midrange-priced access point. *PC Magazine*'s 2002 shootout had this to say about it, "A great price, an easy-to-navigate browser-based management interface, and decent performance make this an easy choice for managers in small to midsize businesses or even small enterprises." The reader can view this review at: http://www.pcmag.com/article2/0,4149,50515,00.asp.

Which Antennas to Select for the Access Points and Client Adapters?

Most vendors now provide 802.11 equipment with antennas because, for most SOHO environments, antenna selection often is not as critical as it is for deployments with large areas or specifically targeted areas. Having stated that, and recognizing that antennas have been covered previously in this work, virtually the only antenna you'll use in a SOHO environment will be an omnidirectional antenna. For indoor use, you may also use a patch antenna where you want to cover a room from a corner or a wall from which you'd install the access point.

For outdoor use when connecting buildings, you likely will be required to select an antenna, and for this a Yagi will do nicely for deployments where you are connecting two buildings. An omnidirectional antenna will still work, of course. You'll probably want to use a parabola if the deployment has distances of a mile or more, poses limitations in gaining enough elevation, has several buildings of approximately the same height, or is higher than one or both of your bridge antenna sites. However, if you're not certain of which antennas to select, you are much better off using a professional installation team.

What Security Protocol to Use?

The issue of security has been covered in detail in previous chapters, but there are different levels of security for different types of uses.

For most SOHO users, even though WEP is a defeated algorithm, it will still keep out freeloaders who want to access your network to connect to the Internet (and who usually do not possess even rudimentary hacking skills). Some may be tempted to rely on what we call the "sardine effect," which is simply to state that there are so many individual users that it's statistically unlikely that you'll run into a hacker armed with RF equipment. The theory is that hackers have too many larger, more accessible, and attractive targets to select from. Nevertheless, no network professional would advise you to disregard matters of security. Thus, 40-bit or 128-bit WEP will do nicely for most home users.

NOTE If you are the owner of a hotspot, you may not want to turn on any measure of security because it will prevent virtually anyone from associating with your access points.

For enhanced security for midsize businesses, there is a wide array of security protocols to select from, such as LEAP, TKIP, mutual authentication, and the scalable management of these protocols. We strongly advise the owners and operators of business-class networks to use the maximum security measures available, while keeping an eye on the balance between security and business efficiency. For networks that include their own server, which includes a surprising number of small-office networks, we advise that you carefully consider incorporating EAP security elements.

For small office networks that have telecommuter access, one of the most widely deployed and simplest security methods that includes a very high degree of security is VPN encryption with an authentication tool like SofToken. This method is very simple to use for the end users, simple to manage for the network administrators, and includes a common user interface across all users, and only a thin software client on the appliance, such as a laptop or PDA. This is the tool used by many large corporations, such as Cisco Systems, which has its choice of security measures.

Self-Installation or Professional Installation?

Odds are that if you've installed your own SOHO network, you'll be more than capable of installing your own WLAN equipment. The site survey is relatively straightforward, and leading 802.11 vendors include easy-to-use site measurement software with their equipment.

Most SOHO deployments involve fewer than three APs, and many use only a single AP. For this reason, some self-installers choose to bypass the site survey entirely. We advise against that strategy, because even if you use only a single AP, you still need to know if there are other 802.11 radios within range of your network, and respond accordingly not only with optimal channel selection, but also by implementing appropriate security measures.

Keep in mind also that performing a site survey should not be limited to a one-time event, generally at the initial deployment. Rather, a regularly scheduled site survey is an excellent diagnostics tool to help you manage the radiating environment in which your network resides. A good site survey will also likely inform you that rogue APs are in use within the radiating environment of your network. Often, one of the most common problems at deployment sites is rouge APs being used not by hackers but by the company's own employees. As stated previously in this work, many 802.11 networks have been deployed simply to minimize the problem of managing well-intentioned employees and contractors who have brought in their own 802.11 equipment.

Who to Call If the Network Goes Down?

Generally, if you have the equipment deployed professionally, you'll be able to call them if your Wi-Fi equipment stops working. By the way, it can be a bit of trick to know whether it's your 802.11 equipment, your server, or your Internet service provider that has gone down, or if in fact your appliance's Windows OS has locked up.

If you have a network upon which you rely a great deal, you'll want to look into having a service contract in place prior to the network developing any problems, because when a network goes down, minutes will seem like hours.

TIP Having network maintenance and troubleshooting support available *before you need it* is a wise idea. There are a number of 802.11 equipment vendors available in your area, even if you live in a small town. Look in the Yellow Pages in your local phone book under Computer Repair, Internet Equipment, and Network Integrators, or contact your local electronics store. For online sources, begin your search with the string network+integrator+your hometown.

Where to Acquire Training for the Devices for Deployment and Use?

Even after more than two decades of involvement in various wireless technologies, the authors still take a course in basic wireless technology on an annual basis. Training on 802.11 equipment is important. Fortunately, some very good classes are available, one of the best of which being offered is from a company called GigaWave of San Antonio, Texas (www.giga-wave.com/index.asp). A considerable number of sources for training on Wi-Fi are available, and we strongly advise that you take at least one multiday class prior to purchasing and deploying the technology.

As your network grows, you'll eventually assign a full-time network administrator, and as the network grows beyond that point, the network administrator will eventually include an 802.11 expert on his or her staff. This technology, while necessarily tightly-integrated into the network LAN, still retains some unique features in terms of propagation, security measures, quality of service, and the various standards, such as 802.11b, 11a, and 11g. These complexities will continue to increase not only in scope, but also in terms of how rapidly they change. In other words, as your network becomes more complex, you'll be including additional IEEE standards-based protocols, which are not necessarily covered under the umbrella of Ethernet LAN comprehension. An investment in relevant professional training will ensure that you and your small office staff have the native expertise to keep your Wi-Fi equipment online, or at least to understand what questions to ask when calling in professional maintenance personnel.

SUMMARY

By way of summary for this chapter, you'll definitely want to include WLAN equipment in your SOHO setting because it enables end users to be untethered to the network. Cisco easily dominates this class with the enterprise-class networking equipment, and while an extensive list of providers has been listed in this chapter, experience has shown that the fewer the different types of equipment in a single LAN, the better the network performs. When selecting equipment for the SOHO deployment, a 6dBi omni-directional antenna will work in nearly every deployment, but you'll want to plan more carefully with regard to coverage, as the number of users on your LAN grows beyond a dozen or so. Understanding how your WLAN will be used and who will access your LAN are some of the important concepts you'll want to evaluate prior to purchasing equipment. There is an array of other considerations, all of which should be dealt with prior to purchasing equipment.

With a little forethought and planning, you'll add a tremendous amount of usability to your network, your end users will enjoy increased productivity, which results in increased job security, increased business velocity, and a better overall economy.

CHAPTER 11

Wi-Fi Security
Best Practices

Throughout this book we've discussed how Wi-Fi LANs provide the enterprise with unprecedented mobility and resulting improvements in organizational efficiency, decision making, and general productivity. However, all of this is moot if the wireless LAN (WLAN) results in an enterprise-wide security breach that either precludes or discontinues its deployment.

Wi-Fi LANs can have a huge and positive impact on an organization. They can also have a correspondingly large negative impact on the organization, one that compromises the security of not only the WLAN but also the entire network, wireless and wired alike. Trade, business, and general media outlets have brought these very valid concerns to the attention of the public. In some cases, though, they have misrepresented WLANs as being fundamentally incapable of being secured. The reality is that although the wireless nature of Wi-Fi presents security problems not found with wired LANs, you can deploy a WLAN of any scale that provides an overall level of security that is equal to, if not greater than, that of a wired LAN.

This chapter outlines the various security tools available today to the IS professional. We'll detail which ones are most applicable to differing client types and applications. We'll discuss the different levels of security that these tools and associated architectures provide as well as how to go about deploying and maintaining them. Various types of network attacks will be discussed as well as how they may be mitigated.

AUTHENTICATION AND ENCRYPTION

When discussing WLAN security systems, the two main areas are *authentication* and *encryption*. Although these areas are interrelated, they are addressed here separately because they constitute different aspects of an overall security architecture.

Authentication

Authentication is the process whereby a device or, better still, an individual is determined to be the entity it purports to be. The concept of authentication is not limited to Wi-Fi or networking in general. Consider these scenarios:

- On a late-night commercial, Crazy Hugo, the owner of a chain of electronics stores, is advertising his annual Arbor Day sale where prices are so low, he's "gotta be crazy." At the end of the commercial, Hugo lets his bleary-eyed viewers in on a secret: If they mention "Crazy Hugo sent me," they'll get an extra-special discount.

- A plainclothes police detective arrives at a crime scene that's ringed by uniformed officers who have never met the detective before. Flashing a badge that contains no more information than a municipality and a number, the detective walks through the security line and gains entrance to the building.

- A patron of the arts arrives at the gate to a symphony concert. The patron hands to the ticket taker a ticket that contains the concert date and the assigned seat. The patron is welcomed into the venue and is ushered to their seat.

- A man knocks on the door of a speakeasy. The door is answered and the man is asked for his name. "Bert," he replies. "Yeah," says the man behind the door, "what of it?" Bert replies: "The monkey flies at midnight." Bert is welcomed in.

- The next night, Bert is at the speakeasy again and a similar exchange takes place. This time when he replies, "The monkey flies at midnight," he's refused admittance. Charlie arrives a minute later and gives his name to the man behind the door. "What of it?" asks the man of Charlie. "I'm the submarine commander in a swimming pool filled with mustard," replies Charlie, who is then shown into the speakeasy.

- A secret agent arrives at a highly classified facility. She first shows her photo identification card to a security guard, who checks her through to an inner room. There, she looks into a viewer that scans the unique pattern of the blood vessels in her retinas. She then types in a number on a keypad, and an automatic door opens, letting her into the facility.

Each of the preceding scenarios is, of course, and example of authentication. In each of the examples, a different type of *credential* is used. In some examples, more than one type of credential is used. Each of these examples has some bearing on the types of credentials that can be used for Wi-Fi authentication.

In the first example, "Crazy Hugo sent me" is a password. Access points can be configured with passwords as well, which are called *service set identifiers* (*SSIDs*, pronounced "sids" and sometimes referred to as ESSIDs, where *E* stands for "extended"). SSIDs are considered by some to be a rudimentary means of security, but in reality are about as secret as Crazy Hugo's midnight message. Access points typically ship with a manufacturer-specific default SSID (typically a single word) that is broadcast as part of the access point beacons. This being the case, if a client adapter is set to "null SSID" by leaving the SSID blank (or having a wildcard name like "any" or "none") in its client utility, it will be able to associate to the access point.

Administrative tools like NetStumbler and even Microsoft Windows XP provide the ability to log all SSIDs within "earshot" of a client and then allow the client to associate to the access point of choice—a nice capability to have in public areas, for example, where more than one WLAN might be installed. Some vendors provide the capability to remove SSID from the access points' broadcast beacons; on one hand, this addresses the security issue, but on the other hand, it removes the ability of a client to find the right network. Moreover, it is common for people to misconfigure access points, leaving the SSIDs in the beacons and broadcasting the password—just like Crazy Hugo. In short, a SSID should be viewed more as a network name than a password. It should act as a means of identifying the access point or, when the same

SSID is added to multiple access points, an entire Wi-Fi LAN. It is typical for an enterprise to put the same SSID on all access points regardless of location.

In the second example, the detective's badge is the sole credential used for authentication. The badge has no identifying characteristics that make it specific to that particular person and, as such, provides a very low level of security—the badge can be counterfeited with relative ease and even shared by a number of individuals seeking to gain unauthorized access to a particular place.

Many Wi-Fi vendors provide the ability to restrict access to the LAN based upon a MAC address inclusion table. MAC addresses are the unique numeric identifiers programmed by manufacturers into LAN devices like wired and wireless network interface cards (NICs) as well as switches, routers, hubs, and access points. MAC address numbers are similar to badge numbers. With this feature, you can enter a number of MAC addresses or a range of MAC addresses into an access point or number of access points, thus allowing only devices that have these addresses to associate to gain access to the LAN. While this does provides for some level of security, this approach has two significant shortcomings:

- MAC addresses can be "spoofed." Some client adapters allow their manufacturer-defined universally administered address (UAA) to be overwritten with a locally administered address (LAA). A hacker can use a wireless protocol analyzer to sniff the wireless traffic for a valid MAC address and then simply copy that address to the LAA-compliant client adapter, thereby impersonating the allowed client.

- Separate databases pose administrative problems. Each MAC address table located in individual access points represents a separate database. Although some vendors do provide a means of replicating these tables across a group of access points, this solution is ripe for synchronization and updating problems.

In the third example, the concert ticket is specific to a certain place and for a limited duration. This is roughly similar to a certificate, a "ticket" delivered to a specific device that is valid for a defined period of time. When the user of the device seeks to gain access to the network, the device displays its certificate to an authentication server via the network. Devices containing valid certificates then gain network access. Certificates are but one *authentication type* used by the latest generation of enterprise wireless security systems, which will be discussed in more detail later in this chapter.

As the speakeasy example illustrates, usernames and passwords are a time-tested means of authentication—speakeasies were replaced by bars and pubs with the repeal of prohibition in 1933. Anyone using an enterprise LAN, whether wired or wireless, is familiar with usernames and passwords for authentication. When authenticating to a wired LAN, usernames and passwords are typically used to gain access to server domains at the application layer—access to the wired network itself is typically unrestricted.

Physical Security Is No Security

With wired LANs, network access ports are typically inside of buildings. IS professionals have come to rely on this as a layer of security. The thinking goes that if an organization is concerned about security in a general sense, it will provide some means of physical security for its buildings, such as locked doors, card readers, and security guards. If the building is understood to be secure, then so are the network ports, limiting access to the network. Although you can question the validity of this thinking—locks can be picked, security guards are notorious for their lapses, and so on—the fact is that this remains the predominant means of restricting access to the wired LAN.

Some IS professionals have tried to extend this thinking to the WLAN as well. They have tried to architect the Wi-Fi LAN such that the RF energy stays within the walls of their buildings, thinking that they can continue to rely on physical security. This approach is simply invalid.

One strategy contemplated is to deploy directional antennas like patches indoors but on the exterior walls of buildings, directing the RF energy inward. The problem with this approach is that even antennas designed for directionality have secondary patterns, referred to as *side lobes* and *back lobes*. Although these lobes provide for far smaller coverage areas than the main lobes, the back lobes in particular can easily create a coverage area directly behind the antenna—outside the building.

Remember that all varieties of Wi-Fi, 802.11b, 802.11a, and eventually 802.11g, support lower data rates that provide for additional range. It is typical for Wi-Fi LANs to be architected such that users maintain higher, if not maximum, data rates. Understanding that radio waves will propagate through most walls to varying degrees, it becomes apparent that the ideas of maximizing performance and limiting signal propagation to within buildings are at odds.

To further make the point, assume for a moment that a WLAN is architected such that the signal is "confined" to the building; stated in another way, the WLAN is structured so that typical client devices like laptops and PDAs can only maintain an association within the building. The problem with even this extreme approach, an approach that would provide woefully substandard network performance, is that different antennas have different receive sensitivities. While a standard client antenna might be incapable of receiving a signal outdoors, a more directional antenna will have this capability. A hacker in the parking lot who is armed with a wireless sniffer and a Yagi or dish antenna will be able to intercept the weak signal, maybe even at a higher data rate than the legitimate clients experience!

Usernames and passwords can also be used for access to the WLAN and represent a second authentication type used by enterprise security systems. Authentication takes place not at the application layer but at the physical layer itself, meaning that the unauthenticated user cannot gain access to the network at all.

Continuing on with the speakeasy example, passwords can be permanent or semi-permanent; that is, they remain valid for a relatively long period of time, like weeks or months. Other passwords can be good only for a single use and are referred to as one-time passwords (OTPs). These passwords, sometimes referred to as *soft tokens,* are generated by typing a permanent personal identification number into an application that then generates a single-use password typically from a range of alphanumeric combinations that are recognized by the authentication server. More security-conscious organizations insist upon OTPs for things like remote access, and similarly now demand OTP support for WLAN authentication.

Finally, many of these authentication credentials are not mutually exclusive. As illustrated in the last example, different means of authentication can be used together to add layers of security. Using a personal identification number to obtain an OTP is a simple example. Using a certificate in addition to a username and password represents another example. For public access scenarios (which will be further detailed in Chapter 13), users may be asked to plug a GSM SIM (the authentication chip found in many cellular telephones) into their laptop and then provide a username and password to gain access to the network. Other means of physical authentication are possible, including biometrics like fingerprint and (as in the secret agent example) retinal scans.

Encryption

In much the same way that the WLAN industry has adopted the concept of authentication from a variety of other sources, so, too, has it borrowed encryption. The notion of using a code to hide the meaning of sent messages from unintended or prying parties is nearly as old as the notion of sending messages. Encryption is the practice of changing data so that it is as close as possible to being impossible to read without the necessary information to decrypt it. This necessary information can be a key, a secret, or a code, and may even take the form of a secret decoder ring or a code book. Generally, the more complicated the code, the more difficult it is to break. Additionally, the more complicated the code, the more time consuming (or processor intensive) it is generally to encode and decode the information.

The subject of encryption is quite involved and well beyond the scope of this book. There are, however, some concepts that are important for the IS professional deploying a Wi-Fi LAN to know.

A *cipher* or *algorithm* is a formula that is used to generate a key stream based upon an encryption key. These encryption keys can be measured in terms of their length; in general, the longer the key, the more complicated and more robust the code. In the digital world, the unit of measure used for key lengths is bits. Thus, for example, a

40-bit key is less robust than a 128-bit key. A 40-bit encryption key will yield 2^{40} (just over one trillion) possible combinations. A 128-bit key will yield 2^{128} combinations. Assuming the same algorithm, a 128-bit key is 2^{88} times more difficult to break than a 40-bit key. The United States Department of Commerce, working in conjunction with the National Security Agency, has placed export restrictions on cryptographic technology based on key length, banning the export of many products that use encryption keys greater than 64 bits long, so-called "strong encryption." (Wi-Fi products, which are classified as being retail products by the government, are exempt from this restriction and may be exported even when providing strong encryption.)

To create the encoded message, called the *ciphertext,* the encryption key is combined with the original message, or *plaintext.* There are two main types of ciphers. *Stream ciphers* encode plaintext one bit at a time. *Block ciphers* break the plaintext into blocks and then encrypt it on a block-by-block basis. Stream ciphers are considered to be more efficient and faster, because block ciphers introduce an extra step in the process, which impacts performance but increases robustness. The combination of the encryption key and the plaintext is referred to as an *exclusive OR* (or, more commonly, *XOR*) function (see Figure 11-1). The resulting ciphertext is then, in theory, as strongly encrypted as the number of combinations possible in the key would suggest.

It stands to reason that if the same message is encoded with the same code, the same secret message will result (the same plaintext is XORed with the same key results in the same ciphertext). In networking terms, this plaintext is a single packet, which often is repeated due to transmission errors and resulting resends, as discussed in Chapter 5. This frequent repetition of packets and resulting repetition of ciphertext provides hackers with a better opportunity to break the code.

One way of addressing this issue is through the use of an *initialization vector,* which is a numeric value of a certain bit length that is attached to the encryption key (see Figure 11-2). Unlike the encryption key, the initialization vector is changed on a frequent basis (as often as every packet sent) and is sent in plaintext such that it is known to both the sending and the receiving stations. Changing the initialization vector thereby changes the key stream, which results in different ciphertext even when the plaintext or packet is exactly the same.

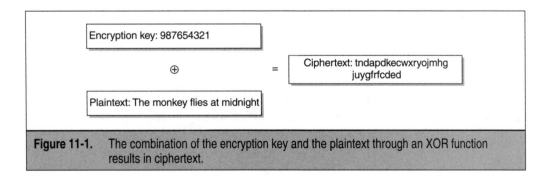

Figure 11-1.   The combination of the encryption key and the plaintext through an XOR function results in ciphertext.

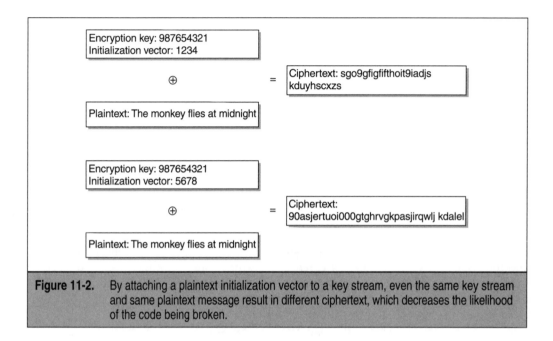

Figure 11-2. By attaching a plaintext initialization vector to a key stream, even the same key stream and same plaintext message result in different ciphertext, which decreases the likelihood of the code being broken.

WEP: When Equivalency Isn't Equal

Security has been part of WLAN standards since the original 1- and 2Mbps 802.11 standard in 1997. It's important to remember the state of the WLAN industry at that time. With relatively low data rates and high prices, WLANs were very much a niche technology, appealing almost exclusively to vertical markets like retail and manufacturing. These markets are characterized by a relatively small number of application-specific client devices, such as bar code scanners and POS terminals, per location. These devices tend not to leave the facility—there's little use in bringing home a bar code scanner for the weekend. In 1997, WLANs were a relatively obscure technology, important to a small number of industries and individuals. In 1997, WLANs were not the phenomenon Wi-Fi is today and people didn't make a hobby out of driving through neighborhoods, shopping centers, and industrial parks looking for wireless networks to hack.

Given how dramatically the WLAN industry has changed over this very short period of time, it's not surprising that the security standard that accompanied the original WLAN standards has become woefully out of date. The initial standard is referred to as Wired Equivalent Privacy (WEP), which at the time was meant to provide reassurance to those sending information such as credit card numbers from POS terminals over the RF. Regrettably, as the standard became increasingly out of step with the rapidly developing market, the name began to look more like empty boasting.

The WEP standard provides for packet encryption using static encryption keys that are shared by all devices on the WLAN, inclusive of both access points and clients.

When applied to the relatively small networks that are typical of applications like retail locations and warehouse facilities, manually installing WEP keys on each client device is not too daunting a task. Indeed, setting up some centralized means of generating and distributing encryption keys could well be argued to be overkill. A very valid concern about storing common encryption keys on client devices is that if a single device is compromised (if the client device gets into the hands of a hacker) that device can be used to decrypt all traffic on the LAN. With shared encryption keys, the implication of a security breach is that all encryption keys on the remaining devices must be changed.

However, the likelihood of application-specific client devices, along with their stored WEP keys, being lost or stolen is fairly low. And even if a device goes missing, changing encryption keys on a dozen or so bar code scanners ruins an afternoon, not a career. In short, the static and shared key architecture of WEP fits well with the security requirements of some applications—applications that once constituted the great majority of WLAN deployments but now represent a small and increasingly niche application.

Imagine the shared and static encryption key option applied to an enterprise Wi-Fi LAN. These networks consist of hundreds if not thousands of WLAN users. Simply installing encryption keys manually on this number of devices is a nearly full-time job. Unlike application-specific devices, laptops and PDAs regularly leave the enterprise facilities, going through airports and being left in cars and in homes. In other words, there is not just a *likelihood* of these devices being stolen, there is an *inevitability* of these devices being stolen which results in a network-wide rekeying being equally inevitable. The static and shared encryption key architecture that is relatively well suited to niche applications is fundamentally incompatible with the scale of enterprise deployments.

In addition to the scalability issues associated with the WEP architecture, the robustness of the encryption keys themselves has been called into question by a number of parties. The encryption keys used for WEP are based upon the RC4 encryption algorithm, a stream cipher designed by Ron Rivest (who is the *R* in RSA Security, a well-known and respected data security company). RC4 (Rivest Cipher Four) is a stream cipher and can be implemented in a variety of key lengths. In addition to WEP, RC4 is used in RSA security products and is the base algorithm for Secure Sockets Layer (SSL), a handshake protocol for securing traffic over the Internet. The most widely used stream cipher, the RC4 algorithm was chosen for WEP in part due to its relatively high speed and its robustness. The point is that the RC4 algorithm is widely used and relatively robust—the shortcomings of WEP should not be attributed to the base algorithm.

The WEP implementation of the RC4 algorithm results in encryption keys that are 40 bits long with an initialization vector that is 24 bits long, resulting in a key that is 64 bits long in total. Many vendors have gone beyond the standard to provide keys that are 104 bits long, resulting in a total key length of 128 bits when the initialization vector is added in. To generate a WEP key, an alphanumeric string is entered—for some vendors, in hexadecimal (numbers, 0–9, plus letters, A–F), whereas for others, any alphanumeric string can be used.

Note that with an initialization vector just 24 bits long, a specific value used for generating the key stream will be repeated every 2^{24} or 16,777,216 times. While this sounds fairly infrequent on the surface, remember that an initialization vector is used for every packet sent. On a fairly typical enterprise WLAN, 16 million packets could easily occur over the course of a single day. In other words, the relatively small number of available initialization vectors limits the ability of the WEP architecture to solve the problem of key repetition—it mitigates it by decreasing repetition but does not eliminate it. To make matters worse, in August, 2001, respected researchers in the field discovered flaws in the key scheduling algorithm used with WEP and postulated that both 40- and 128-bit WEP keys could be broken with as few as 4 million captured packets (a few hours' worth of packets on an enterprise LAN). Soon, an application called AirSnort was posted to the Internet that made real what had only been theorized—with AirSnort, even a casual user, not just a skilled hacker, could intercept and decrypt WEP traffic. The vision of hackers sitting in parking lots easily hacking into a network "secured" with WEP understandably caused a wave of Wi-Fi shutdowns.

After the initial AirSnort attack was publicized, other more involved means of attacking Wi-Fi networks secured with WEP came to light. While the AirSnort attack is a passive attack (based on gathering information from the LAN), this other class of *active* attacks poses even more problems for WEP. These attacks, also referred to as inductive or man-in-the-middle attacks, include the following:

- **Replay attacks**   incrementally build key copies one bit at a time through statistical analysis of predicted responses to plaintext messages sent by the hacker.

- **Bit-flipping attacks**   are similar to replay attacks in that they rely on predicted responses from receiving stations. The hacker modifies a message (flips bits) to elicit an encrypted error message from a receiving station, which can then be compared against the predicted response to derive the key through multiple iterations.

Other forms of attacks on network security, whether wireless or wired networks, exist. These attacks and the ways that they may be applied to WLANs include the following:

- **Denial of service (DOS) attacks**   are designed to force the network offline (not to compromise information). On the Internet, a DOS attack can be accomplished by flooding a server with a storm of data, such as bogus log-on requests. The server is unable to handle and reject the volume of requests and thus either shuts down or is unable to respond to legitimate requests. The wireless twist on this class of attacks is to flood the applicable frequency band with noise. At its most basic, this can be nothing more than placing a 2.4GHz cordless phone within close proximity to an access point and then maliciously initiating a call. The 2.4GHz RF energy created by many cordless phones is sufficient to effectively block much of the access point's direct sequence traffic. More involved DOS attacks can be mounted from greater distances using equipment that generates a greater amount of RF energy across a broader portion of the spectrum inclusive of both the 2.4- and the 5GHz bands.

- **Dictionary attacks**   Based upon the fact that with some authentication models, a password is kept secret but the username is sent in plaintext and easily intercepted. As such, a hacker can obtain a variety of usernames and then begin the (computer-generated) process of guessing at passwords using words in native and foreign language dictionaries. This so-called *brute force attack* can be successful due to the availability of inexpensive processing power and the reality that most users are fairly uncreative in their choice of passwords. Birthday attacks are a similar sort of brute force attack and rise from the frequency at which users select birthdays as their password. Once a hacker has a username and a valid associated password, they can log on to the network, wireless or wired, posing as a legitimate user.

Rogue Access Points

A security problem that is particular to wireless is the rogue access point. As discussed in Chapter 9, it is quite common today for users to attach unsanctioned or rogue access points to the enterprise network—particularly when the IS department is unwilling or slow to meet user demand for wireless connectivity. In the great majority of cases, these rogue access points are installed by legitimate network users and only for the sake of convenience. Naturally, these rogue access points will have few, if any, security features set up. Even if the security features of these typically residential access points are initialized, they are insufficient in the face of a determined hacker.

Hackers can and do make it a practice to "war drive" through areas populated by enterprise networks like office plazas, corporate and educational campuses, and retail areas. Using readily available tools like NetStumbler or even just Windows XP, they search for unprotected or poorly protected access points, with rogue access points being the easiest targets—remember, physical security is no security and a signal from even the weakest residential access point can make its way through exterior walls. Once associated to a rogue access point, the hacker is associated to the enterprise LAN.

Rogue access points are a particularly vexing problem for the IS professional. Due to their small size, access points can be easily hidden under a box, behind a desk, or in similarly inconspicuous places. In the unlikely event that no user in the enterprise has (in the absence of a centrally deployed and IS-managed Wi-Fi network) installed a rogue access point, a hacker need only gain physical access to the building, install and conceal a rogue access point of their own, and then leave. They can then access the LAN from the convenience of the parking lot—with their very own dedicated infrastructure.

IS managers, whether they have deployed Wi-Fi or (in particular) have not, must be mindful of the threat posed by rogue access points. Fortunately, there are steps that you can and should take to mitigate this very real risk:

- *Police the RF.* On a regular and thorough basis, IS professionals should use the same tools used by hackers to scan the 2.4- and 5GHz Wi-Fi frequencies for rogue devices. Legitimate users installing residential access points for their convenience typically broadcast their SSID or have no SSID at all. These devices will clearly show up with tools like NetStumbler or the scanning feature in Windows XP. Using a signal strength meter, you can narrow down the physical location of the rogue access points to within a relatively small radius. From there, it's a matter of turning over boxes, looking behind desks, and knocking on dorm room doors. Rogue access points may be more difficult to find, as they may hide their SSID or use similar means to hide the access point from more popular scanning tools. Although they are expensive, more full-featured RF scanners are available and will display SSIDs and other information in packet headers that will indicate their presence. It's a fair bit of trouble and expense, but if there is reason to believe that hackers can or will install rogues of their own, it could be well worth the effort.

- *Improve physical security.* For the security-conscious enterprise, it's common to have key entry systems and even security personnel on site. While this was a good idea in the days before WLANs, it is today an even better idea. An access point installed and left behind by a hacker amounts to a continual virtual presence in the enterprise and on the network. In addition to all the usual security policies in place, security personnel should be educated on Wi-Fi. They should understand what an access point is, what it does, and the threat that it poses. They should question suspicious (unrecognized, unbadged) individuals installing access points and report it to the IS staff. They should report back to the IS staff any newly deployed access points that look out of step with the organization; that is, those that are installed in an ad-hoc, camouflaged, or generally suspicious manner.

- *Lock down ports.* Rogue access points must, after all, be connected to the LAN via an Ethernet port. Most enterprise switches provide security features that are often little used (given IS professionals' typical reliance on physical security alone). As an example, most switches can limit the number of MAC addresses (the number of individual devices) that can connect to that port. By limiting the number of MAC addresses per port to one, you would allow a user to connect a PC, a printer, or an access point, but this access point (or indeed a wired hub or switch) would be unable to handle any connections itself. While this may be an inconvenience for legitimate user groups who want to share a printer, for example, it may be a small price to pay for the enhanced level of security that it provides. In addition to this, and as will be discussed in the next section, a ratified IEEE standard for port-based authentication exists today but is little implemented. By instituting a policy of authenticating at the edge of the wired network, you can provide much of the flexibility available today on the open port but still greatly enhance the ability to preclude the installation of rogue access points. Finally, even in the absence of these steps, IS managers can and should monitor network logs for suspicious activity on network ports. This can include an inordinate spike in traffic, the use of a previously inactive port, or the use of a port at odd hours.

- *Address the demand.* All the preceding strategies address the problem of rogue access points from the supply side. That is, they presume the existence of demand for rogue access points and seek to limit or eliminate their existence. As any economist or Drug Enforcement Agency agent will tell you, the best, most complete, and long term way to address a problem like this is from the demand side. Focusing just on legitimate users seeking convenience for a moment, you can eliminate the rationale for rogue access points by deploying an enterprise-wide Wi-Fi LAN. From the user's perspective, this will provide them with what they need without personal expense, extra effort, and risk. An enterprise-wide Wi-Fi LAN also tends to "raise the wireless consciousness" among IS staff—their monitoring of the WLAN will likely increase their ability to find rogue access points left by hackers.

Fortunately, help is on the way. Vendors are well aware of the threat posed to the enterprise LAN by rogue access points and that this can negatively impact the continued growth of the industry, but they also know that it represents an opportunity for product differentiation. Means by which access points and even client adapters will continually monitor their environment and report rogue access points are being sought out. It is likely that as Wi-Fi deployments in security-conscious organizations accelerate, new features in enterprise access points and clients will provide for a more streamlined and comprehensive means of dealing with the very real threat of rogue access points.

802.1X Authentication

IEEE 802.1X is a ratified standard from the Institute of Electrical and Electronics Engineers (IEEE) for port-based network access control. Note that it is from the 802.1 working group, and is part of a set of base-level standards that are applicable to a wide variety of networking standards. Indeed, 802.1X was originally intended for use with wired technologies like Ethernet. However, due to IS professionals' typical reliance on physical security for wired ports, as discussed in the previous sidebar, 802.1X was seen by many to be something of a solution in search of a problem.

As has been discussed throughout this book, a theme that runs through the history of WLANs is that of borrowing technologies from different areas to more rapidly address problems. In this fashion, 802.1X was adopted by the wireless industry as the principal means of authenticating users to the LAN.

The 802.1X architecture consists of three main parts: a supplicant, an authenticator, and an authentication server. When applied to Wi-Fi, the supplicant resides on the client devices and the access point serves as the authenticator. The supplicant is typically a small amount of software located in the operating system or in the device driver supplied by the client adapter vendor. The access point acts as the gatekeeper for the LAN, allowing the client device to gain access to the LAN only after the client has been authenticated. Remote Authentication Dial-In User Service (RADIUS) servers, which were initially developed for authentication of remote network users dialing into the network over the unsecure public telephone system, are leveraged to authenticate users accessing the LAN over an equally unsecure medium—radio waves.

The authentication process for 802.1X when applied to WLANs works as follows:

1. The client gains access to the wireless medium via CSMA/CA and makes an association with an access point, as discussed in Chapter 5.

2. The 802.1X-compliant access point accepts the association but places the client in an unauthenticated "holding area." For the unauthenticated client, the virtual port, the gateway, to the LAN is blocked. The access point sends an identification request to the client.

3. The client provides an identification response that contains the username or similarly specific yet not secret identifier. Upon receipt of the identification response, the access point forwards this response across the wired link to the RADIUS server. If an access point is configured to accept only 802.1X-compliant clients and an identification response is not forthcoming from the client, the client remains associated but in the unauthenticated holding area (blocked from network access) indefinitely.

4. The RADIUS server looks up the user ID from a database. It's important to note that RADIUS servers themselves may not always incorporate a database for user IDs and authentication credentials, but instead access these credentials from a separate database such as a Microsoft Windows 2000 Active Directory or NT Domain Services database. The advantage to this approach is that a common, and often preexisting, database can be leveraged to support wireless, as well as wired, authentication. This allows for the centralization of authentication credentials, thereby decreasing administrative burden.

5. Once the user ID has been identified by the RADIUS server, it begins a process of challenging the client (with the access point passing the RADIUS challenge

through to the client). The client responds to these challenges until such time as the RADIUS server determines that the client is indeed the client that it purports to be. Since 802.1X does not specify authentication types, leaving that up to individual vendors, the means by which the client is challenged, responds, and is ultimately authenticated to the LAN vary. These vendor-specific implementations are beyond the scope of this book. What is true in all cases is that information that is meant to be secret, such as passwords, are not passed over the WLAN in plaintext. Understanding that with relative ease information over the RF can be intercepted by hackers, it becomes apparent that sending a password from a client to an access point defeats the whole purpose of a password.

6. With WLANs, not only must the client be authenticated to the LAN, the LAN must be authenticated to the client. That is, the possibility exists that a client could associate with an access point that is not part of an enterprise-wide infrastructure. Indeed, this *rogue access point* could have been purposely installed by a hacker with the intent of intercepting client authentication data. Therefore, when 802.1X authentication is applied to WLANs, it provides for mutual authentication, the client to the network and the network to the client. As such, the client initiates what is essentially the reverse of the challenge and response process with the RADIUS server.

7. Once the client has been authenticated to the network through the access point and the RADIUS server, and the network has been authenticated to the client, the virtual port on the access point is opened up and the client can begin access to the wireless and the wired network.

Dynamic Encryption Keys

While 802.1X authentication addresses the relatively weak authentication capabilities of the original 802.11 standard, it doesn't directly address the issue of encryption keys. More to the point, it does not address the scalability or management issues associated with static encryption keys, which are common throughout the network and stored on all the client devices. What does address this problem is the incorporation of an authentication server to the architecture. A RADIUS server, or for that matter a Kerberos server (an alternative authentication server), provides not only authentication capabilities, but also the ability to generate encryption keys that are specific to that particular client. Centralized key generation is as great an issue when managing remote dial-up users as it is when managing Wi-Fi users, making RADIUS servers a logical choice for this role.

When the client has been authenticated by the RADIUS server after having compared the client credential against the credential stored in the database, the RADIUS server also begins the process of dynamic key generation. As previously shown in Figure 11-3, this key exchange process takes place during the client's authentication of the network. It should be noted that these client-specific keys are *unicast* keys, used only when traffic is directed just at a particular client. *Multicast* keys, used when traffic is broadcast to a number of clients, are shared and have some of the same disadvantages of shared WEP keys.

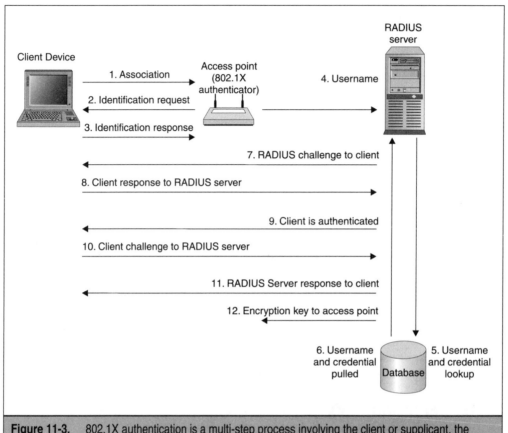

Figure 11-3. 802.1X authentication is a multi-step process involving the client or supplicant, the access point or authenticator, a RADIUS or authentication server, and a database.

The client-specific keys are specific not only to the client but also to a particular client session. Most RADIUS servers provide the ability to adjust the session length, and IS professionals tend to set session timeouts somewhere between a half hour and a full day. The shorter the session length, the fewer number of packets that will be sent with a particular encryption key. This means that hackers will have fewer captured packets to work with, making the job of breaking a key all the more difficult. On the other hand, the shorter the session length, the greater the number of re-authentications over a given period. Depending upon network architecture and load, this can result in performance issues as the RADIUS server is taxed to a greater degree. From a user's perspective, these session timeouts should have little impact; the re-authentication process that takes place at the beginning of the new session typically occurs in the background with, as an example, the user's password being sent from a cache on the user's client device and not manually re-keyed.

By making unicast keys at least particular to a single session and a single user, the severity of a security breach in the event of a key being hacked is greatly mitigated. The breach would result in compromised data for that user only and just for that particular past session. This compares to a compromised static and shared encryption key, which allows the hacker to decrypt packets for all users and for all sessions in both the past *as well as the future*. These dynamic encryption keys "disappear" from the client device at the end of a session or when the client device is powered down—a lost laptop no longer results in a security (and career) disaster.

The 802.11i Standard

Recognizing the need for a far more robust and scalable security architecture for Wi-Fi LANs, the 802.11 group within the IEEE voted to dedicate a task group specifically to security, which had been part of a task of the group dedicated to quality of service. The 802.11i task group (TGi in IEEE parlance) was formed in 2001 and, although it has not to date delivered a ratified standard, has done much to provide *interoperable* enterprise security.

In short, 802.11i specifies 802.1X, coupled with the Extensible Authentication Protocol (EAP), as the means by which Wi-Fi clients and networks mutually authenticate. What is notable about EAP is that the *extensible* aspect of the protocol provides the flexibility to authenticate in a variety of manners. This gives vendors the freedom to provide different *authentication types* or *authentication methods* using different types of credentials. 802.11i specifies RC4, the same encryption algorithm as used for static WEP keys, as the encryption algorithm for single-session, single-user dynamic encryption keys.

Authentication Types

Vendors have taken advantage of the flexibility in the draft 802.11i standard to deliver a variety of authentication types (also referred to as authentication methods). For an 802.11i architecture to function, the authentication types used on the client side must be supported by the RADIUS server. Because access points are, for the most part, simply passing authentication traffic back and forth between the client and the RADIUS server, a single 802.11i-compliant access point is capable of working with client devices using a number of different authentication types, provided that these authentication types are supported by the RADIUS server. RADIUS servers from some vendors have built-in support for multiple authentication types, allowing you to have a single RADIUS server that supports multiple client-side authentication types.

With the delivery of the industry's first (and prestandard) enterprise security architecture in early 2001, Cisco Systems delivered the first authentication type, which came to be known as LEAP (which originally stood for Lightweight EAP but has since been hopelessly obscured). With LEAP, passwords are the authentication credentials, leveraging client-side network login screens and backend network domain databases. Because Cisco is a client-side hardware vendor, LEAP was originally available only with

Cisco client adapters, but now is licensed to and available from other vendors, including Apple Computer Corporation. LEAP is compliant with the 802.11i draft standard, making it one of many authentication types now available.

As part of the Windows XP OS, Microsoft added a second and alternate authentication type to the 802.11i mix. The Extensible Authentication Protocol with Transport Layer Security (EAP/TLS) authentication type relies on certificates instead of passwords as the authentication credential. As discussed earlier in the chapter, the advantage of a certificate over a password is that it requires no user intervention and arguably a greater degree of security as they are far more random than user-selected passwords (see the description of dictionary and birthday attacks earlier in the chapter). On the other hand, certificate-based authentication takes place at the device, not the user level. A thief can authenticate to the network with the stolen device without any special knowledge. Because EAP/TLS is from a software company and because it resides in the OS, it works with essentially any 802.11-compliant client adapter from any vendor. This is an advantage for those IS groups that have little or no control over the types of client hardware on the LAN, which is typical in university settings but common in other enterprises as well.

Initially, EAP/TLS was intended to be available only with Windows XP—you can draw your own conclusions as to whether this decision was technically driven or sales driven. In fairness, Microsoft has since reconsidered this and, as of mid-2002, is in the process of delivering EAP/TLS for other OSes (inclusive of Windows 98, Windows 2000 and various forms of Windows CE) in the form of downloadable service packs.

Other vendors have delivered alternative authentication types, including the EAP with Tunneling Transport Layer Security (EAP/TTLS) authentication type contained in Funk Software's Odyssey client security utility. Meetinghouse Software has similarly delivered an EAP/TTLS authentication type with the Aegis client utility. With EAP/TTLS, a secure authentication tunnel is set up at Layer 2 between the client and the access point using TLS. Having established this secure tunnel, EAP/TTLS then builds upon this, allowing a variety of authentication credentials, including passwords and certificates, to be sent and received through the secure tunnel. EAP/TTLS is a subset of EAP/TLS since it only uses TLS on the server side and not the client. But, by providing for password authentication in addition to certificates, EAP/TTLS is something of an EAP/TLS superset.

A more recent alternative to EAP/TTLS is Protected Extensible Authentication Protocol (PEAP), which is similar to EAP/TTLS in that it too sets up an authentication tunnel, allowing for a variety of authentication credentials. An early implementation of PEAP from Cisco Systems supports OTPs for an even more robust version of user-level authentication. Microsoft has indicated that it will support PEAP in addition to EAP/TLS on selected OSes, thereby providing for not just certificate-based credentials but passwords as well. Many security experts consider PEAP to provide greater security than the earlier EAP/TTLS.

To support these authentication types on the client side, RADIUS server support is, of course, required. Cisco's Access Control Server supports the LEAP and EAP/TLS authentication types. Microsoft's Windows XP server supports EAP/TLS, while Funk Software's Steel Belted RADIUS server supports LEAP and EAP/TTLS, and Interlink's Merit RADIUS server supports LEAP. Many RADIUS servers provide *failover* capabilities, meaning that if an unsupported authentication type is received, it will pass it along to another RADIUS server, if available. In this manner, you can have a single RADIUS server or even multiple RADIUS servers to provide backend support for all client-side authentication types. As shown in Figure 11-4, this provides you with a number of options for deploying an *interoperable* security architecture.

Addressing the WEP Encryption Problem

The various authentication types previously listed go a long way toward providing the interoperable authentication methods required to scale security to enterprise levels. They do not, however, address at all the limitations of the 802.11 implementation of the RC4 algorithm. This deficiency in standards-based security for Wi-Fi LAN is not being overlooked.

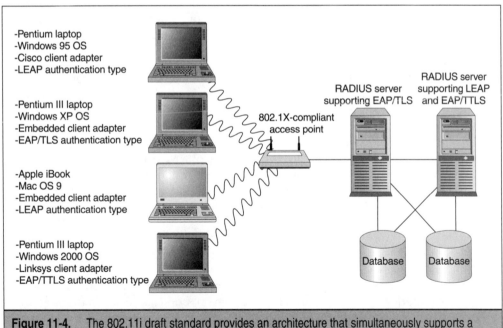

Figure 11-4.   The 802.11i draft standard provides an architecture that simultaneously supports a variety of client-side OSes, client adapters, and authentication types.

The Temporal Key Integrity Protocol (TKIP) is a near-term means of "shoring up" the deficiencies of the 802.11 implementation of RC4 both for static and, more importantly, dynamic encryption keys. As of late 2002, TKIP remained a generally defined element of the 802.11i draft standard. TKIP continues to rely upon RC4 and consists of essentially three major enhancements relative to the initial implementation of the algorithm:

- **Per-packet key mixing** The encryption key is mixed with the sending station's MAC address and a sequential packet number to greatly complicate the base key, making it, in and of itself, more difficult to break.

- **A 48-bit initialization vector** Double the length of the original 24-bit initialization vector specified in the original WEP standard. Remember that key lengths have an exponential effect—while a 24-bit key has approximately 16 million combinations, a 48-bit key provides about 280 trillion combinations. This longer key, coupled with per-packet key mixing makes for encryption keys that are multiple orders of magnitude more robust than previous generation implementations.

- **Message integrity checks (MICs)** Designed to thwart inductive or man-in-the-middle attacks. The TKIP MIC implementation is a next-generation version called (cleverly enough) "Michael." With a MIC, the sending and receiving MAC addresses, as well as other unique information, are integrated into the encrypted payload. Changes to this information, inherent when a packet is intercepted, result in a rejection of the packet and an alert that an attack may be in progress.

Regrettably, TKIP is not yet a complete and ratified standard. In an effort to bring the very much-needed TKIP enhancements to the market faster than is typical through the standards-setting process, a number of organizations have shortcut the process by releasing prestandard solutions. Cisco Systems has released a prestandard, single-vendor version of TKIP. Microsoft put forth Simple Secure Networking (SSN), which is a subset of the 802.11i draft standard but inclusive of a Microsoft implementation of TKIP. Subsequently, SSN was adopted by the Wi-Fi Alliance as an interim security standard, renaming the initiative WPA for Wi-Fi Protected Access. Interoperability testing for WPA is planned by the end of 2002, with mandatory WPA compliance for Wi-Fi certification as early as the middle of 2003.

Despite all the improvements inherent in TKIP and WPA, RC4-based architectures are still considered by many to be fundamentally insufficient for particularly security-conscious organizations. As an example, the various Federal Information Processing Standards (FIPS), which are applicable to many federal government applications including the military, exclude the RC4 algorithm for sensitive but non-classified communications. By extension, the security aspects of the Health Insurance Portability and Accounting Act of 1996 (HIPAA) mandate that patient information be subject to state of the art security—a definition difficult to apply to the RC4 algorithm much less to WEP.

On the other hand, the FIPS-197 standard, published in November 2001, defines the Advanced Encryption Standard (AES), a next-generation encryption standard based upon 128-bit-long keys (minimum) generated by the Rijndael algorithm ("raindoll" and "rhinedahl" are acceptable pronunciations). HIPAA compliance is understood to follow FIPS and therefore AES is likely to be allowable for HIPAA compliance. This development is in keeping with broader industry trends: virtual private network (VPN) vendors who have long used the federally mandated Data Encryption Standard (DES, and the follow-on 3DES or "triple DES") are migrating to AES as a next-generation encryption standard.

There is general agreement amongst those vendors focusing on enterprise-class Wi-Fi offerings that AES is the next-generation encryption standard for WLAN transmission. Given that RC4 is less robust than DES or 3DES and that DES and 3DES are less robust than AES, it follows that by adopting AES, the Wi-Fi industry is essentially leap-frogging a generation of security.

The migration to AES may not be as straightforward as it seems on the surface, and may not be a complete migration at all. As was discussed in Chapter 5, encryption has a significant impact on network performance, particularly when implemented in software and processed on the host. When the relatively "light" RC4 algorithm is implemented in software, the performance penalty can exceed 25 percent. A similarly implemented Rijndael algorithm promises to exact as much as a 50 percent performance hit. As such, a more likely scenario is that the RC4 algorithm (with associated TKIP and WPA enhancements) will coexist with the AES standard. Vendors are planning enhancements to 802.11 beacons that will advertise the security capabilities of the device allowing associated devices to negotiate the highest level of security that is mutually

The VPN Alternative

To those familiar with VPNs, this discussion of WLAN security will have had an element of déjà vu. Indeed, many of the problems inherent in the transmission of secure data over a fundamentally unsecure wireless medium are very similar to the problems inherent in transmission of secure data over the fundamentally unsecure Internet. This begs the question: why not simply use existing VPN technology to solve the problem of wireless security? Why not, indeed.

Many organizations have chosen to ignore the developments being made in Wi-Fi specific security and simply layer a VPN over the completely unsecured Wi-Fi physical layer. There are a number of advantages to this approach:

- VPN technology is relatively mature. With years of experience in securing sensitive data over the Internet, VPN vendors have encountered and mitigated most, if not all, the sorts of attacks that are being made against the WLAN. Today, VPNs provide a variety of authentication methods coupled with DES, 3DES, and AES encryption.

- A VPN approach leverages existing security infrastructure and staff knowledge. Many enterprise organizations have come to rely upon VPNs for remote access in lieu of expensive and non-scalable leased lines and private circuits. At a conceptual if not technical level, these investments can be leveraged to address wireless clients as well.

- With VPNs, there is interoperability of a sort. While it is the case that no truly interoperable standard exists for VPNs, vendors have, to a degree, overcome this with technical and marketing solutions. VPN solutions consist of a client-side application and a backend hardware concentrator or software-based server application. Most VPN client-side applications operate on a very wide range of client-side OSes and are available at little cost, if not free. In so doing, VPN vendors can address the major shortcoming of nonstandard technologies—interoperability. What's the interoperability issue of a VPN client application if it's free and operates on all client devices?

There are, however, drawbacks to a VPN solution to WLAN security issues:

- VPNs are for the most part designed with fairly limited or occasional network access in mind. From the user's perspective, invoking the VPN client typically requires additional steps, an inconvenience that is inconsistent with the freedom of WLANs. On the administrative side, while VPN-specific equipment or hardware dedicated to VPNs may be already in place for remote access, it is unlikely that it is capable of handling the traffic associated with Wi-Fi LANs—a primary local access technology. Hardware VPN concentrators have a fixed number of clients supported—there is a definite cost associated with each additional client supported. Software-based VPN servers may similarly have a finite "seat count." Leveraging VPN technology to support WLANs will, at the minimum, require a significant infrastructure scaling.

- The "interoperability" advantages of VPNs are their disadvantage. That is, because VPN clients reside in software and use the host's processor, their operation will exact a performance penalty far greater than solutions that implement encryption in hardware. While this is true on the client side, it is far more the case with VPN server software in the infrastructure.

- VPNs are limited in that they do not provide for the packet prioritization that is required for time-sensitive traffic like voice and video. VPNs support only IP unicast traffic and do not support other protocols like IPX and AppleTalk.

In short, you should consider both the advantages and the disadvantages of deploying or leveraging a VPN to address the security requirements of the WLANs. It should be noted as well that a VPN and WLAN-specific security solutions are not mutually exclusive. For applications even within the same organization, VPNs may represent a better solution than WEP, TKIP, and WPA—and vice versa.

possible. Vendors are, moreover, developing hardware-based AES implementations that are likely to be available in mid-2003. In much the same way that hardware-based encryption engines provide better performance for the RC4-based WEP, these next-generation encryption engines will provide an even more needed assist for the Rijndael-based AES, providing for a high level of security with minimal performance impact.

Different Types of Security for Different Applications

This chapter has thus far discussed a number of different security architectures, each consisting of various means of authentication and encryption keys. Here, we'll focus on the applicability of each. In any scenario, the first thing you should keep in mind is that *something is better than nothing.* That is, a cursory glance at the trade and business media might lead you to believe that it's pointless to make any attempt at securing the Wi-Fi LAN. This is, of course, simply not the case—even with flawed tools, a good deal can be done to mitigate, if not eliminate, the possibility of being hacked.

Small Offices

First, a distinction should be made between small offices and branch offices. With the former, the entity is autonomous and not connected over the WAN to a centralized network as is a branch office. Small offices can be in the home or outside the home; there's nothing intrinsically different between the two from a security perspective. The simplifying aspect of a small office is not that the data is any less sensitive—patient records, as an example, are every bit as sensitive for a psychiatrist in private practice as they are for a multiunit hospital system. Rather, the simplifying factor is that of scalability—a small office has a very limited number of users and therefore has little need for a scalable solution.

As such, a reasonable security architecture would be to start with some level of authentication. Although the deficiencies of MAC address authentication are well known (they can be easily spoofed), it represents some small degree of security. Better still, going forward, vendors are likely to integrate RADIUS servers directly into the access point, a very useful feature for small autonomous networks. Although static WEP keys can be compromised, they should still be used, particularly since their scalability limitations are not an issue with a small LAN. Remember that key attacks are mostly based upon collecting a number of packets, which, on a busy enterprise LAN, can take but a few hours, with these collection intervals shrinking to a matter of minutes. Collecting this same quantity will take far longer on a relatively small, lightly traveled LAN. By changing the static WEP keys out on the access point and the small number of clients on a frequent and regular basis, you can go a long way toward mitigating an attack.

To a degree, Wi-Fi security is like a car alarm—the point isn't to make it theft proof but rather to make it more theft resistant than other targets. WPA and the inherent TKIP advancements are applicable to both static and dynamic encryption keys. Even small office installations should upgrade to WPA or even a prestandard TKIP implementation as soon as it is available.

Branch Offices

From a physical perspective, a branch office can look absolutely identical to a small office. Indeed, a single spare bedroom can change from being a small office to a branch office depending upon which spouse is using it—the corporately employed wife or the independently consulting husband.

The major difference is that a compromised branch office carries with it the possibility of compromising the enterprise network as a whole, whereas the implications of a security breach to a small autonomous network are far more limited. Branch offices do, however, have the advantage of being able to leverage to a degree the enterprise security infrastructure. To be precise, a branch office can take advantage of a complete 802.1X-based security architecture *provided that authentication across the WAN provides acceptable performance and reliability.* Remember that mutual authentication takes place at the beginning of every session and, at your choosing, can occur multiple times over the course of a day. The implication is that there can be noticeable latency when an authentication is taking place across a WAN, particularly with the low-speed frame relay, ISDN, cable, or DSL carriers that are common for branch offices.

Latency is an even greater issue with more transaction-oriented client devices like bar code scanners, making authentication over the WAN an impracticality for retail stores, which are branch offices of sorts. Worse still, in the event of an interruption in wide area service, the branch office user will be unable to authenticate to the *local* area. This means that if a WAN link goes down, a Wi-Fi user could literally be unable to print a file on a printer located across the room.

Branch offices, which combine the dispersed nature and size of small offices with the security implications of the enterprise, represent one of the most challenging Wi-Fi security applications. If you deploy centralized authentication across the WAN, you must consider the reliability of the link and manage user expectations for performance and reliability. Using different client-side profiles (a feature provided with many client adapters), you should consider a fallback means of local authentication. For larger branch offices, deploying stand-alone RADIUS servers at the local sites may be an option, although there are severe administrative issues and security implications of distributing authentication credentials to this degree.

Going forward, more intelligent standards-based authentication mechanisms will provide branch offices with centralized authentication and resilient authentication services when connectivity to the central server is unavailable. For smaller branch offices, you can consider a VPN-based security architecture; that is, a small office type of security architecture for local traffic with a VPN client invoked when communicating exclusively over the RF to the enterprise LAN. If you assume (or better still mandate) that all local traffic is non-sensitive, non-enterprise traffic, this can be an effective solution.

The Enterprise

The 802.1X-based security architecture was designed with the enterprise in mind and is most applicable to this sort of Wi-Fi deployment. The centralized nature of the architecture addresses the administrative, security, and scalability requirements of the enterprise all while leveraging tools and skills that may well be already available to the IS staff. The issues associated with the architecture—lack of a ratified 802.11i standard, a patchwork of authentication types, and a questionable implementation of the RC4 algorithm—are all being addressed on a literally month-by-month basis. Vendors are providing frequent updates to their various components, making the architecture increasingly viable for the enterprise.

Other security approaches are possible. Some larger organizations continue to struggle with static encryption keys, literally devoting staff members to manually keying thousands of individual client devices. Some organizations continue to ignore the 802.1X architecture in favor of a VPN approach for local Wi-Fi authentication and security. Within the vendor community at least, these approaches are viewed as interim solutions that will eventually be replaced in the enterprise as 802.11i gains full ratification and increased vendor support.

Public Access

As will be further discussed in Chapter 13, the commercial deployment of Wi-Fi in public areas like airports, hotels, convention centers, and even coffee shops is an exciting industry development. With public access, there are really two elements to security, one that impacts the organization that is providing the service, and another that impacts the users of the service and their organizations.

For the service provider, the primary issue is to allow access only to those users who are authorized, typically those who have paid for the use of the public network. This comes down to authentication of the user, providing the user with the services for which they're authorized, and then generating the accounting records needed for billing purposes. These three functions are available in a single server called, appropriately enough, a Triple A server, for authentication, authorization, and accounting. RADIUS servers are a subset of Triple A servers, indicating that while Triple A servers can be used for service provider applications, they are by no means limited to this and are also commonly used in the enterprise.

An alternative to a Triple A server is a service selection gateway, a tool that redirects a user to a specific web page. With this architecture, the user is allowed access to the public LAN but is allowed access to a single web site. This site would typically request some form of payment for use, such as a credit card number for per-use billing or a username and password if a membership business model is employed. In either scenario, the user is allowed access to the whole Internet after payment has been received.

Note from the preceding discussion that no encryption is taking place and that, from the service provider's perspective, security is essentially about allowing (or disallowing) use of the service and then billing for it. Having gained access to the public network, the user must then provide their own security. For casual web surfing, perhaps no additional security measures are necessary. When logging in to an enterprise network, a VPN becomes a logical choice in the same way that it is the logical choice when communicating via the Internet over a wired connection.

CHECKLIST

Security is today the single largest issue facing the Wi-Fi industry. This chapter is intended to provide an overview of the subject and is by no means comprehensive. The subject moreover is in a rapid state of evolution and improvement. As such, before embarking on an enterprise-wide Wi-Fi deployment, you're urged to solicit additional information to make for a more successful, scalable, and robust security architecture.

- ☐ Authentication is the means by which a user is verified to be a valid network user. Authentication is common on both wired and wireless LANs. Many different authentication credentials are available, such as passwords and certificates.

- ☐ Encryption is complementary to authentication and is the process of encoding information to keep it secret from unauthorized parties. Encryption is not as common on wired LANs as is authentication, since many IS professionals count on physical security for wired LANs. Physical security cannot be counted on for wireless LANs at all.

- ☐ Rogue access points present a very real threat to wireless security. Users are well advised to take precautions to minimize, if not eliminate, their proliferation throughout the enterprise.

- ☐ The 802.11 WEP standard was developed at a time when WLANs addressed a very different set of applications. As such, it is ill-suited at an architectural level to enterprise deployments. Moreover, WEP encryption has been found to be relatively easy to break. In summary, it is not advisable to deploy WEP in the great majority of enterprise applications.

- ☐ The 802.1X standard for port-based authentication has been adopted by the Wi-Fi industry. Applied to Wi-Fi, 802.1X involves the client or supplicant, the access point or authenticator, and an authentication server, and provides for mutual authentication. 802.1X coupled with EAP provides for a number of different authentication methods, including passwords and certificates.

- ☐ The 802.11i standard is expected to be ratified in 2003. It provides vendors with the flexibility to deliver alternative authentication methods while still allowing for interoperability.

- ☐ TKIP addresses many of the shortcomings of the WEP implementation of the RC4 algorithm to make for a much more robust means of encryption. A Microsoft implementation of TKIP, originally called SSN and later changed to WPA by the Wi-Fi Alliance, is expected to be available by the end of 2002 from a number of different vendors. The Wi-Fi industry further intends to provide AES encryption for an even greater degree of security.

- ☐ Different applications call for different security architectures. Small offices, branch offices, enterprise offices, and public access scenarios all suggest different security architectures.

CHAPTER 12

QoS in Wireless LANs

As discussed in Chapter 5, the media access method for 802.11-based wireless LANs is CSMA/CA (Carrier Sense Multiple Access with Collision Avoidance) and the related Distributed Control Function (DCF). This architecture is very efficient, democratic, and, in a way, polite. It allows each station on the network to send data when it has data to send. It does not require the station to wait its turn or first ask permission from some higher authority like an access point. It does, however, require that the station first listen to make certain that no other station is using the medium before transmitting. If the channel is busy, the station must monitor the medium continuously until it is idle and then transmit after a random backoff period. *Each station on the network is an equal, meaning no station has higher priority or importance than any other.*

Therein lies the rub. It's implicit in this statement that if every station has equal priority, so then does all data have equal priority. An "instant" message from a company's CEO to the CFO has the same priority as an audio file being downloaded from the Internet by an intern. Voice over Internet Protocol (VoIP) or even a videoconference would have the same priority as any other packet. While in general democracy and egalitarianism are noble ideas, there are some stations on a LAN that have greater importance than others. There are some types of packets that must have greater priority than others. The general concept of providing these differing levels of priority, and therefore differing levels of performance, is referred to as *quality of service (QoS)*.

As Wi-Fi networks are installed in a larger number and greater variety of organizations, they are called upon to handle a greater variety of applications and to carry data of relatively greater importance, or *mission-critical* data. Organizations want to get the most out of the wireless LAN infrastructure that they have deployed—in much the same way as organizations are leveraging their wired infrastructure to support multiple types of traffic, so too are organizations looking to run voice, video, *and* data over the WLAN. With a WLAN, a voice client can provide the same convenience as a cordless telephone in the home (relative to traditional and fast-disappearing corded handsets). Video over the WLAN enables the sort of next-generation "gee whiz" applications that make computers and data communications so exciting—imagine standing a PDA on a conference room table and having a remote colleague's voice coming from the speaker and their face on the display with the microphone serving as their ears and the embedded camera serving as their eyes.

With the current 802.11 standards alone, QoS for such voice and video applications is not supported, although it is possible on lightly loaded networks. This architecture provides no more than *best effort* service, a polite way of saying "I'll get it to you when I can." You wouldn't accept this level of service for an appliance delivery, and you can't for the delivery of voice, video, and even some data packets.

A Trio of Parameters

One way to better quantify QoS is to define what it is that QoS is managing and then measure it. The three parameters that QoS manages are packet loss, delay or latency, and delay variance, which is referred to more commonly as "jitter." Stated another way, packet loss, delay, and jitter are the three things that impact the QoS on the LAN as perceived by the user. Users of different services, say voice rather than data, will have different perceptions and expectations of quality.

As the name suggests, *packet loss* is simply a quantification of the number of packets lost during transmission and is typically expressed as a percentage of all packets. As discussed in Chapter 5, the loss of a packet (a "dropped" packet) will be recognized by a receiving station, resulting in a resend. With data, this represents little trouble. With voice, there is little time to resend a packet such that it can be reinserted into the right sequence, into the right point in the conversation.

Different types of network traffic dictate an acceptable level of packet loss. Standard data traffic allows for a relatively high number of lost packets, more than 1 percent of all sent. "Highly available" networks, such as those handling transaction-based processing like traffic back and forth between a bar code scanner and an inventory system, should lose less than 1 percent of all packets. Voice, naturally, has the most stringent requirements for packet loss; the number of packets lost when handling voice traffic should approach zero. Losing a packet when transmitting over an unlicensed portion of the radio frequency spectrum is far more likely than when transmitting over a copper wire. Managing packet loss and resulting QoS over a wireless LAN is more challenging than over a wired LAN.

Delay is a quantification of how long it takes for a packet to go from one station on the LAN to the next. Also referred to as *latency*, this amount of time has an absolute minimum that is a function of the network protocols. The far more important quantification, and the one that is more difficult to manage, is the latency that results from network congestion. For voice packets, this latency should be no more than 150ms (15 percent of 1 second), which is a pretty short period of time, particularly when a station is continually waiting to send due to a high amount of network traffic.

Streaming voice and video differ from more standard data transmission in that the receiver must generate the original stream from a playback buffer, where the required size of the playback buffer is determined by measured delay. As such, the *delay variance*, the amount of variance between each packet's delay, has an impact on the perceived quality of the transmission. Jitter can result for a congested network, particularly one that is congested with "bursty" traffic such as video or some types of data. For voice traffic, jitter should be kept to below 30ms.

IDENTIFYING TIME-SENSITIVE TRAFFIC

Before packets can be prioritized, they must first be identified as having greater or lesser priority than others. Better still, prioritization can be more of a spectrum than an absolute—with degrees of priority assigned to specific packets. This is referred to as *class of service (CoS)* and represents one element of a QoS architecture. Different types of traffic require different levels of priority.

The type of traffic that requires the lowest level of priority is referred to as *asynchronous*, meaning that it has essentially no temporal requirements. Traffic in this category would include common data traffic like e-mail, file transfers, and web surfing that, in relative terms, can arrive as network availability allows.

Traffic with a higher level of priority, such as streaming video and audio, is referred to as being *isochronous* (from the Greek words for "equal in time"), meaning that it needs to arrive at a receiving station at a rate similar to the rate at which it was sent and in the proper sequence. The consequences of isochronous data arriving at a slow rate or out of order is known to most who have experienced streaming video over the Internet or over a wireless link.

The type of traffic that requires the highest level of priority is referred to as being *synchronous*, meaning that the processes are interrelated with the beginning of one process being dependent upon the completion of another. A typical example of this sort of traffic is interactive voice.

IEEE standards that address CoS include 802.1Q and 802.1D. Note that these are not wireless-specific 802.11 standards; indeed, these standards were first developed for, and deployed on, wired LANs. In the tradition of the Wi-Fi industry, vendors are "borrowing" preexisting standards and applying them to wireless.

The IEEE standards that rely upon priority tags include 802.1Q and 802.1D. The 802.1Q standard defines a means of establishing separate "priority" queues for different types of traffic. The 802.1D standard provides for a means of expediting QoS traffic across bridge links, providing a solution to a problem that is similar to expediting time-sensitive traffic across a wireless link.

The CoS tags that are used by 802.1Q and 802.1D are sometimes referred to as 802.1p tags and are specified in the packet headers defined in the 802.1Q and 802.1D standard. With eight priority levels, outlined in Table 12-1, these tags can be assigned in 3 bits, making them relatively small and network efficient. The 802.1Q and 802.1D tag definitions vary, but show a similar progression for packet types with increasing criticality.

In addition to tagging at the MAC layer via 802.1Q and 802.1D, IP packets can be tagged as well with a differentiated service code point (DSCP), an element of the differentiated services (diffserv) initiative that is part of the Internet Protocol, version 4 (IPv4). With 6-bit DSCPs, 64 levels of priority are available, which is more than would ever be required. On the other hand, unfortunately, there is no standard for these priority levels or for mapping DSCP values to 802.1D CoS values. As such, vendors can and do release their own specific and non-interoperable tags.

CoS Priority Tag	802.1Q Packet Type	802.1D Packet Type
7	Reserved for Network	Voice
6	Reserved for Network	Voice
5	Voice	Video
4	Video Conferencing	Video
3	Call Signaling	Video Probe
2	High Priority Data	Best Effort
1	Medium Priority Data	Best Effort
0	Low Priority Data	Best Effort

Table 12-1. 802.1Q and 802.1D Tag Definitions

PRIORITIZING TRAFFIC

Having assigned a means of identifying a packet's priority via a tagging system, the Wi-Fi devices can now identify and then prioritize packets based upon the time criticality of the packets. There are a number of means by which a station or a packet can receive priority treatment, which can be classified as being *statistical* or *deterministic* in nature. With statistical prioritization, the likelihood of a time-sensitive packet being afforded special consideration is increased but not insured. With deterministic prioritization, a device (an access point for Wi-Fi LANs) takes on a controlling role, scheduling the transmission order of packets. Statistical prioritization, while not absolute, adds less overhead to the medium than does deterministic prioritization, which relies upon additional management and polling packets that add to network traffic.

The 802.11e Standard and WME

As of the latter half of 2002, two standards are being developed that provide for QoS over Wi-Fi LANs, 802.11e and wireless multimedia extensions (WME). The former is, of course, a task group within the 802.11 group and one that is dedicated to QoS. As the *e* designation suggests, this is one of the earliest task groups, indicating the importance placed upon QoS by the 802.11 group. Given that the standard is not yet ratified, it is also an indication that this particular task group has spent a considerable amount of time on the issue without resolution. As a response to that, a group of vendors that includes Agere, Atheros, Cisco, Intel, Intersil, and Microsoft has proposed WME, which is in large part a subset of the current 802.11e draft.

The central idea behind WME is to bring forth a standard that can be implemented in the nearer term than 802.11e, to deliver QoS to customers earlier. In this regard, WME is similar to the SSN/WPA security "standard" discussed in Chapter 11. As of this writing, 802.11e is not yet ratified and WME is not yet finalized. The WME initiative has resulted in a move within 802.11e to simplify the standard such that it can be more quickly ratified and implemented. As an example, features designed to provide 802.11 QoS in consumer electronics–type products and forward error correction (FEC) have been removed from the draft standard. It is now possible that 802.11e could achieve ratification prior to the finalization of the WME specification. To the extent that WME will still be necessary after 802.11e is ratified and broadly implemented, WME (while currently a subset of 802.11e) could diverge into an alternative, non-IEEE standard.

SpectraLink and Prestandard QoS

SpectraLink Corporation is a manufacturer of 802.11-compliant wireless VoIP telephones, serving a number of markets including manufacturing, retail, and logistics. Given that today there is no ratified 802.11 standard for QoS, SpectraLink developed its own means of prioritization over Wi-Fi LANs and has been successful in having a number of vendors support it, including Avaya, Cisco, Enterasys, and Intermec.

Its prioritization mechanism is called SpectraLink Voice Priority (SVP). Given that the sole goal of the system is to prioritize voice and that the success of the company is dependent upon its ability to get third-party vendors to support it, the mechanism is very straightforward yet effective.

To prioritize voice traffic, an access point must first be able to identify a packet as being a voice packet rather than a data packet. In the SVP system, this is addressed by filtering the IP packet headers for voice packets, a function supported by many access points regardless of their support for SVP.

Having identified voice packets, SVP provides for voice prioritization in two main ways. First, it addresses the random backoff times that are part of the 802.11 standard. As was discussed in Chapter 5, as part of the collision avoidance aspect of CSMA/CA, a sending station waits some random period of time between packet transmissions. This randomization is a relatively effective way to decrease the likelihood of stations sending at the same time. With SpectraLink telephones, their backoff period is always zero; that is, they will not wait between packet transmissions. Similarly, an access point that supports the SVP system will not back off between transmissions when the next packet to be sent is a voice packet.

The second means of prioritization is to move voice packets to the "head of the line" for transmission. This can be accomplished either by moving all voice packets to the top of a single transmission queue or by setting up a second queue specifically for voice packets that will always have transmission priority over the data queue.

This approach, while effective, has its limitations. The prioritization is binary—there is only one priority level for voice and no prioritization levels for voice or video (understandable given the voice-centric goal of the mechanism).

The other main limitation applies to any prioritization system: a large number of prioritized packets can have the effect of "starving out" unprioritized data packets—continually moving them down the transmission queue such that they are never sent. To address this, access points supporting the SVP system often include a means of limiting the number of SpectraLink telephones associated to a single access point. This is an imprecise tool at best, because it is not the number of voice devices that can lead to a starve-out effect but rather the number of voice packets that they produce. The maximum number of telephones is therefore a function of how frequently the telephones are being used and how many resulting voice packets are competing with data packets for airtime. This makes the specification of an absolute number an impossibility. Still, as a rule of thumb, it's inadvisable to plan for more than ten SpectraLink telephones on a single access point. The means by which you can architect the Wi-Fi LAN to better support this lower number of devices are outlined in Chapter 9.

Enhanced Distributed Control Function

Both 802.11e and WME specify a statistical means of prioritization, referred to as enhanced distributed control function (EDCF). As discussed in Chapter 5, DCF is closely related to the CSMA/CA method of media access and provides very efficient use of available bandwidth. DCF does not, however, provide for any means of prioritizing traffic. EDCF addresses this limitation by providing new parameters for media access, which can be modified to provide for earlier (or later) access to the wireless medium. With DCF, there is essentially one access category. As shown in Table 12-2, EDCF defines four additional access categories, which can then be mapped to the eight QoS priorities defined within the 802.1D specification (which in turn can be mapped to the priorities defined in the 802.1Q specification). DSCPs, from IP packet headers, can be mapped to 802.11D tags, which in turn can be assigned to an access category. These four access categories represent four additional unicast queues over and above the legacy (and lowest priority) DCF unicast queue.

To provide for the relative prioritization of the packets within the EDCF access categories, adjustments are made to a variety of parameters. As discussed in Chapter 5, the collision avoidance aspect of CSMA/CA relies upon the stations having random backoff times between transmissions. With DCF, all stations, which have equal priority and equal access to the medium, select from the same range of backoff times. With EDCF, higher-priority transmission queues select from a range of backoff times that are shorter in duration than the backoff times within the range used by lower-priority queues.

By waiting a shorter period of time between transmissions, the stations with packets in higher-priority queues have greater access to the medium and deliver their packets at a greater and steadier rate than stations with lower-priority packets. These ranges of

802.1D CoS Priority Guideline	EDCF Priority	EDCF Designation
7	3	Voice
6	3	Voice
5	2	Video
4	2	Video
3	1	Video Probe
2	0	Best Effort
1	0	Best Effort
0	0	Best Effort

Table 12-2. Mapping of EDCF Access Categories to CoS Priorities Specified in 802.1D

backoff times are referred to as *contention windows,* the period of time during which the station is contending with other stations for access to the medium. Each priority queue is assigned a minimum contention window value, called CWmin, and a maximum contention window value, called CWmax. The lower the CWmin and CWmax values, the shorter the backoff times within the range and the higher priority afforded to packets within the queue.

The arbitrary inter frame space (AIFS) is another parameter that can be adjusted between different access categories to provide varying degrees of priority. The AIFS is the amount of time that a station will remain idle between the transmission of frames or packets. The shorter the AIFS, the closer the station gets to continual, uninterrupted transmission. The danger inherent in reducing the AIFS is that a station using a very short AIFS could effectively "capture" the medium, locking out all other stations (even those waiting to transmit higher-priority packets) until the station has completed the whole transmission.

With EDCF, access points advertise their access parameters, the CWmin, CWmax, and their AIFS, as well as their transmit opportunity (TxOP) limits, TxOP budget, and load. These six parameters are specific to each access class, meaning that a total of 24 parameters will be advertised by an 802.11e- or WME-compliant access point. A *transmit opportunity* is the amount of time that an access point will provide to a sending station each time the station successfully contends for the medium (gains control of the medium to send a packet). TxOP limits are the quantification of this period of time. TxOP budgets are the number of TxOP limits the access point has available per access category. The load information the access point provides includes the number of associated stations within each access category and their aggregate utilization of the access point's available resources.

TxOP and load information are important for *admissions control* purposes. With admissions control, either a client or an access point can elect to initiate an action based upon the availability of resources within an access category. For example, to provide an acceptable level of voice quality, a VoIP telephone manufacturer could write logic into the device such that it will return a busy signal rather than begin a call if the measured load for the voice access category is high. In this case, the telephone would indicate busy rather than initiate a call that would have an unacceptable level of voice quality. With admissions control, devices on the WLAN can require a certain amount of available resources for a particular action before initiation of the action (if you can't do it well, don't do it at all), providing for a higher level of quality.

HYBRID CONTROL FUNCTION

The initial 802.11 standard called for an alternative to DCF called the point control function (PCF), which was intended to provide for a deterministic level of QoS on Wi-Fi LANs. The performance implications and difficulty of implementing PCF contributed to the fate of this architecture—it achieved essentially no vendor support and is today no more than a footnote. The hybrid control function (HCF) is a part of the 802.11e draft standard that is meant to address the requirements that drove the PCF architecture. HCF introduces a level of deterministic or parameterized QoS to the WLANs to handle the requirements of the most time-sensitive traffic, such as synchronous voice conversations. While statistical EDCF prioritization can handle voice, it is understood that more absolute, parameterized QoS will generally provide a higher level of quality.

With HCF, in much the same way that an access point controls the station's access to the medium, the access point in an HCF architecture prioritizes time-sensitive traffic over other traffic. HCF incorporates a new set of management packets called *action frames*, which contain transmit specifications (Tspecs). Tspecs take the form of Tspec requests from the client and Tspec replies from the access point.

Although RTS/CTS is not part of the 802.11e draft standard (it's a preexisting part of the 802.11 specification itself and is covered in Chapter 5), the existence of RTS/CTS functionality is essentially required for Wi-Fi QoS, as the hidden-node problem becomes even more acute when time-sensitive traffic is present.

A Tspec request contains information as to the quality requirements of an upcoming transmission flow. Again using voice as an example, a Tspec request would be sent from a client to the access point during the call setup. The Tspec would contain information such as the amount of time between voice packet transmission and the data rate at which the client would be sending these voice packets. The access point would then send a Tspec reply to the client with an unconditional acceptance of the client's request, an outright refusal (likely resulting in a busy signal on the telephone), or a conditional acceptance with modifications to the request.

VTGO from IP Blue

The proponents of every new technology look for that one application of the technology that makes it indispensable. For PCs, the indispensable application, the *killer app,* was spreadsheets—how did we ever get by without them? For the Internet, it was e-mail and web surfing. Real-time bar code scanning, as discussed in Chapter 1, was the killer app for WLANs in the retail market. The killer app for wireless in the enterprise is yet to be defined, but early indications are that there could be a winner.

VTGO from IP Blue is a softphone, an application running on a computer that uses the computer's data link to send voice traffic. Softphones have been available for years and are most commonly associated with making free telephone calls over the Internet. Although an interesting use of the technology, softphones have been more of a novelty than a mainstream tool.

VTGO may change all that. It is designed specifically to run on the HP iPaq, a PDA running Microsoft's Pocket PC 2002 operating system that is becoming increasingly popular in the enterprise. For a list price of $169, VTGO essentially turns an iPaq, which is already equipped with a microphone and speaker, into a wireless VoIP telephone. VTGO includes a number of features commonly found in desktop office phones, like hold, call transfer, speed dial, and caller ID. VTGO supports Cisco System's SCCP or "Skinny" protocol, making it compliant with Cisco's Call Manager, a VoIP PBX. For users already carrying a PDA for other purposes, adding cordless office phone functionality for little incremental cost is quite attractive. There is, however, no QoS support over the wireless link built into the application. The ratification and deployment of 802.11e QoS will only further the excitement building around voice over Wi-Fi, which may be the killer app for the enterprise.

Once the Tspec has been accepted by the client, the access point begins sending the client regular transmit opportunities at intervals and of a duration specified in the Tspec. These *polled TxOPs* are similar in concept to an unsolicited CTS. As an example, the access point could signal to a station sending voice traffic that it has contention-free access to the medium by sending a polled TxOP every 30ms to support a data rate of 8–64 Kbps—an interval and data rate consistent with the requirements and capabilities of a wireless VoIP telephone today. Devices other than VoIP telephones could well have different quality requirements that would be included in the Tspec request. So, while HCF is ideal for synchronous voice traffic, it can be used to support other time-sensitive traffic.

CHECKLIST

This chapter discussed the notion of quality of service, including how it is currently implemented and the manner in which it is likely to be implemented in the future. Some key items to remember include the following:

- ☐ The current ratified 802.11 standards contain no implemented provision for prioritizing one type of traffic over another. The point control function contained within the initial 802.11 standards has not been implemented.

- ☐ The parameters to provide for QoS over a network are packet loss, delay (or latency), and latency variance (or jitter).

- ☐ In order of time sensitivity, the types of network traffic are synchronous traffic (such as voice), isochronous traffic (such as streaming audio or video), and asynchronous traffic (such as e-mail).

- ☐ Different traffic types can be identified through a system of packet tags. The 802.1Q and 802.1D standards incorporate the idea of priority tags in packet headers and provide definitions for these tags. Tags at the IP packet level do not have any standardized definition.

- ☐ Once identified, packets can be prioritized via statistical or deterministic means. Statistic means introduce less network overhead but provide for a less absolute level of quality.

- ☐ The 802.11e draft standard and the WME initiative both incorporate enhanced DCF, a statistical means of prioritizing traffic. EDCF provides four access categories for different traffic types and the parameters to give each of these categories relative levels of priority.

- ☐ 802.11e also specifies the hybrid control function, a parameterized, more deterministic means of prioritizing traffic. HCF is better suited for voice traffic, because it provides more absolute prioritization for voice traffic, which is the most time-sensitive type of traffic.

PART V

802.11 and the Last Mile

CHAPTER 13

*Hotspots: Public Access
of Wireless LANs*

As discussed in earlier chapters, Wi-Fi LANs are rapidly proliferating into the places where people live and the places where they work. Wi-Fi is a cost-effective way to share Internet access, files, and printers in the home without the trouble of running new wires. Wi-Fi is becoming increasingly popular in the enterprise as users begin to demand at work the same wireless freedom they've experienced in the home.

But in today's society, the distinction between living places and work places no longer is clear. Business travelers often do a good part of their living and working away from home, staying in hotels. For many business people, attendance at trade shows is a regular part of their job. To get to these hotels and convention centers, some means of transportation is necessary—in North America, the most common means is the airplane, while in other parts of the world, both trains and airplanes are commonly used. Spending time in airports and train stations, before departure or between connections, is a part of life for many people.

The way that people work also is changing. As discussed previously, many people are increasingly working from home, taking advantage of broadband connections, cellular telephones, and laptop computers to bring much of the office infrastructure into their spare bedroom or on to their kitchen table. But in addition to that, people look to public spaces like coffee shops and cafes as alternative places to work—allowing them to mix work with social interaction and the small pleasure of a cup of coffee.

All of this has created a third "space" for Wi-Fi LANs, one that is *between* the places where people traditionally live and work. This so-called public access market is the newest, the smallest, and the most speculative of the three, making this arguably the most exciting of the group. Because Wi-Fi is a *local* area networking technology, these areas tend to have areas measured in the thousands of square feet rather than the wide area footprints of cellular telephone systems, which are measured in thousands of square miles. These relatively small public coverage areas have come to be known as *hotspots*.

In this chapter, we discuss the types of public places where Wi-Fi LANs are being deployed and the business models that are associated with these deployments—to the extent that business models exist. Some of the more visible companies and people driving the public access market will be profiled. We discuss the technical challenges and regulatory issues that must be addressed for a successful public space deployment. Finally, we analyze the way that public deployments of Wi-Fi LANs complement or compete with third-generation (3G) wireless technologies.

WHERE'S THE WI-FI?

For a public Wi-Fi deployment to be successful, a few conditions must be satisfied:

- A sufficient number of individuals must be passing through a public area with client devices such as laptops and PDAs that are Wi-Fi capable.

- A sufficient number of these devices must be Wi-Fi enabled. If the devices are not already capable, the user must have a sufficient need for access that they will enable the Wi-Fi device for public access.

- The individuals must spend a sufficient amount of time in these public areas, either in terms of single visits or in the aggregate, to have the time and the desire for wireless connectivity.

- They, or their organization, must place a sufficient level of value on public wireless access to justify whatever cost is associated with access.

From the preceding list, you can see that many public areas meet, to varying degrees, the conditions necessary for a public Wi-Fi deployment. Within a few minutes, a reasonably creative group could probably brainstorm scores of potential location types. With that said, the most common places today for Wi-Fi hotspots can be summed up as follows:

- **Airports**   A staggering number of laptop-toting business travelers stream through airports around the world every day. With e-mail becoming a nearly mandatory form of business communication and with expectations for responsiveness increasing, even the traveling businessperson needs to frequently download incoming messages and upload their replies. Airlines' frequent traveler lounges are natural places for Wi-Fi deployment since they not only concentrate business travelers but also encourage them to stay a relatively long period of time. Wi-Fi deployments in the more public areas of airports—in the terminal, at the gates, and in the concourses—meet all the conditions outlined previously except perhaps the idea of having sufficient time. Many business travelers without memberships in the airlines' lounges do all that is possible to minimize the amount of time spent in airports. For all the reasons just outlined, train stations are equally viable as Wi-Fi hotspots in those parts of the world where trains are a common form of business travel. The natural extension to Wi-Fi deployments in airports and train stations would be mobile hotspots in the airplanes and trains themselves. Here, the potential customers are typically in the hotspot areas for an even longer period of time and are even more captive than when in the airport or train station. Today, the regulatory issues of Wi-Fi installation in airplanes are being worked out as are the technical challenges of maintaining a broadband link to the Internet from moving airplanes and trains.

- **Hotels**   A regrettable aspect of business travel is that often the only time to catch up on work that would normally be done during the day is in the evenings or early morning. In-room dial-up access has been the traditional way of providing the connectivity often needed. With file sizes and use performance expectations increasing, dial-up speeds are rapidly becoming impractical for e-mail and Web surfing—in-room broadband is an increasing requirement. Given the small size of hotel rooms, the mobility aspect of Wi-Fi is not that great a requirement. Wi-Fi does, on the other hand, provide hoteliers with the ability to provide in room broadband without having to pull Ethernet cable throughout the facility. As Wi-Fi in laptops grows to be as common as

Ethernet in laptops, wirelessly providing in room broadband becomes increasingly viable.

- **Convention centers**   Anyone who has sat through a "breakout session" at a trade show will appreciate the attractiveness of a diversion like reading e-mail or surfing the Web. Convention center operators, show coordinators, and even some exhibitors appreciate this fact, making it increasingly common in some industries for Wi-Fi access to be available on and around a trade show floor.

- **Coffee shops and cafes**   These popular locations for Wi-Fi hotspots are meant to appeal to people who already spend a considerable amount of time over a high-priced latte. These might be younger people including students, writers, artists and others without more traditional workplaces who treat cafes as a workspace as well as business people stopping in for lunch or dinner. Wi-Fi hotspots are understood to be symbiotic to the core business: coffee and the like attracts users and wireless access keeps them there longer, all the while drinking coffee.

- **Open spaces**   Public areas like city parks, gardens, and even traffic circles are areas where urban workers and dwellers often go to enjoy the outdoors. In the same way that university students take advantage of campus-wide Wi-Fi deployments by wirelessly surfing the Internet from the college green, urbanites would be happy to have outdoor wireless access. Public institutions like city governments and larger urban universities are, for the most part, in the early stages of feasibility analyses for this type of service.

BUSINESS MODELS FOR HOTSPOTS

As a fairly recent phenomenon, no one can make any conclusions as to what business model or models will be optimal for Wi-Fi hotspots in the near and the longer term. Currently, a fair bit of experimentation is taking place, with various business models being tried out.

For any organization considering a Wi-Fi deployment, the first business question that should be answered is whether the hotspot is intended to be a direct revenue generator, with a fee charged for use, or an amenity, with no per-use charge but with some indirect benefit accruing to the organization.

There are two direct revenue models, subscription and pay as you go, that are being applied today to Wi-Fi hotspots. A subscription service typically provides some number of minutes (or an unlimited number of minutes) for a monthly subscription fee. This model closely follows the cellular telephone model and provides the hotspot owner with a smoother revenue stream. A per-use revenue model is more apt to attract the occasional user, as they can connect on impulse without any sort of long-term commitment, typically paying with a credit card. These models are in no way mutually exclusive and are often offered as complementary options. As an example, one large provider of Wi-Fi hotspots offers a monthly unlimited subscription for $30 but also offers a pay-as-you-go plan of $2.99 for the first 15 minutes with 25 cents for every minute thereafter. When compared to the per-use rates, the monthly subscription looks like a bargain—which is just the point.

When Wi-Fi is deployed as a public service, the model is similar to that of any other municipal service like streetlights or garbage collection—there is no direct cost to the user, only their indirect contribution to the project through taxes.

SETTLEMENTS AND BILLING

One of the greatest technical challenges facing the broad deployment of Wi-Fi hotspots has nothing to do with radio frequencies. Indeed, installing an access point in a cafe is no more challenging than installing one in a home. Rather, the challenge is to put in place an overall accounting system that allows for the business models discussed previously.

Many systems rely upon an Internet gateway, an application or device between the access point and the Internet itself, that limits traffic to one or a small number of web sites until a credit card number or subscription password is entered. While this means of authentication is viable, other potential Wi-Fi service providers are suggesting that a better approach is GSM SIM, a means of authentication using a physical smart chip embedded in the client device. GSM SIM is one of the more popular means of identifying and authenticating mobile telephones to the cellular network—it's no surprise that the principal proponents of GSM SIM authentication are cellular equipment vendors and mobile service providers. Already in Europe systems are in place that allow Wi-Fi billing to be integrated with mobile telephone billing on a single monthly invoice.

Those who purchase Wi-Fi access subscriptions would naturally want to be able to use their subscription in as many places as possible to maximize the value of their monthly investment. With cellular telephones, this is accomplished through a system of roaming and settlements. While a user might be a customer of Provider A, they may access the network through a cellular tower owned by Provider B. Through a series of agreements and systems, the two providers "settle" their accounts, billing and paying each other for access provided to customers other than their own.

Today, settlement agreements and systems exist only in the earliest stages for Wi-Fi hotspots but are generally understood to be a prerequisite to mainstream demand—just as they were for cellular telephones. Behind the push to adopt GSM SIM authentication is the expectation that a Wi-Fi system using this cellular telephone system could more easily leverage existing backend settlement and billing systems, making possible the "holy grail" of user convenience: a single integrated bill that contains both cellular telephone and Wi-Fi access charges.

Data Must Be Free!

There is another type of Wi-Fi hotspot model that has little to do with business. That is, a small but very visible group of individuals believes that wireless access is something that should be given or shared rather than sold. Rather than trying to limit access to their residential or workplace WLAN through security and authentication, followers of this model leave their connection wide open, often broadcasting their SSID, essentially advertising their availability to anyone within range.

Organizations on a local and even an international basis are popping up to try to organize this anarchistic phenomenon. Freenetworks.org (www.freenetworks.org) is an umbrella organization dedicated to furthering this "exercise in telecommunications freedom." It has more than a dozen local member organizations in places like London, Prague, San Francisco, Toronto, Washington D.C., and even Pittsburgh. In New York City, member organization NYCWireless (www.nycwireless.net) has a web site that displays an area map with the locations and SSIDs of more than 170 open access points in and around Manhattan. Seattle Wireless (www.seattlewireless.net) is another member organization, providing the location of scores of open access points throughout the Puget Sound area.

Not all people are supportive of the idea of free access. Broadband service providers, such as DSL and cable providers, typically limit the degree to which a connection can be shared between multiple clients. Their provisioning models for residential areas are based upon a relatively small number of devices per connection and a correspondingly modest amount of traffic. Of course, sharing existing connections tends to reduce the demand for new connections, which impacts the service provider's revenue. While the service providers have not to date taken any concerted action against community wireless groups or their members, it is well within their capabilities. With common network management software, it's easy to search for telltale inordinately high usage on a single connection. Most service providers are taking a "wait and see" approach, holding off on a potentially unpopular crackdown until free network growth makes it necessary.

The darker side of free wireless access is *war driving*. A derivative of the mostly archaic term *war dialing* where hackers use random dialing sequences to break into remote computers over the telephone system, war driving is the practice of driving around areas looking for open access points. These access points can be purposely left open for sharing or (more typically) inadvertently left open due to insufficient or nonexistent security measures. War drivers often have car-mounted high-gain antennas to maximize the range and effectiveness of their mobile hacking tool. Although the goal of these war drivers is not always to cause damage to the network or steal data from it, their association to the access point is typically uninvited—at best it's impolite and at worst it's illegal. A more recent outgrowth of war driving is *war chalking*. When an open access point is discovered, the war driver/chalker will mark the location in chalk, often displaying the open access point's SSID. War chalking takes the inconvenience of war driving out of do-it-yourself free wireless access.

While the fringe phenomena of free networks and war driving come from almost diametrically different points of view, they are two sides of the same coin. Free networks come from uncommonly altruistic types taking broadband from the presumably rich cable and telephone monopolies and giving it to the deserving common people. War driving and chalking typically are simple mischief and thrill seeking from technophiles with too much time on their hands. But both indicate the desire and nascent demand for inexpensive (well, okay, free) wireless broadband access across a wide metropolitan area. Although it's likely that both of these movements will diminish over time (as service providers begin to enforce their service agreements and wireless security thwarts the casual war-driving hacker), their general thrust may well continue. In a future with broadly deployed and inexpensive broadband wireless access, the free networks and war driving phenomena may well be looked at as unlikely prototypes.

REGULATORY ISSUES

Public access regulations are to a degree set up with cellular telephone systems in mind. That is, they're based upon licensed portions of the frequency spectrum being sold to providers who in turn offer service to their customers for a fee. Swaths of the spectrum have been auctioned off by governments for billions of dollars. As the owners of these bands, the service providers have proprietary rights to these bands.

To manage the public airwaves and perhaps to protect a lucrative source of revenue, some governments have placed outright prohibitions on the whole idea of providing for a fee access to a device that operates in an unlicensed portion (in other words, unpaid for) portion of the frequency spectrum. In at least one example, however, the United Kingdom has removed these prohibitions, paving the way for a nascent Wi-Fi hotspot market in that country.

Some have speculated that Wi-Fi hotspots pose a fundamental threat to the viability of 3G mobile technologies. While 3G promises data rates as high as 1.5Mbps, which is many times greater than most current cellular performance, current Wi-Fi technology provides even greater performance than that, with dramatic increases through 802.11a and 802.11g on the way. Indeed, no less an industry visionary than Nicholas Negroponte, founder of MIT's Media Lab, refers to 3G as a "small, almost irrelevant change" with Wi-Fi representing a third epoch, following digitization, the first epoch, and packet switching, the second epoch. Negroponte believes that in the not-too-distant future, entire regions, if not continents, will be seamlessly covered by a patchwork of Wi-Fi hotspots, providing the nearly ubiquitous broadband wireless coverage that was only recently assumed to have been the birthright of 3G cellular. He believes that Wi-Fi will result in a fundamental restructuring in the way that the frequency spectrum is parceled out by governments, with an increased emphasis on, and greater provision for, unlicensed, free operation.

Others take the more moderate view that Wi-Fi hotspots actually complement 3G services. Hotspots are an incremental way to introduce users to high speed wireless access in the public areas where it's needed the most. With seamless roaming between Wi-Fi and 3G (a capability currently in development), the 3G network becomes a more wide area extension to the Wi-Fi hotspot. The thinking is that once users experience broadband wireless services in say an airport, they'll eventually expect this same level of performance in more remote places that can only be covered by 3G networks.

Keep in mind that all of those operating in unlicensed bands have equal access to the band. There are no access rights based on earlier occupancy in the band. This has already raised issues for Wi-Fi service providers who operate in the 2.4GHz unlicensed band that provides for just three channels. With client devices being able to search for multiple access points, their client utility may well display a number of available devices, some of which provide access for free, some for a fee. While service providers have gamely suggested that users will choose fee-based access over free access due to security considerations and the availability of customer service, the validity of this assertion has (not surprisingly) yet to be proved. Making a business out of providing service in an unlicensed band has far fewer economic barriers to entry than in a licensed band—perhaps the greatest advantage of Wi-Fi hotspots and its greatest potential threat.

EARLY WI-FI SERVICE PROVIDERS

As 2002 draws to a close, the telecommunications industry is in the midst of what can only be described as a depression, and the resounding burst of the Internet bubble is a painful echo. Wireless public access is one of the few bright, exciting opportunities available, drawing an interesting assortment of companies and characters.

No one draws more attention than Sky Dayton, a self-described "über-aggregator" and founder of the Wi-Fi service provider Boingo (www.boingo.com). His business plan is closely modeled on Earthlink, his earlier startup, an Internet service provider that integrated a patchwork of small ISPs into a cohesive national entity. With Boingo, the general user proposition is that they can use their Boingo subscription for wireless access from hundreds of otherwise independent providers. For providers, Boingo is something of a franchise opportunity, with Boingo providing the national brand recognition and billing in exchange for a percentage of the usage fees.

T-Mobile, a division of German telephone provider Deutsche Telecom, and the ubiquitous coffee shop Starbucks have combined to deploy Wi-Fi hotspots in the thousands of Starbucks locations. T-Mobile indirectly acquired much of this Starbucks infrastructure from MobileStar, an early pioneer in Wi-Fi hotspots that, like many pioneering companies, went bankrupt after having overbuilt the infrastructure well ahead of user demand and revenue. With their global reach, companies like T-Mobile can deploy Wi-Fi hotspots on a literally worldwide basis further increasing the value of a subscription to their service.

In Asia, Yahoo Japan has teamed with McDonalds to deploy Wi-Fi in thousands of these locations. In Korea, Korea Telecom is in the early phases of a similarly ambitious deployment. There is widespread speculation that large technology and telecommunications companies are interested in entering the market. Project Rainbow, an initiative rumored to include Intel, IBM, AT&T Wireless, Verizon Communications, and Cingular Wireless, has gained a lot of media attention but little confirmation from its presumed backers. However, what is clear is that there is a growing interest among traditional companies in Wi-Fi, a technology, an opportunity, and maybe even an epoch.

CHECKLIST

This chapter discussed the places where Wi-Fi hotspots are being deployed and the associated business models. The systems required to support these models as well as regulatory issues were discussed. Finally, a few of the current Wi-Fi providers were briefly profiled. Some key points to keep in mind include the following:

- [ ] A successful hotspot requires a sufficient number of Wi-Fi–enabled users with the time and the means to take advantage of the service.

- [ ] Wi-Fi public access locations, commonly referred to as hotspots, are becoming more and more common in places like airports, train stations, hotels, convention centers, coffee shops, and public parks.

- [ ] Billing can be done on a pay-per-use basis and a subscription basis. The two models are more complementary than competing.

- [ ] Wi-Fi hotspots can be free, offered by altruistic individuals as a means of sharing their connection or by public agencies like city governments. Service providers may well crack down on these free networks in cases where they violate their service agreements.

- [ ] War drivers and war chalkers create their own free networks by hacking into unsecure Wi-Fi LANs.

- [ ] Current regulations don't match up well with the Wi-Fi hotspot phenomenon. Indeed, some believe that the notion of providing service in unlicensed bands has the potential to fundamentally disrupt the current regulatory paradigm.

- [ ] A number of high-visibility companies are currently deploying ambitious networks of Wi-Fi hotspots. Other companies are rumored to be interested.

CHAPTER 14

802.11 In the Service Provider Market

In this final chapter, we look at the wireless technology that arguably has won the minds, hearts, and purchase orders of broadband providers not only in the United States, but worldwide. The fact that 802.11 is more broadly deployed than multichannel multipoint distribution service (MMDS) in the United States is an amazing development given the investment of several billion dollars and the efforts of many very bright, motivated, and capable individuals to help make MMDS as common as the copper broadband medium. This phenomenon extends well past the shores of the United States to broadband rich countries like Korea, Germany and Singapore. This chapter reviews an excellent and highly adopted use for the 802.11 bridge—connecting small and medium enterprises with fiber points of presence. Most if not all of this chapter focuses on 802.11 bridging as opposed to the use of this standard in an access point.

One of the important things to note is that not all 802.11 is U-NII, and vice versa. One would do well to remember that 802.11 is fundamentally a radio protocol, born of the IEEE while U-NII is a carrier frequency protocol born of the Federal Communications Commission of the United States. While these two standards very commonly cross over, i.e., 802.11 radios now include the FCC U-NII specification, 802.11 radios, at this writing, carry the 2.4GHz carrier frequency much more commonly.

U-NII, 802.11A AND THE LAST MILE

During the Internet bubble of 1999 through 2001, service providers scrambled to provide final mile access to bandwidth and speed-hungry customers. At that time, approximately two thirds of all the potential DSL customers were out of the reach of DSL-based service, and little has changed in that regard in the two or so years following the burst of that bubble. Further, the DSL meltdown in areas within reach of the telco plants has generated considerable amounts of bad publicity regarding the miscues by the telcos in their attempt to deploy DSL (upon which was piled the executive misadventures of WorldCom). Among the customers' concerns are the long wait for installation, the lack of installation quality, and an apparent lack of communication and consistency within the telcos who install broadband to residential sites, like that of this author.

In 2000, the author waited for nearly six months for a DSL line to be installed, only to have the installation technicians arrive on the day he was relocating out of state. However, the telcos should be congratulated for their tenacity once they get an idea going because once they began attempting to install DSL in my vacant residence, it took no fewer than three phone calls to get them to discontinue installation. Not much has gotten better. At the time of this writing, the phone company made several miscues when installing my current DSL line, after which I received not one but two separate notices by mail that my DSL line was about to be installed within the following week, even though it was up and running two weeks prior to the mailing of the notices. This most recent development occurred the very day I began to write this chapter. Whereas in previous eras, some adults would begin a conversation with perfect strangers with, "You know, my spouse is driving me crazy…" it's now more socially acceptable, and probably a more common occurrence to begin the same lament with, "You know, my service provider is driving me crazy... ."

Rant ends. And now, to the present. Given that over 80% of all the MMDS spectrum in the United States is owned by Sprint and MCI WorldCom, and that LMDS and other millimeter wave equipment is too expensive and suffers from poor range capabilities (not to mention the enormous financial burden carried by license holders simply for the licenses themselves which must be purchased before any equipment or other assets), unlicensed bands have hands down won the undeclared competition between licensed and unlicensed broadband wireless technologies.

The U-NII band has an additional feature that is highly attractive to service providers: it does not require the purchase of a broadcast license. These licenses typically cost millions or even tens of millions of dollars. Further, licensed broadband fixed wireless (BBFW) links must reside within tightly defined geographical areas called Basic Trading Areas (BTAs). Figure 14-1 highlights some of the expenditures made on spectrum licenses.

Although companies like Sprint had, at one time, expansive plans to deploy licensed links over enormous regions of the United States, few believe it will happen within the next decade or more. Even if they had the capital, they will eventually approach maximum market penetration in their BTAs. At that point, two of their key options will be to either purchase additional spectrum or add BTAs in which they

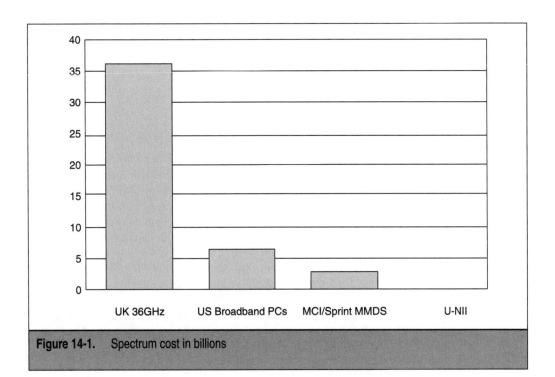

Figure 14-1.   Spectrum cost in billions

do not have licenses by using unlicensed spectrum. In the latter case, U-NII would appear a compelling choice because it does not require additional cost for the spectrum, and importantly, it can be deployed in any strategic BTA selected by the company, thereby making it possible to have as many contiguous BTAs as possible.

Having BTAs that are contiguous offers significant advantages in terms of backhauling because the links can be connected to fiber nodes that reside along a common fiber route. Further, having contiguous BTAs reduces the manpower required to physically maintain a network. Finally, this strategy enables companies with licensed spectrum to capture the majority of a common metropolitan area within which resides numerous BTAs.

There is no penalty for using the U-NII band as opposed to a licensed frequency in terms of how it can be used by the service provider. U-NII band service providers utilize policy-related features identical in every manner to those that can be offered on a licensed link. This includes QoS, voice, throttled bandwidth, and identical element and network management resources.

Further, as the U-NII band is well below 10GHz, it is not subject to restrictions based on weather or air pollution. It also has fewer multi-path characteristics than the MMDS frequencies because it operates at a lower power. U-NII can also operate at the same reliability and availability as licensed frequencies; in summary, U-NII has all the benefits of a licensed link without the overhead cost of a license.

Finally on this note, the purchase of an MMDS or other license can be delayed through negotiations, litigation, and complications such as purchasing the license from an entity in bankruptcy. State-of-the-art BBFW systems have indoor gear which is independent of the carrier frequency. This means that the user can install U-NII until the licensed spectrum is made available for purchase. When the licensed spectrum becomes available, the service provider can either redeploy the U-NII equipment to another site, or leave it in place while bringing the licensed equipment online. However, it's not likely, under most circumstances, that once a service provider installs a link, regardless of the frequency, it will be replaced by another radio technology or frequency unless there is a very compelling reason such as an enormous amount of interference that is impinging on very high-value traffic such as business continuity and storage links.

There are four major unlicensed bands in the United States. The ISM bands cover the spectrum between 2.4GHz and 2.485GHz and were covered in a previous chapter . The U-NII spectrum covers three separate allocations which are indicated in Figure 14-2.

Unlicensed band users in the United States primarily have Apple Computer and the Wireless Information Networks Forum (WINForum) to thank for the existence of U-NII. WINForum requested 250MHz of spectrum at 5.10- to 5.35GHz in May 1995. At approximately the same time, Apple Computer requested the allocation of 300MHz in the 5.10- to 5.35GHz and 5.725- to 5.875GHz ranges to establish a new unlicensed radio service to promote full deployment of the U-NII.

The 5.725 to 5.825 band was already in use by amateur HAM radio users, but there hasn't been much publicity about the decision, and with rare exception, U-NII service

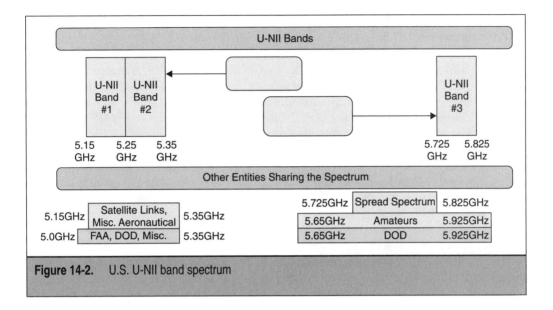

Figure 14-2.   U.S. U-NII band spectrum

providers and HAM radio operators seem to co-exist peacefully and without interfering with one another. Part of this may be due to the fact that HAM radio operators tend to use their radios in the evenings and on weekends, while most U-NII users at present are in the MxU market space and therefore use the frequency primarily during normal business hours. It should be noted of course that most of those relatively new to HAM radio have purchased their equipment instead of building the radios, consequently the prospective issue of co-channel interference between HAM operators and U-NII operators continues to decrease.

This effort to lobby the FCC in the U.S. to make the two lower U-NII frequencies available took approximately two years of effort and was formally introduced to the public in January of 1997. The upper U-NII band (5.725- to 5.825GHz) was already authorized by the FCC in the U.S. under its Part 15 Rules.

One of the interesting aspects of the FCC allocation was that it did not specify a channeling plan (how the radios break the entire spectrum into subsections), spectrum modulation efficiency requirements or even spectrum etiquette. Instead, the FCC focused only on limiting the power output and power spectral density (a definition of how many watts of power per hertz of spectrum can be used) or, in other words, how much energy per single burst of frequency can be used). Rather, the FCC left this up to the industry to resolve through technological- and community-based diplomatic means.

The initiative by Apple was originally called Unlicensed Personal Communications Services (Data-PCS), and was intended not only to provide classroom wireless connectivity to the Internet but also to have what Apple called *community networks*. It is an essential part of what was then called the *National Information Infrastructure*, which is to be a subset of what was then called the *Global Information Infrastructure (GII)*.

One portion of the band (5.150GHz to 5.350GHz) was already earmarked in Europe for a proposed standard called *HyperLAN*. The U-NII band allocation incorporates the European standard and will allow its use in the U.S. It also means that U.S. designers and manufacturers can offer competitive products for the European market. The upper U-NII band is already in use in the U.S., Canada and Australia.

Table 14-1 outlines the summary characteristics of the U-NII band.

U-NII 1, or sometimes referred to as the *low U-NII band*, was designated primarily for indoor use while U-NII 2 was designated for campus use (building to building within a campus). U-NII 3 is sometimes referred to as the *upper U-NII band* and was designed for community networks. Through development and substantial processing gain in addition to spreading technique schemes such as OFDM, it now has the ability to cover distances up to or exceeding 20 miles in a line-of-site environment or 3 to 5 miles in a non-line-of-site environment, depending on the nature of the obstructions.

The reason the FCC allocated the U-NII bands was to promote the following concepts:

- Sharing of spectrum
- Mobility of wireless applications
- Efficient use of spectrum through intermittent use
- Innovation and research for new fixed wireless devices and applications

Promote Sharing of Spectrum

In virtually all frequency bands in use today, one of the most carefully preserved management elements is that the total amount of spectrum is relatively limited. By offering a small portion of the spectrum that many people can use in relatively common geographies, the government preserves other spectrum blocks.

Radio spectrum is highly valuable commodity to a government and billions of dollars are generated for the government from the sale of spectrum to commercial

Characteristic	Band 1	Band 2	Band 3
Frequency (GHz)	5.125–5.25	5.25–5.35	5.725–5.825
Radiated power	50mW	250mW	1W
With 6dB antenna gain	200mW	1W	4W
Applications	Indoor	Campus and small neighborhood as well as indoor WLANs	20 miles point-to-point, ~6 miles point-to-multipoint

Table 14-1. U-NII Bands Summary Specifications for the U.S.

interests. Providing even a limited amount of spectrum to the commercial industry that does not generate revenue for the government has the effect of placing a prospective premium on the balance of the spectrum simply because there is less total spectrum available.

The way the FCC in the U.S. authorized the use of the U-NII band and intentionally provided it with as few guidelines as possible also reduces the governmental costs and resources required for monitoring users, and hearing and resolving complaints. It also reduces cost of government participation in that it is less likely to have to pass future laws which feature greater amounts of specificity and penalties for use outside the intended boundaries. The continual addition of rules requires somewhat of a proportional increase in applying penalties, both of which increase the cost to the government of maintaining this asset.

Promote Mobility of Wireless Applications

Broadband mobility, as mentioned earlier, is a feature that enables users to move their laptops or even office phones from location to location. The U-NII band is ideally suited for both broadband mobility and pervasive computing because U-NII has relatively good propagation characteristics—it has a decent range for a given power and can penetrate some walls close to the transmitter, yet does not generate as much multipath as transmissions at lower frequencies.

Promote Efficient Use of Spectrum Through Intermittent Use

One of the intents of the government was to enable the use of the spectrum through intermittent use. This can be overcome by using spreading or other modulation techniques and it forces the equipment providers to advance research and product development that enables the users to fill the airspace with transmissions for the least possible amount of time.

Promote Innovation and Research for New Fixed Wireless Devices and Applications

When this spectrum became available, industry gambled on it being valuable to the service provider and other industries. This sets off a wave of development and innovation which is not only applied to this spectrum but often crosses over to products in other frequencies and products which can be associated with U-NII radios such as PCMCIA cards, wireless bridges and antennas.

The drawbacks of U-NII—or any unlicensed spectrum—have been discussed at great length publicly and in the halls of virtually every technology company intent on providing this technology to the market place. There are two prospective drawbacks to the use of the unlicensed spectrum: the potential for co-channel interference, and coexistence with other U-NII networks.

Potential for Interference and Coexistence with Other U-NII Networks

State-of-the-art 802.11 systems have an array of "tools" that can be implemented as required to resolve for co-channel resolution. These methods are:

1. The transmission and reception frequencies can be adjusted at the command line interface to a channel that is non-interfering; this is specifically a challenge in hidden node architecture, or possibly with two separate 802.11 sources to avoid interference from another U-NII broadcast source.

2. The packets include a header address that enables the system to discriminate native transmissions from non-native transmissions. This process is accomplished at the digital signal processor portion of the wireless line card.

3. Obstructions (buildings and foliage) can provide substantial protection from competing U-NII transmissions. Transmission power drops by the square of the distance in a line-of-sight link and drops even faster when obstructions are present (by the fourth or fifth power of distance). Therefore even if non-native but distant transmitters happen to be in the beam path of the native receiving antenna, obstructions will reduce their signal to insignificant levels in a great many cases. One of the many advantages, though not well known is that OFDM enables RF network users to deploy antennas at relatively low elevations thereby using obstructions to even greater advantage. The "magic" in this is relatively straightforward and reviewed in detail earlier in this work; one of the key benefits of using an OFDM spreading technique is its exceptionally high bit-recovery capability.

4. The statistical probability is actually quite slight that two competing U-NII links will operate within a few hundred feet of each other within a metropolitan area. To paraphrase the comedian Steven Wright, "It's a small world, but I wouldn't want to have to paint it."

As outlined in Table 14-1, some companies like Cisco Systems use all three of the U-NII bands, the upper band strictly for bridging, the middle band for both indoor and outdoor use, and the lower band, or U-NII 1 band, for indoor use only.

U-NII-based BBFW links perform as well or better than those in the MMDS spectrum and those in the "B" LMDS licensed spectrum (which has 300MHz of spectrum). U-NII customers can receive speeds ranging from 128Kbps up to 45Mbps depending on equipment type. According to a report by The Trategic Group entitled "U.S. Fixed Wireless: Unlicensed Spectrum," dated March 8, 2001, "Despite billions of dollars poured into U.S. broadband wireless licenses, unlicensed wireless technologies maintain a clear lead in terms of deployments to date."

This comes as no great surprise to those close to the industry especially when one considers that at least in the United States, the majority of the optimal frequency for a nationwide deployment is owned by only two companies at this writing, Sprint and MCI WorldCom. The combination of these two entities owns more than 80 percent of the total amount of MMDS license in the U.S.

Both of these companies have been bogged down with numerous deployment issues including the selection of a radio that meets all of their requirements, sufficient deployment resources and sagging economic market conditions which place a strain on deployment budgets and customer acceptance rates. At the same time, both Sprint and MCIWorldCom face considerable competition from a very wide array of smaller competitors which are more nimble and that do not have to amortize the enormous overhead associated with purchasing fixed wireless licenses.

The total amount spent by both of these companies is in excess of $2 billion (refer to Figure 14-1). Most of the licenses owned by these companies were acquired through the acquisition of a large number of smaller licenses; in other words, both companies adopted the strategy of purchasing the rights to MMDS in as many BTAs as they could possibly muster. The competitors to Sprint and MCIWorldCom vary in size from a very wide array of smaller start-ups to multi-billion-dollar companies such as AT&T and SBC.

Although the amount of spectrum available in unlicensed channels is less than their licensed alternatives, depending on the equipment purchased and the area covered, U-NII links can outperform licensed links. Figure 14-3 provides a snapshot of the amount of spectrum available in the U-NII band compared to other common allocations.

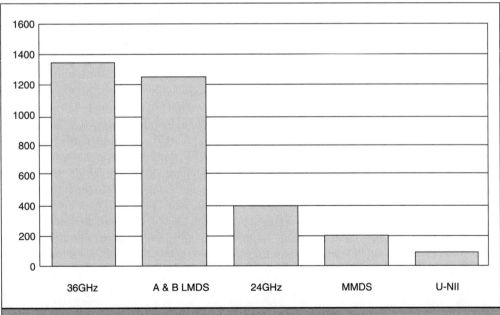

Figure 14-3.   Comparable spectrum allocations in the U.S. in GHz

There is a great amount of mythology about how unlicensed BBFW links compare to those that have licenses. Table 14-2 provides a snapshot comparison of the two approaches.

100 Percent Availability

It is virtually impossible to guarantee 100 percent availability over an extended period of approximately 12 months or longer because there are so many elements in the radiating environment that can easily compromise a link. If one thinks out of the box for a moment, these elements would include items as simple as a lightning strike; this would certainly damage or destroy outdoor equipment and perhaps some indoor equipment at the same time, such as cabling and lightning arrestors.

There can also be failures in the indoor equipment such as with the modem cards that are used in some systems, and even outages on networks with single points of failure such as those that do not have auxiliary power supplies to provide uninterrupted power in the event of a power outage to the network.

Events other than network failure can have a significant impact on the overall availability of the network. While most multi-path challenges can be accommodated through careful link planning (incorporating sufficient performance margin into the link plan to compensate for random drops in link performance that usually occur without notice) and monitoring, there can also be such catastrophic link events as a building being placed directly in the path between the two antennas. This type of event could block the signal entirely, dramatically changing the multipath properties. This would require either a recalibration of the equipment or relocation of the outdoor equipment, specifically the antennas, and easily resulting in a relocation of the radios and other equipment if the leads between the antennas and radios resulted in too much line loss. 802.11 outdoor links are also subject to acts of nature such as fire, earthquakes,

Issue	Licensed	Unlicensed
100 percent availability	No	No
High pre-equipment investment	Yes	No
Guarantee from interference	No	No
Guarantee from link degradation	No	No
Restricted footprint	Yes	No
All Layer 3 options	Yes	Yes
Recourse for co-channel interference	Primarily legal/diplomatic	Technological—nine different ways to mitigate
In-band market competition	Limited	Yes

Table 14-2. Snapshot Comparison of Licensed vs. Unlicensed BBFW

tornadoes and so forth. Neither licensed nor unlicensed links are immune to the effects of one or all of these phenomenons.

The catastrophic effects of these items listed can be mitigated through the use of strategies such as *path diversity*, which is the concept of having two independent paths between two sites. This requires independent sets of 802.11 gear as the links are physically separated from each other and usually take very different physical paths between two end points. Load balancing can be accomplished at either the bridges or the Ethernet switches, or with edge routers. Load balancing ensures the highest level of performance for hot standby, and also increases radio performance and range due to the reduced speed requirement common to load balancing.

You also can utilize increased antenna height, extra gain (sensitivity) and additional link margin (additional link performance margin) but you must take care not to overcompensate for events that have a statistically low probability of occurrence. Excessive insurance measures lead to unnecessarily lower levels of performance. There are also element redundancies such as back-up power supplies and redundant Ethernet switch cards that can be built into the LAN, but ultimately there is no guarantee that a link will never go offline or incur substantial bandwidth or speed degradation—regardless of whether a link uses licensed frequencies or 802.11.

High Pre-Equipment Investment

One of the advantages to having an unlicensed system is that there are no up-front costs or project delays associated with purchasing a license, although up-front costs for evaluating the environment to ensure that the spectrum is clear and available for use should be anticipated in virtually all link deployments. MMDS, LMDS and other licenses are very expensive can easily run into the millions or tens of millions of dollars. However, "quick licenses" can be purchased for the 6GHz and 23GHz frequencies, as well as other frequencies in only a few weeks for modest prices in the $5,000 range.

Using an 802.11 over even a low cost licensed link means that fiscal resources can be used directly and immediately on equipment, deployment and network equipment purposes as well as making the necessary investments in personnel and overhead costs such as office sites.

Guarantee From Interference

A widely held myth is that licensed radio frequency links are immune to interference. What they are intended to be immune from is co-channel interference from competitors who are broadcasting in the same frequencies.

RF links, both licensed and unlicensed, can be interfered with by the effects of multi-path and from high-emission sources which may be either adjacent to the site or in the site path near one of the antennas. Adjacent channel interference can also be a problem for both types of links where a broadcast does not occur directly over the licensed or unlicensed frequencies, but rather adjacent to those frequencies.

Guarantee from Link Degradation

As stated previously, the probability of link degradation increases over time as the radiating environment through which the information is transmitted changes. Links can also require re-engineering if the traffic migrates from latency-tolerant traffic such as e-mail to latency-intolerant traffic such as voice and video. Adding to the potential of link degradation are the effects of water seeping into connectors, damage to cables from activities not associated with the operation of a outdoor 802.11 network such as construction to the buildings where the antennas and other radio equipment is mounted, and resurfacing of roofs. The multi-path environment may also be changed by resurfacing roof tops, replacing windows with a different reflective quality, or other radiating environmental changes such as the addition of large roof mounted air conditioning units which can readily cause link degradation.

The summary of this issue is that a careful establishment of link baseline performance and the ongoing monitoring and adjustments thereof will likely eliminate or at least reduce the issues of link degradation. This does not mean that all links in every location suffer degradation as a matter of course; rather, a policy of informed observation relative to the probability of a link degrading over time, specifically in a metropolitan environment, is high enough that it warrants the constant monitoring of link margins and performance as well as the accumulation of an archived performance record.

Restricted Footprint

One of the most significant differences between a licensed radio link and 802.11 link is that the licensed link must comply with strict parameters set forth by federal agencies with regard to where it can broadcast. However, in the interest of a balanced presentation, it should be stated that federal regulators place tight restrictions on the output power, and interference propensity of 802.11 systems, a subject that has been treated in detail in this work.

Unlicensed bands such as U-NII and 2.4GHz in the United States generally have no such restrictions in terms of where they deploy for broadcast, although they must not do so in areas or in a manner that causes interference to other users of the unlicensed band, some of whom are users of amateur radios. The essence of the unlicensed bands is that they are unregulated in terms, but what that truly means is that they have fewer compliance issues with regard to where, how and what they broadcast.

Both types of equipment require acceptance testing by laboratories that are licensed by federal agencies to ensure compliance with the radiating output, both intentional and unintentional. As all electronic devices radiate energy, this energy is measured both in terms of frequency and strength to ensure that it does not interfere with other forms of electronic equipment.

Recourse for Co-Channel Interference

In a licensed link, the primary recourse for broadcasts that occur in the same frequency and in the same geographical area may possibly be resolved by diplomacy with any luck, but most likely will be resolved by litigation as one or both of the parties will have paid substantial sums or at least made substantial commitments for the right to broadcast in a reserved frequency. This adversarial approach is expensive and time consuming with one party ending up the loser while only attorneys gain financially through the dispute.

With 802.11 links however, the resolution lies within the technology of the units themselves, in the case of state-of-the-art systems, and as the frequencies are essentially unregulated, the opposing parties are most likely to resolve the matter diplomatically. This diplomatic resolution would be based on a common agreement to share the spectrum in such a manner that they would not interfere with each other. Figure 14-4 illustrates how the U-NII band might be broken up to accommodate two parties.

Two parties can readily agree on how to allocate frequency in a common geographic area and they can also agree to divide a larger common geography among them.

In-Band Market Competition

By definition, a licensed band operator has no competition within one or more BTAs—*in the same frequencies*. While they are free from competition in the same BTA for a given frequency such as MMDS, they are not free from competition from the U-NII- and ISM-based service providers, who, with today's equipment, can provide the same services at the same speeds to the same customers. Nor is the licensed band holder released from the issue of incumbent transmitters in the licensed band. This is a very real issue in the MMDS band where ITFS one-way video exists in many communities. As a quick note, neither ISM nor U-NII is typically competitive with LMDS, as LMDS has much more spectrum with their "A" license. LMDS "B" license spectrum which is much more on the order of MMDS and U-NII, may find competition within their BTAs from service providers capable of offering services in the unlicensed bands.

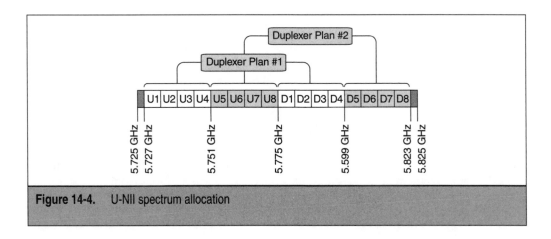

Figure 14-4.   U-NII spectrum allocation

The 802.11b ISM band, while commonly used for data by ISPs at this writing, does not carry voice traffic currently, though it is gaining favor with ISPs and other users of that frequency and has a steadily rising number of competitors in that frequency. The 802.11 band, however should be considered quite competitive with U-NII, MMDS and the LMDS "B" block of spectrum.

802.11 As Final Mile for Fiber Lateral Bypass

One of the architectures being touted by some of the major equipment providers is connection of fiber nodes to MxUs. While fiber trunks are virtually ubiquitous in every major metropolitan area, trenching a fiber connection between a trunk and an MxU site even over short distances requires no less than 90 days and can take as long as six months or more at cost that can exceed $1 million per mile.

Connecting 802.11 bridges to a fiber node, which then communicates to either a point-to-point device at an MxU site or to a small array of point-to-multipoint 802.11 bridges, is a compelling architecture. It solves a number of problems rather elegantly:

- The fiber provider can't access large buildings fast enough
- The BBFW service provider often requires a large backhaul pipe
- The tenants in the large building wish to bypass the local telco exchange

The Fiber Provider Can't Access Large Buildings Fast Enough

One of the largest problems for fiber providers is increasing the extent of their market penetration. Fiber is virtually always laid in areas where there is existing competition from DSL and it has significant advantages in both cost and speed over DSL. Trenching is expensive and time consuming and it is reasonably straightforward to connect a building with an 802.11 bridge to a fiber node via a device like Cisco's 15454 chassis. Cisco in fact offers an 802.11 bridge as a bundled option with its 15454 router. This architecture provides immediate access to large buildings within a two to five mile radius, assuming there are no line-of-sight issues. For point-to-point architectures, assuming the service provider has access to suitable elevation, buildings can be accessed at distances of 20 miles or more on a point-to-point basis with speeds at 11Mbps with 802.11 radios, and at higher rates for 802.11g and 11a radios, though at this writing there is little to confirm that the 11a radios will have ranges for a given speed common to the 11b and 11g radios.

The BBFW Service Provider Often Requires a Large Backhaul Pipe

One of the largest challenges for service providers is aggregating backhaul for either point-to-point or point-to-multipoint architectures. Having access to fiber nodes virtually eliminates this problem and also eliminates the need to lease copper from the local telco exchange, which has a material effect on the profitability of the service providers (in other words, fiber is generally less expensive to lease than copper).

The Tenants in the Large Building Wish to Bypass the Local Telco Exchange

MxU tenants using the local telco exchanges for DSL broadband generally pay a premium for speeds that are typically less than those afforded by an 802.11/fiber hybrid architecture. The cost savings are significant and the transfer to 802.11/fiber access can be effected in a very short time, often less than a week.

802.11 for Extension of DSL and Cable

An interesting use for 802.11 bridges is and will continue to be the extension of service areas by DSL and cable modem operators. A point-to-point link can be installed at the edge of a DSL or cable service area and the service extended to other areas as far as 20 or more miles away. This eliminates the need for trenching or leasing copper lines from a third party, which would require an ongoing monthly fee.

Often, 802.11 point-to-point links can be amortized over approximately 90 days. This is a vast improvement in the amortization cycles of 18 to 24 months common to MMDS or other licensed links. Obviously once the equipment is paid for, the monthly operating expense (opex) of the equipment is significantly reduced.

The DSL and cable modem operators can also use a point-to-point 802.11 link as an interim medium until they have other copper or trenched assets in place. Given that the 802.11 equipment is not restricted to any physical location as would be the case for a licensed link (though some licensed links can be redeployed to new geographies), it can easily be redeployed to a new site once fiber or copper broadband has been laid. Having stated that, the fact is that network managers typically don't like to take links down even if there is a second and faster link available as the 802.11 link can be left in place for business, traffic, or redundancy- continuity purposes.

Practical Considerations for Using 802.11b for Final Mile

The number of 802.11b bridges sold is not inconsiderable in the market space, and may represent as much as 30 percent of all 802.11b sales. It's common for reputable vendors to encourage prospective customers to abandon or at least revise their expectations with regard to the use of the 802.11b standard for final mile use.

Let's begin with the basics as they pertain to both point-to-point (often referred to as pt-pt) and point-to-multipoint architectures (often referred to as pt-mpt). A pt-pt bridge is the simplest bridge: it involves only two end points, whereas a pt-mpt architecture involves a primary bridge (called a *root bridge)* and up to approximately five non-root bridges. While the standard will support many more bridges than a handful in a pt-mpt architecture, the contention for the right to transmit becomes unserviceable, as the bridges are connecting disparate LANs, which in turn are populated by up to hundreds if not a thousand or more users.

While a root bridge more often than not will use an omni-directional antenna, the non-root bridges will almost always use parabolic antennas. Point-to-point bridge links also almost always use parabolic antennas in order to maximize gain, which has a direct link-to-link margin, transmission/reception speed, bit error rate, and reliability. The advantages of a narrow beam versus energy radiated in directions for which there are no receivers are not inconsiderable.

In a pt-pt bridge architecture, for every dB of the transmission that occurs below 30dBm, the antenna gain may be increased from the standard 6dBi maximum, by 3dB. For example, a 29dB transmitter could be assembled with a 9dBi antenna, whereas a 28dB transmitter could use a 12dBi antenna, and so forth. The Cisco Systems BR-350 bridge product is set to transmit from the factory at 20dBm, which is 10dBm below the 30dBm level, and so the end user could use up to a 30dBi antenna. It should be noted, however, that Cisco does not ship an antenna with gain greater than 21dBi, not because the regulations won't allow it, but only because Cisco has not certified the radio with that much gain, and it would need to do so prior to offering it to the public. At the time of this writing, the market has not demanded this configuration, and a 30dBi antenna is not likely be offered.

In pt-mpt systems the FCC has limited the maximum EIRP (the measurement for how much energy density is put out from the radio which is calculated as transmit power plus antenna gain) for systems sold in the United States to 36dBm. The reader will recall that 3db is a logarithmic gain of twice the energy. Also note that pt-mpt systems have a substantially higher energy density allowed for the same space radiated. This is to be expected, because a pt-mpt system will direct a lot more energy in directions without receivers. The allowable gain for a pt-mpt system when the transmission is below 36dBm is 1dB for every 1dB of raw (no antenna) transmission power.

There is an interesting twist on the rules for pt-mpt architectures that can be harnessed quite nicely by the savvy user of this technology. Consider a pt-mpt scenario, where there is one root bridge (the bridge to and from which all other bridges communicate) and 3 *non-root* bridges. The root bridge, which we will call Bridge A will communicate with three other bridges which we'll call Bridge B, Bridge C, and Bridge D. The radio at Bridge A will communicate with Bridges B, C, and D and is therefore in a pt-mpt configuration. However, as bridges B, C, and D are only communicating with a single bridge, Bridge A, they are actually considered as pt-pt bridges. Therefore, the radios in Bridges B, C, and D can be configured at the higherpower setting of a pt-pt bridge.

Amplifiers

One of the common questions asked of 802.11 equipment vendors is, "Can I use an amplifier on my bridges?" The answer can be found in Part C of FCC regulation 15.204 which states, "External radio frequency power amplifiers shall not be marketed as separate products... ." Part D of FCC 15.204 states, "Only the antenna with which an intentional radiator (transmitter) is originally authorized may be used with the intentional radiator." What this means is that if an amplifier is to be attached to the radio between the transmitter and antenna, it must be sold by the equipment vendor, the equipment vendor must have this configuration certified by the FCC, and the amplifier must be sold with the other equipment and not as an optional device. On a more practical front, even with an amplifier, the maximum allowable energy gains must still be adhered to for both pt-pt and pt-mpt systems in the U.S. While it is acknowledged that there are amplifiers on the market for 802.11 systems, they are not to be added onto the radio and no law-abiding 802.11 vendor in the U.S. will sell amplifiers in a manner contrary to FCC rules and regulations. Some vendors will refuse to sell equipment to a customer if they believe the customer will be using amplifiers.

Bridge Data Rates Above 11 Mbps

802.11 radio bridges are a bargain by virtually any definition when it comes to connecting two or more remote sites. They have two key additional benefits, as mentioned previously, which include the ability to be deployed very rapidly, and to be deployed with essentially zero resources dedicated by the end user for licenses and other applications for use (other than construction permits where required, of course). The result of this in part is that some customers would like the value and simplicity of an 802.11 bridge, but at data rates above the 11Mbps standard.

The reader will recall that the 802.11 standard includes channelization of the radio such that there are three non-overlapping channels (Channel 1 at 2412MHz, Channel 6 at 2437MHz, and Channel 11 at 2462MHz). By combining up to three bridges at 11Mbps of speed per bridge, the user can achieve data rates of 33Mbps, with throughput at approximately half that. Care should be exercised with the construction of such a link by ensuring each of the three antennas are installed with at least 2 meters of space between them and that if the reader is using omni-directional antennas, that the antennas be located in a vertical manner, i.e., with a vertical stack of omni-directional antennas, spaced at least 2 meters apart, as opposed to lining them up on a common horizontal plane. With bridges now on the market for less than $1,000, a 33Mbps link for approximately $6,000 is a very high performance bargain. The radios at each end of the link are aggregated into a simple Ethernet hub, with corresponding software at each end. This is yet another example of where purchasing 802.11 from a genuine network vendor as opposed to a radio vendor makes a substantial difference.

Channel Reuse

One of the oldest and most elegant approaches to maximizing the number of available channels with an 802.11 bridge is that of channel reuse. Figure 14-5 provides an indication of how channels can be reused in a manner such that a very considerable area can be covered, even with as few as three non-overlapping channels to work with.

The allocation of channels such that they do not impinge on adjacent cells is very important. It is equally important to use the right amount of gain in the antennas. Too much gain could result in stray energy into an adjacent cell, or two cells over. Path loss

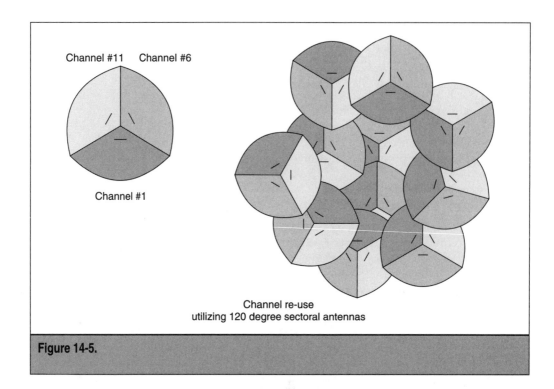

Channel #11   Channel #6

Channel #1

Channel re-use
utilizing 120 degree sectoral antennas

Figure 14-5.

calculations that occur at the early cell-planning stage should indicate at least 90dBm of loss at an area where common frequencies could reside. Too little gain could have the same effect. Proper planning of the physical area, plus an understanding of antenna performance and radio configuration should always be confirmed by a site survey.

Backhaul (getting the data to and from the covered area) must also be considered when frequency planning. For many deployments, backhaul over copper has the advantage of freeing up a radio channel. For deployments where fewer than three channels can be used satisfactorily, and with a minimum probability of the requirement for additional speed in the future, using one of the channels for backhaul is cost effective and relatively easy to do.

Downtilt

One of the most interesting and perhaps one of the most common mistakes made with regard to outdoor deployments of bridges is that of downtilt. The authors have seen more than one site survey where the technicians have not remembered the issue of antenna downtilt. Figure 14-6 illustrates this.

What is important to remember is that the larger the area that the bridge will cover, the larger the null (area of insufficient energy) near the base of the transmitting

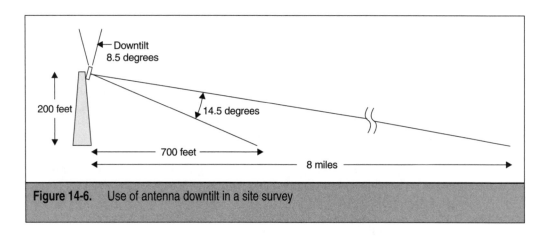

Figure 14-6. Use of antenna downtilt in a site survey

antenna will need to be. The amount of null area immediate to the base of the transmitter is proportional to the total area radiated by the transmitter. Where this has practical limitations is for campus-type networks where the users might be situated near the base of a tall building or structure where the antennas are mounted.

Two Notes of Advice for Final Mile and Service Providers

There are two concepts the authors have seen repeatedly, both in good economic times and during the more challenging economic times where return on assets is analyzed much more critically and a very short time frame is allowed for paying off the equipment (generally now in the 90 day range—down from the former requirement of 18 months or more). In general, telcos often have much longer cycles than 18 months, but many of the service providers no longer do; at least the ones that have remained in business, which are, more often than not, the very small regional and independent service providers.

Bridges to Client Adapters for Service Providers

The first concept for a service provider to consider carefully if planning to use 802.11 as a revenue-generating medium, is that it is generally a lot more difficult than it seems to build a dependable high-speed network by deploying client adapters to condominium, apartment, or single residence dwellers than it appears. The authors have seen dozens of excited would-be entrepreneurs arrive with plans to roll out networks that feature the occasional bridge to a widely deployed set of client adapters. The short version here is that while there are certainly a very limited number of locations where this will work, it rarely if ever scales to the size of an operation where revenue is considerable. The primary reason for this is the amount of path loss from an outdoor bridge to an indoor located client adapter is often greater than –90dBm, which is generally far beyond the capability of a client adapter for upstream transmissions, even if it can receive sufficient downstream signal—which it usually can't. Client adapters with external antennas mounted outside the building will work, but this is awkward and you might as well mount an outdoor antenna to an access point or bridge and remain untethered to your indoor-based LAN by using a standard client adapter interface to an access point in your residence or business.

Another detailed item here is that the externally mounted antenna would have to be on the optimal side of the building facing the outdoor bridge. Line-of-sight issues cannot be overemphasized in this scenario, and the probability of an externally mounted antenna being on the correct side of the building is about one in four. This means that whatever prospective customer uptake you might envision for a geographic area would be further reduced by approximately 75 percent. Pretty measly odds in any event.

This concept should not be confused with that of hotspot locations. The major difference there is that the client adapters are brought to the access point site, such as an airport lounge, hotel, or convention center setting. In this environment, there are generally few line-of-site or path loss issues.

The other caution to offer prospective service providers is to ensure you have a well-established and fully capable call center. 802.11 devices tend not to be very user friendly, and you can bet you'll get good use out of a call center. Knowing how to do this takes an exceptional amount of business savvy; it's not something to try even if you have deep pockets. Poor customer service will bring down a prospective 802.11 service provider network nearly as fast as a lightning strike.

Wide Area 802.11 Service Provider Coverage

The other note of hard-earned advice for prospective 802.11 service providers is to carefully consider the issue of getting line of sight to a large enough customer base make the business. Remember that literally billions were spent on getting broadband fixed wireless into single-family homes and the concept cratered in a most spectacular manner. If the largest of companies like Sprint, MCI, and Cisco who put some absolutely brilliant minds on the project, fueled by amounts of money that would make even an OPEC baron feel faint failed, it is reasonable to consider that there are entirely non-trivial technological hurdles to clear. The first is getting line of sight to enough customers—nothing shot the multi-billion dollar attempt down more completely than the laws of physics which dictate path loss. A key item to remember is that MMDS radios also had an enormous amount of power that could be transmitted—up to 50 watts compared to the 1watt maximum of U-NII 3. The issue of having customer premises equipment that was too expensive is probably the central issue that 802.11 service providers can readily resolve, but in the end, the simple matter of having trees, rooflines, and hills were too much to overcome for not only the MMDS grand adventure, but for other frequencies, as well.

Where the 802.11 service provider can find a target-rich environment is in connecting small and medium businesses to fiber points of presence. The SMB/SME customer will pay more for installation, preventive maintenance, support, and bits per second than a residential user, who is still primarily an AOL customer.

Venture Capital Aspects of Unlicensed vs. Licensed Spectrum

The venture capital industry has taken as much of a drubbing as the technology industry itself during the two or so years previous to this writing, and at this writing there are very few publicized VC-backed 802.11 deals. However the issue of venture capital is well within the scope of comparing unlicensed to licensed spectrum, as without this element, there would be no financing of unlicensed links. There are elements associated with the capitalization of unlicensed links that are unique to that sector of the broadband industry.

There is an increasing level of communication between the industry that provides complex communications equipment and the venture capital (VC) industry. This stemmed originally from the fact that virtually all of the major Internet equipment companies are publicly traded and the financial community actively observed the industry to gather intelligence on which they based investments.

However, even with the largest companies, such as Cisco and Lucent, the great preponderance of sales are not multi-billion-dollar ventures, but rather more commonly in the millions or hundreds of thousands of dollars.

At this writing, even Cisco makes most of its revenue from the enterprise market and it's a rare enterprise deal that goes beyond the tens of millions of dollars; most of the revenue for Internet equipment companies comes from relatively small deals.

What this means to the VC community is that virtually all of the deals are made with VC funds from the tier-two and -three VC companies as opposed to the major houses like Smith Barney, and so forth. Most, if not all of the 802.11 outdoor projects are in fact bootstrapped by the service providers themselves because the expense isn't that great relative to other technology rollouts, and presently service providers are showing tentative, cautious, and very conservative build-out plans.

It is the authors' opinion that the equipment manufacturers, the largest of which are also common sources for financing equipment, must play an ever-closer role with the VC and banking communities. This not only will better facilitate the funding of emerging companies, it will also help prime the pump in terms of getting greater numbers of 802.11 links into the marketplace and online. It will also assist the emerging companies in making a transition from VC sourcing to routine and conventional banking sources which are generally more cost effective and less onerous to the emerging companies.

There are four major entities required to make a telecom venture operate. While there are arguably additional entities such as those for deployment and integration, the primary ones are the following:

- Equipment manufacturers
- Service providers or enterprise customers
- Retail or end users
- Financiers: the venture capitalists and bankers

Of these four entities, the equipment manufacturers, in particular the smaller ones, are generally the first to advance the state of the art in equipment. Either these smaller entities are purchased by the larger entities or the larger entities build similar equipment. The people in this industry fully understand not only the technological advantages of their equipment, but also the economic and social ramifications brought about by their technology offerings.

There are typically two types of service providers and enterprise customers: early adopters of technology, and those who wait a year or so until the technology has been proven. Service providers and enterprise customers, both of the early adopter mentality as well as the more conservative variety, are in constant contact with the equipment providers and are therefore, also well informed about the economic and other potentials afforded by state-of-the-art equipment. The service providers and enterprise customers of the equipment providers commonly supply guidance in terms of technology features, price, and other key aspects.

This leaves the remaining two entities of the four, both of which are generally not technically literate, or at the least are late in coming to the table in terms of gaining literacy on 802.11.

An example of end users would be those with a small business LAN. Quite arguably, these individuals should find the technology as transparent as possible, and not require a deep or even cursory knowledge of 802.11 equipment. Their focus should primarily be on the services and traffic carried by the system as opposed to having a deep technical knowledge of the equipment. It is important to remember that it is this entity that ultimately pays for the equipment and services as no company can be grown for a sustained period on outside capital alone—it must be grown from the profitable engagement of end users.

The final entity is the VC industry and in general they arrive last or second to last in terms of being literate on not only the 802.11 equipment, but on how the technology translates to profitable business strategies.

On one hand, the VC mission is to successfully invest funds from which they grow their capital base and redeploy it in similar or other ventures. On the other hand, they must possess at least a working knowledge of the technology they are interested in. This is more difficult than it seems, as the breadth and depth of knowledge required to fully understand a technology or a technology strategy is quite deep.

The VCs are also compelled to move very quickly, and therefore often do not have the time to truly understand 802.11 technology in general, much less the differences between funding a licensed operation versus an entity that wishes to use 802.11 as their primary carrier band. The number of VC firms is not increasing; in fact it can be claimed that this number is decreasing. Further, most of the VC firms are fully subscribed with the amount of capital they have to dole out. However, it's probable that the number of personnel with backgrounds in engineering and technology management have increased modestly to moderately. Manufacturers as well as the service providers or enterprise players need personnel who understand how to reduce key technological elements such as COFDM to the straightforward business operating terms that are native to the investment community.

The authors have spent many hours with venture capitalists from all sizes of VC firms, and have found them substantially lacking in understanding of the value of an 802.11 outdoor operation. This is for the following general reasons:

- 802.11 is still an emerging broadband medium
- They view a broadcast license as an asset
- Resolution of co-channel interference
- Competition from numerous U-NII regional service providers
- Underestimating value of management execution over frequency selection

802.11 Is Still an Emerging Broadband Medium

Most VC firms are still catching up on the fundamental concepts of how to run a copper- or fiber-based broadband operation. The recent market crash of the spring of 2001 occurred during the writing of this book and it is clear that at least part of the blame resides with the VC community, which made investments in fixed wireless and other businesses with poor business plans, weak management teams, and in too many cases, virtually no radio expertise.

Even though 802.11 technology is sold in the billions of dollars around the world, it is still very much an emerging technology. One of the key reasons for this is that there remains a dearth of 802.11 client cards installed in laptop computers and PDAs. This is in the process of changing, though, as Intel recently announced it would be including 802.11 technologies as part of the chip that will replace the Pentium 4. This means that by mid-2003, the great preponderance of laptops will have native 802.11 capability, just as the ether port has become a standard item on laptops today. This is a very favorable development for the 802.11 industry, and the providers of access with this technology such as hotspot providers like Surf and Sip out of the San Francisco Bay Area.

The unlicensed version of this medium is only one of the latest aspects of a medium that at best is not well understood by the VC community. In other words, the VC community has had to work hard at becoming conversant in copper- and fiber-based broadband technologies; they're generally even farther behind in their understanding of BBFW.

They View a Broadcast License as an Asset

VCs rightfully view a broadcast license such as that for MMDS as an asset. Again, these assets are tangible in that they can be sold and have a market value for many years. An 802.11 service provider operator has no such asset, but does have the advantage that capital can be applied directly to the deployment of assets that generate revenue, such as equipment, personnel, and right-of-way access.

Resolution of Co-Channel Interference

State-of-the-art equipment can mitigate the issue of co-channel interference with a very high degree of resolution, as noted previously in this chapter. Perhaps no issue is less understood by the VC market than this and it is this issue upon which the authors have spent the most time briefing VC personnel.

Competition from Numerous 802.11 Regional Service Providers

This is an appropriate concern for VCs but one that is commonly overestimated because of the fact that demand for broadband remains pent up for small and medium business users, business parks, and the residential unit from single family dwellings to condominiums, apartments, and even hotels. The number one question asked of telcos at this writing by customers is "When can I get broadband to my home or business?" Those who are purchasing homes now commonly consider broadband availability as important as electricity and air conditioning. This translates to a high market penetration rate for the first 802.11 providers—if they are careful not to get caught in the line-of-sight issues so prevalent for deployments, especially the residential market. If the service provider can retain a reasonably high degree of customer satisfaction, though easier said than done, there is a reduced risk of churn. This is primarily due to the fact that once users experience broadband, they find it difficult to return to dial-up speeds and Internet access that is not always on.

This is one of the key reasons why 802.11 providers should target markets in which there is no broadband service, and do so where there is not likely to be competition from copper within twelve to eighteen months. The smaller the geographic market, the better, and the farther from DSL and cable modem service the better. This translates to distances of at least twenty to thirty miles at a minimum from large metropolitan areas.

Finally on this point, there is more market opportunity than can be serviced by even the largest service provider and having 802.11 competition in the same region actually validates the concept rather than threatens it with an eroded customer base.

Underestimating Value of Management Execution over Frequency Selection

An 802.11-based service provider operation is an execution operation which means that the potential for success is more incumbent on a winning and experienced management team that is well funded than on having a wireless license. Even the largest and best-funded service providers are struggling financially, while many smaller 802.11 service providers are thriving. As stated earlier in this work, according to a March 2001 report by Strategis, unlicensed fixed wireless deployments far outnumber licensed deployments.

For the reasons outlined in this chapter, one of the most important elements in the worldwide fixed wireless market will be the use of unlicensed spectrum links as either the primary medium or to augment licensed wireless architectures. In spite of its relative obscurity at this writing, especially given the headlines generated when companies pay billions of dollars for a spectrum like MMDS, the 802.11 bands are poised for considerable press exposure. For virtually all but a very few service providers, 802.11 technology is the only fixed wireless radio technology that can be given serious consideration.

APPENDIX A

Audio, Video, Voice, and Data to a PDA over 802.11 at a Nuclear Power Plant

Where the subject of 802.11 WLANs becomes the most exciting for most people and the easiest to understand is when the discussion turns from how the network is designed, configured, and deployed to *how it will be used.* This appendix will cover the following six items:

- General site and industry considerations

- Site survey considerations

- Hardware

- Software

- Costs and benefits

- Typical uses for 802.11 at a nuclear power plant

General Site and Industry Considerations

While nuclear power plants commonly use a number of types of wireless technologies, including cellular phone and two-way radio systems for plant maintenance, management, security operations, paging, radiation protection and monitoring management, and operator logs, in addition to other uses, this appendix will focus on the use of an 802.11b installation for data, voice, and video at a United States nuclear power plant.

For security reasons, neither the name and location of the power plant nor the timeline for this installation will be disclosed in this appendix, but suffice it to say that this deployment is quite indicative of the capabilities of an 802.11 network when properly deployed. One other key point is that there is a major difference in equipment among different vendors. In this case, the vendor was Cisco Systems for the 802.11, Ethernet, and other equipment. The sources of the video back-end equipment can be sourced satisfactorily from a number of vendors, and the architecture in this deployment remains relatively consistent regardless of the video vendor.

The nuclear power plant industry in the United States in the new millennium is primarily focused on providing electrical energy to consumers and commercial customers, as well as providing an attractive and secure investment for their shareholders as a public utility. These sites operate under the mandates of a number of regulatory agencies, including local and state entities and, of course, the Nuclear Regulatory Commission. The matrix of rules, regulations, and compliance issues is myriad and highly complex. Sites must provide enormous amounts of energy to customers over vast areas covering multiple states, and they must do so in a highly-secured, predictable, and controlled manner, with a dedication to safety policies and procedures that match any industry in the world.

Deploying 802.11 technology at a nuclear power plant requires a highly-developed competence in general network technologies. Further, and most importantly, one must be aware that deploying this technology at a nuclear power plant requires a great deal of extra care and deliberate advance planning—far more in general than virtually any other type of deployment site. This is due in part to two issues, the first being that every single piece of hardware deployed within the power block must be fully characterized, field-proven, and documented in terms of its performance, thermal, and other energy output, redundancy, and configuration. This is in order to mitigate the number of variables that might occur during a nuclear anomalous event.

The second reason 802.11 deployments at this type of site are very expensive is because nuclear plant operators are exceptionally reluctant to add, modify, scale, or migrate technologies within the power block. The movement of even empty conduit requires numerous meetings and concurrences from a wide array of committees and personnel. In other words, the deployment of technology within a power block must be very well thought out in advance—this isn't a deployment where you can "wing" the design, architecture, and network elements.

The rationale for deploying 802.11 technologies within this industry include the typical ones that center on increasing efficiencies and reducing operating expenses, but one other interesting factor is evident within this industry, which is that according to estimates from personnel within the site in review in this appendix, approximately half of the nuclear-qualified personnel are scheduled to retire within the next 10 years, and there is a shortage of new people entering the field to replace this talent. The need for autonomous and smart systems that are augmented with communications networks that are highly-efficient, ubiquitous, high-performance in nature, and robust will help mitigate this increasingly important problem. Increasing the reach of this "institutional memory" is one of the objectives of 802.11 technology at this deployment.

Communications are a mission-critical element at a nuclear power plant, both in the course of routine plant operations, but even more so during a security or operational anomaly, at which time speed, accuracy, and reliability cannot be compromised. We will first consider the WLAN function as it pertains to the general facility. There is a considerable array of buildings at the site in which a wide range of functions occur, from human resources management to the management of the nuclear reactor itself. The 802.11 network therefore performs two essential functions: a bridging function between buildings and as a WLAN within the various buildings. Neither of these functions is remarkable in and of itself, but in order to understand the implications of a deployment at this type of setting, it's important to understand the structures and general lay of the site.

There are essentially two types of buildings at a nuclear power plant, and they are differentiated by function. The predominant building by far is what is called the *power block,* which is the building in which the nuclear reactors and steam turbines and generators reside. The first impression one has when seeing the power block is that it is a formidable structure indeed. Its size and scale can perhaps be summed up by an experience the author had while accompanying a colleague to the site to perform work on the project. As we entered the campus area, my colleague said to me, "It doesn't look that big," to which I responded, "Amigo, we're half a mile away from that building." Upon hearing this, my colleague went slack-jawed and then appreciated just how enormous the facility is. The exterior of the facility is probably 200 feet high at its peak, and encompasses approximately one million square feet of space.

The power block on the campus in discussion here contains two enormous reactors designed and built by Westinghouse. They each put out approximately 9 *billion* kilowatt hours of electricity per year. Adjacent to the power block is a complex of high-voltage wires that introduce the electricity onto the regional power grid, and when you're present at the facility, you can't help but feel dwarfed by the immensity of the complex.

There are two types of nuclear reactors. Both types operate on the same principles, which are either *boiling water reactors* or *pressurized water reactors*. Both are cooled by ordinary water, which is the link between the fission energy released in the reactor and the rotation of the turbines that spin the generator. Contrary to popular belief, it is not the reactors that generate the electricity; rather, the job of the reactors is to heat water in order to rotate turbines that then rotate power generators, which are the devices that actually produce the electricity. In boiling water reactors, the water is heated by the nuclear fuel and boils to steam inside the reactor. The steam is then piped to the turbine via a pair of stainless pipes that are approximately one meter in diameter and which are clad in insulation and stainless steel sheeting for thermal safety.

Pressurized water reactors are the kind used at the site in review in this section. In this type of power plant, the water is heated by fission but kept under pressure to prevent it from boiling. From the reactor vessel, the hot water is pumped to a steam generator at which point a supply of cool water is applied which then creates steam. The steam spins the turbine, driving the electric generator, producing electricity.

The Power Block

As you can imagine, physical entry to the power block is *extremely* highly-controlled, and compliance to all security measures is undertaken with a full measure of soberness, precaution, and a disregard as to whether or not you are in a hurry. Again, for security reasons, the details of gaining access to the power block will not be covered. Upon gaining entry inside the power block, you will notice two things, the first being that there is a lot of background noise from the power generation equipment, and secondly, the entire facility seems to hum with a very slight vibration. The power block is comprised of literally hundreds of rooms, each separated with walls that are 2 to 3 meters of very heavily-reinforced concrete. The default condition of the doors between these rooms is that the doors remain closed at all times during plant operation. The doors themselves are very substantial, comprised of thick layers of steel, and each door we passed through required careful compliance to access policies and procedures. An interesting element of a power block that is relevant to the deployment of an 802.11 network is that the site management has the option under an extreme emergency to simply flood the entire power block with water and then cease operations while leaving the complex under tight guard in perpetuity.

The reason this option is relevant to the deployment of a WLAN is that the doors between the rooms in the power block are not only substantial, they remain closed at all times except to allow the passing of pedestrian traffic.

What this description should tell the reader in part is that getting an 802.11 network to operate at its full level of efficiency requires very thorough and comprehensive planning. While most of the rooms is essentially its own unique radiating environment, there are two additional factors to consider: that some of the rooms are interconnected with large holes approximately 3 meters square, which enable the steam pipes to cross from one side of the room to another, and that many of the rooms are virtually filled to each corner with either stainless piping or other equipment that essentially eliminates any line of sight to the workers or 802.11 appliances. It seemed evident upon visual inspection that multi-path would be an enormous problem if it weren't for the very small size of the rooms (given of course that the radio waves travel at the speed of light).

Other unique problems include the concept that once located, the access points can not be moved without requiring approval from numerous plant operational and safety committee hearings. Every piece of equipment in a power block must be documented in terms of not only its location, but also its thermal output, power requirements, and other safety parameters such that if there was a nuclear event of an anomalous nature, plant personnel could carefully and accurately predict how each piece of equipment in the plant would function.

The cost of wiring for the access points is non-trivial in WLAN deployments, and this project was no exception. An estimated $5 million was spent on providing both power and signal cabling to the 700 access points used on this project, of which approximately 450 were used inside the power block. A quick calculation would indicate that for every dollar the customer spent on APs (list price), they spent approximately $5 on installing cables.

The walls, which as mentioned previously are enormously thick and strong, have small conduits through which some cabling can be passed. Interestingly enough, and with no small degree of irony, there is not a single 100-VAC outlet in the power block itself, which is a humorous fact given that the output of that facility will provide power to literally millions of common wall outlets in homes and businesses across numerous states. This means that all of the APs have to be powered from junction boxes, which is fairly typical in an enterprise or campus deployment.

Other Campus Buildings

The other buildings on the campus are fairly typical commercial structures in their size, material composition, and layout. This should not come as much of a surprise given that they are used for normal business and plant operations efforts. They are located in the general vicinity of the power block, and some of the buildings are within a dozen or so meters of the power block. Among the different types of buildings on the general site are vehicle and equipment maintenance buildings, general office facilities, and a building approximately 2 kilometers away that is used for semi-off-site training.

Site Survey Considerations

As part of the deployment effort, the management of the site spent approximately $80,000 on a site survey—a sum that is all but unheard of in the 802.11 industry. The author won't comment as to whether that price was a good value or not, but what is interesting is that the site went through two different vendors prior to the contract for the network (not the site survey) being awarded to Cisco Systems. Neither of the first two vendors questioned the site managers as to what type of traffic would be carried on the WLAN network within the plant. This is an essential issue to cover, because a site survey for a WLAN that will carry low-latency traffic such as voice and video needs to be much more conservative in terms of link margin and AP coverage overlap, and low-latency traffic is what the nuclear plant operators will be migrating toward.

The Cisco team provided audit services on the original site survey to ensure appropriate coverage and cell overlap. What is interesting to note is that the company that performed the initial site survey did so with a FHSS modulation scheme in mind. The Cisco Systems equipment uses DSSS with state-of-the-art bit recovery. The DSSS modulation and award-winning performance of the Aironet equipment ensured that the site survey that was performed for equipment turned out to be a conservative set of measurements because of the nature of the higher performance equipment from Cisco.

Having stated the above, the preparations prior to a site survey are extensive and non-trivial in scope if the survey is to accomplish all that it can. One could use the analogy of painting a room or a car in reference to performing a site survey, which is that the quality of the deliverable is very much proportionate to degree of preparation before the first signal is even transmitted and measured. A wide array of issues should be resolved prior to performing a site survey, and while such issues are worthy of detailing on their own, the list should include the following:

- Have you published a wireless strategy?
- What wireless technologies, 802.11 and other, have you deployed or are you planning to deploy?
- What network elements will be supported by your wireless technology, if any?
- Has your organization developed any mobility applications?
- Have you deployed any 802.11 components previous to this site survey?
- Have you considered the issue of rogue (unauthorized) access points in use at your facility?
- What are the specific areas you will need to cover?
- What are the priority sites for deploying your 802.11 equipment?
- What type of traffic will be carried by your 802.11 elements in the next 12 months?
- What type of traffic will be carried by your 802.11 elements in the next 24 months?
- What 802.11-compliant devices, such as voice and PDAs, will you deploy?
- What coverage will you require for such mobility devices as 802.11 phones and 802.11 compliant PDAs?
- What is your budget for this technology over the next two years?
- How do you accommodate training for this technology?
- Do you deploy the technology, or will you contract to a third party?

- Who will perform the security and site survey audits on a forward going basis?
- What are your network security requirements?
- Who will author and maintain your 802.11 documentation?

The aforementioned questions were extensively discussed at the nuclear plant site and at regional office before, during, and after the site survey occurred.

Within the power block, many of the rooms were approximately 75 feet square by 30 feet high, although many were a lot larger, and some were smaller. What made the prospect daunting upon the initial site visit was the fact that many of the rooms were nearly completely filled with steam pipes that are approximately 36 inches in diameter, and clad in stainless steel. Some of the rooms were so filled with these high-pressure pipes that there remained little room for walking or working. To the eye—something one should trust little with regard to 802.11 surveys—it was a daunting environment for two radios to communicate because there seemed to be little line of sight available. However, what mitigates this is the general limited size of the rooms; this allows for the radio energy to propagate rather well.

An 802.11 survey usually takes into consideration areas that are generally, but not always, limited to a single room, although the "room" can be as large as a warehouse or large manufacturing facility. Having stated that, in general, physical elements at ranges farther than 400 feet don't affect the performance of either access points or client adapters. One of the prospective concerns inside the power block was that while many of the rooms were sealed most of the time with heavy metal doors, there were a number of rooms that were interconnected by openings in the floor, wall, or ceiling, which were sometimes as wide as 15 feet. For that reason, care had to be taken with regard to the frequency planning so that none of the adjacent rooms utilized the same radio channel.

State-of-the-art 802.11 systems include site survey software, and it's far easier to use than that required in outdoor service provider links.

There are three important criteria with regard to a link: signal strength, noise floor, and signal-to-noise ratio. This again proves that a signal can be strong but include a considerable amount of noise that must be resolved by the receiving processing capabilities.

With the continuing emphasis on the inclusion of low-latency traffic such as voice and video, there is both a tendency and a requirement to install 802.11 networks that feature more densely populated areas with access points.

Just prior to the site survey performed by Cisco Systems at the nuclear plant site, the Cisco team wanted to ensure that the following were in place:

- Possession and review of detailed building drawings
- Site tour
- Test equipment and antenna selection
- Training session with nuclear plant personnel
- Planning sessions with network managers and technicians

Building Drawings

One of the most important assets to acquire while planning an 802.11 network at a nuclear plant, or any other site, is a set of drawings for the entire building. It's preferable to have a set of drawings that can be dedicated to the project and therefore can be marked with the locations of access points, power lines, and items such as pillars, ceiling components, or beams to which the access points can be attached. Also inclusive of this are the wire trays that will carry and protect the ether and power cables to and from the access points. The nuclear plant site is very complex in its layout, and accordingly, numerous drawings were reviewed in detail.

Building drawings can also show rooms that have large built-in elements such as heavy equipment and ducting. If a person is performing a site survey in a particular room, he or she may not be aware of its contents and use of an adjacent room, but this is generally not the case at the nuclear plant site because the walls are 4-6 feet thick with small portals of approximately 6 inches which act as sites for bulkheads through which the various cables pass through from one end of the plant to the other.

Building drawings also indicate relative distances between areas and the size of rooms to be covered. This will assist both the experienced and inexperienced installer in determining how many APs to use and where to locate them for optimal WLAN performance. Figure A-1 is typical of what might be used in a site survey.

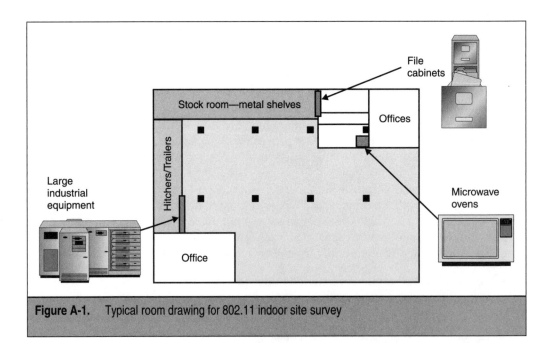

Figure A-1. Typical room drawing for 802.11 indoor site survey

Having a set of drawings for the project that has been marked up during the planning and site survey portion of the WLAN deployment also serves as an important aid should a team be required to return to the site later to either scale up the network or troubleshoot a problem. The value of accurate documentation that "stands alone," or in other words, is complete in and of itself and can be understood by a person not familiar with the project, is very important in the maintenance of this long-term asset.

Site Tour

A site tour with a knowledgeable person enables the survey and installation team to be aware of what operations occur in adjacent rooms and floors, as well as the contents of adjacent rooms and floors. Building drawings typically don't indicate installed equipment and are limited to floorplans. We took a detailed tour of the power block, and during the tour, the author of this appendix was reminded again of the value of a digital camera and hand-held voice recorder to document items which must be accounted and planned for during the actual site survey, including the need for ladders, further building blueprints, and the location of power and cable trays.

One additional item to consider when reviewing building drawings, which is ensured by an advance site survey tour, is that not all sets of building drawings reflect *as built* configurations. While the access points in use at the nuclear power plant in question do not require cables for power and signal, most access points do in fact have a requirement for separate lines in this regard. In any event, the walking tour helped ensure that the AC was located and was consistent with the indicated drawings. It should be noted that in many 802.11 deployments, building drawings are not always available.

Test Equipment

802.11 site survey equipment is much more manageable, easier to use, and far less expensive than that required for non-802.11 outdoor RF links. While this type of gear can be used, and is typically centralized around a hefty spectrum analyzer, it is not generally necessary, because 802.11 site surveys are typically performed with the actual equipment that will be placed in service. What is required is an access point, an array of antennas, and a laptop or palmtop computer with a PCMCIA card installed, along with the client utilities, and of course the capability to pass traffic between the client and the access point (this occurs with the site survey utility when using the Cisco ACU).

It's also a good idea to procure some duct tape and tie wraps to hold antennas in place during the site survey; by doing this, the site survey team will be able to use one less person. Based on experience, two other items that are useful are a common flashlight to see above the ceiling area, which typically isn't lit (and, in some cases, you'll need it to see the space between floors), and an auxiliary battery pack for access points that will be placed in locations for site surveys where there is no local AC outlet. There are now site survey kits on the market from Cisco Systems and other companies, although for most deployments, they're cost-prohibitive at approximately $5,000. The site survey kit the authors' team used at the nuclear plant included the following items:

Cisco AIR-AP352E2RA-K9	Access points
Cisco AIR-PCM352	PCMCIA client Adapters
AIR-LMC352	350 series adapter DSSS PC card–no antenna
Cisco AIR-ANT4941	2.2 dBi dipole antenna (Rubber Duck)
Cisco AIR-ANT5959	2.0 dBi diversity omni ceiling mount antenna
AIR-ANT2506	5.2 dBi omnidirectional mast mount antenna
AIR-ANT3213	5.2 dBi pillar-mount diversity omni antenna
Cisco AIR-ANT2012	6.0 dBi diversity patch wall mount antenna
Cisco AIR-ANT3549	8.5 dBi hemispherical patch antenna
Cisco AIR-ANT1949	13.5 dBi Yagi mast mount antenna
Cisco AIR-ACC55959-072	Aerial cable for console port configuration
Cisco AIR-420-1625-0500	RP-TNC connector assembly (5 inches)
Terrawave TW-SSBP-001	Site survey battery pack for the 350 AP with inline power
Terrawave TW-IPMB-001	Industrial-purpose mounting brackets
Terrawave TW-RSA-3510	Attenuator
Terrawave TW-AATC-001	Airline-approved travel case with foam cutouts for all listed equipment
Terrawave TW-SSMW-001	Site survey distance measuring wheel
Terrawave TW-ASKIT-001	Misc. accessories: duct tape, zip ties, velcro, pens, 50 AP mounting location markers, colored tape rolls

Most of the items included in a site survey kit, such as the one provided by Terra Wave (www.terra-wave.com) which arguably provides one of the most comprehensive site survey kits on the market, and a terrific carrying case that you can ship.

Planning Sessions with Network Managers and Technicians

Initial meetings with the network managers and technicians are crucial prior to the site survey because the installed 802.11 equipment will become an extension of the existing network. One of the purposes of the site survey is to ensure that 802.11 elements have a maximum degree of performance and reliability as fully-integrated extensions of the network.

Network administrators, site managers, construction specialists, security managers, and others contribute planning details on such items as the location and traffic loads on existing ether lines, optimal locations for mounting access points to connect the access points, future plans for physical area configurations, and so forth.

The network managers will be able to inform the site survey team as to where the areas of coverage will be, which as stated previously in this book is based fundamentally on the physical traffic patterns of the end users. While the users will be able to roam significant distances from the access points, the system should be designed with a focus on the areas where the users will spend most of their time. High-use areas may call for the installation of extra access points in order to accommodate a greater number of users or to cover the area appropriately if it is an odd shape. such as a long rectangle or an area divided by floor-to-ceiling metal shelves. Even the location of microwave ovens, such as in employee lunch areas, should be considered for high-use areas.

Typical Site Survey Steps

A typical site survey occurs in the following order:

1. Commit to purchase equipment from the vendor.
2. Study the building drawings with building and network managers.
3. Identify possible obstructions not shown on drawings and mark up drawings.
4. Build layout of site on drawings.
5. Perform site survey.
6. Select antennas.
7. Write final report.

Commit to Purchase Equipment from the Vendor   It doesn't happen very often, but occasionally there will be a site survey that is not followed up by the purchase and installation of equipment. It is this author's opinion that because site surveys require a lot of time and effort, if no guarantee has been made by an account to purchase the equipment, the survey team may want to prioritize that account below accounts that have already purchased the equipment or at least placed orders for it. In this economy, this may be less of an issue, as many site surveys are commonly performed by integration specialists who charge a reasonable fee for the performance and documentation of this work.

Site survey teams charge approximately $5,000 to perform a survey of a facility that requires 20 or more access points, so you can understand the scope of the effort required for the $80,000 charge for performing a site survey at the nuclear power plant. The site survey audit performed by the author's employer was done so at no charge, but was performed with the understanding that Cisco equipment would be installed at the site.

While the occasional customer will demand that the site survey be done at no charge, to determine how an 802.11 system might perform in their facility and to then base a purchase decision on that, it is the author's opinion that a customer who balks at paying a site survey fee of $5,000 probably isn't a solid customer in any event, because the customer will have very substantial expenditures in other areas such as networking equipment, laptops for employees, and modest construction costs to accommodate the new network devices.

Build a Layout of the Site on Drawings   Once the preliminary meetings have occurred with the appropriate building and network managers, and possible obstructions have been identified and marked up on the drawings, it is time to build a layout of the system on the drawings.

There are three key items that must be included on as part of the marking up of drawings relative to the site survey, which are:

1. Access Point location

2. AC power sources if not using Ethernet switch power sources

3. Frequency planning

NOTE Remember that the primary purpose of a site survey is to confirm the advance planning with regard to the build out of an 802.11 network.

The site survey audit team in this case was aware and asked a lot of questions about the prospect of unforseen physical items that could affect the site survey measurement and build-out performance, from items such as elevator shafts, large metal shelving structures, and walk-in coolers to x-ray rooms and large metal cabinets. These items can effectively seal off a room from local access points and sometime require dedicated access points.

Perform the Site Survey The classic approach for an indoor 802.11 site survey is to measure by placing the access points high in the corners of each room and directing their energy to the center of the room. The measurements in this case were made with both a laptop and an iPAC PDA into which was loaded an 802.11 PCMCIA card and drivers. By walking around with them and a Palmtop computer while taking measurements, a site survey team assembled readings that were most like those that would occur during the actual use of the system.

After this, the team confirmed the areas of coverage on the building drawings, and then tagged each location at which an access point was to be installed. Each location was marked with a tag that included the access point type, the channel to be used, and an address location within the building. This tag was then digitally photographed and included in the documentation package.

The site survey team confirmed that each access point overlapped at least one other access point. This ensured that there were no *nulls,* or areas with reception that is too weak for use. Figure A-2 illustrates what a drawing might look like after mapping the coverage from various access points. This figure indicates four access points mounted, one in each corner. The drawing also indicates which channels would be used in which areas.

Select Antennas During the site survey, an experienced team generally knows in advance what antennas will work best for a given area or use. However, as each site survey is unique, the final antenna selection is generally not selected until after the site survey has been completed for each area.

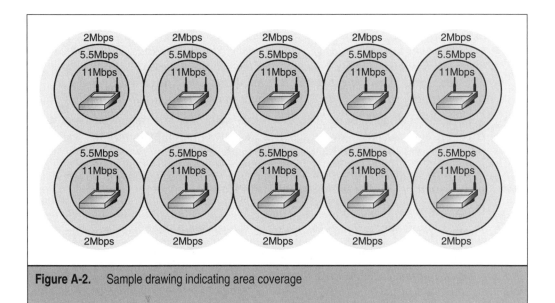

Figure A-2.   Sample drawing indicating area coverage

NOTE   One of the tasks confirmed during a site survey is that of final antenna selection. While indoor deployments nearly always use either omni-directional or patch antennas; the *gain* selected has an enormous amount to do with the performance of the network as the importance of optimizing the *shape of the coverage* is as important as virtually every other element of the planning.

The antennas selected for the power block were almost all omni directional antennas, although there are also a number of patch antennas included in the design.

Write the Final Report   Following the site survey, a final report is written. In the case of the nuclear power plant, a fair amount of the documentation existed from the initial site survey, but the power plant personnel augmented that which was written by the initial site survey team with finalized details on access point location, channel selection, antenna selection, and digital images of the installation locations.

In most professionally performed site surveys, copies of the documentation are distributed among key members of the customer's business, and the site survey team keeps a master copy. If the installation team is not the same as the site survey team, then a copy can also be given to the installation team, or the installation team can acquire a copy from the customer.

It is often a good idea to include in the report writing a senior member or project manager from the installation team, whether or not it's the same team as the site survey team, because they will have information to contribute along with the customer network manager or technician.

A well-written final report will include at least the following information:

- Location of access points, as shown on the coverage drawings. Distances from at least two walls or other permanent elements are necessary to pinpoint location. Some site survey teams place small markers with a felt-tipped pen, or use other permanent or semi permanent marking, such as pins with tags.

- Antennas designated for each access point—critical to ensure performance and coverage as indicated in drawings. It is important to remember that access points can only be ordered with specified antennas.

- Suggested configuration of each access point, including speed, channel, and security settings and selected security protocols

- Drawings of coverage areas

- Photographs of the unique antenna or access point locations and mounting

- Number of packets sent to each access point during the test

- Channels and datarate configurations

- Packet size setting

- Data retries for each access point

- Packet success threshold

The configuration, packet size, and other information, such as delay between packets, will be gathered from the site survey utility. The report also indicates not only AC power sources, but also their associated cable routings as this is considered critical documentation in a nuclear power plant.

TIP One of the most important concepts to retain while assembling a site survey report is that it must pass the "man on the street" test. In other words, an individual who is not familiar with the actual site survey and deployment (but who is a network professional, of course) should examine the document and *not* need to contact the site survey or integration team with fundamental questions about the technical details of the work previously performed.

Another good reason to assemble a final report with as much detail and clarity as possible is that, as in this case, the installation was not scheduled to be completed until some months following the site survey. Fortunately a nuclear power plant site is very stable in terms of the physical geography. In other environments, such as "cube farms" in office buildings where the physical area can change considerably over several months, some or the entire site survey may need to be audited or repeated to ensure its accuracy. In all deployments where more than a few access points are to be deployed, a relatively recent site survey, or a site survey in an area that has not changed, is an important element of owning and maintaining a highly robust 802.11 system.

CAUTION   Movement of large objects such as file cabinets, metal shelves and so forth need not take place in the area of *intended* coverage; rather, movement of large objects in an adjacent room or floor can also have an impact on the area of coverage.

The good news about having a lag period of weeks or even a few months between the time of site survey to the time of installation is that the system will be tested during installation and checked against the site survey information. Adjustments to optimize areas of coverage are typical, but should not occur as a matter of routine during the installation as long as there have been few changes to the physical area that underwent the site survey.

Hardware

The hardware in use at the nuclear power plant included the following elements:

- Access points
- PCMCIA client adapters
- Bridges
- Security cameras
- Mobile access router
- 802.11 phones

The most common element other than PCMCIA client adapters are the access points that are installed at nearly 500 different locations at the nuclear plant site, which in this deployment includes both internal to the power block as well as the normal office settings throughout the campus. Most of them are the Cisco 1200 series access points, but many of them are the more commonly-deployed AP-350.

The PCMCIA client adapters selected are the Cisco PCM-350 adapters, which are presently the most commonly sold client adapter into the enterprise market. They feature award-winning performance along with the highest degree of interoperability with other 802.11 compliant devices. These client adapters will be deployed in laptops and PDAs on the site.

A number of the buildings will be connected by 802.11 bridges—in particular, a training facility situated away from the main campus across a body of water and farther down an access road of approximately half a mile. One of the many advantages a nuclear power plant has is that of elevation. In other words, a number of the buildings have more than enough elevation to support outdoor bridges.

The security cameras used at the nuclear power plant site are not provided by Cisco or any other 802.11 vendor, but rather by one or more video vendors which specialize in video cameras that have pan/tilt/zoom (PTZ) features as well as thermal imaging, motion detection, and variable resolution. What is unique about these cameras is that the latest generation are now mounted in security vehicles, interconnected by 802.11, and their output can be received by iPAQs or other PDAs outfitted with an 802.11 card. This enables not only real-time remote monitoring of high security areas, but also provides for campus perimeter security with patrolling vehicles.

Mobile access routers play an important role in this capability, and this device, while palm-sized, has the same performance of a Cisco 3640 router—very considerable by any measure.

The concept behind an MAR is to combine such disparate communications mediums and protocols as 802.11, satellite, cellular, and public emergency frequencies onto one easily-managed platform. A number of devices can be attached to the 3200, specifically, in this case, a security video camera and an 802.11 mini-PCI card, the combination of which enables the nuclear plant to have real-time video on a roving basis. The final 802.11 element to consider in this deployment is an 802.11 phone.

An 802.11 phone is a particularly interesting 802.11 device because it takes 802.11 usage to unprecedented heights, as 802.11 users can now communicate effectively with each other over the 802.11 infrastructure. This is of particular value at the nuclear plant site for two compelling reasons, the first being that the Motorola two-way radios have a lot of time on them, although they still perform admirably well in spite of their age, which is well in excess of 10 years. The second, and arguably the more compelling rationale for going to an 802.11 phone over a conventional two-way radio inside the power block, is that the conventional two-way radios won't work in areas where the rooms are effectively sealed in a manner such that radio waves are essentially constrained to the rooms. An 802.11 phone, of course, features connectivity to an access point which is hard wired to the existing intranet which enables the phone to communicate effectively to devices outside of water tight rooms with thick steel doors an walls of concrete in excess of a meter in thickness.

Software

Like any other 802.11 deployment, the software featured at this site center on three different types, which are drivers, security, and management.

The software drivers exist to enable the 802.11 hardware on the selected user platform, and also to enable the configuration and local management of same through the setting of preferences. The security software is layered over the management software, or integrated as separate software. The management software that is used by the network administrators and is the software probably discussed more than the others as it enables the network administrators to manage new users, the performance of the access points, security breaches, and various performance and reliability alarms. Of the three types of software, the management software is often the most faceted and complex and there are versions for small deployments as well as versions for large deployments.

The management software utilized by the nuclear plant network administrators is sometimes provided by a company called Wavelink, which specializes in the management of 802.11 systems in enterprise and campus networks. This software enables WLAN network managers to accomplish five specific tasks, which are:

- Support multi-vendor wireless LAN elements
- Decrease deployment times for WLAN elements
- Maintenance
- Manage remote site WLANs from a centralized location
- Extend and enhance existing WLAN security measures

The nuclear power plant customer specifically did not want to have a mixed vendor environment, but this is somewhat unusual in the campus and enterprise network market, as many customers either migrate from one vendor to another for technology, pricing, or support reasons, and the larger customers commonly require more than a single vendor to help mitigate potential supply and support problems. Wavelink software currently supports all the leading 802.11 vendors such as Cisco, Symbol, Ericsson, and Intel.

Software provided by companies like Wavelink will auto-detect access points as they are turned on, and then automatically distribute predefined settings such as IP address and other configuration parameters instead of having the integration technician configure each access point one at a time as they are turned on and brought into the network. This type of software will also alert network administrators to such network conditions as removal of access points or various failure conditions and performance degradations. These alerts can be sent to network administrators by e-mail or pager or forwarded to an alert monitoring console, similar to how most enterprise and campus networks are managed.

One additional advantage to management software is that all of the WLAN elements can be managed from a single site, even if the access points are other elements that are distributed over a very wide area or in disparate buildings. This provides a clear advantage as opposed to having to visit each radio independently for maintenance or upgrades. Another key advantage is that centralized management is the best way to provide and mange access control lists, which are commonly changed, such that all users have to be authorized from a central office location, which enhances network security. Further, for the networks running WEP security protocol, this type of management software can automatically rotate the WEP keys, the rotation of which is a fundamental security enhancement.

Security

Security, of course, is an element of high consideration at a nuclear power plant. The physical barriers and checkpoints to entry are formidable and will not be disclosed in this appendix for obvious reasons. The complex in general has a number of variable levels of physical security that are designed to provide an optimum compromise between efficiency and operational velocity while yet maintaining the highest degree of physical security within the power block and other areas.

Network security is obviously an issue of prime concern at a facility such as this, and the concept of 802.11 is commonly referred to as the same as having an ether jack in a parking lot or building across the street from the protected area. This, while being technically true, provides an opportunity to reconsider the concept that 802.11 security issues are fundamentally not wireless security issues, but rather network security issues.

Contemporary 802.11 network elements include a protocol called WEP, which stands for *wired equivalent privacy*, and is referred to as a defeated algorithm. This premise is treated in full in the chapter on security in this work.

As the 802.11 equipment on this project was provided by Cisco Systems, the worldwide leader in WLAN security, it's important to note that there are fundamentally three levels of security available:

- Open access
- Basic security
- Enhanced security

Again, as the premise of security has been treated in detail elsewhere in this book, we'll focus on what was deployed at the nuclear plant site, which would, of course, be the enhanced security version of 802.11. This included not only the ability to rotate keys through the Cisco Extensible Authentication Protocol (LEAP), but also includes VPN capability for remote worker access, and Virtual Private Network (VLAN) capabilities. To allay confusion, it's important to note that LEAP is a Cisco proprietary security protocol that is focused on authentication as opposed to encryption. Authentication and encryption are what might be referred to as the twin towers of security, and LEAP provides one of those essential elements.

LEAP is a protocol for enhanced security requirements, and is used by all who lawfully enter the network, whether they access the network onsite or remotely through the Internet. VPNs are more traditionally used for telecommuters and travelers who require access to the network. Again, we can see that these protocols are "wireless" protocols, but rather network security protocols.

The VPN capability is an element provided by the non-802.11 portion of the network, and it requires a thin software client to reside on the client devices such as laptop computers and PDAs.

Perhaps one of the most interesting elements of the 802.11 network equipment is its ability to provide VLAN capabilities. Each access point can support up to 16 separate VLANs, which are unique collision domains that can also be thought of as virtual bridges. One of the key capabilities of this technology is that it enables all the 802.11 voice users to remain on one virtual collision domain, and other users on other collision domains, depending on who they are, the type of traffic they generate, and their location.

A VLAN is a networking capability common to Ethernet switches, especially those from the world market leader in Ethernet switches, Cisco. VLANs allow networks to be segmented on a logical basis, as opposed to a physical basis. In other words, you can have different groups of users in the same common physical area. Each end-user device, such as a laptop or PDA, can be assigned a VLAN identification number (ID), and end-user devices with the same VLAN ID operate as though they are all on the same physical network. Where this is specifically of value is when the network carries more than one type of traffic, and the VLANs can be managed at either Layer 2 or 3, depending on the type of switching technology in use; at the nuclear plant site it is switched at Layer 2. The use of VLANs increases network performance, although it does incur a modest amount of additional complexity at the network management level. Where the VLAN capability truly hits its home run at the nuclear plant is during the two 30-day maintenance shut-down periods where the reactors are shut down and the plant ceases to supply electricity to the regional grid. Thousands of contractors arrive at the site to perform various types of maintenance work, and the ability to have them communicate with their home bases and other sites via the Internet without going directly onto the nuclear plant network is very desirable.

In simple terms, the contractors are given what is termed a "dirty VLAN," which means a VLAN that can be accessed by anyone near the campus, or by Ethernet port. This VLAN is logically separated from the rest of the plant's network, which enables a high degree of network security to remain in place while also providing high speed and cost effective communications for thousands of contractors who are operating under a very tight schedule.

802.11 Network Uses

There is an array of areas in which the site increases productivity, reduces errors, and mitigates the need for increasingly valuable "institutional memory" to be at each and every physical site on the campus to enable day-to-day operational decisions. The key areas in which an 802.11 network enhances the day-to-day operations of the nuclear plant include ubiquitous communications to maintenance, security, and corporate operations.

Ubiquitous high-speed communications translate into increased event velocity. Perhaps nowhere else at the nuclear site is this more imperative, outside of a reactor anomaly. As stated earlier, two of the most critical events at the plant site each year are the bi-annual maintenance shutdown events where the plant ceases to produce electricity in order to complete routine and scheduled maintenance activities. These events are limited to two 30-day durations, and represent an opportunity cost of approximately one million dollars per day of lost revenue. This translates into a time-critical event in which all maintenance functions must be completed before the 30-day period elapses. The value of high-speed ubiquitous communications for both contractors and the plant site are obvious and compelling. With 802.11 devices built into or added onto conventional devices such as laptop computers and PDAs, the need to build temporary communications hard-wired links is obviated. The ability for contractors and employees to be able to communicate with each other regardless of their location inside the power block or anywhere else on the campus is also obvious in its value and ability to increase maintenance velocity.

Velocity in business is a hot topic. The winner in business is not always the biggest, or even the best, but sometimes the fastest. It is publicly known and understood doctrine that the employer of the two authors of this book places a high premium on business velocity, and there is a relentless pursuit of increase efficiency and velocity, and every employee is aware of the metrics which are used to measure this capability, and they are also aware of the efficiency and velocity targets set for the following year.

The ability for an employee to review his or her human resources, healthcare, managerial, task management, and other day-to-day business information in a ubiquitous manner is an important part of continual process improvement. Productivity gains of 45 minutes per day or more are common when employees have access to their intranet and the Internet from virtually any location at their work site. By installing access points at key meeting and work locations, such as conference and lunch rooms, employees gain a new level of access to the information that is vital to them, not the least of which are e-mail communications, and now with 802.11 phones, they can also receive phone calls regardless of whether or not they are at their desk. This concept will become as fondly adopted as that of laptop computers and cell phones over the next few short years.

Security is an item of the highest priority, and in fact ranks equal or asymptotically close to safety as a prime issue of focus at the site. With the ability for all security personnel to observe real-time video of any area of the entire campus from a PDA, the site achieves unprecedented levels of security, and the ability to observe and manage security-related events. The nuclear plant personnel also witnessed a demonstration of voice-activated dialing to an iPAC via an ear-mounted Bluetooth-based device. This capability would enable security personnel to not take their hands off of their weapons or other devices while establishing and maintaining communications with all other security and management personnel at the site, and while performing their nominal security missions. The ability to mount video cameras on patrol vehicles, and even on patrol personnel, is also a compelling and cost-effective technological capability that cannot be overlooked. High-speed, real-time video, voice, and data communications have a vital role to play on the day-to-day operational capability of this site, which translate into enhanced security, safety, and profitability for this important national asset.

APPENDIX B

Glossary

Many of the following terms are generally more often associated with network elements such as routers, switches, and so forth, and many of the other terms pertain to the issue of network security. These terms are intentionally included in this glossary because 802.11 elements, when properly deployed, configured, and managed, are no longer simply "radios," but rather should be considered as essential network elements that operate in a highly secure manner while retaining a high degree of performance. You'll also see some terms of art that aren't necessarily part of either the 802.11 or network lexicons, but are included because they are associated with other closely related subjects.

802.1X An IEEE standard that defines the operation of a MAC bridge in order to provide port-based network access control capability. This standard uses the Extensible Authentication Protocol (EAP), and ties it to the physical medium, be it Ethernet, Token Ring, or wireless LAN. EAP messages are encapsulated in 802.1X messages and referred to as EAP over LAN (EAPOL)

802.11i An IEEE standard that focuses on enhancing the current 802.11 MAC to improve security.

access method Generally, the way in which network devices access the network at large; in other words, the medium that connects LANs. Examples include broadband fixed wireless, DSL, and cable modems.

adjacent channel A channel or frequency that is directly above or below a specific channel or frequency.

AES Acronym for Advanced Encryption Standard. AES is a U.S. Federal Information Processing Standards (FIPS) standard, and specifically refers to FIPS Publication 197, which specifies a cryptographic algorithm for use by U.S. government organizations to protect sensitive, unclassified information. Security experts generally agree that this standard will rapidly be adopted on a voluntary basis by many commercial entities and network development companies such as Cisco and others.

algorithm Well-defined rule or process for arriving at a solution to a problem.

amplitude The magnitude or strength of a varying waveform.

analog signal The representation of information with a continuously variable physical quantity, such as voltage. Because of this constant changing of the wave shape with regard to its passing a given point in time or space, an analog signal may have an infinite number of states or values. This contrasts with a digital signal, which has a very limited number of discrete states.

ANSI Acronym for American National Standards Institute. Voluntary organization composed of corporate, governmental, and other members that coordinates standards-related activities, approves U.S. national standards, and develops positions for the United States in international standards organizations. ANSI helps develop international and U.S. standards relating to, among other things, communications and networking. ANSI is a member of IEC and ISO.

antenna A device for transmitting or receiving a radio frequency (RF). Antennas are usually designed for specific and relatively tightly defined frequencies and are quite varied in design. As an example, an antenna for a 2.5GHz (MMDS) system will generally not work for a 28GHz (LMDS) design.

antenna gain The measure of an antenna *assembly* performance relative to a theoretically perfect antenna called an isotropic radiator (*radiator* is another term for antenna). Certain antenna designs feature higher performance relative to radiating a specific area or with regard to frequencies.

AP Acronym for access point. An access point is a device which commonly connects client devices such as PCMCIA cards to the Ethernet portion of a LAN. An access point generally has an Ethernet port and power port it's backside and includes one or two antennas which transmit and receive RF signals from client devices, other access points, or work group bridges.

application layer Layer 7 of the OSI reference model. This layer provides services to application processes (such as e-mail, file transfer, and terminal emulation) that are outside of the OSI model. The application layer identifies and establishes the availability of intended communication partners (and the resources required to connect with them), synchronizes cooperating applications, and establishes agreement on procedures for error recovery and control of data integrity.This layer corresponds roughly with the transaction services layer in the SNA model. *Other associated terms include* **data-link layer**, **network layer**, **physical layer**, **session layer**, and **transport layer**.

ARP   Acronym for address resolution protocol. An OSI Layer 3 protocol used to map IP network addresses to the hardware addresses used by a Layer 2 data-link protocol. The protocol operates when IP is carried over Ethernet.

ARQ   Acronym for automatic repeat request. Communication technique in which the receiving device detects errors and requests retransmissions.

ASCII   Acronym for American Standard Code for Information Interchange. Specifies 8-bit code for character representation (7 bits plus parity).

ATM   Acronym for Asynchronous Transfer Mode. International standard for cell relay in which multiple service types (such as voice, video, or data) are conveyed in fixed-length (53-byte) cells. Fixed-length cells allow cell processing to occur in hardware, thereby reducing transit delays. ATM is designed to take advantage of high-speed transmission media such as E3, SONET, and T3.

attenuation   Loss of communication signal energy, whether by equipment design, operator manipulation, or transmission through a medium such as the atmosphere, copper, or fiber.

authentication   In security, the verification of the identity of a person or process.

backbone   Part of a network that acts as the primary path for traffic that is most often sourced from, and destined for, other networks.

backplane   Physical connection between an interface processor or card and the data buses and the power distribution buses inside a chassis.

bandwidth   The frequency range necessary to convey a signal, measured in units of hertz (Hz). For example, voice signals typically require approximately 7kHz of bandwidth, and data traffic typically requires approximately 50kHz of bandwidth, but this depends greatly on modulation scheme, data rates, and how many channels of a radio spectrum are used.

baseband   Characteristic of a network technology where only one carrier frequency is used. Ethernet is an example of a baseband network. Also called *narrowband*.

baud Unit of signaling speed equal to the number of discrete signal elements transmitted per second. Baud is synonymous with bits per second (bps) if each signal element represents exactly 1 bit.

BBFW Acronym for broadband fixed wireless. One of the most commonly used terms in the fixed wireless industry. In general, it implies data transfers in excess of 1.5Mbps.

beamwidth Refers to the "directiveness" of an antenna, more specifically used in regard to a parabola or yagi and is defined as the angle between two half-power (–3dB) points on either side of the main lobe of radiation.

BER Acronym for bit error ratio. Ratio of received bits that contain errors compared to bits received without error.

best effort The type of traffic that has the lowest priority between two or more devices. Best effort traffic is commonly data that is not sensitive to delay. E-mail is generally the best example of this.

bit A contraction of *binary digit*, which is the smallest possible unit of information a computer can handle. An alphabetic character or number is generally made up of 8 bits, which comprise 1 *byte* of information. Therefore, a single character, such as the letter *b*, requires a combination of eight 1s and 0s.

block A *block* of information is that of a certain size which is treated as a single unit. For example, 64 DES is a common encryption method used on the Internet, and is termed *64 DES* because it encrypts 64 bits at a time. While even a single bit can be encrypted, it would be rather easy to decode; that is, the solution would likely be the opposite of that which is shown. In other words, if the encrypted bit is a 0, the decoded value would be a 1.

BootPC Short for Bootstrap Protocol-Client. BootPC is a boot protocol used to acquire a number identifying a server or other platform. Other information is also acquired by this protocol such as IP number, as well as setting up DNS. In order to boot over the network, the computer must usually acquire three things: 1.) an identity, 2.) an operating system image and 3.) usually, a working filesystem.

BootPS Short for Bootstrap Protocol-Server

BPSK Acronym for binary phase shift keying. A digital frequency modulation technique used for transmitting information. This type of modulation is less efficient but more robust than similar modulation techniques, such as QPSK and 64QAM.

bridge Device that connects and passes packets between two network segments that use the same communications protocol. Bridges operate at the data-link layer (Layer 2) of the OSI reference model. In general, a bridge will filter, forward, or flood an incoming frame based on the MAC address of that frame.

broadband In general, describes a data system that has a constant data rate at or in excess of 1.5Mbps. Its corresponding opposite is *narrowband*. Historically, it refers to a transmission system that multiplexes multiple independent signals onto one cable, or, in telecommunications terminology, it refers to any channel having a bandwidth greater than a voice-grade channel (4kHz). In LAN terms, it can refer to a coaxial cable on which analog signaling is used. Also called *wideband* (by LAN definition).

broadcast In general, the opposite of *narrowcast* and infers that a signal is sent to many points at the same time and/or is transmitted in an omnidirectional pattern. In the radio world, "broadcast" is a term of art, which means it has a special meaning relative to a specific technology. A "broadcast" signal is one that's intended for reception by the general public. This should not be confused with the term "multicast," in which a single originating point connects with multiple sites; in the networking world, "multicast" and "broadcast" are synonymous.

BTA Acronym for basic trading area. The geographical area frequently used by the FCC for assigning licensed frequencies. BTAs are typically contiguous counties or trading areas and were first described by the Rand McNally mapping company. Rand McNally eventually licensed these area descriptions to the FCC.

buffer Storage area used for handling data in transit. Buffers are used in internetworking to compensate for differences in processing speed between network devices. Bursts of data can be stored in buffers until they can be handled by slower-processing devices. Sometimes referred to as a *packet buffer*.

byte A series of consecutive binary digits that are operated upon as a unit (for example, an 8-bit byte).

caching Form of replication in which information learned during a previous transaction is used to process later transactions.

CALEA Acronym for Communications Assistance for Law Enforcement Act. A set of federal laws enacted within the United States that requires that all BBFW providers that can carry voice over their networks be able to intercept and deliver to law enforcement agencies detailed information on voice calls that originate or terminate within their area of geographic coverage.

carrier frequency The frequency of a transmitted signal that would be transmitted if it were not modulated. Some BBFW systems also have intermediate frequencies, which reside between the indoor equipment and the outdoor equipment. Carrier "frequency" can be either a single frequency or a range of frequencies carried at one time between the transmitter and receiver.

Category 5 cabling One of five grades of UTP cabling described in the EIA/TIA-586 standard. Category 5 cabling can transmit data at speeds up to 100Mbps.

CBR Acronym for committed bit rate. A prioritization of information that is higher than BE-type traffic, but lower than unsolicited grant service (UGS). In ATM networks, CBR refers to constant bit rate and is used for connections that depend on precise clocking to ensure undistorted delivery.

CDMA Acronym for Code Division Multiple Access. A transmission scheme that allows multiple users to share the same RF range of frequencies. In effect, the system divides a small range of frequencies out of a larger set and divides the data transmission among them. The transmitting device divides the data among a preselected set of nonsequential frequencies. The receiver then collates the various data "pieces" from the disparate frequencies and into a coherent data stream. As part of the RF system setup, the receiver components are "advised" of the scrambled order of the incoming frequencies. An important aspect of this scheme is that the receiver system filters out any signals other than the ones specified for a given transmission.

certificate A digitally signed statement from one entity saying that the public key of some other entity has some particular value. Certificates are a common concept in modern society. We use them for drivers licenses, for club memberships, and as identification. These items bind a public key to an individual, position, or organization.

channel A communications path. Multiple channels can be multiplexed over a single contiguous amount of spectrum. It also refers to a specific frequency allocation and bandwidth. As an example, downstream channels used for television in the United States are 6MHz wide.

checksum An integer value computed from a sequence of octets taken through a series of arithmetic operations. The value is recomputed at the receiving end and compared for verification. Checksums are used as a method for checking the integrity of transmitted data.

cipher A key that converts plaintext to ciphertext. This is not to be confused with some forms of secret codes in which certain words or phrases are replaced with secret code words or phrases.

ciphertext Text that has been *ciphered*, or encrypted. While the ciphertext contains the same information as the plaintext, it may or may not be the same number of bits. Certain lower-end systems may have difficulty accommodating encryption, the technical term being *data expansion ciphering*. Ciphertext always requires a key to determine the plaintext.

CLI Acronym for command-line interface. Where the network technicians control the actual radio settings. Resides on the routers or switches at each end of the BBFW. Commonly and appropriately screen-saver, username, and password protected.

coaxial cable The type of cable used to connect BBFW equipment to antennas and indoor/outdoor gear. Coaxial cable, or *coax*, usually consists of a center wire surrounded by a metal shield with an insulator separating the two. The "axis" of the cable is located down the center of the cable. "Coaxial" means that there is more than one conductor oriented around a common axis for the length of the cable. Coaxial cable is one of the primary means for transporting cable TV and radio signals.

collision domain In Ethernet, the network area within which frames that have collided are propagated. Repeaters and hubs propagate collisions; LAN switches, bridges, and routers do not.

convergence Speed and ability of a group of internetworking devices running a specific routing protocol to agree on the topology of an internetwork after a change in that topology.

converter Converts the intermediate frequency to and from the carrier frequency. Some RF systems have two fundamental frequencies: one that is sent over the air (carrier frequency) and another that is sent back and forth between the indoor equipment and the outdoor equipment (intermediate frequency. (Also referred to as *up/down converter* or *transverter*.

cookies Store information that users provide to a web server at some point. Each time a web site is accessed, a trail about the user is left behind. This could include the user's computer name and IP address, operating system, and the URL of the last page visited. While cookies themselves are not gathering data, they can be used as a tracking device. A cookie cannot read data to find out your identity or your home address. But, if you provide that information to a site, it could be saved to a cookie. As more information is gathered, it is associated with the value kept in your cookie.

CRC Acronym for cyclic redundancy check. Error-checking technique in which the frame recipient calculates a remainder by dividing frame contents by a prime binary divisor, and compares the calculated remainder to a value stored in the frame by the sending node.

cryptanalysis An analysis of the strength of the cryptography used to secure information. Cryptanalysts continually evaluate the manner in which codes are broken in order to produce even more sophisticated ciphertext, which is often eventually broken, thereby fueling rounds of "cat and mouse." In the end, however, true data security is established not by the sole use of a highly sophisticated encryption technique, but rather by maintaining a minimum level of security for the entire operation. Also referred to as *code breaking*.

data-link layer Layer 2 of the OSI reference model. Provides reliable transit of data across a physical link. The data-link layer is concerned with physical addressing, network topology, line discipline, error notification, ordered delivery of frames, and flow control. IEEE divides this layer into two sublayers: the MAC sublayer and the LLC sublayer. Sometimes this is simply called the link layer. It roughly corresponds to the data-link control layer of the SNA model.

data encryption key Used for the encryption of message text and for the computation of message integrity checks (signatures).

dB Abbreviation for decibel. A unit for expressing a ratio of power or voltage in terms of gain or loss. Units are expressed logarithmically and typically in watts. dB is not an absolute value, but rather is the measure of power loss or gain between two devices. For example, –3dB indicates a 50 percent loss in power, and +3dB indicates a doubling of power. The rule of thumb to remember is that 10dB indicates an increase (or loss) by a factor of 10; 20dB indicates an increase (or loss) by a factor of 100; and 30dB indicates an increase (or loss) by a factor of 1000. Gain or loss is expressed with a + or – sign before the number. Because antennas and other RF devices/ systems commonly have power gains or losses of four orders of magnitude, dB is a more easily used expression.

dBi Abbreviation for decibels of antenna gain referenced to the gain of an isotropic antenna (hence the *i*). An isotropic antenna is a theoretical antenna that radiates with perfect symmetry in all three dimensions. Real-world antennas have radiation patterns that are far from symmetric, but this effect is generally used to advantage by the system designer to optimize coverage over a specific geographic area.

dBm Abbreviation for decibels of power referenced to a milliwatt; 0dBm is 1mW.

dBW Abbreviation for decibels of power referenced to 1 watt.

demodulator The part of a receiver for assembling signals from the radio into a format usable by the network or device attached to the radio. The corresponding device on the transmission side of a system is a *modulator*.

DES Acronym for Data Encryption Standard. Standard cryptographic algorithm used by the U.S. National Bureau of Standards. In networking terms, DES also stands for destination end station.

DHCP Acronym for Dynamic Host Configuration Protocol. Provides a mechanism for allocating IP addresses dynamically so that addresses can be reused when hosts no longer need them.

domain A general grouping of LANs based on organization type or geography.

downtilt The downward angle used on directional antennas, such as parabolas or yagis, which enhances coverage closer to the base of the antenna mast or tower. Typically, most antennas have zero to six degrees of downtilt, but this greatly depends on the application and deployment scenario.

DNS   Acronym for Domain Name System (as well as Domain Name Service).

DS-0   Acronym for Digital Signal level 0. Framing specification used in transmitting digital signals over a single channel at 64Kbps. Compare with DS-1 at 1.544Mbps (commonly referred to as 1.5Mbps), and DS-3 at 44.736Mbps (commonly referred to as 45Mbps).

DSSS   Acronym for direct sequence spread spectrum. A spreading technique in which various data, voice, and/or video signals are transmitted over a specific set of frequencies in a sequential manner from lowest to highest frequency, or highest to lowest frequency. *See* **spread spectrum**, **FHSS**.

E-1   Wide-area digital transmission scheme used predominantly in Europe that carries data at a rate of 2.048Mbps. E-1 lines can be leased for private use from common carriers.

EAP   Acronym for Extensible Authentication Protocol. Ensures mutual authentication between a wireless client and a server that resides at the network operations center (NOC). EAP by itself does not provide mutual authentication, as is evidenced by EAP-MD5. The server for an 802.1X authentication type does not have to reside at the NOC.

EAP-MD5   Acronym for Extensible Authentication Protocol Message Digest 5. An IETF standard for carrying various authentication methods over any Point-to-Point Protocol (PPP) connection. EAP-MD5 is a username/password method that incorporates MD5 hashing for security.

EAP-SIM   EAP for use in GSM-type phones, which are predominantly in Europe and Asia, though becoming more common in the United States. SIM refers to the SIM cards that imbed manually into phones and other devices and contain user information and certain security elements. EAP-SIM is a protocol that would enable devices such as mobile phones to authenticate to 802.11 networks.

EAP-SIM6   Same definition as EAP-SIM except that it refers to the emerging IPv6 network protocol.

EAP-TLS   Acronym for Extensible Authentication Protocol-Transport Level Security. A protocol that provides for mutual authentication, integrity-protected cipher negotiation, and key exchange between two end points.

EIRP Acronym for effective isotropic radiated power. Expresses the performance of a transmitting system in a given direction. EIRP is the power that a system using an isotropic antenna would use to send the same amount of power in a given direction that a system with a directional antenna uses. EIRP is usually expressed in watts or dBW. EIRP is the sum of the power at the antenna input plus antenna gain, expressed in dBi.

electromagnetic spectrum The full range of electromagnetic (same as magnetic) frequencies, a subset of which is used in commercial RF systems.

encapsulation Wrapping of data in a particular protocol header. For example, Ethernet data is wrapped in a specific Ethernet header before network transit. Also, when bridging dissimilar networks, the entire frame from one network is simply placed in the header used by the data-link layer protocol of the other network.

encryption Application of a specific algorithm to data so as to alter the appearance of the data, making it incomprehensible to those who are not authorized to see the information.

equalization Technique used to compensate for communications channel distortions.

Ethernet Baseband LAN specification invented by Xerox Corporation and developed jointly by Xerox, Intel, and Digital Equipment Corporation. Ethernet networks use CSMA/CD and run over a variety of cable types at 10Mbps. Ethernet is similar to the IEEE 802.3 series of standards.

ETSI Acronym for European Telecommunication Standards Institute. Organization created by the European PTTs and the EC to propose telecommunications standards for Europe.

Fast Ethernet Any of a number of 100Mbps Ethernet specifications. Fast Ethernet offers a speed increase ten times that of the 10BaseT Ethernet specification, while preserving such qualities as frame format, MAC mechanisms, and MTU. Such similarities allow the use of existing 10BaseT applications and network management tools on Fast Ethernet networks. Based on an extension to the IEEE 802.3 specification.

FCC Acronym for Federal Communications Commission. U.S. government agency that supervises, licenses, and controls electronic and electromagnetic transmission standards.

FDM   Acronym for frequency division multiplexing. The modulation scheme that divides the total available spectrum into subsets, which are commonly used in parallel across one or more links.

FH   Acronym for frequency hopping. Frequency hopping is where a transmitter sends bits of information sequentially over a number of radio channels in what is called a pseudo-random order; i.e., there are so many combinations of the radio channels that it appears to be random, but it is vital that both the transmitter and receiver know which channel to be on and for how long at any given point in time.

FHSS   Acronym for frequency hopping spread spectrum. A spreading technique in which various data, voice, and/or video signals are transmitted over a specific set of frequencies in a pseudo-random order, rather than in a sequential manner from lowest to highest frequency, or highest to lowest frequency, as with DSSS. The signals are spread in the time domain, not the frequency domain. *See* **DSSS** and **spread spectrum**.

file virus   The most common kind of virus, which typically goes after a file with a certain extension, such as .doc or .exe. File viruses attack by overwriting parts of the file such that the file becomes unusable or highly unstable, which then crashes the PC, server, or router. File viruses, as with sector viruses, can often reside in the RAM portion of the PC, server, or router, and thus care needs to be taken in rooting them out during the repair phase.

FIPS   Acronym for Federal Information Processing Standards. FIPS refers primarily to standards with regard to information security.

firewall   Router or access server, or several routers or access servers, designated as a buffer between any connected public networks and a private network. A firewall router uses access lists and other methods to ensure the security of the private network.

fixed wireless   The type of wireless in which both the transmitter and receiver are nonmobile. BBFW is always broadband wireless; in other words, it is capable of data rates in excess of 1.5Mbps, though the links can be throttled to data rates below that, but typically not less than 256Kbps downstream and 128Kbps upstream.

flow control   Technique for ensuring that a transmitting entity, such as a modem, does not overwhelm a receiving entity with data. When the buffers on the receiving device are full, a message is sent to the sending device to suspend the transmission until the data in the buffers has been processed.

footprint   The geographical area covered by a transmitter.

Fourier transform   Technique used to evaluate the importance of various frequency cycles in a time series pattern.

fragmentation   Process of breaking a packet into smaller units when transmitting over a network medium that cannot support the original size of the packet.

frame   Logical grouping of information sent as a data-link layer unit over a transmission medium. Often refers to the header and trailer, used for synchronization and error control, that surround the user data contained in the unit. The terms cell, datagram, message, packet, and segment are also used to describe logical information groupings at various layers of the OSI reference model and in various technology circles.

frequency   Number of cycles, measured in hertz (once per second), of an alternating current signal per unit of time. For example, a 1MHz frequency would have a full cycle (a complete sine wave) pass a given point in space at the rate of one million cycles per second. A 1GHz frequency would have sine waves pass a given point in space at the rate of one billion times per second, and so forth.

frequency reuse   One of the fundamental concepts on which commercial wireless systems are based, which involves the partitioning of an RF radiating area (cell) into segments of a cell, which for BBFW purposes means the cell can be broken into up to 13 or more equal segments. Notably, most RF cells are segmented into either three or four segments. One segment of the cell uses a frequency that is far enough away from the frequency in the bordering segment that it does not provide interference problems.

Frequency reuse in mobile cellular systems means that each cell has a frequency that is far enough away from the frequency in the bordering cell that it does not provide interference problems. Identical frequencies are used at least two cells apart from each other. This practice enables cellular providers to have many more customers for a given site license.

Fresnel zones Theoretically, ellipsoid volumes that reside in the space between a transmitting and a receiving antenna. The industry rule of thumb for line-of-sight links is to leave 60 percent of the centermost part of the first Fresnel zone free from obstruction. There are many Fresnel zones within an RF link, and they are often referred to as the First Fresnel Zone, Second Fresnel Zone, and so on as the area referred to is farther from the center of the beam path.

FTP Acronym for File Transfer Protocol. Application protocol, part of the TCP/IP protocol stack, used for transferring files between network nodes.

full duplex Capability for simultaneous data transmission between a sending station and a receiving station. Half duplex is where only one side of a link can transmit at a time; simplex is where there is only one transmitter and one receiver in a link.

FWA Acronym for fixed wireless access. Also referred to as BBFWA (broadband fixed wireless access).

gain For an amplifier, the ratio of the output amplitude of a signal to the input amplitude of a signal. This ratio is typically expressed in decibels. For an antenna, the ratio of its directivity in a given direction compared to some reference antenna. The higher the gain, the more directional the antenna pattern.

Gb Abbreviation for gigabit. Approximately one billion bits.

Gbps Abbreviation for gigabits per second.

GHz Abbreviation for one billion cycles per second.

goodput The net amount of data transmitted minus the overhead traffic to manage the link or connection. Sometimes referred to as **throughput**.

GRE Acronym for generic routing encapsulation. A protocol which allows an arbitrary network protocol to be transmitted over any other network protocol. This is accomplished by encapsulating the packets of the source network within GRE packets, which are carried by the receiving, or transit network.

headend Main point of a BBFW network. All CPE units transmit toward the headend; the headend then transmits toward a number of CPE devices.

header Control information placed before data when encapsulating that data for network transmission.

HSRP   Acronym for Hot Standby Routing Protocol. HSRP allows for redundant paths for information on a "hot standby" basis. If the primary route goes down, the packets will be sent over a secondary path with no apparent delay or disruption to the network users.

HTTP   Acronym for Hypertext Transfer Protocol. HTTP is a low overhead protocol that allows for text and images to be carried over a wide array of different information systems. It is a generic object-oriented protocol that may be used for many similar tasks such as name servers, and distributed object-oriented systems, by extending the commands, or "methods," used.

IAPP   Acronym for Inter Access Point Protocol. A protocol proposed by the largest providers of 802.11 equipment with the intent of having a high degree of interoperability with regard to security, mobility, handover, and other higher functions that are not generally addressed by the Wi-Fi certification provided by the Wireless Ethernet Compatibility Alliance. It is an extension of the IEEE 802.11 implemented on top of IP and uses UDP/IP and SNAP as the transfer protocol.

IEEE   Acronym for Institute of Electrical and Electronics Engineers.

interference   Unwanted communication noise that decreases the performance of a link or prevents a link from occurring.

IOS   Acronym for internetwork operating system.

IPSec   Short for Internet Protocol Security.

ISM Bands   It is generally, but not always, agreed that the Industrial Scientific and Medical bands are 902- to 928MHz; 2.4- to 2.485GHz; 5.15- to 5.35GHz; and 5.725- to 5.825GHz.

isochronous transmission   Asynchronous transmission over a synchronous data link. Isochronous signals require a constant bit rate for reliable transport. Compare with asynchronous transmission.

ISP   Acronym for Internet service provider. An ISP is a provider of Internet access such as Earthlink, MSN, or AOL.

ITU   Acronym for International Telecommunication Union. International body that develops worldwide standards for telecommunications technologies.

IV Acronym for initialization vector. An external value needed to start off cipher operations; in other words, a mathematical value upon which the ciphertext depends for encrypting. An IV often can be seen as a form of message key. Generally, an IV must accompany the ciphertext, and so always expands the ciphertext by the size of the IV. In 802.11 networks, it is recommended that a unique IV be deployed on a per-packet basis to eliminate a predetermined sequence that hackers can exploit. In particular, this makes it difficult for hackers to write or use attacks that use mathematical tables that simply cycle the number of key combinations until one or more are discovered that work.

IXC Acronym for inter-exchange carrier. Common carrier providing long-distance connectivity between LATAs. The three major IXCs at this writing are AT&T, MCI WorldCom, and Sprint, but several hundred IXCs offer long-distance service in the United States.

jitter Analog communication line distortion caused by a signal that is sent in random time occurrences or excessive variances in signal timing. Jitter can cause data loss, particularly at high speeds.

Kb Abbreviation for kilobit. Approximately 1000 bits.

Kbps Abbreviation for kilobits per second.

key Used to "unlock" ciphertext; one may think of it in the same relative terms as a lock and key. A single key can generate a large number of different versions of ciphertext from the same plaintext. There are also different kinds of keys, such as the running key, which encrypts the sequence of a number of bits, and a message key, which is different for each and every message. In the use of keys like message keys, obviously both the transmission source and receiving source must know the order and specific key that is used on each transmission.

LAN Acronym for local area network. High-speed, low-error data network covering a relatively small geographic area (typically up to a few thousand meters). LANs connect workstations, peripherals, terminals, and other devices in a single building or other geographically limited area. LAN standards specify cabling and signaling at the physical and data-link layers of the OSI model. Ethernet, FDDI, and Token Ring are widely used LAN technologies. Compare with MAN and **WAN**.

latency   1. Delay between the time a device requests access to a network and the time it is granted permission to transmit. 2. Delay between the time a device receives a frame and the time that frame is forwarded to the destination port. Excessive latency is not generally a problem with e-mail, but can readily become a problem with latency-sensitive applications such as voice and video streaming.

LEAP   Acronym for Lightweight Extensible Authentication Protocol. A version of EAP (Extensible Authentication Protocol) and should be viewed as a shorthand name for EAP-Cisco Wireless, an 802.1X authentication type developed by Cisco and licensed to a restricted set of vendors, including some Cisco competitors. There are approximately five variants of EAP at this writing, including LEAP, EAP-SIM, EAP-PEAP, EAP-TTLS, and EAP-TLS. *See* **EAP**.

license   The purchased right to transmit RF waves over a given BTA on certain frequencies for a certain period of time. The license tightly governs the design parameters of an RF system and its use. Licenses are usually granted in a way that ensures a greatly reduced probability of interference from other users of the same spectrum. Depending on the licensed service and the country in which the license is issued, the license may be issued as the result of an auction, or as the result of a "beauty contest" in which the regulator evaluates the merits of proposals to use the spectrum. The theory behind auctions is that they use free-market forces so that a spectrum is put to its best use.

LMDS   Acronym for local multipoint distribution service. A relatively low power license for transmitting voice, video, and data. In the United States, there are typically two licenses granted in three frequencies, each to separate entities within a BTA. These licenses are known as Block A or Block B licenses. In the United States, Block A licenses are from 27.5- to 28.35GHz, 29.10- to 29.25GHz, and 31.075- to 31.225GHz for a total of 1.159GHz of bandwidth. Block B licenses operate from 31.00- to 31.075GHz and 31.225- to 31.300GHz for a total of 150MHz of bandwidth. LMDS systems have a typical maximum transmission range of approximately 3 miles, as opposed to the transmission range of an MMDS system, which is typically 25 miles. This difference in range is primarily a function of absorption due to precipitation and other physical phenomena, as well as FCC-allocated output power limits.

load balancing   In routing, the ability of a router to distribute traffic over all of its network ports that are the same distance from the destination address. Good load-balancing algorithms use both line speed and reliability information. Load balancing increases the use of network segments, thus increasing effective network bandwidth.

logic bomb   A virus, similar to a physical bomb planted by an individual, that lies in wait until triggered by an event like a specific date, number of times a program is executed, or even the deletion of a file. These viruses can be very destructive and are often difficult to locate prior to being executed.

LOS   Acronym for line of sight. Refers to the fact that there must be a clear, unobstructed path between transmitters and receivers. This is essential for millimeter wave products like LMDS and most microwave products lacking modulation and other schemes specifically designed to overcome the effects of a partially occluded (blocked) beam path. Having an LOS path enhances general performance in every RF deployment, as opposed to partially obstructed data paths. The opposite of LOS is NLOS, or near line of sight (also incorrectly referred to as nonline of sight).

MAC   Acronym for Media Access Control. The lower of the two sublayers of the data-link layer defined by the IEEE. The MAC sublayer handles access to shared media, such as whether token passing or contention will be used.

MAC address   Standardized data-link layer address that is required for every port or device that connects to a LAN. Other devices in the network use these addresses to locate specific ports in the network and to create and update routing tables and data structures. MAC addresses are 6 bytes long and are controlled by the IEEE. Also known as a hardware address, MAC layer address, and physical address.

macro virus   Resides within an application and is executed when loaded onto a hard drive. Macro viruses are not as well known as other virus types and most commonly reside in Microsoft Office applications such as Word, Excel, PowerPoint, Access, and so on.

Mb   Abbreviation for megabit. Approximately 1 million bits.

Mbps   Abbreviation for megabits per second.

MD5   A protocol that takes a message of arbitrary length and produces as output a 128-bit "fingerprint" or "message digest" of the input. MD5 was developed by Ron Rivest of MIT (who also helped develop RSA). MD5 ensures that no two messages will produce the same message digest, or produce any message having a given prespecified target message digest. MD5 is intended for use where a large file must be "digested" in a secure manner before being encrypted with a private (secret) key under a public-key cryptosystem such as RSA.

MD5 is considered a more reliable way to verify data integrity, than the more simple checksum and other commonly used methods.

MDU   Acronym for multiple dwelling unit. Condominium or apartment building.

MIC   Acronym for message integrity check.

MKK   The Japanese version of the U.S. FCC.

MMDS   Acronym for multichannel multipoint distribution service. A licensed frequency in the United States. The FCC has allocated two bands of frequencies to this service, 2.15- to 2.161GHz and 2.5- to 2.686GHz. Licenses have been assigned by BTA.

mobile wireless   The type of wireless utilized in mobile phones, PDAs, pagers, and other small, portable, battery-powered devices that can transmit and/or receive information by radio.

modem   Short for *mo*dulator/*dem*odulator. Device that converts digital and analog signals. At the source, a modem converts digital signals to a form suitable for transmission over analog communication facilities. At the destination, the analog signals are returned to their digital form. Modems allow data to be transmitted over voice-grade telephone lines.

modulation   Process by which the characteristics of electrical signals are transformed to represent information.

MTU   Acronym for multiple tenant unit. Building with multiple business tenants.

MxU   Acronym for multiple tenant unit or multiple dwelling unit.

NAT   Acronym for Network Address Translation. Mechanism for reducing the need for globally unique IP addresses. NAT allows an organization with addresses that are not globally unique to connect to the Internet by translating those addresses into globally routable address space. Also known as Network Address Translator.

NEBS   Acronym for Network Equipment Building Systems. Covers spatial, hardware, craftsperson interface, thermal, fire resistance, handling and transportation, earthquake and vibration, airborne contaminants, grounding, acoustical noise, illumination, EMC, and ESD requirements.

network layer   Layer 3 of the OSI reference model. Provides connectivity and path selection between two end systems. The network layer is the layer at which routing occurs. *Other associated terms include* **application layer**, **data-link layer**, **physical layer**, **presentation layer**, **session layer**, and **transport layer**.

network management   Generic term used to describe systems or actions that help maintain, characterize, or troubleshoot a network.

NIAP   Acronym for National Information Assurance Partnership. Serves as the joint NSA/NIST program that serves U.S. industry to help define criteria for security measures and algorithms.

NIST   Acronym for National Institute of Standards and Technology. A U.S. federal technology agency that develops and promotes standards in security as well as other standards for measurement, standards, and technology.

NLOS   Acronym for near line of sight; also commonly (and incorrectly) referred to as nonline of sight. The term refers to obstructions located between transmitting and receiving antennas, both physical and nonphysical, such as local interference, an RF path, or a pathway. *See* **Fresnel zone** and **LOS**.

NOC   Acronym for network operation center. Organization responsible for maintaining a network.

OFDM   Acronym for orthogonal frequency division multiplexing. An FDM modulation technique for transmitting signals by splitting the radio signal into various frequencies that are then transmitted simultaneously. One of the key differences between OFDM and DHSS or FHSS is that the signals in OFDM are sent simultaneously as opposed to sequentially over time.

open authentication A type of authentication where an access point will grant authentication to any client, regardless of whether or not it is native to the network of that particular access point. Arguably more common with simple data devices, such as bar code scanners, that have little processing power.

OSI Short for Open System Interconnection reference model. Sometimes referred to as the OSI reference stack. Network architectural model developed by ISO and ITU-T. The model consists of seven layers, each of which specifies particular network functions such as addressing, flow control, error control, encapsulation, and reliable message transfer. The lowest layer (the physical layer) is closest to the media technology. The lower two layers are implemented in hardware and software, while the upper five layers are implemented only in software. The highest layer (the application layer) is closest to the user. The OSI reference model is used universally as a method for teaching and understanding network functionality. It is similar in some respects to SNA. *Other associated terms include* **application layer, data-link layer, network layer, physical layer, presentation layer, session layer,** and **transport layer.**

OSS Acronym for operations support system. Network management system supporting a specific management function, such as alarm surveillance and provisioning, in a carrier network. Many OSSs are large centralized systems running on mainframes or minicomputers. Common OSSs used within an RBOC include NMA, OPS/INE, and TIRKS.

out-of-band signaling Transmission using frequencies or channels outside the frequencies or channels normally used for information transfer. Often used for error reporting in situations in which in-band signaling can be affected by whatever problems the network might be experiencing. Contrast with in-band signaling.

oversubscription The method of having more users on a network than the network can accommodate simultaneously. What makes this work is the premise that rarely, if ever, do all users actually use the network at the same time. Oversubscription is mission-critical to the financial models used by Internet service providers (ISPs) and other entities, and in many cases, oversubscription is what keeps an entity solvent. Oversubscription rates can be anywhere from a factor of 6 to a factor of 50 or more, depending on the class of service the subscriber has agreed to and other factors, including how much bandwidth the subscribers use.

packet   Logical grouping of information that includes a header containing control information and (usually) user data. Packets are most often used to refer to network-layer units of data. The terms *datagram,* **frame,** *message,* and *segment* are also used to describe logical information groupings at various layers of the OSI reference model and in various technology circles.

parabolic antenna   A dish-like antenna that sends and receives radio waves in a highly focused manner. Such antennas provide very large antenna gains and are highly efficient. This antenna is typical to most point-to-point RF systems, but is not the only design available or appropriate for a given RF link. The primary task of an antenna is to provide gain (signal boost) and to radiate in particular directions in accordance with the network's intended use; for example, point-to-multipoint or point-to-point, or to cover a prescribed geographic area.

passband   The frequencies that a radio allows to pass from its input to its output. If a receiver or transmitter uses filters with narrow passbands, then only the desired frequency and nearby frequencies are of concern to the system designer. If a receiver or transmitter uses filters with wide passbands, then many more frequencies in the vicinity of desired frequency are of concern to the system designer. In a frequency division multiplexing (FDM) system, the transmit and receive passbands will be different. In a time division multiplexing (TDM) system, the transmit and receive passbands are the same.

PAT   Acronym for Port Address Translation. A function provided by routers which allows hosts on a LAN to communicate with another LAN without revealing their own IP address. All outbound packets have their IP address translated to the LAN edge routers' external IP address. Replies come back to the router which then translates them back into the internal IP address of the original host within the LAN. Used to enhance security measures.

path loss   The power loss that occurs when RF waves are transmitted through the air. This loss occurs because RF waves expand as they travel through the air, and the receiver antenna only captures a small portion of the total radiated energy. In addition, a significant amount of energy may be absorbed by molecules in the atmosphere or by precipitation when the carrier frequencies are above 10GHz. The amount of absorption due to precipitation depends on the amount of precipitation and is usually a factor only for systems that operate at frequencies above 10GHz.

The amount of atmospheric absorption depends greatly on the particular frequency used. At 12GHz, water vapor absorbs a great deal of energy, and at 60GHz, oxygen molecules absorb even more energy. Systems that operate at those frequencies have very limited ranges.

PDU Acronym for protocol data unit. OSI term for packet.

PEAP Acronym for Protected Extensible Authentication Protocol. Provides mutual authentication and key generation in a manner such that the user authentication phase is protected; for example, the user identity can be kept secret. This protocol is particularly useful for quick reauthentication when a user roams between devices such as access points.

physical layer Layer 1 of the OSI reference model. Defines the electrical, mechanical, procedural, and functional specifications for activating, maintaining, and deactivating the physical link between end systems. Corresponds with the physical control layer in the SNA model. *Other associated terms* **application layer, data-link layer, network layer, presentation layer, session layer**, and **transport layer**.

plaintext The original, readable information. It is usually a set of alphanumeric characters, but can also be other forms of data, such as values or mathematical symbols.

POP Acronym for point of presence. A term commonly used to describe a centralized facility that subscribers use to access the Internet.

POP2 Acronym for Post Office Protocol –2 POP is an Internet mail server protocol that provides an incoming message storage capability. It works in conjunction with the SMTP (Simple Mail Transfer Protocol), to enable the movement of mail from one system to another. The current version is called POP3, as defined in RFC 1939 (Post Office Protocol-Version 3, May 1996).

POTS Acronym for Plain Old Telephone Service.

presentation layer Layer 6 of the OSI reference model. Ensures that information sent by the application layer of one system will be readable by the application layer of another. The presentation layer is also concerned with the data structures used by programs, and therefore negotiates data transfer syntax for the application layer. Corresponds roughly with the presentation services layer of the SNA model. *Other associated terms include* **application layer, data-link layer, network layer, physical layer, session layer**, and **transport layer**.

propagation delay Time required for data to travel over a network, from its source to its ultimate destination.

protocol Formal description of a set of rules and conventions that govern how devices on a network exchange information.

protocol stack Set of related communications protocols that operate together and, as a group, address communication at some or all of the seven layers of the OSI reference model. Not every protocol stack covers each layer of the model, and often a single protocol in the stack will address a number of layers at once. TCP/IP is a typical protocol stack.

PSTN Acronym for Public Switched Telephone Network. General term referring to the variety of telephone networks and services in place worldwide.

PTM Acronym for point-to-multipoint. Common variants include pt-mpt and P2MP. However, all versions denote the same concept, which is a communication between a group of sites that interface a single hub site. PTM is commonly set up in three or four segments to enable frequency reuse, but can be designed for as many as a dozen or more segments within a single cell.

PTP Acronym for point-to-point. A common variant is pt-pt. However, both versions denote the same concept, which is to provide communication between two end points. In the United States, PTP systems are typically found in the ISM, U-NII, and LMDS bands.

PTT Acronym for Post, Telephone, and Telegraph. Government agency that provides telephone services. PTTs exist in most areas outside North America and provide both local and long-distance telephone services.

QAM Acronym for quadrature amplitude modulation. Method of modulating digital signals onto a radio-frequency carrier signal involving both amplitude and phase coding. QAM is a modulation scheme mostly used in the downstream direction (QAM-64, QAM-256). QAM-16 is generally more prominent in the upstream direction. Numbers indicate the number of code points per symbol. The QAM rate or the number of points in the QAM constellation can be computed by 2 raised to the power of *number of bits/symbol*.

QoS   Acronym for quality of service. A feature of certain networking protocols that treats different types of network traffic differently to ensure required levels of reliability and latency according to the type of traffic. Certain kinds of traffic, such as voice and video, are more sensitive to transmission delays and are therefore given priority over data that is less sensitive to delay.

As an example, Cisco Systems PTM BBFW systems traditionally have 4 levels of QoS, but some systems have as many as 13 levels of QoS, depending on how many bits are used to prioritize the traffic. Most systems use either three or four levels of QoS, which are commonly referred to as Unsolicited Grant Service (UGS), Committed Bit Rate (CBR; sometimes referred to as CIR or Committed Information Rate), and Best Effort Rate (BER). USG has priority over CIR/CBR, which has priority over BER. QoS levels are set in Layer 2 (data-link layer) of the OSI reference stack.

QPSK   Acronym for quadrature phase shift keying. A method of modulating digital signals onto a radio-frequency carrier signal using four phase states to code two digital bits.

RC4   A security algorithm used by WEP. Openly considered as a defeated algorithm, RC4 was developed in 1987 by Ron Rivest, for RSA Data Security, and was a proprietary algorithm until 1994, when the code was posted to the Internet, and thus to the rest of the world.

repeater   Device that regenerates and propagates radio or electrical signals between two network segments.

RF   Acronym for radio frequency. Generally refers to wireless communications with frequencies below 300GHz. The term RF is commonly used too broadly to cover all types of wireless.

RFC   Acronym for Request for Comments. Document series used as the primary means for communicating information about the Internet. Probably the best known versions are from the IEEE. Some RFCs are designated as Internet standards. Most RFCs document protocol specifications such as Telnet and FTP, but some are humorous or historical. RFCs are available online from numerous sources.

RJ connector Short for registered jack connector. Standard connectors originally used to connect telephone lines. RJ connectors are now used for telephone connections and for 10BaseT and other types of network connections. RJ-11, RJ-12, and RJ-45 are popular types of RJ connectors.

round A term of art relative to security that refers to a set of encryption operations performed on a block of information. For example, 64 DES uses 16 rounds of operations to produce the final version of the ciphertext, which can then be transmitted over an open BBFW link or other unsecured method of transmission.

RSA A public-key cryptographic system that may be used for encryption and authentication. Named for the inventors of the RSA security technique, Rivest, Shamir, and Adelman.

RTS Acronym for Request to Send. EIA/TIA-232 control signal that requests a data transmission on a communications line. Compare to *CTS, Clear to Send*.

sector virus Sector viruses modify the data that resides within sectors. These viruses are usually far larger than the 512 bytes available in a sector and therefore usually reside within the RAM portion of a PC, server, or router and then go on to affect the data in sectors. Because this type of virus can take up residence within RAM, even if the disc is repaired, they can recontaminate the disc immediately after being repaired.

session layer Layer 5 of the OSI reference model. Establishes, manages, and terminates sessions between applications and manages data exchange between presentation-layer entities. Corresponds to the data flow control layer of the SNA model. *Other associated terms include* **application layer**, **data-link layer**, **network layer**, **physical layer**, **presentation layer**, and **transport layer**.

SID Acronym for service ID. A number that defines (at the MAC sublayer) a particular mapping between two network devices. The term is used in cable standards such as DOCSIS. The SID is used for the purpose of upstream bandwidth allocation and class-of-service management.

SKA Acronym for shared key authentication. SKA requires an AP to demand a WEP key from a client.

SMPT   Acronym for Simple Mail Transfer Protocol.

SNA   Acronym for Systems Network Architecture. Large, complex, feature-rich network architecture developed in the 1970s by IBM. Similar in some respects to the OSI reference model, but with a number of differences. SNA is essentially composed of seven layers which are: data-flow control layer, data-link control layer, path control layer, physical control layer, presentation services layer, transaction services layer, and transmission control layer.

SNMP   Acronym for Simple Network Management Protocol. Network management protocol used almost exclusively in TCP/IP networks. SNMP provides a means to monitor and control network devices, and to manage configurations, statistics collection, performance, and security.

SOHO   Acronym for small office/home office.

spoofing   1. Scheme used by routers to cause a host to treat an interface as if it were up and supporting a session. The router spoofs replies to keep alive messages from the host in order to convince that host that the session still exists. Spoofing is useful in routing environments such as DDR, in which a circuit-switched link is taken down when there is no traffic to be sent across it in order to save toll charges.

2. The input of a hacker illegitimately claiming to be from an address from which it was not actually sent. Spoofing is designed to foil network security mechanisms such as filters and access lists.

spread spectrum   A spreading technique in which data, video, or voice signals are distributed over a wide range of frequencies; the signals are then collected and collated at the receiver.

SQL   Acronym for Structured Query Language. Data manipulation language for searching within relational databases.

SSID   Acronym for service set identifier. An ID that allows logical separation of WLANs. A client such as a PCMCIA card has an SSID that allows the upstream devices, such as the AP, authentication servers, and so on, to become part of the WLAN. Clients are often commonly segregated by SSIDs in a virtual LAN (though there are other ways of segregating VLAN participants).

SSL Acronym for Secure Sockets Layer. A protocol for establishing mutual authentications and encrypted sessions between web servers and web clients. SSL starts with a handshake from the client, and establishes a TCP/IP connection. Next, the server is authenticated to the client by verifying its public key. Once authenticated, the server selects the strongest cryptographic algorithm supported by the client and finally, a shared secret key is generated to encrypt all data flowing between the client and server. Finally, an encrypted SSL connection is established.

station authentication The event of authenticating an 802.11 device, such as a bridge or access point, as opposed to authenticating a client, such as a PCMCIA card.

stooge A security term of art; a network used by a hacker to attack other networks.

system sector virus A system sector virus is a virus that affects not just data, but hard drive sectors. Sectors are not files but instead are areas on a PC disc, server, or router that are read in chunks. For example, DOS sectors are 512 bytes in length. Sectors are invisible to your applications but are vital to the operation of a PC, server, or router because they contain the basic information for applications and data. When the sectors are disrupted, the results are terminal for the performance of the PC, server, or router.

T1 Transmits DS-1-formatted data at 1.544Mbps through the telephone-switching network.

T3 Transmits DS-3-formatted data at 44.736Mbps through the telephone-switching network.

TCP Acronym for Transmission Control Protocol. Connection-oriented transport-layer protocol that provides reliable full-duplex data transmission. Part of the TCP/IP protocol stack.

TCP/IP Acronym for Transmission Control Protocol/Internet Protocol. Common name for the suite of protocols developed by the U.S. Department of Defense (DoD) in the 1970s to support the construction of worldwide internetworks. TCP and IP are the two best-known protocols in the suite.

TDMA   Acronym for Time Division Multiple Access. A technique for splitting transmissions on a common frequency into time slots, which enables a greater number of users to use a given frequency. A technique commonly used as opposed to CDMA and frequency division multiplexing (FDMA).

Telnet   Standard terminal emulation protocol in the TCP/IP protocol stack. Telnet is used for remote terminal connection, enabling users to log in to remote systems and use resources as if they were connected to a local system.

TFTP   Acronym for Trivial File Transfer Protocol. Simplified version of FTP that allows files to be transferred from one computer to another over a network.

throughput   The net amount of data transmitted minus the overhead traffic to manage the link or connection. The more common specification for BBFW links is one that includes overhead traffic, and does not therefore clearly indicate link performance. As a general rule of thumb, overhead represents an additional 30 percent of bandwidth over throughput. (Throughput sometimes is referred to as **goodput**.)

TKIP   Acronym Temporal Key Integrity Protocol. TKIP, like WEP, is based on RC4 encryption, but is enhanced over WEP for reasons that include the generation of new encryption keys for every 10KB of data transmitted.

traffic shaping   Use of queues to limit surges that can congest a network. Data is buffered and then sent into the network in regulated amounts to ensure that the traffic will fit within the promised traffic envelope for the particular connection. Traffic shaping is used in ATM, Frame Relay, and other types of networks. Also known as *metering, shaping,* and *smoothing.*

transport layer   Layer 4 of the OSI reference model. Responsible for reliable network communication between end nodes. The transport layer provides mechanisms for the establishment, maintenance, and termination of virtual circuits, transport fault detection and recovery, and information flow control. Corresponds to the transmission control layer of the SNA model. *Other associated terms include* **application layer, data-link layer, network layer, physical layer, presentation layer,** and **session layer.**

Trojan horse   Named after the wooden Trojan horse that was delivered as a gift to the city of Troy but that secretly contained Greek soldiers. Aseemingly harmless computer program that delivers destructive code, such as a logic bomb, and therefore is a carrier, not a virus. This type of attack appears as a useful piece of software until executed.

truck roll   The concept of "rolling" trucks to the installation site to install, repair, or upgrade equipment.

UDP   Acronym for User Datagram Protocol.

U-NII   Acronym for Unlicensed National Information Infrastructure. Primarily a U.S. frequency band. The wireless products for this are in the 5.725- to 5.825GHz frequency for outdoor use. There are two other U-NII bands: 5.15- to 5.25GHz and 5.25- to 5.35GHz. The 5.15GHz band is for indoor use only in the United States, while the 5.25- to 5.35GHz band can be used either indoors or outdoors in the United States. Both of the lower two sets of U-NII frequencies are transmitted at lower power levels than the 5.725- to 5.825GHz band.

These frequencies do not require the use or purchase of a site license, but the gear does require certification by the FCC and strict compliance with its regulations. U-NII was a term coined by federal regulators to describe access to an information network by citizens and businesses. Equivalent to the term "information superhighway," it does not describe system architecture, protocol, or topology.

UNIX   Operating system developed in 1969 at Bell Laboratories. UNIX has gone through several iterations since its inception.

VDSL   Acronym for very-high-speed digital subscriber line. One of four DSL technologies. VDSL delivers 13- to 52Mbps downstream and 1.5- to 2.3Mbps upstream over a single twisted copper pair. The operating range of VDSL is limited to 1000 to 4500 feet (304.8 to 1372 meters).

virus   Potentially destructive software that spreads itself from program to program, from computer to computer, and from LAN to LAN, most commonly by e-mail attachment.

VLAN   Acronym for virtual local area network. A group of clients that are situated at different physical locations but who communicate with each other as if they were all on the same physical LAN segment.

VoIP   Acronym for Voice over IP. Enables a router to carry voice traffic (for example, telephone calls and faxes) over an IP network. In VoIP, the DSP segments the voice signal into frames, which are then coupled in groups of two and stored in voice packets. These voice packets are transported using IP in compliance with ITU-T specification H.323.

VPN   Acronym for virtual private network. A virtual private network is a private link that resides between two parties but travels across public networks.

WAN   Acronym for wide area network. Data communications network that serves users across a broad geographic area and often uses transmission devices provided by common carriers.

WAP   Acronym for Wireless Access Protocol. A language used for writing web pages that uses far less overhead compared to HTML and XML, making it preferable for low-bandwidth wireless access to the Internet from devices such as PDAs and cellular phones that also have small viewing screens. WAP's corresponding OS is the OS created by 3Com in its Palm Pilot. Nokia has recently adopted the Palm OS for its web-capable cellular phone.

WAP is based on the Extensible Markup Language (XML). XML dictates *how* data is shown, whereas HTML dictates *where* data is located within a browser page.

WEP   Acronym for Wireless Equivalent Protocol. WEP is a security protocol primarily used in 802.11 radios to secure wireless communications from eavesdropping and theft of data, and to prevent unauthorized access to a wireless network.

wireline   The use of copper phone, cable lines, or fiber. Wireline advantages include high reliability, high tolerance to interference, and generally easier troubleshooting. In the case of fiber, wireline also has exceptionally high bandwidth. Wireline is the technological opposite of wireless.

WLAN   Acronym for wireless area network. It generally, but not always, refers to a collision domain of 802.11 devices, i.e., a series of devices that contend for shared connectivity.

worm   A software that makes copies of itself and then distributes those copies, which create more copies, and so on. The typical objective of a worm is to suddenly generate such an enormous amount of e-mail that a system will shut down.

xDSL   Group term used to refer to ADSL, HDSL, SDSL, and VDSL. All are emerging digital technologies using the existing copper infrastructure provided by the telephone companies. XDSL is a high-speed alternative to ISDN.

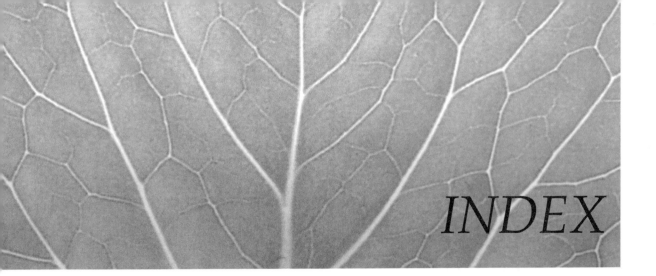

INDEX

❖ B

❖ **C**

❖ D

E

❖ J

❖ K

❖ L

❖ M

❖ Q

R

S

T

❖ U